FRANCE AND ISLAM IN
WEST AFRICA, 1860–1960

AFRICAN STUDIES SERIES 60

GENERAL EDITOR
J. M. Lonsdale, *Lecturer in History and Fellow of Trinity College,
Cambridge*

ADVISORY EDITORS
J. D. Y. Peel, *Charles Booth Professor of Sociology, University of
Liverpool*
John Sender, *Faculty of Economics and Fellow of Wolfson College,
Cambridge*

Published in collaboration with
THE AFRICAN STUDIES CENTRE, CAMBRIDGE

OTHER BOOKS IN THE SERIES

FRANCE AND ISLAM IN WEST AFRICA, 1860–1960

CHRISTOPHER HARRISON

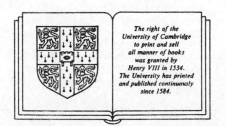

The right of the
University of Cambridge
to print and sell
all manner of books
was granted by
Henry VIII in 1534.
The University has printed
and published continuously
since 1584.

CAMBRIDGE UNIVERSITY PRESS

CAMBRIDGE

NEW YORK   PORT CHESTER   MELBOURNE   SYDNEY

Published by the Press Syndicate of the University of Cambridge
The Pitt Building, Trumpington Street, Cambridge CB2 1RP
40 West 20th Street, New York, NY 10011, USA
10 Stamford Road, Oakleigh, Melbourne 3166, Australia

First published 1988
Reprinted 1990

Printed in Great Britain at the University Press, Cambridge

British Library cataloguing in publication data

Harrison, Christopher
French policy towards Islam in West Africa,
1860–1960 – (African Studies series; 60).
1. Islam – Africa, West – History.
2. Africa, West – Foreign relations – France.
3. France – Foreign relations – Africa, West.
I. Title   II. Series.

Library of Congress cataloguing in publication data applied for

ISBN 0 521 35230 4

CE

For Tom

Contents

Contents

Acknowledgements

This book is largely based on my doctoral dissertation at the School of Oriental and African Studies, University of London. Research for the thesis was undertaken in London, Paris and Dakar. In all three places I owe considerable debts to a number of individuals and institutions. My greatest debt remains to the supervisors of the original thesis, Donal Cruise O'Brien and Richard Rathbone, who having performed the role of midwives to the thesis have been no less comforting as benevolent godparents to the book. For their advice and hospitality I remain extremely grateful. The revisions to my original thesis owe much to the insights I gained through my association with an Anglo-French research project on 'Islam, Society and the State in Africa' funded jointly by the Economic and Social Research Council and the Centre national de la recherche scientifique. In London I should also like to thank Christopher Andrew, Ailsa Auchnie, Louis Brenner, Peter Clarke, Murray Last, Harry Norris, the SOAS History Seminar and the SOAS Postgraduate Forum for their various services as friends and critics.

In Paris I am particularly grateful to Jean-Louis Triaud (University of Paris VII) and to his postgraduate students at the Laboratoire tiers monde with whom I attended a weekly seminar which was both stimulating and a source of Left Bank *camaraderie* in the cold steel of the Jussieu campus. To the staff of the Centre de recherches africaines, I am also very grateful for allowing me to make full use of their library facilities. Of all my fellow students in Paris Tiebilé Dramé became a particular friend who shared with me his enthusiasm for his subject in the face of considerable personal adversity. Vincent Monteil gave me some interesting food for thought at an early stage of my research.

In Paris I was fortunate enough to be introduced to Makane Fall from the Archives nationales in Senegal. Makane invited me to stay with his family when I went to finish my research in Senegal and this proved to be one of the happiest invitations I have received. I know that my stay in Dakar would not have been the same but for the warmth and hospitality of the Fall family and all their neighbours in the Dakar suburbs of Liberté V, Dieupeul and

Acknowledgements

Castors. In particular, I should like to thank Makane's mother, Emily Fall, who combined the arduous task of looking after a large family with a full-time job. I hope that she is now enjoying a happy retirement. The head of the archives in Dakar, Monsieur Saliou M'Baye, was always most helpful. Monsieur Iba der Thiam, now Minister of Education, spared time from his busy schedule in his former job as *Directeur* of the Ecole normale to discuss my research topic. The three-hour midday breaks in the archives afforded plenty of time for more leisurely discussions in the cafes of Gorée with other research students and I know that my thesis owes much to such lunchtime seminars and in particular to conversations with Jim Searing of Princeton.

My debts to institutions are also considerable. Firstly, I should like to acknowledge the assistance of a Department of Education and Science, Major State Studentship which made the research and travel possible. Secondly, I should like to thank the staff of all the libraries and archives I have worked in; the SOAS library, British Library and Rhodes House in Britain; the Archives nationales (section Outre-Mer), Archives nationales, Service historique de l'armée de terre, Institut de France, Institut catholique, Bibliothéque nationale, and the Centre des hautes études administratives sur l'Afrique et l'Asie modernes in Paris; and the Archives nationales de la république du Sénégal and Institut fondamental d'Afrique noire in Dakar. Thirdly, I completed my thesis and undertook all the revision for the book whilst working full time in the African and Caribbean Division of Longman Group publishers and I should like to thank my colleagues in this Division for their encouragement.

To all these individuals and institutions I am very grateful; needless to say they bear no responsibility for any inaccuracies or errors in the present work. My final vote of thanks goes to Liz, my wife, for her support and companionship throughout.

Abbreviations

AEF	Afrique equatoriale française
ANS	Archives nationales du Sénégal
ANSOM	Archives nationales, section outre-mer
AOF	Afrique occidentale française
BCAF	*Bulletin du Comité de l'Afrique Française*
BCEHSAOF	*Bulletin du Comité des Etudes Historiques et Scientifiques de l'Afrique Occidentale Française*
CEA	*Cahiers des Etudes Africaines*
CHEAM	*Centre des hautes études d'administration musulmane.* (After 1958, *Centre des hautes études administratives sur l'Afrique et l'Asie modernes.*)
FD	Fouta Djallon (Futa Jallon)
HSN	Haut Sénégal et Niger
IC	Institut catholique
IF	Institut de France
IFAN	Institut fondamental de l'Afrique noire
JAH	*Journal of African History*
JOAOF	*Journal Officiel de l'Afrique Occidentale Française*
RCBCAF	*Renseignements Coloniaux: Bulletin du Comité de l'Afrique Française*
RFHOM	*Revue Française d'Histoire Outre-Mer*
RMM	*Revue du Monde Musulman*
SHAT	Service historique de l'armée de terre
SOAS	School of Oriental and African Studies

A NOTE ON ORTHOGRAPHY

This book covers a wide range of African languages and I can make no claim to scientific accuracy in the transliteration of any of them. I have simply aimed to be as consistent as possible and to avoid, where it is not anachronistic to do so, the French use of -ou, ou- and dj- where -u, w-, aw- or j- are used in English transliterations. In extracts spellings of proper names and ethnic groups are given as in the original French sources except for the names of the colonies themselves which have been translated into English.

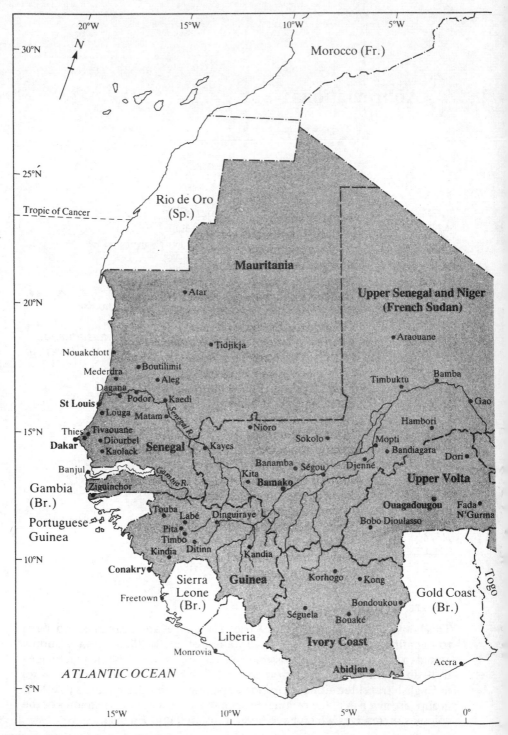

North West Africa, c. 1930.

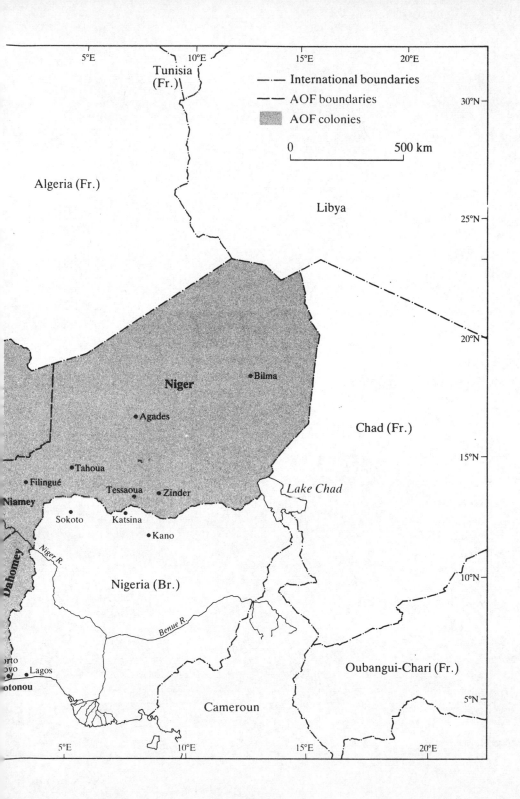

1

Introduction

This study is a contribution to the social, political and intellectual history of one of the largest colonial states in Africa – the Federation of French West Africa (AOF). The Federation grouped together the present-day states of Benin, Burkina Faso, Guinea, Ivory Coast, Mali, Mauritania, Niger, and Senegal. Between them they straddle all the major bands of climate and vegetation that are to be found in West Africa, and the indigenous population is correspondingly varied. Yet this vast and varied area was treated for over fifty years (1904–56) as a single administrative unit presided over by an alien government based in the Federation's capital in Dakar. Muslims were to be found in all the colonies of the group – though the proportions varied from the exclusively Muslim society of Mauritania to the mainly animist and Christian societies of the southern coastal colonies of Dahomey and Ivory Coast. By examining French attitudes and policies towards Islam, it is possible to gain insight into both the political nature and the ideological underpinning of the colonial state of AOF.

A study of French relations with Islam can, it must be said, make little claim to originality. Scarcely had Africa been partitioned before French 'experts' were sent to investigate and report on Islam.[1] By 1915 two doctoral dissertations on the subject had been submitted to French universities.[2] Throughout the colonial period successive administrators, scholars and interested spectators produced a constant stream of works which were designed both to document Islam and to suggest what policies should be adopted towards France's Muslim subjects.

The concern of scholars in the post-colonial era has, not surprisingly, shifted away from the administrative 'problem' of Islam towards an attempt to understand its internal dynamics in sub-Saharan Africa. In analysing what is perhaps its most striking feature, namely the huge increase in conversion to Islam over the past two centuries, scholars have focussed their attention on such themes as *jihad* and Islamic reform movements,[3] the economic and social foundations of the expansion of Islam,[4] the relationship between Islam and slavery in Africa,[5] Islamic response to colonialism[6] and, finally, the political economy of Islam in the twentieth century.[7] At the

1

same time scholars and Muslim leaders have been anxious to reintegrate African Islam – *Islam noir* as it is called in the French literature – into the mainstream of the worldwide Islamic experience.[8] This has been in response to the affirmation of many colonial experts that African Muslims were not true Muslims because they practised a 'bastardised' form of Islam.

The present study is one which in many ways returns to the colonial perspectives but which attempts to take a more detached look by examining not so much the 'problem' of Islam but rather the 'problem' of French understanding of Islam. It is a study which is based, in contrast to most recent writing on African history, almost exclusively upon European written sources. This is not intended to be a boast, but nor is it a guilty admission. This study undoubtedly invites a complementary one of Islamic attitudes and policies towards France but I prefer to leave such a study to others more knowledgable and competent than I.

The need to come to terms not only with the importance but also with the complex and often contradictory nature of the colonial state seems unquestionable, and this constitutes the first of the major themes of this study. The capitalist penetration of Africa that took place during the colonial era, the creation of an infrastructure within the colonies designed to meet the needs of metropolitan capital and the determination of Africa's patently nonsensical boundaries have all had the profoundest of impacts on Africa's political, social and economic development. Claims that the colonial era represented no more than an 'interlude' in African history[9] do little justice to the enormity of change that has taken place over the last century. Yet at the same time it is necessary to add nuance to this 'enormity of change' for it is clear that there was much that colonialism did not change and much that the colonials never saw nor ever heard. Furthermore, change occurred in ways that colonial administrators could not anticipate, for Africans were not the dumb and passive recipients of colonial rule that was often imagined. They – if one may be permitted the generalisation – retained their own identity and took advantage of any new opportunity that colonial rule offered. In this they had much in common with the working classes of industrial Europe.[10]

Nor were the colonials homogeneous and all-powerful. Political intrigue and competition flourished within the small and isolated colonial societies. However much the rhetoric of colonialism may have stressed the altruism of the civilising mission, Frenchmen by and large went to the colonies for career reasons, and their principal concern was to advance as rapidly as possible up the complex hierarchy of bureaucratic promotion. As everybody knows, career building is a vicious and fiercely competitive process – and in the colonies it was no exception. However, at least for the early part of this study, Frenchmen not only had to look over their shoulders to keep an eye on their rivals but they also had to look out for a wide range of fatal diseases. At the turn of the century medicine had advanced sufficiently that Europeans need not expect to die in the Tropics. Nonetheless the death rate was still very high: in 1914 one in ten of the graduates of the Ecole coloniale, the training school for colonial administrators, would die within the first few years of serving in the colonies.[11]

The second general theme running through this study concerns the problem of understanding other societies and cultures. Studies of European perceptions of non-European societies all rightly highlight the Eurocentric and innately racist nature of these perceptions.[12] This study will provide further examples of these characteristic perceptions but it is important to stress, as M. Rodinson has done in his critique of E. W. Said's *Orientalism*, that one should not be tempted into arguing that the perceptions of the western scholar or administrator are inevitably invalidated by his or her race and social class:

> It was entirely true [writes Rodinson] that the conclusions of bourgeois scholars were partially, and to a greater or lesser extent according to the discipline, personality, *conjoncture* and specific cases, influenced by their class situation. But that does not mean that their conclusions were totally without relationship with what one has to call reality.[13]

Nevertheless, it is hard to disagree with Said's basic argument that the Muslim Arab world was grossly distorted in western perceptions, and that these distortions were well-suited to western political designs.[14]

Another point which Said stresses is the ahistorical nature of the western vision of the Arab world:

> The Orientalist attitude ... shares with magic and mythology, the self-containing, self-reinforcing character of a closed system, in which objects are what they are *because* they are what they are, for once and for all time, for ontological reasons that no empirical material can either dislodge or alter.[15]

This ahistorical vision was evident in many European accounts of the African past and was, as we shall see, an important factor in the formulation of policy. However, it is important to recognise that Europeans often regarded their own past through similarly ahistorical eyes: the eighteenth- and nineteenth-century collectors and chroniclers of European popular culture, for example, likewise assumed an unchanging, undifferentiated and timeless bucolic past.[16]

The third theme of this study is closely related to the second and concerns the contribution of the social sciences to colonial rule. The colonial era was characterised by, amongst many other things, a relentless pursuit of facts and statistics. The reasons for this are clear enough. Firstly, at the end of the nineteenth century the Europeans found themselves in nominal governance of vast areas of land about which they knew very little. There was, therefore, a lot of ground to be made up. Secondly, the model of government in Europe, with its increasingly bureaucratic and interventionist states, relied increasingly upon statistics. Thirdly, social scientists themselves made considerable claims for their discipline and at the turn of the century, a time when Durkheim wrote that 'Sociology is on everybody's lips',[17] it was confidently predicted that government would soon be elevated to a science.

However, the forward march of Science was not without its obstacles. A debate between the anthropologist, Malinowski, and the future Governor of Kenya, Mitchell, conducted in the pages of *Africa*, the journal of the International African Institute, provides an excellent summary of the way in which the claims of 'Science' and the 'Practical Man' could sometimes conflict.[18] (Mitchell argued that the 'Scientist' was incapable of reaching his conclusions with sufficient speed to be of any practical use to the colonial administrator and that, furthermore, the 'Scientist' lacked the broad range of skills that were essential to the 'Practical Man'. Malinowski countered that colonial rule urgently needed a base of scientific understanding of the colonised societies if it was to be both efficient and acceptable.) Even with the best will in the world it is not clear that administrators would have been capable of making use of the insights of social scientists. R. Buell, an early American political scientist who made a major study of the 'native policies' of the various colonial powers, reported that 'The French Colonial Office has an immense library and archives, but neither officials nor scholars can make use of them because of the lack of an adequate filing system.' Furthermore, he reported, government expenditure on the library was barely sufficient to cover the costs of book-binding.[19] If this was the situation in Paris one would hardly expect it to be any better in the colonies – but it is, perhaps, as a symbol of the problem of using 'knowledge' in 'government' that Buell's anecdote is best remembered.

A final point related to this theme, and one which relates more specifically to the question of French attitudes towards Islam, is to realise that the positivist social sciences cut in several ways as far as Islam was concerned. For whilst it is true, as Peter Clarke has pointed out, that the commonly held notion that Islam represented a step up from animism owed a great deal to the ideas of Comte,[20] it can also be argued that the developments in the sociology of religion contributed to a more sophisticated understanding of 'primitive' religions in comparison to which Islam no longer appeared so superior. For example, when Durkheim argued that all religions are a means by which societies maintain cohesion and social order he undermined the 'superiority' of Islam over animism. It was now possible to argue, indeed, that animism was a superior religion to Islam because it was better suited to the temperament and way of life of African societies. This apparently academic consideration was to be of considerable practical importance in French policy-making.

The fourth theme of this study concerns the transposition by the French of their own metropolitan preoccupations and political battles to the colonies. Of particular significance were the Dreyfus affair and the battle over the secularisation laws, which between them dominated French political life at the turn of the century, deeply divided France and highlighted a particular conspiratorial style of French politics.[21] Conspiracy was as potent a myth as it was a reality. It provided a useful opportunity to defame one's opponents whilst at the same time galvanising one's supporters into a show of solidarity against a well organised, yet shadowy, conspiracy. As a result a suspicion of conspiracy, verging on paranoia, came to be a characteristic of French political thinking. This tendency was partly a reflection of deep divisions within French society and partly a reflection, too, of the uncertain nature of international relations in Europe and of the widespread fear of German intentions. It is important to understand that the spy scandals and invasion scares which disturbed the peace of Edwardian Britain as much as of the French Third Republic and which provided such wonderful targets for the pens of metropolitan satirists[22] had a serious and direct bearing on events in the outposts of empire.

The fifth theme is more specific. It concerns the attempt to identify the level at which colonial policy in AOF operated. At one extreme AOF represented part of France's world-wide strategic interests. It so happened that France's most important and oldest overseas possessions lay across on the other side of the Sahara desert from AOF and that the indigenous population there was overwhelmingly Muslim. France's 'Muslim Empire' was further increased after the First World War with the share out of the Ottoman Empire between France and Britain. At this level Islamic policy in AOF was practically synonymous with imperial policy. At the other extreme, AOF represented a federation of parochial governments, isolated parish councils whose perception of policy and strategic interest was necessarily limited and for whom the dictates of the imperial bureaucrats in Paris may well have been quite meaningless. The federal government in Dakar was placed between the parish politics of the local *cercles* and the imperial politics of the Empire. This study attempts to cover the totality of this range. By focussing on particular case studies one can appreciate the conflict of interests inherent in the federal government's position as half-way house between the parish pump (or more appropriately village well) and the Colonial Office in the rue Oudinot.

The final theme is the one around which the book is organised: the attempt to impose a sense of periodisation on the events that were taking place and the ideas that were taking shape. The book is divided into four main parts. Part I covers the second half of the nineteenth century as the French started to penetrate into the interior away from their long held coastal trading entrepôts. The coverage of events in this section is not intended to offer a comprehensive account of French relations with all the Muslim societies of the interior but rather to highlight some of the dilemmas facing the French in this first phase of colonial rule. Particular attention is paid to the Algerian experience as this was to be a formative one for colonial rule in West Africa in the early twentieth century. Part II covers the years from around the turn of the century to the start of the First World War in which administrators attempted to apply the knowledge gained by French rule in Algeria and in which, too, the growth of Arab nationalism and

Introduction

Germany's activities in Europe, North Africa and the Middle East preoccupied colonial minds and to a certain extent distorted their perceptions of local realities. The watershed in French relations with Islam is described in Part III which analyses the burst of scholarly enquiry that took place between the start of the First World War and 1920 and which contributed to a significant shift in French appraisal of Islam, leading to the establishment of a stable system of alliances and coalitions based on a commonly held understanding of *Islam noir*. Part IV analyses the operation of what I have called the French stake in African Islam during the 1920s and 1930s. During these years the French administration established very close and very rigid alliances with a limited number of Muslim leaders who to a very large extent had been identified as potential allies by the scholar-administrators described in Part III. Although briefly disrupted by the Vichy regime this highly personalised pattern of relationships continued through to the achievement of independence in French West Africa, and this later period is briefly considered in the Epilogue.

Part I

1850–1898: Nineteenth-century origins of French Islamic policy

Je demeure convaincu que la construction d'une mosquée au Sénégal est un premier pas vers le progrès dans cette colonie. Ne pas adapter aujourd'hui par bienveillance une mesure si utile et si désirée, serait s'exposer à y recourir plus tard par nécessité. . . . On a trop longtemps attendu pour que le christianisme fasse maintenant beaucoup de proselites au Sénégal, la très grande majorité de la population y professent l'islamisme, et parmi cette population se trouvent bon nombre d'individus qui sont en possession de l'estime publique, et qui marchent vers l'aisance et la propriété. Or la propriété engendre le patriotisme chez les hommes . . . et le patriotisme constitue les citoyens utiles sur qui repose l'avenir d'un pays. (Commissaire de la Marine, Rapport à M. le Gouverneur, 16 December 1836, ANSOM Sénégal et Dépendances X, 3 quat.)

Introduction

The French presence in West Africa dates back to 1637 and the establishment of a trading post in St Louis on the mouth of the River Senegal. For the next two hundred years the French remained on the coast where they competed with Dutch, English and Portuguese merchants for a share in the trade in slaves, gold, gum and animal hides. It was not until the early nineteenth century that the French began seriously to contemplate extending their influence to the interior of the country. Colonel Julien Schmaltz, appointed Governor of the colony in 1816, constructed forts in Bakel (1818–19), Dagana (1819) and Richard Toll (1824) which were intended to provide the infrastructure for the exploitation by French colonists of the Senegal River valley. However, construction of the forts met with fierce resistance and within a short space of time the projects for agricultural development were abandoned. French interest turned again to trade.[1]

In the early nineteenth century the gum trade was the most lucrative trade of the region. Gum, which was extracted from the acacia trees which grew wild along the southern edges of the Sahara, was brought by Moorish traders to seasonal markets held in three riverside locations in the lower river valley.[2] The French merchants generally found themselves in a weak bargaining position at the markets: not only were they forced to pay a number of taxes to the Moorish chiefs who controlled the trade, but they also risked losing their share of the trade completely to English traders on the Mauritanian coast if they attempted to put pressure on the Moors to offer better terms. Within St Louis the merchants – dominated by trading companies from Bordeaux – were the most powerful and most stable political force. As such they were able to exercise great influence on the colonial government, especially as there was such a high turnover in colonial officials.[3] In the mid-1830s, the Bordelese merchants persuaded the government to take up arms against the Trarza Moors who dominated the gum trade. However, the fighting remained inconclusive for two decades. In the 1850s the authorities in St Louis, with backing from the Naval Ministry in Paris to whom they were responsible, revived the earlier scheme for expansion into the interior in order to secure French control over the

9

commercial opportunities of the region. The merchants were particularly impressed with the work of the naval engineer, Louis Faidherbe, who was posted to the colony in 1852. When the French suffered unexpectedly high losses in the construction of the latest of the forts in Podor in 1854, Faidherbe won the backing of the merchant community for nomination as Governor of Senegal. In the following decade under Faidherbe's guidance French expansion into the interior was set on a course of no return.

Within the West African interior which the French were now seeking to control, Islamic reform movements had been the most dynamic political force since the mid-eighteenth century.[4] Not only had they created powerful centralised states which nurtured scholarship and greatly widened the sense of Islamic community, but they also established a precedent and a model for warfare for others to follow which had less harmonious results. Indeed, the violence associated both with the waging of *jihad* together with the massive enslavement of conquered peoples to sustain the economies of the *jihad* states had a traumatic effect on West African society.

In the middle of the nineteenth century, the rival imperialisms of French merchant interests and Islamic reformers came into conflict in the upper valley of the River Senegal. By 1855 Faidherbe had conquered the Trarza Moors and was starting to negotiate with leaders in the upper valley who resented the growing influence of al-Hajj Umar Tall who had launched his *jihad* in 1852 on the border between the Futa Jallon and the kingdoms of upper Senegal. By 1854 Umar's forces had conquered most of the eastern Senegambia and in February the following year Umar was writing to the Muslim community of St Louis in the following terms:

> Now we will take action by the power of God. We will not waver until we receive a plea of peace and submission from your tyrant [the Governor], for our Master said: 'Wage war on those who do not believe in God nor in the last judgment, who do not conform to the prohibitions of God and his Prophet and who, having received revelation, do not follow true religion, until they pay tribute, for they are in the minority position.'[5]

For over two hundred years the Europeans had been tolerated by Muslim leaders. For the most part confined to their coastal enclaves and willing to respect the authority of their African neighbours, Europeans could easily be accommodated within an Islamic model of good neighbourliness which had a ready-made place for the *dhimmi* or 'protected person'.[6] However, it was clear that in the second half of the nineteenth century the basis of this relationship was being radically altered as French military imperialism[7] in the Senegambia and in the upper valleys of the Senegal and Niger Rivers was able to impose its own terms of 'good neighbourliness'.

2

French Islamic policy in Senegal and Algeria

In late 1854 Faidherbe was appointed Governor of Senegal with instructions to pursue a policy of expansion into the interior of the colony at minimum cost to the treasury. Within months of his appointment he had successfully brought an end to the war with the Trarza Moors thereby establishing French control over the lower valley of the Senegal River. Faidherbe then waited for the river level to rise to enable him to continue his advance upstream. He immediately made inroads into the Umarian domination of the upper river valley by establishing alliances with Umar's enemies in Medine and Bundu and constructing a fort in Medine.[1] However, back in St Louis the French were acutely aware that Muslims greatly outnumbered Christians and there was very real concern within the French community that the local Muslim population would answer Umar's call issued in early 1855 to reject French rule. This concern was translated into a wide range of opinions about what policy the French authorities should adopt towards Muslims within the town of St Louis. Education policy, which had been the subject of quite heated debate for a number of years,[2] became the litmus test of French attitudes towards Islam in the colony.

There were certainly those amongst the French community who argued that no concession at all should be made towards Muslims. Others expressed pious hopes that eventually French education would train a new class of pro-European Muslims on whom the colonial power could call for support.[3] However, Faidherbe argued that unless French education itself, which at this stage consisted of two mission-run schools in St Louis, was willing to change and moderate the overtly Christian nature of the instruction offered to African pupils, then there was little chance of education ever reaching the minds of young Muslims, let alone transforming them. He, therefore, called for the appointment of two secular teachers to the mission-run schools in St Louis. He told the naval minister in Paris that he would have *liked* to be able to consider Muslims as a 'mere anomaly' in our small Senegalese society but that unfortunately this was unrealistic:

11

> The Muslim element here is by far the most numerous and active and perhaps also the most useful. (I can tell you this in this letter because there is nothing wrong with telling you the whole truth, but I would not make this admission in front of Muslims.) On all sides we are surrounded by Islam. The war we are waging on the lower river is nothing compared to the serious and endless dangers of the Holy War provoked and maintained by Alhadji [i.e. al-Hajj Umar].

And then, in a very revealing appraisal of the French position in Senegal, Faidherbe went on to ask:

> What is the class that is the most indispensable to us in Senegal? It is the admirable *laptots* of the river. They are all Muslims.... If we need volunteers for war with the Trarza or whether even it is a Muslim war as with Alhadji, who is it that responds to our call? The Muslims.[4]

Faidherbe's realism was not universally shared. The former *Préfet apostolique* of Senegal wrote to the Director of Colonies in May 1856 supporting the idea of secular teachers providing they were of 'sure morality' and met with the approval of the Superior of the Congregation of the Holy Spirit. However, he then went on to cite approvingly the opinions of M. Carrère who was the co-author of a book on Senegal which contained violently anti-Islamic sentiments and whose contribution to the debate on education was to argue that 'Serious methods should be employed to destroy the mosque, to reject for ever the idea of a Muslim tribunal, to expel all foreign marabouts and to restrict the areas in which the marabouts of St Louis can teach to two districts of the town'.[5]

Faidherbe, however, had his way. The first secular teacher was appointed in October 1856, and in November the following year Faidherbe reported that the school was doing well with a roll of over 200.[6] Apart from being an interesting insight into French attitudes to education, the debate over the provision of secular teachers provided an early example of the importance of realpolitik in French dealings with Muslims. Faidherbe's recognition of the dominance of Islam in St Louis and of the strategic value of a Muslim alliance generally ran counter to strong ideological pressures against a Muslim alliance, but Faidherbe was able to use his dominant position in Senegalese politics to overcome this opposition.

The debate was conducted against a background of some bitter fighting between French forces and al-Hajj Umar. After some successes in 1856 and 1857, Umar was forced to withdraw after sustaining heavy losses in an unsuccessful siege of the French fort of Medine which lasted from April to July. French forces continued to come into conflict with the retreating *jihad*ists during 1858 and 1859, but by 1860 the costs to both sides of the military campaign together with the realisation that the war was ruining the local economy and destroying trade persuaded both parties to come to an agreement whereby the French were left in control of Senegambia and Umar was left to pursue his interests to the east.[7]

The question of the application of Islamic law to Muslims provoked a debate that was in many ways similar to the education issue.[8] In 1832 St Louis Muslims petitioned the Governor to complain about the application of French Civil Law that had been introduced in 1830. However nothing came of this first petition.[9] Following further petitions in the 1840s a plan was drawn up in 1848 for the creation of Muslim Tribunals with jurisdiction in certain civil matters affecting Muslims but, despite reaching an advanced stage, the plans were not put into practice[10] and the Muslims had to wait until Faidherbe's governorship before they got a sympathetic hearing. Whilst in Paris in September 1856 Faidherbe wrote to the Naval Minister concerning the need for a Muslim Tribunal:

> It seems to me [he wrote] that one can scarcely refuse to the Muslims of St Louis who are sincerely devoted to us . . . and whose support is essential to us . . . what the French government has granted with such good grace to the Muslims of Algeria who are hostile to us from the depths of their hearts.

Faidherbe stressed nonetheless that he regretted 'that we have to make this concession to a religion which offends us by its intolerance'. Back in Senegal he wrote in March 1857 emphasising the urgency of acting upon his recommendation as he had promised a Muslim Tribunal and feared the consequences if he was unable to keep his promise to the Muslims. He did not have to wait long, and in May a Muslim Tribunal was created in St Louis by decree.[11]

However, this Tribunal did not satisfy Muslims as the judge (*qadi*) was not allowed to settle inheritance and to act as ward to fatherless orphans despite the fact that under Qur'ānic law these were included amongst the duties of the *qadi*. In 1865 the Governor was asked to extend the powers of the *qadi*, but M. Carrère, now head of the Judiciary Service in Senegal, was predictably unimpressed by such demands, ascribing ulterior motives to them and arguing that the French had a duty to spread French ideas and culture. He concluded that if in the metropole adherents of all religions had to obey the Code Napoléon then he saw no reason why the same rule should not be applied in the colonies.[12] Pinet Laprade, Faidherbe's successor as Governor, did not agree:

> It would be impolitic to restrict the duties of the *cadi* so soon after the struggles with Alhadji and Maba, when the religious passions which in part provoked these struggles have not yet died down. But I hasten to add that the duties should not be extended but that it will be sufficient to define them clearly in order to give satisfaction to the Muslims of St Louis, the majority of whom, we must acknowledge, have never refused us help against the enemies of the colony.[13]

Pinet Laprade's ambivalence on the issue is suggestive. Clearly aware of the value of maintaining Muslim support in the colony's power base in St Louis, he was not however prepared to make any extra concessions to the Muslim community. Consequently, no change was introduced to the *qadi*'s duties.

When the question resurfaced again in the late 1880s the French

13

administration was much more confident in its rejection. This was partly a reflection of the growing confidence of French imperialism in West Africa generally. Following the 1860 agreement between Faidherbe and Umar, the French had sought to consolidate their position on the lower river and to increase their influence over the groundnut-producing regions of Senegambia. In the last quarter of the century the French military revived the policy of eastward expansion and conquest into the West African hinterland. By the late 1880s the French army was approaching the end of the final conquest of the Umarian empire which under the leadership of al-Hajj Umar's son, Amadu Sheku, was staging a desperate last-ditch attempt to rally the forces of Islam against the onward march of Archinard's men. By the late 1880s, too, construction had begun on a railroad and a telegraph line which would link Dakar with Bamako where the French had constructed a fort in 1883.[14] Thus the French administration in St Louis had good reason to feel that there was less need to make diplomatic gestures to local Muslims. However, the crucial argument of the Head of the Judiciary was that the situation in Senegal was very different to the one pertaining in Algeria where *qadi*s had much greater powers. His argument is worth quoting at length for it was one that was to be rehearsed many times in the early twentieth century and was one of the first signs of the development by the French of a specifically West African perspective on the question of Islam:

> One cannot [he wrote] compare Senegal with Algeria. . . . Islam was the only religion which existed in Algeria at the time of the conquest. It was natural as much as it was prudent to respect it and even facilitate the practice of its laws. . . . But it is not the same here . . . and we are not bound by the same obligations. Senegal is a colony created by France; the town of St Louis was shaped by the French and it was only gradually, indeed clandestinely, that Islam filtered into the black population of the town. . . . [Islam] does not, therefore, have freedom of the town and cannot claim the same rights to those in Algeria. Here, more than anywhere else, the Muslim as a result of his profound ignorance which his fanaticism has encouraged is absolutely hostile to our ideas, our usages, our language, our customs and our civilisation.[15]

This report was presented to a special commission charged with reorganising the Muslim judicial system in Senegal. The commission included the *qadi* of St Louis, and for his benefit the substance of the report was translated into Arabic. However, the less than complimentary remarks about Islam and the ignorance of the Senegalese Muslims were tactfully left untranslated![16]

The discussions on the provision of special educational and judicial facilities for Muslims in nineteenth-century Senegal were very revealing of French attitudes not just towards Islam but towards colonial policy generally. The discussions raised the fundamental question of whether ideological or confessional preferences should be allowed to dominate wider strategic interests. They also revealed that relations between the French authorities and the African Muslim communities lacked stability. There was no obvious continuity in French thinking about Islam in West Africa as pragmatic gestures aimed at forging an alliance with the Muslim community were followed by acts which could only antagonise these same people. If we are to find a serious and sustained development in French policy towards Islam in this period that goes beyond the whims of individual administrators and soldiers, we have to look north to Algeria where a definite consensus about the position of France with regard to Islam had emerged by the end of the century.

The French experience in Algeria is widely accepted as having been a major influence in the colonisation south of the Sahara. Georges Hardy, one-time Inspector of Education in AOF and colonial historian, argued that:

> It was Algeria that served as a testing ground for political and economic doctrines.... Whether for good or for evil ... the mark of Algeria's colonisation is to be found in all parts of the French domain.[17]

It was certainly true that many of the French military personnel who served in Senegal had gained their first experience of Africa in the Algerian campaigns. The best known of these soldiers was Faidherbe himself. In October 1859 he bluntly informed the Naval Minister that:

> The analogies between Senegal and Algeria are complete. Senegal must be assimilated to Algeria and not to the other colonies. Senegal should be no more than a sub-division of Algeria.[18]

FRENCH CONQUEST AND ADMINISTRATION OF ALGERIA: PIONEERING AN ISLAMIC POLICY

It was not until ten years after the initial military expedition against Algiers in 1830 that the French began to penetrate into the Algerian hinterland.[19] In the decade that followed the capture of Algiers, the French were content to control the town and the coast surrounding it, allowing the principal Algerian leader, Abd al-Qadir, to build up a sphere of influence in the interior. However, the appointment of General Bugeaud to the command of the French army in Algeria was a signal of France's intention to pursue the conquest further inland. Throughout the 1840s Bugeaud led a brutal military campaign, particularly during the years 1841–2 when he initiated a scorched earth policy that soon sapped the will of Abd al-Qadir's followers to resist. In April 1845 Bugeaud justified his policy in language that was to become familiar later, south of the Sahara:

> We have never obtained anything from these people except through force. In vain we have often tried means of persuasion. Either there was no response at all or they told us that we would first have to fight and that if we triumphed, then they would submit.[20]

15

However, it would be a mistake to imagine that the French actions in Algeria during the 1840s were characterised by nothing more subtle than blind fury. From a very early stage Bugeaud recognised the need to be well informed about the nature of the society he was in the process of conquering. The mechanism for acquiring this knowledge were the *bureaux arabes*, established by ministerial decree in 1844. Every administrative area within the 'military territory' of Algeria was allocated a *bureau arabe* which reported directly to the commanding officer of the area. In practice this was an extremely powerful position as the army was wholly dependent upon the *bureaux* for information and advice. The *bureaux*, staffed by specialist officers who had acquired some knowledge of Arabic language and culture, were credited in their early days with being 'a paternalist authority' taking a sympathetic interest in Arab affairs and as such were resented by the early colonists in Algeria who accused them of being arabophile.[21]

Bugeaud's career in Algeria ended in 1847 when he was asked to retire – a few months before Abd al-Qadir's eventual submission. The 1848 Revolution in France brought with it a new Republican Constitution in which the colony of Algeria was accorded the same status as a metropolitan *département*. (At the same time a similar status was given to the four Senegalese communes of St Louis, Dakar, Gorée and Rufisque.) The Algerian policy of Emperor Napoleon III, who seized power in 1852, was a paradoxical one. He shared the optimism of the St Simonians in the possibilities of a planned and rational colonisation that, as a result of providing the necessary infrastructure (particularly railways) to encourage industry, would benefit the indigenous and settler population in equal measure. To the dismay of the settlers he encouraged the idea that Algeria was not so much a colony as an 'Arab kingdom' that was worthy of respect and protection. Examples of this paternalist attitude can be seen in the establishment and financing of several *médersa*s – Muslim colleges named after the Arabic *madrassa*, a school – where the French hoped to train an indigenous civil service; in the law or senatus consulte of 1863 which was intended specifically to protect Arab land rights and in the senatus consulte of 1866 to extend French citizenship to Arabs. However, such paternalist liberalism merely antagonised the settlers who wasted no time in finding ways of interpreting the new laws to their advantage: the 1863 law on land rights, for example, was used to *reduce* the amount of land available to Arabs. Likewise, the senatus consulte of 1866 was ironically to prove to be one of the corner stones of settler domination in the colony as its requirement that Muslims would have to forfeit their personal Muslim status in order to become French citizens was unacceptable to the vast majority of Muslims.

Around this time the *bureaux arabes* began to go into decline as their earlier reputation for concern for the Algerian population was tarnished by cases of cruelty and corruption. In the end the *bureaux* alienated both the indigenous and the settler population. The remarks of one long-serving officer in 1870 illustrate the disillusion that had set in about the wisdom of the philosophy behind the *bureaux*, and it was a sentiment that was to be expressed later in West Africa:

> As a result of my experience I would say that the indigenous society is in a permanent state of conspiracy against us and that any organisation that is built on the native element rests on an unstable base.[22]

Although reforms of 1867 and 1870 abolished the upper sections of the *bureaux*, they nonetheless remained a distinct feature of the colonial administration in Algeria which continued to employ and train large numbers of specialist officers. During the Algerian War (1954–62) the *bureaux* reappeared under the new name of Sections administratives specialisées.[23]

The years 1830–70 were ones of great uncertainty in terms of French colonial policy in Algeria. Although the increasing power of the settler population in the 1860s provided some clues, what the exact nature of the colonial state was to be was far from clear. However, in the course of the two decades following the fall of Napoleon III in 1871, the confusion resulting from the dual heritage of a paternalist military administration and an anti-Arab civilian administration was to be resolved very definitely in favour of the European settler population.[24]

The genesis of *Algérie française* does not directly concern us here, but other developments in the last quarter of the nineteenth century were of considerable significance in helping to define French attitudes towards Islam. The first of these developments concerns the attempt by the civilian administration to argue that indigenous Algerian society was neither wholly Arab nor Muslim but that it was made up of a number of different ethnic groups of mixed Berber and Arab origins.[25] This was, of course, quite true but the argument was taken a stage further by its most extreme advocates who suggested that the Berber Kabyles, through a common Roman ancestry, had more in common with French than with Arab culture. Attempts were made to introduce French food and to encourage inter-marriage between French and Kabyles in order to rescue the latter from the 'decadence' caused by an overlong contact with Arabs. It is apparent that such views were also sometimes used deliberately by the civilian administration in order to discredit the military administration, particularly the *bureaux arabes*, whose administrative system presupposed a more or less uniform Arab Muslim culture and which the civilians held responsible for 'Arabising' and 'Islamising' Algerian Berbers. As we shall see later in this book, there was a widespread fear in sub-Saharan Africa that the expansion of Islam was more than anything else due to the misguided encouragement of previous French administrations who had been unwilling or unable to recognise the essential heterodoxy of the religious and ethnic make-up of the local population.

The second development concerns the attitude of the Catholic church towards Islam in Algeria. Until the late 1860s the church had confined its activities to the European population, but the elevation of Mgr. Lavigerie to the Archbishopric of Algiers in 1867 signalled a change in policy. Lavigerie immediately embarked on a campaign to convert Muslims: during the famine of 1868–9, he adopted over 1,700 Muslim orphans, baptised them and placed them in newly created Christian Arab villages. He, too, made use of the 'Kabyle myth' in order to justify his missionary zeal, claiming that he was merely reclaiming the souls that in the fourth century AD had belonged to the Augustinian Church in North Africa. The civilian and military administrators soon developed serious doubts about Lavigerie's eagerness to evangelise amongst the Muslims and attempts were made to restrain him. However, Lavigerie, with the full backing of Rome, went on to found two religious orders specifically for the task of converting Muslims. Of the two orders the White Sisters worked mainly in the Christian orphanages, but the White Fathers were sent south into the Sahara desert with instructions to take their mission as far as Timbuktu. Lavigerie stated explicitly that he regarded Algeria as a base from which to spread the Christian faith across the whole of Africa:

> Algeria is no more than a door, opened by Providence, to a barbarous continent of two hundred million souls. It is there above all that we must carry the work of the Catholic apostolate.[26]

The fact that several missionaries were killed by hostile Tuareg as they attempted to reach Timbuktu did not deter young idealistic Frenchmen from joining the new order. Lavigerie, who argued that 'All Blacks would become slaves' if Islam was allowed to spread throughout Africa, benefited in particular from the strong abolitionist current of late nineteenth-century Europe.[27] Lavigerie's career illustrates well many of the paradoxes in the relationship between the Church and the colonial state that were to reappear later in West Africa and which consisted chiefly in the fact that however well his charitable activities fitted with the rhetoric of the civilising and liberating mission of colonialism and however much his anti-slavery campaigns fired the imagination of the metropolitan audience, the colonial authorities were nonetheless, with good reason, fearful of the political consequences of allowing the missionaries a free hand in strongly Muslim areas.

Finally, it is important to recognise the development of scholarship in relation to Islam in Algeria. Although the *bureaux arabes* had fallen into disrepute by the 1870s, they had nonetheless established a tradition of detailed administrative research. Furthermore, the liberal ideas which to a large extent underpinned the *bureaux* survived as the largely metropolitan-based *indigènophiles* raised public awareness about the situation of Muslims in Algeria and pleaded for a colonial policy that was more sensitive to Muslim feelings.[28]

The appointment of Jules Cambon as Governor-General of Algeria in 1891 seemed to suggest official awareness of the need to adopt a more conciliatory approach to Algerian Muslims.[29] Cambon arrived in Algeria with a specific brief to implement a 'native policy', and this was immediately seen in his dealings with Muslims. In the southern territories of Algeria where French control was far from complete he made efforts to establish good relations with the powerful Sufi brotherhoods (*tariq*, pl. *turuq*) of the region and to Algerian Muslims generally, he offered assistance to pilgrims to Mecca and allowed pupils to stay away from school on religious festivals – a minor concession which in the past had been consistently refused by successive administrations.

Cambon also obtained a *fetwa*, or ruling, from the Sherif of Mecca declaring that it was permissible for Muslims to obey a non-Muslim government. Cambon hoped that this would sufficiently impress the Muslims of southern Algeria that armed conquest of the region would no longer be necessary – a hope that betrayed a basic and widely held misconception that equated the role and power of the Sherif of Mecca with that of the Pope in the Roman Catholic church. In any case, Cambon was pre-empted by the army which made a start on a military campaign in the south before he was able to distribute the *fetwa*. Somewhat aggrieved he nonetheless had fifty copies printed and offered them to other French colonial administrations including those of the Ivory Coast, Guinea, Senegal and French Sudan. The offer met with a mixed response: in the Ivory Coast and Guinea it was welcomed but in the Sudan the Governor, Grodet, thought that most of the local Muslim leaders were mere 'ignorant fanatics' and incapable of understanding the document.[30] A relatively minor incident but one which nevertheless illustrates well certain European concepts of Islam: Cambon's over-estimation of the power of the Sherif of Mecca and Grodet's refusal to recognise African Muslims as Muslims worthy of the name constitute two distinct views of Islam which continue at least to the end of the colonial period.

Cambon's concern with the brotherhoods derived in part from the opinions of Louis Rinn, the head of the Native Affairs Department, who had published a major study of Islam in Algeria in 1884[31] in which he argued that France should combat the Sufi brotherhoods with an official salaried Muslim clergy. Rinn's definition of the Sufi brotherhoods was somewhat vague but he was in no doubt that they were powerful and well organised and that they exercised a very pernicious influence on society:

> Their aim is the exploitation of human stupidity and of the most ridiculous superstition. Their practices ... are more often than not noisy and theatrical. ... Almost everywhere the active members of these brotherhoods are itinerant musicians, singers, dancers, snake charmers, jugglers and acrobats who mix in with their acts the better known prayers and verses from the Coran to which all of their spectators listen with respect.[32]

Cambon's willingness to do business with the Sufi brotherhoods in southern Algeria suggests that he did not agree with Rinn's damning analysis, but his eagerness to distribute the sherifian *fetwa* indicated perhaps that he shared Rinn's hopes in the possibility of sponsoring an official Muslim 'clergy'.

Rinn's study of Islam was succeeded thirteen years later by an altogether more substantial work which was to be of the greatest influence in the development of French understanding of Islam. O. Depont and X. Coppolani's *Les Confréries religieuses musulmanes* was the result of an official investigation into the state of Islam in Algeria which had been initiated in February 1895 by Cambon himself. Its two authors were respectively a senior administrator of a mixed Franco-Algerian district and a young and very ambitious civil servant.

Xavier Coppolani, the junior partner in the writing team, was one of the more colourful characters of the French colonial administration at the turn of the century.[33] He was born in a small Corsican village in 1866 where he stayed until the age of ten when his parents decided to emigrate to Algeria to join other members of the family. Coppolani's early childhood appears to have been dominated by his pious mother who, despite his later marriage, was to be the only woman about whom he ever spoke with any affection. Her simple piety together with the strong superstitions of the Corsican villagers served as models of popular religion which Coppolani later applied to his analysis of Islam. In Algeria Coppolani studied at the Ecole normale in Constantine and by the time he started his administrative career as Secretary in the *commune mixte* of Oued Cherg in 1889, he was a competent speaker of Arabic. He was, however, soon frustrated by his lowly position and began to look out for a patron willing to help him in his career. He succeeded in attracting the attention of Depont, and when in February 1895 Governor-General Cambon issued directives for a major study of the Sufi brotherhoods in Algeria it was to Depont and his young protégé that the mission was entrusted. Coppolani had got the break he was looking for.

Robert Arnaud, a friend, colleague and biographer of Coppolani, claimed that Coppolani did most of the research and that Depont's role was to lend an air of authority to the conclusions that would otherwise have been lacking. Certainly the language of *Les Confréries religieuses musulmanes* is similar to the language used in Coppolani's later reports and, like all of his writings, it contains a large element of propaganda for his own career. Coppolani, with his humble family background, needed more than a patron, he also needed a *raison d'être*. Islam or, more precisely, the Islamic threat was to be that *raison d'être* as Coppolani put himself forward as a person uniquely qualified to deal with the Muslim populations of north-west Africa.

Although it is clear that to a certain extent the book merely confirmed popular prejudices about Islam,[34] it was nonetheless in scientific terms a distinct improvement on Rinn's idiosyncratic study. It was also one of the clearest statements of what one can call the 'Algerian school's' understanding of Islam. Broadly speaking, this was an understanding which emphasised the power of Islamic structures and which attached particular importance to the role of the Sufi brotherhoods in providing the organisational infrastructure and the inspirational ideology.

In their introduction Depont and Coppolani warned:

> [Brotherhoods] are by their very nature the enemies of all established power, and Muslim states, as well as European powers which rule over Muslims, have to reckon with these anti-social preachers . . . the very soul of the pan-Islamic movement.

Sounding the crusader's trumpet, they continued:

> There is a work of justice and compassion to be done here which must be carried through without weakness. We must tear away from the rapacious hands of merciless and oppressive bigots a population which for too long has been encouraged to attack our institutions by the words and deeds of this politico–religious madness.[35]

The account of the Islamisation of the Maghreb conceded, however, that Islam was not the all-conquering force it might seem to be. Islam, they argued, was brought to the Maghreb by Arabs 'holding the Coran in one hand and the sword in the other' but met with stiff resistance from the indigenous Berbers before finally, and here the authors stressed that there was a lesson for the French, the Arabs, realising the dangers of a religiously, motivated resistance, compromised with the local beliefs and customs.[36] The power of superstition was, they argued, universal: 'Humanity is everywhere the same: Man, no matter to what category he belongs, poses himself . . . insoluble questions and even the most sceptical amongst us, in the midst of his pleasures, thinks of the Invisible and gives himself up to Nothingess.'[37] These remarks are indicative of an erosion of a positivist confidence in a clearly defined hierarchy of civilisations and cultures, and the point about the powerful influence of pre-Islamic custom was one that was to be well taken by later Islamicists in West Africa.[38]

Depont and Coppolani were impressed, too, by the ability of the brotherhoods to assimilate traditional beliefs and rightly saw this as one of their greatest strengths. They warned that when the Sufi formula for spiritual regeneration was preached to an ignorant and, they conceded, often an ill-treated populace,[39] then their message became 'extremely dangerous':

> One can sense. . . all the extreme exaltation of religious madness in which the echo of Islam is unfortunately always to be found and which demonstrates that we should never cease our vigilance, that we should on the contrary always prepare ourselves against the surprises that Muslim fanaticism has in store for us. The principal agents of this fanaticism are the brotherhoods, compact bundles of politico–religious forces which have seized hold of the minds of the masses whom they dominate and direct as they wish.

No longer able to mount open resistance – the French were too strong – they acted as 'secret societies agitating in the shadows and exploiting the Orient's proneness to *mahd*ism and pan-Islamism'.[40]

The danger represented by the brotherhoods was, therefore, vividly portrayed, and Coppolani was to make much of it over the next few years. The reader may well have trembled as he read such dire warnings which

21

probably confirmed all his worst suspicions of Islam but ... Depont and Coppolani had a remedy!

In the course of the description of the brotherhoods some hints were dropped that their fanaticism was measured and could be controlled. Firstly, although the authors stated that the strongest opposition to European expansion had been offered by the brotherhoods, they admitted that not all had been equally hostile and that in the conquest of Algeria, for example, the French had been able to form an alliance with the Tijaniyya.[41] Secondly, despite the susceptibility of the Algerian masses to mystic appeals, Depont and Coppolani argued that:

> Happily, the human soul has some penchants which not even the purest morality or the most austere doctrine can always succeed in controlling. Many of the founders of the brotherhoods whom posterity has painted as saints emerged occasionally from their solitude ... and abandoned themselves to the enjoyment of earthly pleasures.[42]

Earthly pleasures which in this material age the French could now offer in exchange for a little worldly obedience.

Tribute was also paid to Cambon's successful collaboration with some of the brotherhoods, and in their conclusions Depont and Coppolani sketched out the principles for policy in the future. They emphasised that history had shown that it was futile to attempt to destroy the brotherhoods and that, therefore, the French should try and work with rather than against them. Discreet official sponsorship of education together with subsidies for the construction of lodges for the brotherhoods were favoured as the methods of gaining future political control. By faithfully pursuing such policies France would do much, they concluded, to remove the threat of a pan-Islamic rebellion and would be assured of a broad sweep of allies rather than having to rely on a handful of proven collaborators.

Les Confréries religieuses musulmanes was an extremely important work and it contains a wealth of detail that has been used by successive generations of students of Islam in Algeria. For our purposes, however, it is more interesting to see it for its ideological content, as a sophisticated statement of the beliefs of the 'Algerian school'. One of the most striking aspects of the book was the emphasis placed on the Sufi brotherhoods, to the extent that other forms of Islam were almost wholly ignored. The accent on Sufism is significant partly because it exaggerated in the European's mind the mystical and mysterious origins of Islam and partly, too, because it encouraged a belief in the innately conspiratorial nature of Islam. On the northern shores of the Mediterranean the idea of a 'secret society agitating in the shadows' was common currency and referred, according to one's convictions, either to the Freemasons or the Jesuits. (For someone with Corsican origins it might, of course, have had other more sinister Godfatherly connotations!) The year after the publication of Depont and Coppolani's work, France was divided over another great scandal full of accusations and counter-accusations of conspiracy and treason as the

Dreyfus affair broke upon the political scene. A few years later with the advent of the Bloc républicain to power in France a four-year battle was engaged between the government and the Church. The first attack was made against the monastic orders – the *congrégations* – the same word that was often used to designate the Sufi brotherhoods. Depont and Coppolani's work – indeed the whole question of French understanding of Islam in this period – must be seen in this context.[43]

Thus, although the Algerian experience undoubtedly consisted of many different strands there was nonetheless a clear evolution in official policy towards Islam. This official policy was most explicitly stated in the conclusions to Depont and Coppolani's study but one should also stress the tradition of administrative scholarship associated with the *bureaux arabes*, administrative unease about the potentially disruptive effects of militant Christianity in a Muslim society and, finally, the obvious eagerness to recognise ethnic variations of Islam within the colony. As the inexperienced French administration in West Africa looked for a policy to apply towards its Muslim subjects, it was natural that they should look first towards Algeria. How long Algeria would remain an acceptable model for the French West African administration will be seen in Part II of this book.

Part II

1898–1912: The fear of Islam

Depuis notre conversation, tous les passants que je rencontre je leur trouve je ne sais quoi de louche dans l'allure. Je m'inquiète s'ils me regardent; et ceux qui ne me regardent pas, on dirait qu'ils font semblant de ne pas me voir. Je ne m'étais pas rendu compte jusqu' aujourd'hui combien la présence des gens dans la rue est rarement justifiable. (André Gide, *Les Caves du Vatican*, 1914.)

Introduction

By the turn of the century the era of overt military conquest had come to an end. The conquest of the western Sudan had created heroes – Archinard, Gallieni and Marchand amongst the best known – but the financial strain it imposed on the colonial budget made these heroes the enemies of the colonial accountants in Paris. By the 1890s economy was the order of the day, and Chaudié, the Governor-General of AOF, was expected to restrain the activity of his military colleagues.[1] The other imperative, linked to the need for economy, was organisation. Military conquest had not only been costly but it had also been haphazard. Legislation passed between 1895 and 1904 gradually imposed order on the situation with the creation of a federal government headed by the Governor-General based in Dakar. By 1904 the federal government had effective political control over the local governments of the various colonies of the Federation. Through its control of the federal budget, to which all colonies contributed their revenue raised from custom duties, the federal government also exercised economic control. The system survived more or less intact throughout the period covered in this study.[2]

One aspect of the transfer of power from the military to a civilian administration was a change in attitude towards Islam. Chautemps, the Minister of Colonies in the mid-1890s, gave specific instructions to Chaudié not to underestimate the power and authority of Islam in West Africa and to accord it the respect it deserved.[3] However, these instructions and the attitude that lay behind them require qualification and explanation. They were directed principally at the administration of the French Sudan and were derived from an influential body of opinion in Algeria where a similar antagonism existed between advocates of military conquest and diplomatic persuasion as in West Africa.[4]

The link between Algeria and sub-Saharan Africa was to be personified in Xavier Coppolani whose work in Algeria had come to the eye of the administration south of the Sahara. Coppolani, having been entrusted with a mission to investigate the state of Islam in the French Sudan, formulated a grandiose Islamic policy which he argued would guarantee French supremacy over the whole of north-west Africa.

27

However, his scheme foundered, partly as a result of tension and conflict within the French community and partly as a result of its innate impracticability. Thus the hopes expressed by Chautemps and others in the 1890s that the final stages of the 'pacification' of African Muslims could be achieved without bloodshed were abandoned. Chapter three is chiefly concerned with the intense anxieties that succeeded the early optimism about Islamic policy. In the first decade of the century, events throughout the Muslim world caused considerable alarm amongst colonial powers, and the French moved from a tentative policy of co-option to one based on close surveillance of Muslim leaders. They were also years marked by an intense hostility to marabouts, and the chapter discusses aspects of this peculiarily French distaste for what was termed *maraboutage*.

Chapter four examines the question of education: at a time when religious legislation over education was dividing opinion in metropolitan France, French attitudes to Muslim education were particularly illuminating and revealing of the often very contradictory way in which Islam was viewed by France's so-called anti-clerical colonial administration. Chapter five, concerning events in the Futa Jallon in 1909–11, is a case-study of the consequences of a combination of French anxieties about Islam generally, an overriding acceptance of racial and ethnic stereotypes and, again, conflicting ambitions within the French administration.

3

The fear of Islam

The decade before the First World War was rightly seen by the European powers as a time of great unrest in the Islamic world. Dramatic and alarming metaphors abounded in the numerous articles written about Islam as the rumblings in the officer messes in Turkey and in the nationalist printing presses in Alexandria were widely supposed to be the first signs of a 'volcanic explosion' within the world of Islam, unleashing all the latent fanaticism of the 'Mohammedan peoples' against the ill-prepared defences of Europe.

European fears were founded on the revolutions in Persia (1906), the deposition of both the Ottoman and the Moroccan sultans (1908), the growing radicalism of the Egyptian nationalists and the first Italian–Sanusiyya war, all of which combined to add a fresh sense of urgency and a new dimension to traditional European Islamophobia. The Japanese defeat of the Russians in 1906 was also a severe blow to European confidence about its ability to contain the diverse forces of the 'Orient'.[1]

Missionaries came to see their major enemy as Islam, and two Protestant conferences in Cairo (1906) and Lucknow (1911) addressed themselves specifically to the problem of evangelisation amongst Muslims.[2] Even the scholarly *Revue du Monde Musulman* had a special issue in 1911 devoted entirely to 'La Conquête de l'islam'.[3] Snouck-Hurgronje and C.-H. Becker, the most respected experts on Islam in Holland and Germany, were employed by their respective governments as advisers on Islamic policy, and their articles were swiftly translated into other European languages.[4] There was then a perception of a struggle which opposed Christian Europe against the Muslim 'Orient': a struggle which, it should be stressed, the Europeans by no means felt entirely confident about winning. To a certain extent this perception was merely a continuation of a suspicion and fear of Islam that dates back to the Crusades, but in the early twentieth century the fear was not so much of what Islam was (or what the Europeans believed it to be) but of what, mixed up with nationalism, it might become.

Colonial rivalries of the past thirty years were not, however, swept aside in the face of the common enemy of Islam. In particular, the French, whose colonial expansion had been so intimately linked with the experience of metropolitan humiliation in 1870–71,[5] were ultra-sensitive to European challenges to their Empire. Since Fashoda and the establishment of the *entente cordiale* (1904), French suspicion of 'Perfide Albion' had been tempered. Rather it was the Germans, the new lords of Alsace–Lorraine, who caused the greatest headaches for French colonialists as French and Germans clashed in two areas in Africa. In Wadai and Tibesti in Central Africa, the French suspected that the Germans were intriguing with local chiefs against the infant French presence. The area on the eastern border of the French Empire was of symbolic interest to French colonialists: a plainly barren land, it nonetheless represented an important link in the chain of French territories running from the Mediterranean to the Congo.

Morocco, the other area where French and German interests clashed dramatically, was altogether different.[6] Never part of the Ottoman Empire, its independence had been respected by the Europeans during the 'Scramble for Africa', but during the reign of Sultan Mawlay Hassan (1873–94) European interest in Morocco increased greatly. For example, between 1864 and 1894 the European presence in Morocco increased from 1,350 to 9,000 as new commercial and administrative possibilities were provided by the Sultan's schemes for modernising the country. As the French reconciled themselves to British pre-eminence in Egypt and the Sudan, their eyes turned to Morocco. Treaties were signed with both Britain and Spain in 1904 which prepared the way for an eventual French occupation of the bulk of the country. The occupation was justified by the French on the grounds of the anarchy of the Moroccan state where political stability had deteriorated during the reign of Mawlay Hassan and showed no signs of improving under his young successor, Abd al-Aziz (1900–8). Only the Germans stood in the way of the smooth diplomatic relations for the carve up of Morocco. In April 1905 Kaiser Wilhelm II landed in Tangiers and proclaimed German support for an independent Moroccan state. A diplomatic crisis ensued before the Algeciras conference of the following year provided an acceptable compromise. Meanwhile, French plans for occupying Morocco moved on a stage as troops arrived in Casablanca and Oujda, on the Algerian border, ostensibly to protect French citizens. In 1908, Abd al-Aziz, whom the French had supported, was deposed and replaced by his younger brother, Mawlay Hafiz. The new Sultan, however, was no more able to defend himself against his (Moroccan) enemies than his brother had been. In 1911 he found himself besieged in Fez and had to be rescued by a French military expedition. The Germans responded to the French march on Fez by sending a gunboat to Agadir, and a new diplomatic crisis ensued. The following year the myth of Moroccan independence was finally given the lie, and a French Protectorate was declared. Resistance to French rule was stiff in the traditionally unruly *Bilad al-Siba* ('Land of Disorder'), particularly in the south and in the Rif mountains in the north, and it was not until 1934 that the whole country was eventually 'pacified'.

French commentators did not doubt that these events in the Islamic world were of direct consequence to themselves. A. Le Chatelier, the editor of the *Revue du Monde Musulman*, argued that:

> Through Algeria and its proximity to Morocco, through Senegal and through the new provinces in Chad, France is an African Muslim power.[7]

As a 'Muslim power' itself France was bound to take an interest in what was happening in other Muslim countries. In a later article Le Chatelier warned of the great unity within the Muslim world:

> From Morocco to China, from South Africa to Siberia, the Muslim of one country feels quite at home in the country of another Muslim, just as the Englishman [feels at home] from Vancouver to Hong Kong, from Cape Town to Nepal. Like the Englishman, too, the Muslim considers himself above all other varieties of the human species. And finally, like the Englishman, once he has finished praying and praising the Prophet, the Muslim has one overriding preoccupation, that of profit.[8]

This argument is a clear suggestion that wider issues of national self-image were at stake. On one level Islam was part of the hostile world which surrounded France's natural borders but on another it offered France (now transformed into a 'Muslim power') a unique opportunity to increase her influence throughout the world – and score a few points against some old enemies.

It was perhaps in West Africa at the turn of the century where one of the most optimistic views of France's relations with Islam was taken. Although there was a considerable variety of opinion there was nonetheless an influential body of opinion which took an essentially positive view of Islam. Le Chatelier had written an impressive general study of Islam in West Africa in 1888, but had delayed publication for over ten years because he was not confident of the accuracy of his findings.[9] His chief cause for doubt lay in the fact that his conclusions – that the Sufi Muslim brotherhoods played a relatively minor role in West Africa – contradicted the received wisdom of the Algerian school of thought. Le Chatelier argued that the hierarchically minded Algerian administration had a tendency to exaggerate the power and organisation of the brotherhoods.[10] He conceded that some brotherhoods did combine great political and religious strength but argued that 'that does not mean that all Muslim brotherhoods should be considered as immense temporal religious associations sending out their masonic roots throughout the Mahommetan world'.[11] However, Le Chatelier (who was very impressed with the *cultural* power of Islam throughout the world) forecast that the poor organisation of the brotherhoods would not prevent Islam from spreading rapidly across West Africa.[12] One of the reasons for his confident prediction was his conviction that Islam was far superior to traditional African religious beliefs which, he said, entirely lacked 'a philosophical system',[13] In a paragraph which candidly expressed the European dilemma, he wrote:

> When one studies the African races or when one lives amongst them one cannot help but be struck by the superiority of the Muslim over the fetishist.

> The former is sometimes a great cutter of throats, a slave dealer and a rebel but he has always a more open intelligence and a less primitive civilisation. *Even when seen as an enemy it is nonetheless to him that we give our preferences.*[14]

This piece of advice was offered more in the spirit of common sense than of scientific enquiry, and its common sense was echoed in a manual published in 1902 which offered a wide range of practical advice to Europeans living in Africa.[15] Most of the book was taken up with medical advice, for European mortality rates were still high and epidemics of Yellow Fever could still decimate the populations of towns, Nonetheless, Islam did have a place even here, and the opinions of the practically minded Dr Barot are of considerable interest. In his chapter on 'social relations' between Europeans and Africans he wrote:

> Relationships with Europeans are codified, Islam being a religion recognised in the same way as any other. . . . Negro Muslims, who are distracted from the influence of Turkish and Moroccan sultans, are not hostile to us. On the contrary, by a wise and just administration we should win their confidence and assume the leadership of Islam in West Africa. It is a considerable and vital force which is easy for us to turn to our profit. . . . One day [Islam] could assure us supremacy over all this continent.
>
> The fetishist peoples who have lived some time in contact with us have assumed all our vices, particularly alcoholism. . . . They obey us through fear of the policeman. . . . It is necessary to consider and treat them like children. Only a slow adaptation over three or four generations will lead them to a conception of social duties and moral laws.
>
> Amongst the fetishist peoples whom we are in the process of conquering we have to struggle against the enormous influence of witches. . . . In the countries still to be explored we cannot count on anything except luck and chance; for the *griot* bought one day with the price of gold will declare himself against us the following day if the white rats, the kolas, or the other oracles give an unfavourable opinion. Many explorers have been the victims of the idiotic capriciousness of fetishists.[16]

For early European administrators worried about their health and generally impatient to return to the metropole, animist beliefs and rites must have been not only incomprehensible but also at times simply terrifying. One should not be taken in by the bravado of colonialist rhetoric and believe that all Europeans were self-confident and unquestioning exporters of an hegemonic culture: fear and insecurity as much as arrogance made up the colonial psyche.

Dr Barot's book contained a preface written by Louis Gustave Binger who was Director of the Africa Department in the Colonial Ministry from 1902 to 1906.[17] Binger himself had written two slim volumes on the subject of Islam in Africa based on his observations as an explorer and administrator. The first book was published in 1891 and dealt with the issue of slavery[18] and the second, published in 1906, considered the possibility of pan-Islamic rebellion.[19] On the subject of slavery Binger challenged Christian self-righteousness arguing that on the whole slaves were better treated in Muslim Africa than were the unemployed of Paris. The second book, with the ironic title of *Le Péril de l'islam*, was similarly dismissive of another major European obsession with Islam – pan-Islamism. Binger, who identified strongly with the secularist movement in France (he was on the Comité de patronage of the Mission laïque[20]), argued for a policy of strict religious neutrality which avoided the dangers of persecuting Islam:

> It would [he said] be unjust and pointless to encourage a combatative attitude towards Islam: unjust because intolerance should be banished from the human heart; pointless, because one does not make a religion disappear through persecution.

Binger was confident that 'progress' – a combination of railways and schools – would ensure that Islam would eventually decline in Africa.[21]

It would be unwise to label Le Chatelier, Barot and Binger too closely together. With their very different backgrounds and purposes the three men would certainly be surprised today to find themselves classed together. Nonetheless, their views at the turn of the century do add up to a picture of Islam in Africa which was generally positive about its virtues and not unduly concerned about its vices.

However, such views failed to convince administrators and scholars in Paris and the various administrative centres of AOF. Instead, the pre-war period came to be characterised by intense suspicion of all forms of Muslim activity, as French officials listened attentively for echoes of the Alexandran printing presses in the back streets of Dakar and Conakry. The unease caused by the events in North Africa and in the Middle East was compounded firstly by the conspiratorial climate of metropolitan politics, secondly by the idiosyncracies of the Frenchmen in charge of advising the colonial government on Islamic affairs and, thirdly, by the turn of events in West Africa itself.

XAVIER COPPOLANI AND THE 'PEACEFUL PACIFICATION' OF MAURITANIA

As the nineteenth century drew to a close and the accountants in Paris began to reckon up the cost of military conquest of the western Sudan, pressure was applied to the local administrators to find cheaper methods of maintaining French rule.[22] This was particularly important for the administrators on the limits of the French African Empire. At the turn of the century vast areas of land on the Saharan fringes lay outside effective French control. A French trader who had spent eighteen years in the region advocated starving the Tuareg into submission along with the marabouts, whom he described as 'a vermin that becomes dangerous unless it is crushed'.[23] However, the Governor of the Sudan, General de Trentinnian, was of a more liberal and tolerant disposition and was hopeful that a less drastic method could be found to obtain the submission of the Tuareg. He identified Islam as the key factor and reflected in his annual report for 1898 that:

> The influence of Islam has almost always been a powerful lever used against us; it is an inexhaustible seam for the marabouts who exploit the credulity of the naturally simple and good Blacks as well as the instincts of the Tuareg, so proud of their independence and so ardent in war and pillage.... The utilisation of Islam ... is a question of prime importance. It has become the object of the constant preoccupation of the government of Sudan.[24]

In a letter to the Commander of the north and north-east region of the Sudan he wrote that:

> Religion which looms up in front of us like an insuperable barrier can, in capable hands, become a precious instrument [of conquest]. By making ourselves the protectors of Islam we shall get to know it better, we will make use of its resources ... and with perseverence, we shall be able to draw towards us certain influential men who still appreciate the goods of this world.[25]

Trentinnian followed up these optimistic remarks by inviting Xavier Coppolani to go on a mission amongst the Moorish and Tuareg tribes of the Sahel in the hope that Coppolani's Algerian experience would enable him to negotiate a settlement with the local leaders that would leave the French in effective control of the region without the expense of a military campaign.

Although Coppolani had hoped that the Foreign Ministry would send him on a world-wide study tour of Islam,[26] he nonetheless welcomed the chance to put some of his knowledge to a practical test. It is also clear that he sensed right from the start that a successful mission would do his own career prospects no harm at all. As self-publicist Coppolani had few rivals. In his report on the mission he argued that a military expedition would have been out of the question as it would have provoked the suspicion of the tribesmen and condemned the mission to costly failure:

> No [he continued in language that speaks volumes about his modesty]. My role was greater. My action was to be one of energy, tolerance and humanity towards the untamed Muslims who were waiting for me. I had to inspire confidence in them and to achieve this it was necessary to surprise them ... as a friend, in the name of the Governor of Sudan, their natural protector. I needed confidence in myself, and this confidence was never found wanting. I knew from experience that these fanatics who had generally been described to me in a bad light were for the most part men appreciative of our sentiments of justice and wisdom. Furthermore, I was only too well aware of their divisions, their interests and their misery not to worry for a moment about the welcome they were to keep for me.[27]

However, Coppolani's report was distinctly vague about the details of his mission. It seems he left Nioro on 19 January 1899 and returned barely a month later having obtained the submission of the principal tribes of the region, the Mechdouf and the Allouch, without a shot having been fired. According to Coppolani he simply rode out and met the chiefs who everywhere gave him a warm welcome because 'in their eyes I was the happy messenger who brought lasting peace and the hope of tranquility that was so necessary in their tribes'.[28]

Even greater confusion surrounds the second part of Coppolani's mission amongst the Tuareg, north of Timbuktu, as there appears to be no surviving report and very little correspondence between Coppolani and his colleagues. The two most illuminating accounts are contained in personal letters to Auguste Terrier, President of the Comité de l'Afrique française, written by two observers of the mission. Curiously, their accounts are almost wholly at odds with each other.

The first letter was written by Robert Arnaud, who was a great admirer of Coppolani and who accompanied him on the mission. Addressed to 'Mon Capitaine' it described how Arnaud and 'Coppo' had arrived in Timbuktu having successfully completed the earlier part of the mission around Nioro:

> At Tombouctou serious problems were waiting for us. Up until our arrival the policy followed had been to consider the nomad as the enemy and to protect the Negro excessively. This had naturally alienated us from the white populations, Moors and Tuaregs, and one couldn't wander outside Tombouctou without danger. We had to do something about this because of the great interest there is for France in winning the sympathy, the alliance or the clientele of the tribes who belong as much to the south of Algeria as they do to the north of Sudan. An officer was there, a Captain Henrys, who agreed completely. . . . Coppo had worked upon the Moors. . . . The Tuareg as well had come to terms with us. To this end we left at the end of March in the direction of the eastern wells where we were supposed to find the main dissident tribes. The chief of the Bouamine came with us. One by one the chiefs of the Kel Antasar arrived to ask for *amam* and offered serious guarantees of submission provided that we gave them justice, that is to say provided we didn't shoot them at random and that we stopped raiding their women in order to satisfy the ardours of men starved of white flesh and that we designated them land for transhumance. Their demands were too reasonable not to be accepted, and an order has just been sent from Tombouctou designed to prevent the capture of white women in the future, and women held are to be released.
>
> In short our tour has been most fruitful. The Regagda have joined the Kel Antasar in seeking peace; in this country of so-called savages there was only one cry, – 'Give us tranquility!' . . . The famous Sakraouai, chief of the Igoudanen, came to pay hommage and complete his submission. It was truly a fine sight; there were just the two of us, alone without escort or arms, alone in the middle of a hundred warriors armed up to the teeth, all arrogant with great black eyes [and] long medieval spears. Before returning to Tombouctou Coppo was able to open negotiations with the Aouelliminden who had been upset by a recent patrol, but the submission of this great tribe will be a matter of time.

After a perilous trip back in a leaky canoe they returned to Timbuktu where:

35

> Coppo had a hard task, he had to have the treaties ratified, receive dele-
> gations, reassure the chiefs and put up with all sorts of dirty handshakes.
> Finally . . . all has been brought to a happy conclusion!
>
> However, the shortcomings of the old days when policy consisted of not
> having one and saying 'Kill everything!' have alienated the chief of the
> Berabiches; he has been writing insolent letters . . . and making a nuisance of
> himself. We had to change his ideas and so we are going to Araouan. We are
> leaving this evening in the company of Moors for the town (?) or village (?) of
> Araouan. If we get there we shall be the first Frenchmen since René Caillié to
> have done so, if we get there that is, for one must not forget that Major Laing
> was killed on the way.[29]

Arnaud's letter is interesting on several counts, not the least of which is as
an insight into the character of the author who shortly afterwards became
the chief adviser to the government of AOF on Islamic affairs. The
unflattering comments on previous administrations are particularly note-
worthy, and the final evocation of Caillié and Laing remind us that at the
turn of the century European knowledge of certain parts of Africa was far
from complete and it could still *almost* be said that 'Geographers in Afric
maps/With savage pictures fill their gaps'.[30] But despite Arnaud's enthusiastic 'Boy's Own' description, the mission did not appear to have had any
concrete results.

This suspicion is reinforced not only by Coppolani's own curious reti-
cence about the second half of the mission but above all by the second letter
to Terrier, written by Captain Henrys (whom Arnaud had mentioned in his
letter as an admirer of Coppolani). Henrys reported that:

> From Tombouctou to Bamba, Coppolani has only had dealings with com-
> pliant regions and has obtained the submission only of the Kel Antasar, who
> had already submitted. Then we went on to Araouane but he did not enter the
> town. The chief of the Berabiches forbad him to enter and made him establish
> his camp more than a kilometre from the town. . . . Unable even to take a
> photographic view he returned as quickly as possible and not in the least bit
> reassured. . . . I scarcely believe more in what he has done in the Sahel than
> the results obtained here.[31]

In a sense both letters were political and are probably more acurately seen
as attempts by civilian and military interests to lobby the metropolitan
colonialist pressure groups. As was to become clear over the next few years
little love was lost between Coppolani and the French military who
regarded each other from a position of mutual scorn.

Coppolani returned to Paris in the late summer of 1899 somewhat
chastened by his experiences and entirely convinced of the superiority of the
'white' Moors and Tuaregs over their black neighbours.[32] In Paris he began
to lobby strenuously for a more active French involvement in the area of
contemporary Mauritania and for the creation of a unified north-west
African Empire stretching from the Mediterranean across the Sahara to the
banks of the Senegal and Niger rivers. Despite long-standing trading
interests along the coastal and riverain regions of Mauritania, the French

had never been tempted to venture into the interior of the country. In Paris there was certainly support for the idea of a unified empire which bridged the natural barrier of the desert,[33] and it seems that Coppolani was able to win over the newly-elected Prime Minister, Waldeck Rousseau. However, equally there was no shortage of opponents to the scheme for more direct French involvement in Mauritania. The Foreign Office, with the memory of Fashoda still recent, was anxious about the consequences of such a policy on the diplomatic relations with Spain and Britain, both of whom had interests on the coast of the western Sahara, and in Africa itself the government in St Louis simply did not think that it was worth it.[34]

The balance of attitudes was reflected in the eventual compromise solution as the Colonial Ministry agreed – but with some reluctance – to the creation of a new administrative unit known as Mauretanie occidentale which was to be governed by a civilian *résident* based in St Louis and appointed by the Governor-General. In addition, a new department 'designed to centralise all the documents relating to Islam, the brotherhoods and the topography of the Saharan regions' was created and called the Service spécial des affaires musulmanes.[35]

Coppolani, who had hoped for the establishment of a full protectorate over Mauritania, reluctantly accepted the outcome.[36] However, he continued to lobby for a more positive policy but faced increasing scepticism from the authorities in Africa who were being severely shaken by the Yellow Fever epidemic (1900–2) in St Louis. In addition, traditional objections to the occupation of the interior of Mauritania, based on the warlike reputation of its inhabitants, were reinforced by the failure of a recent expedition which had set out in an expansionist mood (backed by a particularly chauvinist campaign in the national paper *Le Soleil*) to investigate the possibility of a trans-Saharan railway but which soon succumbed to illness and only narrowly escaped destruction at the hands of the followers of Sheikh Ma el-Ainin, the most powerful of the Mauritanian chiefs.[37]

In order to overcome official scepticism Coppolani was forced to resort to increasingly optimistic prognostications in order to stir up some enthusiasm. Islam, and in particular the Islam of the Sufi brotherhoods, was the essential feature of his optimism as Coppolani, in his first major report as *résident*, argued that:

> With their co-operation we shall have peace, the security of the caravan routes and the solution to the problem of our north-west African Empire. Without their help we shall have Holy War involving a disproportionate expense of men and money. It would mean a step into the unknown and would cause a permanent state of hostility with the Saharan and Moroccan populations.
>
> Fortunately, Muslims have more or less the same character under different latitudes. These white races whose adventurous and commercial spirit has, we believe, been wrongly presented to us as that of untamed Muslims lost on the so-called Saharan steppes are no other than those Arabs and Berbers of the tent that all Algerians have seen. . . . We have found amongst them the same tribes, the same language, the same morals and the same religion, albeit with a

> more liberal element than amongst their brothers of North Africa. What has
> enabled us to traverse without conflict the principal Moor and Tuareg camps is
> the presence of those same brotherhoods and those same religious groups that
> we have studied in Algeria and that we found there just as interested in serving
> our cause.[38]

This argument was further refined in his report of October 1901 to an
Interministerial Commission which had been created (partly at Coppolani's
suggestion)[39] to investigate the problems of north-west Africa. In his report
Coppolani argued that there was a sharp distinction between the societies
on either side of the Senegal River – 'a demarcation line between Whites
and Blacks that not even el-Hadj-Omar and his Toucouleur were able to
cross'. He also stressed that the social structure in Mauritania lent itself
naturally to an Islamic policy. The particularity of the Moorish social order
which justified his argument was the distinction between the warrior
Hassanic tribes and the clerical (or, in the parlance of the day, maraboutic)
tribes. The distinction, he argued, was simple:

> A warrior is neither a trader nor a manufacturer, he can neither read nor
> write. He is the master of the gun, the representative of force and con-
> sequently the defender of the country. . . . The clergy is represented by
> veritable tribes of learned men. They are independent of the Hassania, never
> take part in war but rather dispense justice and are mediators of peace. Their
> rosary replaces the gun. . . . The action of the religious leaders is preponderant
> over the masses and often over the warrior chiefs as well. They have become
> the auxiliaries of our policy and could become the precious instruments of
> pacification if, bearing in mind the rivalry between warrior tribes, we combine
> the various elements and attack the question with determination and unity of
> views.[40]

Coppolani's explanation was a crude simplification of the social structure of
Moorish society. The caste system of many of the societies of the southern
Sahara did indeed distinguish between a warrior and a religious nobility; but
in practice the distinction was often blurred as there were clerical groups
who took up arms just as there were warriors who forsook them.[41]
Furthermore, the ability of clerical leaders to prevail over warriors was by
no means certain, and Coppolani's assertion that 'the action of the religious
leaders was often preponderant over . . . the warriors' was little more than
wishful thinking in the somewhat anarchic circumstances of the early
twentieth century.[42]

One of the most striking examples of Coppolani's simplistic analysis was
his statement that 'Sheikh Ma el-Ainin is the brother of our friends and
protégés Sheikh Saad Bu and Sheikh Sidi el-Kheir and is consequently our
ally'.[43] In fact Sheikh Ma el-Ainin and his son, el-Hiba, were to be the most
bitter opponents of French rule in Mauritania and Morocco.

Before returning to Mauritania Coppolani, along with some other
like-minded persons in Paris, founded a new journal called the *Revue
Franco-Musulmane et Saharienne* of which thirteen issues were printed

between 1902 and 1903. It enjoyed the patronage of the leading lights of the Parti colonial[44] and called for greater French involvement in the Muslim world, but particularly in north-west Africa, and for a policy based on respect for Islamic values.[45]

In October 1902 Governor-General Roume appointed Coppolani as his civil commissioner in Mauritania and entrusted him specifically with the task of bringing stability and security to Trarza, the area with which France had the most contact and to whose leaders France was still paying an annual custom duty for the right to take part in trade. During the last quarter of a century the deteriorating political situation in Trarza was both symptom and cause of the decline in the gum trade. Leadership within Trarza was fiercely contested, and of the six emirs who ruled between 1885 and 1903, five had been assassinated by a blood relative.[46] Coppolani's brief was to prop up the ailing government of the Emir Ahmet Salum, who was facing family pressures of the most unenviable kind. A military expedition sent to deal with the problems in February 1902 had failed to deter Ahmet Salum's opponents,[47] and by October, when Coppolani took charge, the Emir's situation was very precarious indeed. However, within five months Coppolani had convinced Roume that he had the situation under control. The Governor-General wrote enthusiastically to the Minister in Paris that Coppolani had been able to exploit the divisions between the clerical and Hassanic tribes and to take full advantage of the negotiating skills of the country's leading marabouts, Sheikh Sidia and Sheikh Saad Bu, in order to restore effective French authority. Roume was bullish about French prospects in Mauritania and urged Paris to agree to a more positive policy to ensure that the colony would fulfil its promise of becoming 'one of the finest provinces of West Africa'.[48]

However, despite these optimistic prognostications it soon became clear that French control of the area was far from complete, and with this growing realisation, Roume's confidence in Coppolani began to falter. The military lobby in West Africa were also highly critical of Coppolani whom they suspected, quite justifiably, of trying to carve out a little empire for himself in Mauritania. Furthermore, the St Louis based trading houses were by now openly trying to discredit Coppolani, especially after his attempt to control the lucrative arms trade in June 1904. Throughout 1903 and 1904 the French were involved in various skirmishes with a number of different Moorish groups. The most serious of these was an attack on the French post of Aleg in December 1903 by an alliance of Ahmeidu, a former emir of Brackna, and the Hassanic Edawich tribe. As the skirmishes continued Coppolani's critics became more vocal since it became apparent that the supposedly inexpensive and peaceful occupation of the interior of Mauritania was not as simple as some had hoped.[49]

Nonetheless, by the end of 1904 Coppolani had succeeded in winning qualified support for establishing French posts in Adrar, the hinterland region of Trarza and Brackna, where opponents of the pro-French emirs were able to take refuge.[50] In December 1904, Coppolani wrote that 'Respect of the religion, morals and customs of the population, backed by a sufficient defensive force, will be a guarantee of success'.[51] Within a few months the mission had been assembled, and by April 1905 Coppolani had reached Tidjikja where he was forced to make an unscheduled stop to wait for some supplies which had been delayed. The delay was to have disastrous consequences for the mission: on the night of 12 May, Coppolani was attacked and killed by a Muslim belonging to the Ghoudf brotherhood who had successfully penetrated the defences of the camp.[52]

Coppolani's death at the hands of a Muslim highlighted the fragility of the base on which he was seeking to unify the French north-west African Empire and seemed to discredit the whole idea of a Muslim policy. Undoubtedly, Coppolani, in the pursuit of his own career interests, raised hopes of such a policy too high with his optimistic and simplistic pronouncements. The reality of the situation was that Moorish politics were of an exceptional complexity in which alliances were generally insecure and short-lived. There was a strong suspicion, particularly among the military, that the clerical tribes had been taking the French for a ride, posing as the innocent victims of Hassanic marauders. Captain Frèrejean, one of the soldiers most active in the Mauritanian campaigns, considered that:

> The marabouts have done everything to exploit the initial profound ignorance of the French, posing as victims whereas too often they were merely trying to enlist our support in their illegitimate refusal to pay their suzerains for the protection which had been afforded them for centuries.[53]

This attitude was reflected in the subsequent policy of involving the warrior tribes in a much more active role in the 'policing' of the desert regions, as warriors were integrated into the French army in *meharist* units as early as 1906.[54]

Paradoxically, the legacy of Coppolani – the first of a long line of Islamic 'experts' hired by the administration in West Africa – was one of insecurity as much as knowledge about Islam. Whilst his close relationships with leading Mauritanian marabouts such as Sheikh Sidia were a positive achievement, Coppolani's obvious failure to bring security to the area combined with the manner of his death became object lessons in the complexity of Islamic politics.

THE DEVELOPMENT OF FRENCH SUSPICIONS

Coppolani's death came at a time when the French were having a lot of other misgivings about the role of Islam in all aspects of colonial affairs. Coppolani's belief in the positive contribution of Islam to African civilisation was not shared by his colleagues on the other side of the River Senegal. One of the key personalities in Coppolani's Mauritanian policy was Sheikh Saad Bu, whose authority as one of the leading Qadiri marabouts extended far beyond the confines of Mauritania.[55] Early in 1905 Sheikh Saad Bu started to make arrangements for his annual tour to collect alms from disciplines on the left bank of the Senegal. Coppolani raised no objection to the tour but when news of the Sheikh's intentions reached the Lieutenant-Governor of Senegal, Camille Guy, objections were immediately voiced. Apart from anything else Guy was upset by Coppolani's lack of courtesy in failing to consult him about the tour which he considered would only serve to further impoverish the people of Senegal.[56] These objections were shared by the administrator of the *cercle* of Thies, M. Jacques. Reporting on his meeting with the Sheikh, who openly admitted that he had come to collect alms in order to repay debts in St Louis, M. Jacques explained:

> Cheikh Saadaibou exercises a great influence on black Muslims. . . . For these people his arrival was a holiday, a day of celebration. Quiet and tranquil in his camp he received numerous presents either in silver or in kind, some of them even from the far side of Baol. Every day sees emissaries bringing more offerings than the previous day. The traders, who are somewhat unhappy, go as far as saying that the natives sell their groundnuts in order to get money which they can then offer to the great marabout. I think that they are exaggerating but it cannot be denied that many natives bring him presents and that his passage through the colony will to a certain extent have made money rarer.[57]

Similar arguments were advanced later in the year when two of the Sheikh's envoys arrived in Cayor to collect alms. Guy was on leave, but his interim complained that although he was aware that 'this religious chief enjoys considerable political influence in Mauritania' and that he did not want to be 'ungracious about the services he has rendered on the right bank', nonetheless he did not see why he should be permitted to collect alms from a population which he considered to be over burdened as it was with taxation.[58] On his return to Senegal the following year, Guy took up the argument again pointing to the damage caused, firstly by the drain of money away from the colony as a result of the tours and, secondly, by the damage done to France's political authority by the apparent French 'subservience' to 'certain Muslim chiefs'.[59]

Although this particular issue was never clearly resolved the debate does serve to illustrate the fundamental difference in approach to Islam between the Senegalese and Mauritanian administrations. Whereas in Mauritania men such as Sheikh Saad Bu were regarded as influential leaders whose support was crucial to French domination in the area, in Senegal the same men were regarded at times as little more than idle scroungers. The image of the marabout from Mauritania as a peace-loving scholar was transformed totally south of the River Senegal where *marabout* and its associated concept of *maraboutage* came to take on a very particular meaning, a meaning which represented a peculiarly French interpretation of an African reality.

41

One part of the French definition of the marabout related to the supposedly parasitical nature of his existence. Implicit comparisons were drawn between the marabout in Africa and the village *curé* in France, and at a time of strong anti-clericalism in France this was intended to be a critical rather than complimentary comparison. Like the village priest, the marabout was accused of obfuscation and of leading a life-style which was essentially exploitative of the mass of believers. The role of the supernatural – in the form of amulets and special magic formulae – was seen to be as common a feature of rural French Catholicism as it was of popular Islam in Africa. Likewise the use of the two languages, Latin and Arabic, in the two religions could be interpreted as being intended to keep the masses in a state of ignorance and to encourage exaggerated reverence for those religious men who were masters of these esoteric tongues. However, to this long-established and almost universal image of a parasitic priesthood there was added a less common and more sinister portrait of politically motivated conspirator. Just as in metropolitan France there were numerous stories of Jesuit plots against the whole fabric of society, so too in West Africa in the decade before the First World War there were constant fears of a vast Islamic conspiracy orchestrated by malicious foreign agents. The marabout was seen to be a key personality in maintaining the various conspiratorial links between the masses of believers on the one hand and the international directors of the conspiracy on the other.

Islamic conspiracy was widely thought to be particularly dangerous because its cutting edge was based on religious fanaticism which rendered its followers senseless to rational persuasion. Above all it was the figure of the *mahdi* which haunted the European powers. For the British in the early twentieth century the *mahdi* had very particular connotations, namely Muhammed Ahmad el-Mahdi, the leader of resistance to British rule in the Sudan and the man held responsible for the death of the Victorian hero, General Gordon. For the French, however, the *mahdi* was a rather different character. Altogether more parochial in his aspirations he could be regarded as more of an irritant than a serious threat to the might of imperial France, the *mahdi* was identified as virtually a universal character of village Islam. Nevertheless, it was accepted that the mahdist phenomenon and its associated climate of messianic expectations were a serious problem – particularly in the outlying regions of French rule.

In the months following Coppolani's death the French authorities in Dakar received numerous reports which suggested an increase in all forms of Islamic activity.[60] Governor-General Roume responded to these various warnings with a number of measures. Firstly, he issued a circular requesting local administrators to send in information about Muslim personalities. He wrote that as Africans themselves were unable to understand they were being cheated by their marabouts, it was necessary for the French to take action on their behalf:

It is necessary to get to the root of the evil. As soon as the presence of a foreign marabout effecting unauthorised alms-collecting tours is communicated to you, you should immediately put them under surveillance and obtain more complete information about them. Whether the marabout is a peaceable man or whether he is considered as a dangerous individual, you should draw up a personal file, if possible with a photograph attached.

The files were then to be sent to Dakar where other documents concerning Islam were to be centralised and where they could be used to combat Muslim proselytism which Roume considered to be 'a constant threat to the tranquility of our domination in Africa'.[61] This collection of files formed the basis of what was later to become the Service des affaires musulmanes.

Secondly, Roume sent Robert Arnaud on a mission to investigate the state of Islam throughout the West African colonies and to draw up a manual of Muslim policy for the use of French administrators in AOF, Arnaud was given a wide-ranging brief which included historical research into the Mali and Songhay empires. However, the main thrust of the mission was to collect information on marabouts – a fact which underlines the growing administrative preoccupation with the personalities rather than the structures of West African Islam.[62]

Robert Arnaud was in many respects a natural choice to undertake this mission. Born in Algiers in 1873,[63] Arnaud studied Arabic before attending the Ecole coloniale from 1895 to 1897. He did not complete his diploma at the school but nonetheless went straight into the Algerian administration in 1898 as an *administrateur adjoint* of a *commune mixte*. At the end of the same year he was chosen to accompany Coppolani on his mission to the French Sudan. It is very probable that he had first met Coppolani through his father who had translated many of the documents used by Depont and Coppolani in their study of Islam in Algeria. In 1905 he was a member of Coppolani's mission into the interior of Mauritania and was present in Tidjikja at the time of Coppolani's death. No one could, therefore, dispute Arnaud's qualifications – even if his experience had been gained predominantly in Algeria.

However, there was another side to Arnaud which perhaps made him a less suitable choice for the job. There can be no doubt that he was profoundly influenced by Coppolani not merely from an intellectual but also from a spiritual point of view. Coppolani was more than a tutor in Islam for Arnaud; he was also a very great friend whose death Arnaud quite consciously set out to avenge.[64] The other great influence in Arnaud's early life was Isabelle Eberhardt, a young woman of mixed Russian and German parentage who emigrated to Algeria where she converted to Islam, married an Algerian and rode about the Algerian countryside disguised as a young Muslim man. She wrote articles for the liberal Franco–Arab newspaper *Akhbar*, and in the tense political climate in Algeria at the turn of the century her journalistic activity led to her expulsion from the colony. Arnaud had spent some time with her in 1902 (and had lent her his copy of

Thus Spoke Zarathrustra which was one of his favourite books). Soon after her clandestine return to Algeria, Isabelle Eberhardt was drowned in a freak storm at the age of twenty-seven in 1904. In the last years of his own life Arnaud wrote biographies about his two mentors to defend their reputations against some of the many charges that had been levelled against them both.[65]

Arnaud also fancied himself as a poet, philosopher and man of letters. His first novel, *Rabbin*, a mildly anti-semitic tale of marital woe, was published in 1896 and from then until his death in 1946 he published a further twenty novels and collections of poems under the pseudonym of Robert Randau.[66] His favourite subject matter – indeed, his only subject matter – was colonial life as he attempted to write a sort of *comédie humaine* depicting the lives and loves of French colonial society north and south of the Sahara. Both Coppolani and Eberhardt, called Antonetti and Sophie Peterhof respectively, appear frequently in highly glamorous roles, and Arnaud, himself, under the name of Cassard or Lemare appears in almost all of the novels. Arnaud saw himself as one of the leaders of a new and youthful 'colonial' school of literature which rejected both the dilettante life-style of the metropolis and the transient fancifulness of the popular 'exotic' writers such as Pierre Loti in favour of a tougher, heroic, patriotic and, it was claimed, realistic portrayal of 'Africans' (as the French colonials liked to call themselves). Arnaud's 'Africans' were almost a race apart – Arnaud, for example, described himself as a Franco–Berber – and they were characterised in his novels by a seemingly unquenchable appetite for sex and drugs and an apparently limitless capacity to talk earnestly about Kant and Nietzsche whilst sailing down the Niger or crossing the Sahara on camels. Strong, intelligent and beautiful – a master race, indeed.[67]

Arnaud's literary *oeuvre* has quite deservedly sunk into obscurity. Even in his own lifetime it is doubtful that his readership extended beyond a certain sector of colonial society and it is probable that readers were attracted, if they were attracted at all, more by the numerous descriptions of Arnaud's beautiful wife stepping out of her bath rather than by his philosophical discourses on the human condition. What is interesting for our purposes is to see to what extent Arnaud's enthusiastic, impressionable and essentially adolescent view of the world permeated his analysis of West African Islam.

In 1906 Arnaud published his *Précis de politique musulmane* which was the manual on Muslim policy that Roume had requested the previous year. Its scope was perhaps more limited than Roume would have hoped as it dealt specifically with the Moors of the right bank of the River Senegal only. However, it also contained some interesting general points about Islamic policy. After an introductory chapter on the nature of colonialism it went on to discuss the history and dogma of Islam. A chapter on 'Prophetism' denied that Sufism belonged to the Islamic orthodoxy and urged the need for the 'strictest prudence' when dealing with important Sufi figures. Luckily,

Arnaud wrote, few Sufis were indifferent to material persuasion and so it was up to the French to calculate exactly how much each Sufi leader was worth and then extract the maximum possible advantage from him.[68] On the brotherhoods themselves, Arnaud made a firm and classic distinction between the Qadiriyya ('broad-minded and philanthropic') and the Tijaniyya (distinguished by their 'extreme intolerance and their appeals to violence against all Christian domination').[69] Again Arnaud showed that he had been an attentive and receptive pupil of Coppolani when he went on to argue the folly of attempting to destroy the brotherhoods: 'As long as they continue to exercise an undeniable political influence we have to make use of the brotherhoods and attempt *to reduce them to simple and purely local associations that are not at the beck and call of outsiders*'.[70] There then followed several chapters detailing precise colonial policies ranging from ensuring that each outpost was staffed with an African Muslim nurse through to granting honorific titles to the heads of the brotherhoods and above all encouraging divisions between Muslims. In many ways the book was little more than a tribute to Coppolani and rehearsed Coppolani's central argument of the importance of winning the allegiance of a handful of Sufi leaders. However, Arnaud also stressed the need to encourage the particularism of West African Islam which was a significant departure from Coppolani's emphasis on the uniformity of Islam in north-west Africa. Arnaud, for all his idiosyncracies, represented an important link between the former Algerian consensus on Islam and the development of a specifically West African perspective which came to be known as *Islam noir*.

THE *MAHDIST* 'PLOT' OF 1906

In December 1905 two *gardiens de cercle* were killed in Djerma in Upper Senegal and Niger. At first the French thought that it would be sufficient to send out a force of fifty soldiers to restore order. However, by March it was believed that the problem was more serious and that the killings in December were the first shots in a wider rebellion masterminded by an itinerant marabout called Sahibu. William Ponty, the Lieutenant-Governor of the colony described him to Roume as 'this marabout, or rather this charlatan, ventriloquist and adept trickster [who] thanks to his talents was easily able to involve the natives in an anti-French movement'.[71] Reinforcements were sent to the region, and Sahibu was forced to flee across the border to northern Nigeria, where he made contact with Malam Isa, the chief of the village of Satiru situated some fourteen kilometres north of Sokoto. The British immediately sent out a force to arrest the two men but the force was ambushed and twenty-eight were killed, including Hilary the acting resident of Sokoto. This seemed to confirm the worst fears of the French and British alike that a widespread religious uprising was being planned. Shocked by the ambush of the initial force, the British quickly amassed a much larger force with the help of the Sultan of Sokoto who regarded Sahibu as much a threat to his authority as to the British. The combined forces of the British and the Sultan marched on the village of Satiru, razed it to the ground and killed over 500 of its inhabitants. Sahibu was captured and later beheaded.[72] Roume had kept in touch with his British counterpart, Lugard, and offered him assistance against a movement which, he said, was 'certainly of a religious character directed indiscriminately against Whites, whether they are English or French'. Roume's offer was appreciated but not taken up by Lugard who believed that the rout of Sahibu's forces had effectively put an end to the rebellion.[73]

However, within a month the French believed that they had stumbled across another religiously motivated plot against European rule. Their suspicions were alerted by a clumsy assassination attempt in early March on Captain Lefebvre, the *commandant de cercle* of Zinder. A force under the command of Major Gadel was sent to Zinder and on 30 and 31 March twelve people were arrested, including Ahmadu, the Sultan of Zinder. At this stage concrete evidence was almost totally lacking, but Gadel listed nine 'moral and material' proofs. Although these nine 'proofs' were in fact all based on rumour, Gadel believed that they were sufficient to justify the execution of nine of the people arrested, including the Sultan. Although he promised that he would not act without further orders he did consider that these facts, combined with evidence that the chief of the Tuareg, Imezureg, was also plotting with the Sultan against the French, pointed to the urgent need to occupy Agades in the north.[74] In May Gadel was confident that he had obtained 'absolutely convincing material proof' of the guilt of the arrested men and of the connection between events in Zinder and the earlier unrest in Djerma and Sokoto.[75] This evidence consisted of a confession extracted from the Sultan's messenger that he had carried letters between Zinder and Sokoto in November 1905. The Sokoto letter was said to have contained instructions to Zinder to attack the 'Whites' in mid-April. The Sultan of Zinder had been tempted to attack on 7 March, but according to Gadel, he was persuaded at the last minute to follow the Sokoto instructions. Gadel claimed to have a further oral testimony which implicated the Kano emirate in the plot as well.

Gadel and Lefebvre compiled an enormous dossier containing approximately 250 pieces of evidence which was intended to prove beyond a shadow of a doubt that the Sultan of Zinder was guilty. The 205th item of evidence was a one hundred page report by Captain Lefebvre which explained how his suspicions had been alerted after someone had tried to poison his milk. There was, however, no evidence of a coordinated conspiracy. Lefebvre argued that although the Sultan had a personal grudge against him for having reformed the anarchic system of tax collection which had been a lucrative source of income for him, this was not the fundamental cause of the revolt. Rather, he continued:

> It is an undeniable fact that in all the regions where Islam is profoundly rooted we are held in the greatest scorn by certain marabouts. The biggest danger is

that there is in this country a form of bastardised Islam, a mixture of religion and ridiculous superstitions, a superficial religion in which the marabouts and the pseudo-marabouts who abound in this country are the carriers of malicious rumours, maintain the credulous people in sentiments of hatred against us and work towards the brutalisation of the race by superstitious practices. This element is perforce hostile to us. The chiefs need these marabouts who distribute a thousand *gris-gris* for the success of their pillages and, in exchange, these marabouts enjoy numerous privileges.[76]

As reports continued to come into the federal authorities of the activities of itinerant marabouts causing unrest in various part of AOF, Robert Arnaud was sent to investigate the unrest in Niger. He confirmed the alliance between the aristocracy and the marabouts against the colonial authorities who had liberated their slaves. Interestingly, Arnaud revised his earlier distinction between the Qadiriyya and the Tijaniyya, and the Umarien branch of the Tijaniyya was now described as the only truly loyal brotherhood in AOF. The Qadiriyya's reputation had, it seems, been tarnished by the alms-collecting tours of Sheikh Saad Bu and its relationship to the Ghoudf brotherhood which was blamed for the death of Coppolani. Arnaud concluded that the French had been lucky in Djerma and warned that:

In a maraboutic revolt it is not the rebels killed that one should count; whether a hundred or a thousand are killed it still won't stop the other *exaltés* following the first imposter to appear. One has to go straight to the chiefs. Behind the sheeplike crowd we find ... the local chiefs; the present Sultan of Sokoto, the Sultan of Zinder, the chief in Karma and all the Hausa and Djerma nobility. The most guilty of all, the man who wanted to reconstitute the old empire was Sahibou.

Since the second half of the nineteenth century, he continued, Africa had become 'the chosen land of *mahdis*'. All this was serious enough, said Arnaud, but it was exacerbated by the influence of pan-Islamist agents in the pay of the German ambassador in Cairo, Baron von Oppenheim.[77]

In one of his later (1931) novels Arnaud mocked the local administrator who was obsessed by the threat of a pan-Islamic revolt.[78] In defence of Arnaud's fictitious administrator it should be said that Arnaud himself at the time shared this obsession. His report not only confirmed, but also amplified, Major Gadel's suspicion of a vast conspiracy; for Gadel never suggested that Baron von Oppenheim was involved. However, neither Gadel nor Arnaud succeeded in entirely convincing Gadel's commanding officer, Lieutenant-Colonel Lamolle, who had to admit that proof of the Sultan of Zinder's guilt consisted in a bundle of circumstantial evidence rather than in concrete proofs. Nonetheless, the French did believe that it would be prudent to exile him and early in 1907 Ahmadu and his 'accomplices' were duly sentenced to varying lengths of imprisonment in the Ivory Coast.[79]

Arnaud's introduction of a German element into the conspiracy reflected anxieties in Paris about 'Perfide Teuton'. The government had received information about a German mission in Ottoman Tripolitania and had decided that it should take all measures necessary to prevent the Germans obstructing the link between Algeria and Lake Chad. Dakar was accordingly instructed to prepare immediately for the occupation of Bilma, Kawar and Tibesti leaving the Algerian authorities responsible for the security of Djanet and south-west Wargla.[80]

The Paris analysis coincided happily with military demands for a second occupation of Agades which had been briefly occupied in 1904. The civilian authorities in Upper Senegal and Niger were still very dubious about the merits of further military action, and William Ponty urged restraint in the use of force.[81] It is perhaps in this context that we can best understand the military response to the so-called Zinder 'conspiracy'. Major Gadel and Captain Lefebvre had been convinced for some time of the need to establish a greater military presence in the region of Ahir but they found it difficult to convince the civilian authorities. The uncovering of a widespread 'conspiracy' provided them with exactly the sort of evidence which seemed to justify their demands for a more active role in the area. One of the first conclusions reached by Gadel and Lefebvre was, significantly, that Agades should be reoccupied. This demand was backed up with the exceptionally voluminous dossier of evidence designed to prove beyond a shadow of a doubt that the Sultan of Zinder was guilty of conspiracy against the French and which in hindsight seems to have been a distinct case of overkill. It would not be unreasonable to assume that Gadel and Lefebvre were to a certain extent engineering a little conspiracy of their own against their traditional enemies – the civilian bureaucrats and accountants.

However, we should not submerge ourselves in conspiracy theories: fear and a sense of isolation are equally plausible explanations of military actions. Proof of a widespread conspiracy would provide justification for a widespread mopping-up operation; justification, that is, for more soldiers. A fascinating insight into the anxieties of soldiers in the region is contained in a letter written by Captain Lefebvre to a friend in which he described how the 'plot' had been uncovered:

> We have made a rich catch; proofs abound, information, guns found in the Sultan's residence, the lies of the accused – there will be some sensational confrontations. Everybody has been compromised because it is a great religious movement which has been simmering for three months. . . . I have been lucky enough to escape three assassination attempts. . . . A charming country! You see, my dear Jean, we have narrowly escaped a disaster. But consider our situation 800 kilometres from the nearest telegraph – when will we receive instructions from the government? We should put the whole country under a state of siege and establish a court martial, otherwise we will never see the end of it.[82]

Such anxieties were not of course unique to French soldiers. In Natal in 1905, for example, rumours of a Zulu rebellion evoked a similar pattern of emotions amongst the white settlers.[83]

Did the Djerma and Zinder conspiracies really amount to anything more than a handful of letters and a bowl of 'poisoned' milk? Whilst it is undoubtedly true that there was enormous resentment of the European conquest of the Sokoto Caliphate and that many of the people who had followed the defeated Caliph Attahiru into exile cherished hopes of reviving the caliphate even after Attahiru's death in battle in 1903, it is unlikely that there was any concerted strategy. Letters expressing hostility to the Europeans and issuing a general call to arms may indeed have been circulated in the region – it would be surprising if they weren't – but they hardly constitute a conspiracy in themselves. A recent account[84] has suggested that one of the key pieces of evidence against Ahmadu – a letter implicating him in a plot with Sahibu – was fabricated by Ahmadu's chief adviser (*bellama*) in an attempt to curry favour with the French whom he knew to be dissatisfied with Ahmadu. The strategem appears to have worked for the *bellama* was made *chef de province* after Ahmadu was deposed and the sultanate abolished. This same account also suggests that shortly after the supposed assassination attempt on him, Captain Lefebvre's alarm was augmented by the sight of the arrival on horseback in Zinder of one of the town's richest traders, Malam Yoro, accompanied by his large retinue of servants whom Lefebvre mistook for *mahdist* rebels. Whatever, the veracity of these accounts it is clear that, as in Mauritania, the political situation was much more complicated than the authorities imagined and that the nuances of Islamic response were much too subtle for the handful of soldiers stationed in the outposts of the Empire. The traumatic changes that the region was undergoing as a result not only of European conquest but also of the decline in the trans-Saharan trade routes were in themselves sufficient explanations for the various incidents without us having to construct a conspiracy theory which in its most extreme form implicated the German consulate in Cairo. The Zinder 'conspiracy' tells us much more about the French than it does about Muslims in Niger.

WILLIAM PONTY AND ISLAM

One of the main actors in the Zinder drama was William Ponty, the civilian Lieutenant-Governor of the colony of Upper Senegal and Niger. His main role was to exercise a restraining hand on the military, warning them against excesses in their actions. He does not seem to have been entirely convinced by their 'conspiracy' theory, but he nonetheless did have very strong feelings on the subject of Islam.

When Governor-General Roume was forced to retire at the end of 1907 through illness Ponty, despite his youth, was the automatic choice as successor and he remained as Governor-General until his death in 1915. Ponty had enjoyed rapid promotion since he entered the colonial office of the Marine Ministry as a law graduate at the age of twenty-two in 1888.[85] In 1890 he was appointed Colonel Archinard's personal secretary during the campaign against Samori from which Ponty emerged with the prestigious Légion d'honneur. In 1896 he was posted to Madagascar but returned the following year to West Africa to take up a post as *commandant de cercle* in Djenné where he maintained his record of impressing his superiors with his hard work and good manners. In 1899 he became Governor of French Sudan, the largest of the West African colonies where he remained until his final promotion to Governor-General early in 1908. Clearly a man of considerable administrative ability, Ponty was among the most influential of all Governor-Generals as he was one of the few men to occupy this position who had a distinct vision of the nature of African society. This vision was a product both of his own early experience of Africa gained in the campaign against Samori and of his personal political sympathies.

Ponty believed that the French were witnessing the death throes of a feudal society which had been created by the *jihad* states of the eighteenth and nineteenth centuries, in which the nobility and the marabouts had joined forces to exploit the masses. Slavery was the key to this analysis of society.[86] At the turn of the century the western Sudan comprised a very substantial slave population – in some towns of the valley of the middle Niger the proportion of slaves is estimated to have been as high as two-thirds. Although the slave population had recently been enormously swollen by Samori, it is nonetheless clear that the labour needs of the region had for some time been met by slave and other forms of unfree labour. Faced with this situation the French, like their British counterparts, were placed in a dilemma: on the one hand they did not want to be seen by their metropolitan observers to be condoning the system of slavery but, on the other hand, in the 1890s they could not afford to antagonise African rulers by liberating their slaves. Furthermore, they had labour needs of their own – porterage, railway construction etc. – which were most conveniently met by use of unfree labour. The way out of this dilemma was a fudged compromise consisting of abolitionist rhetoric (and a certain amount of legislation) to satisfy the metropolitan audience and a policy of non-intervention in the affairs of master and slave. Although the French did undermine the position of slave-owners by refusing to recognise the legal basis of the state of slavery (1903) and by a formal abolition of the slave trade (1905), it is clear that it was the slaves themselves who took the initiative in deserting their masters in their thousands in the early years of the century.[87] Ponty's analysis of a social revolution in West Africa was accurate but it was a revolution which had taken place as much in spite of, as as a result of, French policies.

In this social revolution it was convenient for the French to tar Islam with the brush of slavery. By arguing that Muslim unrest was essentially the expression of a privileged class of marabouts disgruntled by their loss of status and wealth, the French were able to ignore other factors behind the widespread Muslim unrest of the early twentieth century. The argument – as with so many other colonialist analyses – was founded on fact: namely the historic links between Islam and slavery in Africa, but the reasoning was contrived. As we shall see, many of the Muslim rebels were made up of the poor and hungry, including many former slaves. However, it was more comforting for the colonial power to stick to its stereotypes.

Ponty set about eroding the alliance of the marabouts and chiefs by redefining the basis for chiefship in AOF. Instructions were issued in September 1909 to ensure that Muslims were not placed as chiefs over non-Muslim peoples. Ponty stressed that this was necessary because:

> More scrupulous and more familiar with our manner of conceiving the principle of authority ... Muslims quickly manage to acquire a political hegemony in a country where fetishists are in a majority. It happens then that without ourselves gaining any advantage ... we are encouraging the extension of Muslim clericalism.[88]

Ponty's policy of ethnic particularism became known as the *politique des races* and remained a central plank of 'native administration' of successive administrations in AOF at least until the Second World War.

The encouragement of ethnic particularism was also applied to Islam. Although the marabouts were generally regarded as posing the greatest threat to French rule, the French drew some comfort from their belief that local West African Islam was not as dangerous as, for example, the Islam of North Africa. In 1911 Ponty wrote to François Clozel, Lieutenant-Governor of Upper Senegal and Niger, that:

> Luckily the Islam of our West Africa still retains a rather special character which we have the greatest interest in preserving. Our Muslims have not accepted the pure Coran, whatever their devotions they have wanted to preserve their ancestral customs.[89]

However, in the same letter he also listed three personalities likely to disturb this happy state of affairs: Baron von Oppenheim, the Sultan of Constantinople and the Khedive of Egypt (who 'under the inspiration of Lord Cromer dreams of becoming the Commander of the Faithful in Africa'). If the 'Islam of our West Africa' was to be kept unsullied by foreign influences then it was essential that the linguistic barrier between black Africa and the Arab world should be maintained. However, since the time of Faidherbe, Arabic had been used as the most convenient language for transactions between the French and African rulers and, as late as 1906, Arabic was still regarded as being one of the most important parts of the curriculum at the Ecole normale in St Louis.[90] Increasingly over the next few years the stress was put on the importance of teaching French and on the unsuitability of Arabic for Africans. In 1910 Mariani, the Inspector of Muslim Education in AOF, wrote to Ponty that 'Knowledge of the French language is the best possible antidote against the danger of a retrograde Islam'.[91] In May 1911 Ponty issued a circular banning the use of Arabic in judicial and administrative matters arguing that:

> Arabic only enters into African countries with Muslim proselytism. For the Black it is a sacred language. Even indirectly to oblige those under our jurisdiction to learn it in order to maintain official relations with us comes to the same as encouraging the propaganda of the votaries of Islam. . . . We must not appear to take sides in religious questions which can only interest us inasmuch as they assume a political character. Furthermore, most of our clerks cannot speak Arabic and are consequently incapable of exercising control over documents written in this language. . . . The few Arabic-speaking natives are most commonly religious persons, marabouts often under surveillance, and people moreover who very often have a very mediocre understanding of the language in question. We should not tolerate having to rely on such 'scholars' for the honest communication of our intentions.

Ponty contrasted Arabic with French which he said was a much easier language for Africans to learn and to pronounce and which he was pleased to see was establishing itself as the lingua franca in the region. Although the reform was clearly motivated by anxiety about having to rely on intermediaries whom the French did not think were trustworthy, it made good sense for many areas of AOF where the use of Arabic was wholly inappropriate.[92]

In addition to restricting the use of Arabic, Ponty also attempted to exercise greater control over the importation of publications in Arabic, particularly ones which had taken an anti-French position on the Morocco question. However, censorship of the Arab press was not always easy: in Dahomey, for example, there was nobody in the administration able to read Arabic and so the Lieutenant-Governor asked for a simple list of the anti-French papers.[93]

The French were concerned not only with the written word but also with images. The following incident reveals the extent to which all branches of the administration – in Conakry, Dakar, Cairo and Paris – co-operated in order to control 'subversive' propaganda. In 1911 several caseloads of engravings depicting the Ottoman fleet outside Constantinople were seized in Dakar and Conakry. The engravings were printed on the presses of the *Cairo Punch* in Bologna and so the Colonial Ministry wrote to the Foreign Ministry to ask for information about the paper. The Foreign Ministry asked the French plenipotentiary in Cairo to investigate and his findings were duly communicated to Dakar. Ponty decided that the best way to fight this insidious propaganda was to fight kind with kind and therefore commissioned some colour engravings of portraits of French heroes and the interior views of French factories. In July 1912 the Colonial Ministry approved the payment of one hundred francs to 'Cantin Bros.', lithographers of 104–5 rue Oberkampf in Paris, for the supply of a quantity of these improving engravings.[94]

The local administrations in Guinea and Upper Senegal and Niger seem to have got carried away in their enthusiasm to stamp out Arabic in their respective colonies. In Guinea, the Lieutenant-Governor, Guy, regretted that the laws on the freedom of the press prevented him from banning the sale of 'Arabic works, Corans, books of prayer etc.' and proposed adopting a similar decree to one used in Madagascar in 1901 which gave Governors powers to decide what books written in a foreign language were to be allowed to go on sale in the colony. Ponty agreed that 'We should not neglect any opportunity to combat an ardent proselytism which is hostile to our influence and to European domination' but felt obliged to remind Guy that a distinction should be made between religious and political works.[95] In Upper Senegal and Niger, Clozel was worried about the increased sales of Qur'āns through representatives of the 'Maurel and Prom' and 'Dutheil and Rochene' trading houses and thought that the two houses should be requested to forbid their African agents from trading in Qur'āns. Ponty replied to Clozel's interim that whilst Clozel did well to investigate such matters the sale of Qur'āns was not illegal – 'officially at least'.[96]

The growing concern about the importation of Arabic publications was closely connected to concern about the increasing numbers of immigrants and traders from elsewhere in the Arab world. The single largest group were Levantines – both Christian Maronites fleeing persecution and Muslims. The first recorded arrivals were in Guinea in 1897 and by 1919, according to an official report the following year, the Levantine population (986) of the colony exceeded that of the Europeans (963).[97] Most of the early arrivals had probably intended to travel on and cross the Atlantic to America but they soon found that there were rich pickings to be made on the West African coast. The same report revealed that a Levantine trader could expect to make his fortune in a third of the time it would take in the United States. Initially they were welcomed to AOF as they provided a valuable service for the European trading houses, acting as middlemen between the African producers and the European merchants. In Guinea they helped to monetarise the trading network in rubber – buying rubber from Africans for barter and reselling it to Europeans for currency. However, the smaller European traders very quickly sensed the threat which they posed to their position, and the first petition against the Lebanese was organised in 1898, only a year after the first arrivals. Nevertheless it was not until 1910 – a critical year both politically and economically in Guinea – that there was more concerted official action against the Levantine traders as stricter immigration controls and more restrictive trading rules were introduced. In Senegal, the other colony with a large Syrian and Lebanese population, opposition seems to have been muted until the depression of the 1930s.[98]

Libyans and Moroccans were also included in the list of suspect Arab groups in AOF, and it is interesting to follow the correspondence in 1911 concerning a Moroccan trader called Abdul Karim Mourad who had been trading along the West African coast for several years. In August 1911 the Lieutenant-Governor of the Ivory Coast wrote to Ponty to warn him that Abdul had left Abidjan bound for Dakar. Ponty passed the information on to the Lieutenant-Governor of Senegal, who wrote back to Ponty in

October to inform him of Abdul's arrival. 'I do not believe' he said, 'that this Moroccan can be considered as a disturber of public order and I do not believe that he has ever taken part in any anti-European propaganda but I consider that he should, in the words of Monsieur le Commissaire, be considered as an "undesirable".' He proposed to make use of the fact that his immigration cards were not in order to expel him from the colony. Ponty wrote to the Lieutenant-Governor of the Ivory Coast to warn him that the unfortunate trader might be back after a stay in Senegal in which 'under the cover of commercial operations he has been taking part in active Muslim propaganda, very probably of an anti-European nature'.[99] This correspondence is interesting as evidence not only of a rudimentary intelligence service but also of the quite arbitrary way in which it worked. On the admission of both the Lieutenant-Governors of the Ivory Coast and Senegal there was no real reason to suppose that Abdul Karim Mourad was anything other than a trader yet Ponty portrayed him, relying more on innuendo than fact, as a subversive character. His real crime was to have been a Muslim who travelled widely.

Despite these obvious anxieties about 'foreign' influences it remained the case that the administration was still primarily concerned with domestic Islam. Between 1905 and 1910 there were reports from all over AOF of disturbances in which marabouts were said to have taken a leading part. In Senegal the authorities were disturbed about the continuing popularity of the exiled Mouride leader, Sheikh Ahmadu Bamba.[100] In Bamako the local administrator described marabouts as 'parasitic nuisances and charlatans'.[101] Even in the Ivory Coast where the Muslims formed a small proportion of the population administrators expressed their anxiety about Islam. In the *cercle* of Bondoukou in the north-east of the colony the administrator, Benquey, confessed that he was becoming 'a little sceptical about the beneficial and civilising influence of Islam on the Blacks' and proceeded to relate a harrowing tale of human sacrifice committed by pious Muslim Dyula.[102] Two years later Benquey was administrator of the north-west *cercle* of Korhogo, and what had started as a twinge of scepticism was now a fully-fledged conviction: 'Islam is perhaps a perfect religion in theory,' he wrote, but one had only to cast one's eyes around to realise that in practice it offered 'very little from a political point of view and nothing from a moral one'.[103]

In May 1907 in Guidimaka on the right bank of the River Senegal, the local French administration feared that they had been the victims of a Muslim conspiracy after they became aware that a local marabout had been preparing magic potions to rid the country of the French. According to the official French account,[104] the names of M. Dupont, the resident administrator, M. Audan, a junior official, and Malami Tandia, the interpreter, were all engraved on the skull of a hyena which was thrown into the well along with the putrefying entrails of the decapitated animal. A few days later M. Dupont fell gravely ill and the other members of the residence complained of upset stomachs. This evidence of the efficacy of the marabout's positions persuaded the local Sarrakole population to step up the pressure by attacking Africans who worked with the Europeans before a force of forty *tirailleurs*, sent out to assist the beleaguered residence, succeeded in restoring order.

In Dagana, a river port some fifty miles upstream from St Louis, there was a minor revolt in 1908 led by a marabout called Aly Yoro Diaw who claimed to have been to Mecca and that he was the *mahdi* sent to chase away the Europeans whose guns, he promised, would be useless against him and his followers. In the beginning of March he succeeded in resisting a small force sent out to arrest him but when, a few days later, he launched a direct assault on the French post in Dagana the attack was easily repulsed; Aly Yoro and twenty-eight others were killed, sixteen were wounded and four were taken prisoner. The revolt came after a period of drought, made worse by an invasion of locusts, and Aly Yoro's supporters were said to have been 'common and poor ... certainly men of little means'. However, Van Vollenhoven, the interim Lieutenant-Governor of Senegal, appeared to discount the possibility that social hardships were a contributing factor to the unrest.[105]

Later in 1908, in the Mossi region of Upper Senegal and Niger, a Muslim who had been trying to convert the animist Mossi and to persuade them not to pay their taxes was killed as he led a force of some 2,000 men against the French.[106] There was also evidence of Muslim discontent in the Futa Jallon in Guinea where a French administrator, M. Bastié, was killed in March 1909.[107] Finally, in 1910 the French authorities in Niger again claimed to have uncovered a vast spy network centering on Abidin, the great grandson of Sheikh Sidi Mokhtar al-Kunti. The report on the spy network admitted that the evidence against Abidin and his followers was not conclusive but concluded that 'Nonetheless their guilt was evident'.[108]

Although it is doubtful that the French considered any of these incidents to be in themselves a major threat, there is no doubt that their cumulative effect on French attitudes to Islam was considerable. In the short term they also pointed to a failure in French Muslim policy. In 1911 Ponty complained to Clozel that he had received very few of the personal files on marabouts that had been requested by Roume in 1906.[109] He therefore reissued the request in a circular in December 1911 which left no doubt about his opinion of the West African marabouts:

> Maraboutic propaganda – *the hypocritical facade behind which are sheltered the selfish hopes of the former privileged groups and the last obstacle in the way of the complete triumph of our civilising work based on the respect of justice and human liberty* – will disappear completely when all its activists, identified and closely watched, are no longer able to pass through the gaps in the vast network which surrounds them throughout the entirety of our West Africa.[110]

It is this 'hypocritical facade' which most succinctly states the consensus prevailing in the Ponty administration about the nature of Islam. It was a view which represents a marked shift from the widespread feeling at the turn of the century that Islam, whatever its faults may have been, was nonetheless a positive factor in West African society. It was certainly a far cry from the optimism of Coppolani that Islam was France's most powerful ally in the conquest of north-west Africa. The change in attitude can be explained by a wide range of factors: partly it was the French response to the undoubted increase in millenarian Muslim activity in the first decade of the century; partly it was a reaction to the optimism of people such as Coppolani; partly it was a reflection of ideological changes within a French administration headed by the Freemason, William Ponty; and partly it was the consequence of the increasingly polarised and conspiratorially minded nature of pre-war French politics. All these are considered in detail in the case-studies of the next two chapters.

4

Education policy and Islam

Education has always played a peculiarly important role in French society and politics[1] and it is not surprising that the establishment of an educational system in AOF preceded the final administrative organisation of the Federation itself. The various *arrêtés* of November 1903 provided a structured system of education, from the village schools at the bottom to the Ecole normale in St Louis at the top, with curriculum and personnel appropriate to each type of school.[2] Until these reforms French education had been left to private, mainly missionary, initiative but the combined pressure of metropolitan secularisation laws and the growing realisation of the urgency of finding new alternatives to military conquest forced the colonial authorities to take a more active part in the education of its newly conquered subjects. The moral conquest of the Africans had explicit political and economic aims: Governor-General Clozel's preface to a book by Georges Hardy, the Inspector of Education in AOF, stated plainly that 'the first requirement of the education which we give in our colonies should be one of practical utility, first of all for us and then for the natives'.[3] In an earlier survey of the colony of Niger it was argued that 'To instruct the natives is to augment their economic value'.[4]

In no case was the political aspect of education reform more clear than in the question of Muslim education. Camille Guy, who as Lieutenant-Governor of Senegal appreciated the low cost of mission education, was reluctant to allow the traditional Qur'ānic schools to go untouched whilst at the same time being forced to close down the mission schools and in July 1903, along with his Inspector of Education, Risson, he drew up a decree designed to control and restrict the number of Qur'ānic schools. Schools with less than twenty pupils were outlawed, the pupils were not allowed to beg, teaching during French school hours was forbidden and evidence of pupils' attendance at a French school became an essential requirement if the marabout was to be allowed to continue teaching. Finally, the marabout's competence to teach was to be examined by local Muslim scholars. In the Four Communes only fifty-one of the 202 marabouts recognised by the French authorities as directing Qur'ānic schools were authorised to continue. In the rest of Senegal only twenty-eight of the ninety-five teacher marabouts received official authorisation.[5] A year after the *arrêté* was issued Guy wrote triumphantly to Roume that the question of Qur'ānic schools 'can finally be considered as closed in Senegal'.[6]

However, the triumph – if triumph it was – was more apparent than real. In reality the French authorities were wholly incapable of regulating Qur'ānic schools – a huge task even for a large and dedicated administration. As later reports recognised, the existing administration could not seriously hope to restrict or even control Qur'ānic schools.[7]

In any case Guy's views on the relative merits of mission and Qur'ānic education were not universally shared. Mairot, the Algerian-born Inspector of Education in AOF,[8] was not impressed with the standard of mission education:

> 'What decadence. What apathy!' he wrote to Roume early in 1905, 'have I seen in the schools directed by the missionaries in the Sudan. Classrooms, dormitories, they all breathe of neglect. In Kita the children have classes at most one hour a day.... So the general results are not as satisfactory as those obtained in the modest official school directed by native monitors.[9]

Ponty also thought that the educational achievements of the *Pères blancs* had been paltry and scarcely justified further official subsidies.[10]

A more serious objection raised by both Mairot and Ponty was that the mission schools created a barrier between France and her African Muslim subjects:

> It is difficult for them [Ponty wrote] to believe in our religious tolerance and our respect for freedom of conscience as long as we appear to favour the proselytism of the missionaries.[11]

Mairot made a similar point and warned Roume that:

> Wherever the Muslim natives – more intelligent than the fetishists – dominate, the country remains absolutely hostile to all forms of religious proselytism attempted by the missionaries ... What an error it would be, and perhaps also what a danger if the government favoured Christian teaching in Muslim country, if they also let it be supposed that in making common cause with the missionaries they were also encouraging the spread of Christianity.[12]

Coppolani had spoken optimistically of what could be achieved by a policy of co-operation with the Qur'ānic schools,[13] and Mairot wholeheartedly agreed. In an official report he urged the French not to underestimate and despise traditional Qur'ānic education but rather to regard it as a 'moral force' which should be exploited:

> France, he continued, the natural guardian of her Muslim subjects in Africa, has always protected their doctrines and their customs ... In AOF the Peuhls, Toucouleurs and the Woloffs represent an intellectual and military élite who would be glad to see the local government interest themselves in the doctrines of Islam. Let us raise their children in sentiments of respect towards France. Let us collaborate with the marabouts in the education of the Muslim youths

... Let us make our collaboration serve the development of French influence, otherwise the Muslims will continue to raise their children away from us and left to themselves the Coranic schools will conserve their predominantly religious influence. To suppress the schools would be dangerous, to abandon them to themselves would be folly.[14]

So although the Qur'ānic schools continued to irritate the French – one of the most unchanging features of colonial rule were the derogatory adjectives used to describe the schools – no serious effort was made to close them down. The French could not afford to do so, they were not able to do so and they had nothing to put in their place.[15] Furthermore they were left untouched by the various secularisation laws that had been passed in France.

The secularisation laws were a central plank of the Radical and Republican programmes and were the most important and controversial pieces of legislation of the governments of Waldeck–Rousseau (1899–1902) and the Bloc Républicain of Emile Combes (1902–5) and Maurice Rouvier (1905–6).

In July 1901 the attack on the clerics was opened with a law (*Loi sur les Associations*, 1 July 1901) designed to regulate the religious orders whose wealth and power had increased greatly over the last quarter of a century and whose schools were attracting increasing numbers of pupils. However, the law was without a cutting-edge until a series of ministerial decrees in June and August 1902 led directly to the closure of over a hundred Congregational institutions. In 1904 Congregational education was outlawed. Finally, under pressure from the free-thinkers and the Socialists and incensed by the apparent desire of the Vatican to interfere with the government's religious policies, the government took the decision to proceed to the dissolution of the Napoleonic 'Concordat' between the Roman Church and the secular government and to promulgate the separation of the Church from the State. The law of 1 December 1905 promised to assure freedom of conscience and declared that the government would neither subsidise, recognise nor pay the officers of any religious belief.[16]

In April of 1905 Clementel, the Minister of Colonies, wrote to the various Governor-Generals for information on 'native associations and secret societies – especially Chinese Congregations and Muslim Brotherhoods' and for suggestions as to how these institutions should be treated legally. Roume, having consulted with the colonies of the Federation, replied that the secularisation laws should be applied with little modification to AOF where, despite the fact that missionaries did some good work, their presence aroused the suspicions of Muslims and made the task of recruiting Muslim pupils for French public schools very difficult.[17] In reply to a later question about the applicability to Senegal of the law separating Church and State, the Lieutenant-Governor of Senegal told Roume that with a few qualifications the law could be applied in Senegal and that within four years all state financing of priests could be withdrawn.[18]

However, the Lieutenant-Governor emphasised that the law was entirely inapplicable to Islam:

> The Muslim religion has been in Senegal since time immemorial. Almost all the natives practise it with a fervour bordering on fanaticism. The Muslim cult does not have any clergy ... The pecuniary resources of the Muslim cult in Senegal are almost nil; they are made up of offerings by the faithful and are used for the benefit of the needy amongst their fellow Muslims.[19]

The description of Islam as a poor and rather humble religion which used what money it did have for the relief of the needy contrasts sharply with the far more commonly expressed opinion that Islam enabled a handful of corrupt and scheming marabouts to exploit the poor, not help them. Evidence perhaps of pro-Islamic, anti-clerical colonial officials? Roume echoed the Senegalese Governor's doubts about the applicability of the separation law to Islam. He told the Minister of Colonies that:

> The Muslim brotherhoods which exist in Guinea, Ivory Coast, Dahomey and in Upper Senegal and Niger exhibit, like those of Senegal, the same characteristics which clearly differentiate them from any other religion ... Furthermore, reasons of a political nature oblige us not to apply the law of 9 December 1905 to the Muslims. These people, particularly secretive in their faith ... would misconstrue the measures laid down in this text and would see in it an attack on their secular traditions.[20]

Those opposed to the secularisation laws in France saw in them the hand of 'satanic Freemasonry' (the phrase is taken from the Papal encyclical of Leo XIII, *Humanum Genus*, 1884) and the subsequent decision that in the colonies Islam was to be spared, confirmed opponents of the laws in their belief that the priests were being victimised by an anti-clerical, atheistic even, colonial administration. The belief was a strong one which was restated at regular intervals over the next decades. In a series of lectures delivered at the 'Institut catholique' in 1933, J. Maze, a White Father, denounced French colonial education policy again and again speaking of:

> The monstrosity of the fact that in the French colonies the conversion of a Pagan or a Muslim to the Catholic religion is considered as an act of rebellion against France ... France, alone amongst the great colonial powers, rejects the help of the missionary Church in the so difficult and yet so important task of the education of the natives.[21]

Another White Father accused the Education Inspectorate of being run by anti-clerical Freemasons and argued that:

> This Islamophile position was convenient for all those who did not want the Catholic religion to spread in our colonies. At this time of most violent anti-clericalism in France, in the colonies even if administrators felt closer to the missionaries because of the small numbers of Frenchmen nonetheless they were happy to seize a supposedly scientific reason to refuse them all support.[22]

Mgr. Bazin, the head of the White Fathers in AOF in 1908, warned dramatically that 'Islam is the sin of Europe in Africa. She may well yet pay a high price for it'.[23]

The 'Islamophilia' of the administration was, and still is, greatly exaggerated. Whilst it is true that there were Freemasons and anti-clericists in the colonial administration, perhaps especially in the Educational Inspectorate, it should not be imagined that this automatically meant that they were in any way pro-Islam. It has often been said that some administrators favoured Islam 'pour embêter les curés' but in practice this was seldom the case. If an anti-clerical administrator wanted to annoy priests there were far simpler ways of doing so as the complicated etiquette of colonial 'society' afforded ample scope for discreet social snubs. Most anti-clerical administrators regarded marabouts as being just as offensive as Catholic priests and, as we shall see, did as much as they could to combat them. It is understandable that the Church made the accusations it did for the secularisation laws in France were an ideological and divisive piece of legislation. However, the decision not to apply them to Islam was based on *raison d'état* and nothing more.

The whole question of the applicability of the secularisation laws to the colonies was in any case a vexed one which divided otherwise united pressure groups, including the Parti colonial. The semi-official wisdom that 'anti-clericalism was not an article for export' appeared not to have been seriously contested in the last quarter of the nineteenth century. The Alliance française, founded in 1883 to encourage the spread of the French language and culture throughout the world and whose membership was dominated by patriotic Republicans, refused to adopt an anti-clerical position with regard to mission-run schools. Even the Mission laique, founded in 1902 with the intention, as its name suggested, of bringing a missionary zeal to secular education was not as resolutely opposed to mission schools outside France as one might have suspected. Indeed, its first President, Eugène Etienne (one of the leading lights in the Parti colonial) voted for an amendment to the law of 1904 which exempted the noviciates, which trained missionaries for sending overseas, from the ruling which outlawed Congregational education. Etienne's justification was that if France stopped French mission education in the colonies and was at the same time unable to provide sufficient secular education to meet the needs of its colonial subjects, then it would leave the field open for foreign missionaries: 'national defence' required the secularists to make a compromise. However, Etienne did not convince everybody in the Mission laique and the following year he gave up the Presidency. Thus, despite the polarisation of camps in France over the secularisation laws, in the colonies there was still room for nuance: indeed, economic considerations demanded it.[24]

Neither Mairot nor Ponty (a member of the Comité de patronage of the Mission laique) approved of simply giving marabouts *carte blanche* in the field of education. Mairot argued strongly in favour of creating the post of Inspector of Muslim Education and the inclusion of 'French' subjects such as 'theory of agriculture and elementary notions of social hygiene' in the curriculum of the Qur'ānic schools.[25] However, a scheme in 1906 to encourage the teaching of French in Qur'ānic schools by offering a small financial incentive of not more than 300 francs per annum to marabouts who gave two hours of French instruction a day failed to attract any support. Camille Guy, the architect of the scheme, reissued the relative *arrêté* the following year, but again there were no takers.[26]

However, the idea of offering a reward to marabouts who taught French was not entirely abandoned. In August 1910 Ponty wrote that:

> We cannot subsidise Coranic schools and we should avoid the appearance of encouraging the development of a religion whose followers to say the least are not always favourable to our influence or to the new ideas of which we are here the representatives. But if we are obliged to continue observing the strictest confessional neutrality we should not abstain from rewarding the efforts of the teachers who wish to help us. Not all the marabouts are hostile to us and I even believe that there are some amongst them who ask for nothing more than to get along with us and who would willingly send their pupils to our schools and take lessons in French themselves.[27]

Coppolani's plan for Franco–Arabic universities was more realistic, based on the experience of similar institutions known as *médersa*s in Algeria. In 1906 Clozel was sent to Algeria on a mission to study the workings of the *médersa*s. In his final report he included a copy of the lengthy (300+ pages) report made in 1891 by the then Senator, Emile Combes, who had argued that the *médersa*s should seek not just to train Muslim administrators but that they should also act as 'an effective instrument of pacification and *rapprochement*'. If France was prepared to act resolutely, he concluded, these institutions would assure France control of Algerian Muslims as their leaders would no longer have to leave the colony in order to complete their studies. Clozel agreed that providing a suitable balance was kept in the curriculum between, on the one hand science and French and, on the other, Islamic doctrine and law, the *médersa* should be introduced to AOF as well.[28]

The first *médersa* to be formally opened in AOF was in Djenné, in the colony of Upper Senegal and Niger where Ponty was an enthusiastic supporter of the idea. The *médersa* had two aims specifically stated in the *arrète* by which it was founded. It had firstly 'to develop higher Muslim education and train the teachers of Coranic schools' and secondly 'To teach an élite of young Muslims how to speak and write in French and at the same time to give them proper views on the civilising role of France in Africa'.[29] At the end of the year Roume reported optimistically to Paris that 'The young men who are educated in this establishment will be able in a few years time to expose the marabout preachers of Holy War and to reveal their true nature to the credulous mass of natives. The *médersa* at Djenné will be our most effective answer to Islamic propaganda'.[30]

The first year's recruitment was not easy, and Ponty regretted that of the thirty pupils admitted only six had had experience of schools other than traditional Qur'ānic education. Nevertheless he remained optimistic that:

In a few years time the *médersa*'s [education] will deservedly be respected by all the Muslim population of the colony and that it will contribute immensely to the raising of the moral level of our natives, enlightening them about the dangers of fanaticism and showing them that the duties of a good Muslim are not in the least incompatible with their duties as French subjects.[31]

Mariani, the Inspector of Muslim Education, reported that initially many of the locals had been hostile to the project as there had been widespread rumours that its first director, Mohammed Merzouk, the 22-year-old Algerian *répétiteur* of the Ecole des langues orientales vivantes in Paris, was a Christian, but that now that the rumour had been scotched 'The Djenninkes . . . are starting to show pride in their *médersa'*. He warned that with the limited resources available the French should not try and make the *médersa* a carbon-copy of the Algerian *médersa* but rather they should more modestly seek to 'Train according to our methods young men capable of giving a liberal interpretation of the Coran and of spreading in our language our ideas of justice and of tolerance'.[32]

In St Louis the possibility of creating a *médersa* to complement the existing Ecole de fils des chefs and the Ecole normale had been discussed since 1906,[33] but it was not until 1908 that it was finally created. The Ecole de fils des chefs appeared incapable of training Arabic interpreters, and in 1906 only three of the eighteen candidates for the final exam – introduced for the first time that year and consisting of a simple translation from Arabic to French – achieved a reasonable standard. Roume wrote to the director of the school when he heard of these results to emphasise the importance of Arabic instruction and asked him 'To neglect nothing that might raise the level of Arabic studies in the minds of the pupils and of your colleagues'.[34] Mariani also urged Roume to create a *médersa* at St Louis arguing that it was the best way of combatting the marabouts. He stressed that the *médersa* should not just be a centre of Islamic learning but that rather the 'French spirit must give it life. Conceived in the manner of the reformers Combes and Houdas . . . the *médersa* will always be the most logical form of education in Muslim country, the only one capable of usefully serving our policy whilst at the same time flattering the vanity of the natives'.[35] A measure of the 'life-giving' French spirit can be seen in the proposed curriculum for the *médersa*. In addition to traditional Islamic subjects, first-year pupils were to be given elementary French language lessons including explanations of such mysteries as white men's houses, the postal system, work, travel, hunting and fishing. The second-year pupils were to learn about agriculture and hygiene and the third-year pupils about the geography of the colony, AOF, France, the countries of Islam and a history of the French conquest.[36]

In the first years of its existence the *médersa* underwent something of an identity crisis as it was not clear whether it was intended to supplant or to complement the existing Ecole de fils des chefs. Initially pupils were recruited by means of an exam but following the decision to close the Ecole in 1909, exam entry became less common and pupils to the *médersa* were recruited on the same basis as had been used for the Ecole de fils des chefs. At the same time the period of study was lengthened to four years and there were some changes in the curriculum – tacit admissions perhaps of the lower standards of the new intake.[37]

In 1910 there were fifty-six pupils at the *médersa* of whom twenty-three were the sons of chiefs, five sons of *qadis*, thirteen sons of marabouts or Arabic teachers, three sons of traders, six sons of farmers and six from other backgrounds. Over half were in their early twenties. Forty-five came from Senegal, nine from Mauritania and two from Upper Senegal and Niger. Most of the Senegalese received a grant (thirty-two full grants) but the non-Senegalese had to fend for themselves.[38] These figures reveal the uncertainty in French minds about whom the *médersa* was supposed to educate in these early days of its existence.

But whether the pupils were sons of chiefs or sons of traders the pupils were to learn the same basic lessons that loyalty to France need not be at the expense of abandoning the duties of a good Muslim. As important as encouraging loyalty to France it was also hoped that the *médersa* would encourage the development of a more 'progressive' Islam, open to the latest discoveries in science.[39] Mariani wrote that he considered 'The installation of *médersas* in AOF as a laicisation of Muslim education'[40] – in other words that the obscurantist marabouts would be replaced by a new generation of open-minded, free-thinking Muslim teachers,[41] just as in France the village schoolteacher was replacing the village priest as the spiritual guide of the nation's youth.

The *médersa* was intended both to diffuse the Islamic threat and to give the French some control over the Muslim leadership. Mariani was concerned about the inability of the French to contain the increase in the number of Qur'ānic schools. In the French Sudan he observed that 'The attendance of the Qur'ānic schools has become increasingly significant in Tombouctou and in the regions of Djenné. This situation concerns us for, if Islam represents a progress from fetishism, Muslims in general are difficult to handle and they have a tendency to consider themselves superior even to us, simply because they were born Muslims'. His solution to the problem was to propose the creation of another *médersa* in Timbuktu for he argued that money spent on the clergy (in December 1908 the Conseil général voted to renew the allowance of 38,000 francs to the Catholic clergy with a further 2,000 for the Protestants and 3,000 for the *Tamsir* of St Louis) would be better spent on teaching French: 'The study of a living Christian language is the most effective remedy to Muslim fanaticism ... The Mahommetans who know French or English are less fanatical and less dangerous than their co-religionists who can only speak Arabic, Berber or Turkish'.[42] Two years later he argued that 'Knowledge of the French language is the most effective antidote against the danger of retrograde Islam'.[43] Thus it was hoped that the *médersas* would be a step towards the creation of a liberal pro-French Islam in black Africa.

However, such developments could only be in the long-term. In the short-term the *médersa*s were intended to train a pro-French Muslim élite who on completion of their studies were intended to take up positions in the administration.[44] However, the French could not guarantee that there would be jobs available. At first Ponty believed that former pupils of *médersa*s should not be given automatic preference for jobs over other candidates, but when he learned that only two of the seven pupils who had left the St Louis *médersa* in 1910 had found jobs he became anxious and asked the Lieutenant-Governor of Senegal if the other five graduates could not be made monitors in schools. The Lieutenant-Governor regretted that the colony's education budget was insufficient to make this solution possible but he believed that in time suitable jobs would be found. Ponty was not satisfied and thought that the time had come to give pupils of official French schools some help in their search for jobs and issued a circular stating that henceforward all candidates for administrative jobs were to provide proof of two years consecutive study in an official French school.[45]

As we shall see the concept behind the *médersa* was by no means universally accepted. The decision not to attempt to apply the laicisation laws to Islam and at the same time to create official schools where religious instruction inevitably took up a large part of the time might appear incongruous from an administration which otherwise appeared to identify Islam as the greatest threat to French security in AOF. Some saw in this educational policy the cynical influence of Freemasonry. More accurately it represented a combination of *raison d'état* and wishful thinking: *raison d'état* because to have assimilated the position of Islam in AOF to that of the Catholic Church in metropolitan France would have been not merely inaccurate but also extremely foolish; wishful thinking because the French never ceased to think of themselves as 'the natural guardians of Islam'. The logic behind this belief was perverse and based on the fact that by a process of often bloody conquest France ruled over the Muslim population of Algeria. France was thus a 'Muslim power' with not only a right but also a duty, so the theory ran, to direct the evolution of its Muslim subjects. In Black Africa this often meant that the French had a duty to 'purify' *Islam noir* – and the place to start this was in the *médersa*.[46]

The *médersa*s were, however, only one part of French educational policy towards Islam. Whatever encouragement may have been given to the higher level of Muslim education, at the other end of the scale, attitudes to the mass of Qur'ānic schools remained suspicious and hostile. In April 1907, Roume, prompted by information which 'leaves no doubt about the organising effort of the muslim brotherhoods in AOF' issued a circular requesting details of Qur'ānic schools:

> It is important, he wrote, to be informed exactly on the number of schools. (These schools disseminate religious doctrines and the political suggestions issued unknown to us by the more or less secret agents of the big religious orders.) It is also important to make enquiries about the very personality of

> the marabouts who teach in the schools so that we know something of their origins, degree of learning, their means of instruction, their local influence and of any contact they may have kept with their former teachers ... From another point of view the administration wishes to know what subjects are being taught, what books are used and what categories of pupils the schools are designed for (children, adolescents, adults). And when a French school exists in the locality, or in a neighbouring one, it is necessary to find out whether the pupils of the Coranic schools come to complement their religious education or, if they do not attend the European school, to discover the reason for their refusal to attend.

The task, he said, required a great deal of tact on the part of the researcher but it was a very important task which would enable the administration to establish as accurately as possible 'the size of the forces at the disposal of the brotherhoods and the means of action they have available through the intermediary of the teaching and preaching marabouts'. The results were to be sent to the Governor-General marked 'Very Confidential'.[47] The attitudes expressed in the circular were entirely in keeping with the administration's anxieties about Islam at this time as the Qur'ānic schools were suspected of being a crucial link between the foreign directors of the brotherhoods and the mass of credulous African Muslims. The role of French administrators making discreet enquiries for their very confidential reports was almost as mysterious and as exotic as that of the 'more or less secret agents' of the brotherhoods. The reality was no doubt more prosaic. However, at the time the French felt a great need to have as much information as possible on Islam.

The practical results of the survey of the Qur'ānic schools are hard to gauge but if nothing else the piles of statistics which were sent at regular intervals over the following decades to the Governor-General must have been reassuring – evidence, perhaps, that the secret agents were becoming less and less secret.

Less spectacularly the Qur'ānic schools continued to be accused of severe pedagogical shortcomings. Cor, Lieutenant-Governor of Senegal from 1911 to 1914, declared that:

> Nobody is unaware of the unfortunate effects which these schools have from both a social and a political point of view, on the one hand depriving the numerous pupils who frequent them of the benefits of French instruction and, on the other hand, as a result of the confessional education, raising a veritable barrier between the young generation and ourselves.

He commissioned Souleyman Seck, the Arabic teacher at the St Louis *médersa* and M. Zanetacci, also from the *médersa*, to make an inspection of the Qur'ānic schools of St Louis. They described a 'typical' school where children were taught all about the Muslim obligation to wage Holy War in physical surroundings of the most extreme squalor:

> Cows, calves, sheep and goats graze peacefully beside the pupils who frequently have to brush away the accumulated excrement of several months, even years, before sitting down. Flies and insects of all kinds go from one dirty

child, stricken with leprosy or scabies to a clean and healthy child . . . and all
this little world lives, unconscious of the dangers surrounding it, mechanically
repeating to each other words of a language which is not theirs and which they
can only memorise with the greatest difficulty.

Cor wrote to Ponty that 'These revelations show a most critical situation
which the public authorities cannot ignore any longer' and he drew up a
proposal of legislation designed to regulate the schools, introducing
minimum standards of hygiene, etc. However, Ponty noted in the margin to
the letter that he considered the proposals 'utterly impossible – especially at
the moment this measure would not be wise because it would be considered
as the start of a persecution. That is what we must above all avoid. I repeat,
especially at the moment'.[48] The events to which Ponty referred which
made Cor's proposals so inappropriate were those that had taken place a
few months earlier in the Futa Jallon in Guinea and it is with these events
that the next chapter is concerned.

5

French Islamic policy in crisis: the Futa Jallon 1909–1912

The Futa Jallon region of the modern state of Guinea (Conakry) has a rich and important history. It is the most mountainous area of the western Sudan and, indeed, it is in its hills that the two great rivers of West Africa – the Senegal and the Niger – have their source. The two dominant ethnic groups are the Fulbe and the various Mandinka groups known collectively as the Jallonke from whom the region gets its name. The Jallonke agriculturalists invaded and settled on the plateau of the Futa between the eleventh and thirteenth centuries. Between the fourteenth and sixteenth centuries animist Fulbe pastoralists followed but, preferring to graze their livestock on the higher hills, did not seriously clash with the Jallonke. In the seventeenth century Muslim Fulbe, coming from either Macina or the Futa Toro, defeated both the Jallonke and the animist Fulbe and imposed their suzerainty over the area exacting tribute and taking slaves from the defeated tribes. Despite their great numerical inferiority they succeeded in imposing themselves as the dominant political force in the region in the course of the century. A further grouping which deserves comment were the Jakhanke, a clerical group belonging to the Soninke people, who settled in the Futa in the eleventh century and founded the town of Touba which acquired a reputation as a centre for Islamic learning, attracting visitors from all over West Africa.[1]

Towards the middle of the eighteenth century the head of the Futa state (who took the title *almamy*),[2] Karamoko Alfa, organised the Futa into seven provinces or *diwal* each of which had its own chief and which together formed the Futa Jallon federation which lasted more or less successfully until the French conquest. When Karamoko Alfa was forced to give up through ill health in 1751, the 'Council of Elders' elected a relation, Ibrahim Sori Mawdo, to be *almamy* as Karamoko Alfa's son, Alfa Saadibu, was too young. This decision led to disputes between the two families known henceforward as the Alfya and Soriya. The dispute was eventually settled by an arrangement whereby an *almamy* was chosen from each family, the two of them taking it in turn to reign for a period of two years at a time. This original system lasted a remarkably long time and it was not until 1888 that it finally collapsed. Whilst it survived the Futa constitution was, in David Robinson's words 'a triumph of balancing'. T. Diallo, a Guinean historian, described the period when the system worked properly as the 'most glorious of nineteenth century Futa history'. Marty, although less enthusiastic, argued that the Futa federation was a more impressive state than those of either Ashanti or Dahomey.[3]

However, by the last quarter of the century the Futa was in serious decline, and the central authorities were increasingly vulnerable to pressure both from within and from outside the federation. Above all the intense factionalism of the ruling families which had always been one of the striking characteristics of Futa politics provided the ideal opportunity for French intervention. The timetable for the final collapse began in 1886 when the *almamy* designate of the Soriya family, Mamadu Paathe, was ousted by his younger brother, Bokar Biro, who shared power with the Alfya *almamy*, Ahmaadi Ahmaadu, until 1895 when the regional chiefs of the Futa rebelled. During this time the French had been signing treaties with the various *almamy*s of the federation but this diplomatic pressure was not sufficient to bring Bokar Biro to terms. A year after the regional chiefs rebelled against the central authority, the French, too, decided on the use of force. In 1896 Bokar Biro was defeated and killed in a battle against an alliance of the French and regional chiefs.

In 1897 a Protectorate Treaty was signed in which France agreed to recognise the heads of the two ruling families of the Futa, Umaru Bademba for the Alfya and Sori Illili for the Soriya, and to respect the original constitution of the federation. However, the latter promise was soon neglected as the French decided to divide the Futa into two administrative provinces, Timbo and Mamou, under the leadership of Sori Illili and Umaru Bademba respectively. The chiefs who had fought alongside the French were similarly rewarded with recognition of the 'permanent' quality of their chiefships.[4]

By the end of the nineteenth century the Futa was undoubtedly in a state of crisis. There were several strands to this crisis: economic, political and religious changes resulting from the growing influence of the French and the simultaneous collapse of central authority within the Futa combined to create what Lamine Senneh has called 'a crisis in authority' as various groups jostled for the power and authority once held by the *almamy*s. At the turn of the century, Sanneh suggests, the two main contenders were the French and a new religious élite based on a rural network within the Futa of radical Muslim communities composed of disaffected peasants and freed slaves.[5] However, the French, whilst recognising that the situation in the Futa was certainly fluid, appear to have been satisfied that the old structures were still sufficiently strong for them to recognise and make use of existing chiefs. Writing to the Colonial Minister to report on his recent visit to the Futa, the Governor-General explained his policy of indirect rule and respect for the status quo. In Timbo he was met by a delegation of chiefs, who, he said, all expressed themselves enthusiastic supporters of the French:

> I would even go as far as to say, he continued, that if I had pressed them it would have been easy to make the Malinkes, who constitute the base of the working population of the Fouta say 'Free us from the Foulahs', to make the Foulahs say 'Free us from the chiefs', the chiefs say 'Free us from the *almamys*'. But the moment is not ripe for such a radical social revolution and I believe that we should govern thc Fouta Djallon with the social organisation that we found there. Without in appearance changing the actual institutions we will remain the only masters of the country through the intermediary of the *almamys* who can only remain in power thanks to us and who will succeed in place of us in doing the police work necessary to maintain the tranquillity of the populations and the security of the roads.[6]

That such a policy involved turning a blind eye to despotism cannot be doubted. For example, Alfa Yaya who was confirmed as chief of Labé, Kade and Gabu after the defeat of Bokar Biro enjoyed two years of absolute rule:

> During these years, Marty later wrote, when Alfa Yaya was the uncontested master of Labé he earned himself the reputation of a prize tyrant and bandit which has perhaps been exaggerated. Like all African potentates, Alfa Yaya didn't hesitate to cut off a few heads and to seize the goods of his victims but at the same time he introduced order and tranquillity into the country, encouraged agriculture and kept war outside his frontiers. These procedures of summary justice ... the very product of the feudal organisation of the Fouta should be judged with the indulgence required of the surroundings.

Furthermore, tax receipts between 1898 and 1903 increased from 250,000 francs to over a million – and for this the French would forgive anything, as Marty admitted: 'We were very happy with the financial results and we didn't attempt to discover by what methods ... the tax was collected'.[7] Umaru Bademba, who had been made sole *almamy* of Mamou, appears to have gone too far even for the indulgent French administration: 'His countless exactions, his abuses of power and his acts of cruelty were such that he had to be deposed in 1900'.[8]

However, the wisdom of using the existing chiefs soon came to be doubted. The accession of Frezouls, a Radical Republican, to the Lieutenant-Governorship of Guinea in 1904 played a part in this change of heart.[9] Certainly in the case of Alfa Yaya it was reported that he felt vulnerable as a result of changes in Conakry.[10] But Alfa Yaya's unpopularity with the French was, it seems, as much due to his claim to one-tenth of all tax receipts and to suspicions that he was intriguing with the Portuguese, who, under new boundary arrangements, had been given control over a large section of Labé, as it was to the arrival of new Radical Republican ideals in Conakry.[11]

In October 1905 Alfa Yaya was arrested on charges of plotting against France and sentenced to five years internment in Abomey.[12] How much can this be imputed to Frezouls' Republicanism? Frezouls was not the first person to clash with Alfa Yaya. As early as 1896 de Beeckman, the administrator who had been given the task of drawing up the treaties with the chiefs of the Futa Jallon, was accused by Cousturier, the Governor of Guinea, of pursuing a personal attack against the chief of Labé.[13] Nor was Frezouls exactly consistent in his treatment of the chiefs of the Futa. In the same year that Alfa Yaya was deported, Umaru Bademba, the deposed *almamy* of Mamou, was made chief of Dare, Telike and Pale Sara.[14] So one should be wary of imagining that the arrival of a good Republican as Lieutenant-Governor of Guinea automatically spelt the end of an era for the chiefs of the Futa. In practice such changes as occurred in chiefship depended on a host of factors which combined to form the political make-up of the colony, of which the chiefs were themselves an important part and not just the more or less passive victims of changing ideological currents in Paris or even Conakry.

In purely ideological terms Radicalism, in any case, was probably not as important as the ideas held by the administration on religion and race. Such ideas were particularly strong in relation to the Fulbe of the Futa Jallon. Early European travellers were struck by the fairer skins, fine features and apparently higher social and political organisation of the Fulbe. In the early nineteenth century the French explorer, René Caillié, had, for example, been very impressed but he added that 'The Foulahs are proud, suspicious and liars'.[15] These same characteristics of, on the one hand, an apparently superior intelligence and, on the other, of a passion for intrigue and an abhorrence of work continued to impress European observers. By the first decade of the twentieth century early ethnologists had drawn up a hierarchy of African ethnic groups, and although opinions differed about the exact ordering and about what criteria should be used for judging, all agreed that the Fulbe came at the top of the black African races.[16]

The classification was both 'scientific' (i.e. based on observation of physical characteristics) and moralistic for although the Fulbe were regarded as being beautiful and clever (Fulbe women were particularly recommended as native wives for French administrators for both these reasons),[17] there was also a sense in which they were seen to be too clever for their or anybody else's good. Frobenius was the least equivocal of the moralisers as he drew a sharp distinction between the state-forming but lazy 'Hamitic' peoples and the non-state-forming but hard-working 'Ethiopic' peoples.[18] Others made similar judgements. Tauxier, for example, writing in a journal pioneering the 'method of observation' in the infant social sciences declared that:

> The Foulah is cunning and two-faced; superficially he will show a deferent, even obsequious submission to the French authority, but inside he will be determined to do nothing that he is commanded to do. He makes a lot of promises but keeps none of them. By contrast the ordinary Black obeys and once he has promised, keeps his word ... In short, the Mande makes less

objections to our authority and gives us better services.... The Foulah is more intelligent and scholarly as a result of the superiority of his blood and the nordic [*sic*] influence ... He is more authoritarian and knows how to command in his family and in his state. This Foulah who is so intolerant of our authority, is very authoritarian in his own home ... It is this quality which has made the Foulah capable of founding a small empire in the Fouta Djallon and which has made them dominate politically and militarily over their Mande neighbours.[19]

In a history of Guinea, published in 1911, the author described the pre-colonial administration of the Futa Jallon in the most unflattering way:

The shameful exploitation of the people became the principle of an administration which had forgotten that its primary task was the defence of the tribe. To this abuse of power the Peuhl replied with perfidy, lies and inertia all of which he considered as qualities. Intrigues, armed struggles and assassinations became increasingly frequent ... Thus Dochard could write of the feudal inhabitants of the Fouta Djallon in 1817 that 'their distinctive character is cunning and two-facedness'.[20]

The ability of the Fulbe to form states commanded respect from the French but their admiration was qualified by their insistence of, on the one hand, the near anarchy of the states and, on the other, of the Machiavellian virtues by which the state was created. Witness a monograph on the history of the *cercle* of Timbo written in 1908:

During all this history of the Fouta Djallon ... anarchy ruled supreme. As a result of circumstance however, and partly due to the influence of an advanced religion, customs and traditions established themselves which finished by giving this society an organisation which was less rudimentary than those of other native peoples. Moreover there was nothing surprising in this; less primitive than most of the Blacks, intelligent and double-dealing, as lazy as he is proud and greedy the Foulah was bound to reserve an important place in his life for political affairs.[21]

The Fulbe were also generally described as being fervent Muslims. P. Guébhard, whilst the interim commandant of the *cercle* of Timbo, wrote that 'The greatest part of the existence of a Foulah is passed with the Coran in his hand, whether as a child bleating out verses, or as a *talibé* [pupil] ... or finally as an old man thumbing through the yellowing pages of the family book in between the hours of prayer'.[22]

Another French administrator wrote that;

All travellers to the Fouta have been struck by the depressive influence that religious practice seems to have on the Peuhl. Go to the mosque when the *calyo* calls the faithful to prayer. You will see the natives going there walking slowly, muscles languid, back bent, shoulders hung and head low. The expression on the face is fixed, the eye is dull and the mouth (Oh, that mouth!) always open. It seems as though the blood has been drawn from their veins ... Look at them pray. Whether they say the words out loud or whether they whisper them . . . not a muscle on their face moves. And when they tell their beads nothing can disturb them from their imperturbable gravity of thought. Truly they give the impression of being saintly men.[23]

Some suggested that this attachment to Islam constituted a threat to the French. Captain Normand, writing in 1902, warned that 'The marabout is slowly creating a force which can only be hostile to us and which to my mind will always be a worry for the future of French Africa. For let us not forget the words of Bugeaud: "Boil up the head of a Christian and the head of a Muslim together for a week, the stocks will never mix".'[24]

However, it should be said that the Fulbe of the Futa Jallon were not invariably accused of religious fanaticism. Another essay written soon after the establishment of French rule noted that although music and singing were rare in the Futa this was not so much a result of fanaticism but rather of the puritanism of the Fulbe character. 'Respectability' the author argued was one of the distinguishing features of a Fulbe village.[25] According to the official guidebook to Guinea produced for the 1906 Marseilles colonial exhibition, the Fulbe of the Futa were not in the least bit fanatical in their religion, and the author was pleased to note that the *almamy* openly drank wine and alcohol and enjoyed talking religion with Christians.[26]

Finally a word should be said about the way in which the political organisation of the Futa Jallon as a whole was regarded by the French. The existence of a military and religious aristocracy of a minority ethnic group, the Fulbe, alongside a subordinate and often completely enslaved population who performed all the manual labour, not unreasonably reminded contemporary observers of what can loosely be called feudal society. It would perhaps be more accurate to say that they likened it to the pre-1789 situation in France – Marty, for example, entitled his chapter on the nineteenth-century Futa Jallon, the 'Ancien Régime'. A positivist view of history demanded that there should be a 'third estate' to secure the progression of society from the absolutism of the Fulbe aristocracy to a more just system based on self-determination. However, in the absence of an obvious candidate for the 'third estate', the French took it upon themselves to play the part, and the most explicit statement of such a doctrine is to be found in Ponty's *politique des races* circular. As we have seen in 1897 the French – or at least the Governor-General – did not think that the time had come to introduce a social revolution into the affairs of the Futa Jallon. Ten years later official policy had changed – though as has been emphasised this did not necessarily mean that all chiefs of the *Ancien Régime* were out of a job – far from it. Nonetheless there existed at this time a very special sense of the *mission civilisatrice* – more fundamental than the construction of schools, hospitals, etc. – which related to the wish to engineer a social revolution in Africa, to bring in other words 1789 to the Futa Jallon.

This has been a lengthy but necessary introduction to the events of 1909–11. Two main themes should be emphasised. Firstly, whatever may be said of the anarchy of the pre-colonial Futa Jallon, it was a powerful and well organised state which the French had never conquered but which they had been able to control only by entering into the local power struggle against Bokar Biro. The loyalty and the value of their alliances were as a result far from certain, and, indeed, the French were very suspicious of many of their allies, especially Alfa Yaya. Secondly, there existed a whole string of stereotypes, which contained elements of reality but which, like all stereotypes, ultimately confused rather than illuminated.

As early as 1899 the government in Guinea had been alerted to the possibility of an Islamic uprising. Noirot, the resident in the Futa Jallon, warned the Governor that Tierno Ibrahim, the *wali* of N'Dama,[27] who had been given an important position by the Senegalese administration, was causing Alfa Yaya trouble in Labé and that in the tradition of al-Hajj Umar, Ma Ba Diakhu and Mahmadu Lamine, he was planning to wage Holy War against the French.[28] Again in 1900 the Governor was worried by rumours of Islamic rebellion in Kankan, rumours that were especially worrying in view of the labour difficulties on the recently started Conakry to Niger railway.[29] However, the administration must have been reassured in 1903 by answers it received from *commandants de cercle* to questions it had sent out concerning the state of Islam. Almost without exception the local *commandants* replied that Islam was not a serious threat to the French.[30]

However, in March 1909 a French administrator, M. Bastié, was killed in an ambush and as a result the French became less complacent about Islam. The murder had a traumatic effect on the Europeans in Guinea. Marty described it as 'a unique event' in the history of the colony.[31] At first it was assumed that the murder was committed for personal reasons as Bastié was a man of violent temperament, disliked the Fulbe and was willing to take bribes. However, personal vendetta was ruled out as a motive for the murder, which quickly came to be seen as an act inspired by religious fanaticism as suspicion fell on a marabout, Tierno Amadou Tijani, a member of the religious community (*missidi*) in the village of Goumba.[32]

The person most responsible for this line of argument was Mariani, the Inspector of Muslim Education, who happened to be on a mission in the Futa Jallon at the time. In particular he accused Tierno Aliou, the *wali* of Goumba of master-minding an anti-French conspiracy throughout the Futa Jallon. Born around 1820, Tierno Aliou was an elderly man and apparently nearly blind when the Bastié murder took place.[33] He was born in the province of Ditinn in the Futa Jallon and was initiated into the Shadhiliyya – a brotherhood of North African origin which 'emphasised in devotional exercises the cultivation of inner resources alongside involvement in secular affairs'. It had been introduced into the Futa by 'Ali le Soufi', a Fulbe from Labé, and in the nineteenth century it was the brotherhood with the largest following in the Futa. However by the beginning of the twentieth century it had lost ground both to the Qadiriyya and to the Umarien Tijaniyya.[34] Having got involved in the political in-fighting of the mid-nineteenth-century Futa, Tierno Aliou moved from the centre of the Futa and around 1880 settled in Kindia where, bringing men and cattle, he was welcomed. His first contacts with the French date back to 1885 and from the start he was on best of terms with the Europeans in Conakry. He then moved, with French permission, to Goumba where he attracted a large following especially from amongst the Hubbu. The Hubbu movement in the Futa Jallon was a direct challenge to the central authority of the Futa state. Composed mainly of ex-slaves and disaffected peasants many of whom were recent converts to Islam and living in rural Islamic communities such as the one directed by Tierno Aliou in Goumba, the Hubbu explicitly denounced the corruption of the Futa aristocracy.[35] It is not surprising, therefore, that with such followers Tierno Aliou was regarded with intense suspicion by the *almamys*. The local *almamy* of Timbo was particularly hostile and intrigued with the neighbouring Sussu against him. However, benefitting from his French alliance, Tierno Aliou was able to beat off the Sussu attacks, and the last decade of the nineteenth century was something of a golden age for the *zawiya* (a Sufi centre, meeting place, lodge or seminary) of Goumba. The *missidi* constructed by Tierno Aliou[36] and his followers became a religious centre for lower Guinea and in a monastic atmosphere the daily routine in Goumba was dedicated to prayer and agriculture. From 1900 onwards Tierno Aliou was acknowledged as a saint – hence the name by which he was most commonly known, the *wali* of Goumba.

The fact that he enjoyed good relations with the French seemed to be proven once again when he quickly handed over his disciple, Tierno Amadou Tijani, whom the French had identified as the murderer of Bastié. However, Mariani saw only fanaticism and intrigue at work in Goumba. A week after Bastié's murder he warned the *commandant* of Kindia that:

> Although the people of this country are very docile, unfortunately they all become dangerous and incapable of reason when under the pretext of religion they are encouraged to wage Holy War against the infidel. Now the marabout of Goumbo is a past master at egging men on. On leaving my residence yesterday he didn't stop shouting 'Allah Akhbar' in a loud voice as if he was leaving for Holy War. Three times a day the vaults of the vast mosque echo with chants in honour of the prophet. I haven't come across anything like it elsewhere in AOF. To conclude, I tell you, something is going on in the *missidi*. The *Ouali*'s intentions may momentarily change but he must be closely watched. You must be careful of such a man agitating in such a fanatical environment where everybody obeys him blindly.[37]

The following day in another letter to the *commandant* of Kindia he regretted that the French 'had foolishly allowed a sort of theocracy to develop in *missidi* ... Death alone will rid us of this astute saint who is already very old and it's only after his death that we can seriously go about reducing the prestige and influence of his successors'. However, such prudence was not necessary outside the *missidi* and in other areas Mariani concluded 'It is up to us to ruin his good reputation completely'. Such warnings were also telegrammed to the authorities in Conakry and Dakar.[38]

In the wake of the Bastié murder, Liotard the Lieutenant-Governor of Guinea, decided to send Bobichon, the Inspector of Native and Political Affairs, on a tour of the *cercles* of Ditinn, Timbo, Labé and Yambering. Bobichon agreed that the *missidi* of the *wali* of Goumba was a centre of religious fanaticism, but he maintained that the murder of Bastié was the isolated act of a fanatical individual for which Tierno Aliou could not be held responsible. He further emphasised the uneasy relations based on fear and mutual suspicion which had developed between the French and the religious leaders of the Futa since the murder of Bastié. Liotard issued a circular to the local *commandants* asking for more information on the state of Islam and forwarded Bobichon's findings to Ponty, adding that he agreed with Bobichon's analysis, although he also stressed that Islam was more fervently practised and better organised in the Futa Jallon than in other parts of AOF.[39]

Mariani, however, continued to be very preoccupied with the question of Islam in the Futa Jallon. In two letters written at the end of July to the Governor-General he again stated his beliefs and fears. There was, he argued, no real danger in Guinea or anywhere else in AOF of a serious pan-Islamic revolt organised by the brotherhoods but, nonetheless, Islam could be a nuisance in the hands of certain individuals. 'In this time of social changes' he said, 'one would be wrong not to try and discover the political, economic or religious reasons which can lead men such as the *ouali* of Goumba into becoming or attempting to become at once a temporal and a spiritual chief'. According to Mariani, Islam was on the increase in Kindia as the Bambara and Sussu were forsaking their ancestral religions. Any satisfaction which the French may have felt about the moral and social improvement which, said Mariani, attended conversion to Islam soon went when 'entering the *missidi* one realises with what little regard we are viewed by the natives who only have as much respect for us as the *ouali* chooses to allow'. Mariani concluded that there were two imperatives: to create a *médersa* in Labé and to give more power to traditional chiefs to act as a counterweight to the likes of the *wali* of Goumba.[40]

Mariani's analysis of the social situation in the Futa struck a chord with the administration in Dakar. On the advice of Fournier, the head of the Bureau of Native Affairs, Ponty wrote to the Lieutenant-Governor of Guinea about the issues raised by Mariani. He argued that what was happening to the Muslim populations of Guinea was similar to the pattern elsewhere in AOF where, he said, the French were attacking the position of certain privileged minorities who lived at the expense of the masses. The Muslim question was therefore a social question which required a great deal of thought and attention. A month later Ponty wrote again to Liotard to emphasise his view: 'To maintain in the Fouta Djallon the hegemony of the Peuhl race is' he argued, 'to maintain with all its inconveniences the existence of the kingdom of the *almamy*s'. France needed to fight the alliance of the aristocracy and the marabouts, and the most effective weapon available to the French was to eradicate slavery, the basis of the aristocratic and maraboutic wealth. Deprived of their wealth the Fulbe *almamy*s would no longer be able to maintain their political hegemony, and each race would become its own master. Islam had been the only factor which had been able to unify the *almamy*s but it was, said Ponty:

> Islam based on slavery and we cannot allow it to prevail. The Islam which we protect, without actually helping its propaganda, is the modern Islam which does not permit tyranny and which abolishes captivity.[41]

All this was of course a familiar argument of the Ponty administration and was the essential feature of the stereotype of the *mission civilisatrice* discussed above. Superficially attractive, both as a description of the state of affairs and as a prescription for the remedy of social inequality, it was as we shall see deeply flawed in both respects.

Islam continued to be a major preoccupation in 1910. In April the political report from the *cercle* of Mamou warned of 'A veritable clerical peril which has found a well prepared terrain in the hostile dispositions of the Foulah leaders, discontented by our intervention'. The marabouts – led by the *wali* of Goumba – were all in regular correspondence and often read out each other's letters at Friday prayers. Even if the contents of the letters were not subversive they were still dangerous simply because, the argument ran, the native Africans held the written word in such reverence: 'The letters open the door to excitement or crime, to insurrection, to the preaching of Holy War. That's why one cannot be too careful about maraboutism and even if it is true that black Muslims, even the Foulah are not fanatics, the same cannot be said of the professional marabouts'.[42] Ponty warned the Lieutenant-Governor of Guinea that 'The example of two or three major Mauritanian marabouts whose very real services to us are known throughout AOF, should not delude us about the temporal role that certain religious notables, profiting from what they imagine to be weakness in our part and which in reality is tolerance, would like to play, serving as intermediaries between us and the mass of natives'.[43] In his instructions to Guy, the new Lieutenant-Governor of Guinea, Ponty spoke of the reported maraboutic activity in the *cercle* of Mamou and continued:

> We must put an end to this Islamic clericalism, which is a vulgar deformation of the Muslim doctrine. Responsible for the assassination of the administrator Bastié, it will cause a lot of damage if we leave it free. Of course, we shouldn't imagine that it will cause a generalised movement against the French but it does increase the natural suspicion of the native. Through the contagiousness of the fanaticism it inspires it could, if we don't take it seriously, cause numerous local troubles.[44]

Specifically French attention was directed at the *missidi* of the ageing *wali* of Goumba whose every action was now being ascribed a sinister ulterior motive. Marty wrote later that 'The most ordinary and benign statements of the marabout were interpreted in a tendentious way'.[45] Yet there was really very little evidence that Tierno Aliou had moved from his lifelong position as a supporter of the French. Indeed, M. Sasias, the *commandant* of Kindia who at the end of 1910 was sent to investigate the *missidi* of Goumba admitted that:

> I have never had the proof that he has acted against us or that he took part whatsoever in the assassination of M. Bastié ... The Foulah of Goumba seem absolutely tranquil, and the *ouali* whose body is covered with ulcerated wounds finds it impossible to leave his house or even to get up. His health is very poor and in the *missidi* every one expects him to die soon. Certainly no one has been able to give me information as to his intentions but I doubt that having been in such pain for so long he has thought about stirring up agitation amongst the Foulah of this and of neighbouring *cercles*.

But Sasias added as a qualification: 'It seems that he is surrounded by six or seven thousand men, all well armed and ready to march and that he possesses large numbers of weapons. Finally I have seen for myself the swiftness with which the smallest orders are carried out'.[46] Sasias made a further visit – taking all his family – and again found the *wali* apparently loyal to the French.

In July the assistant administrator of Kindia, Roberty, went to investigate rumours of arms purchases and reported that the *wali* was friendly but suffering from bronchitis and a thigh wound that wouldn't heal.[47]

However, French anxieties increased as the year drew on and the date of Alfa Yaya's return from exile drew nearer. The administration in Conakry would have preferred to have postponed Alfa Yaya's return, but to each of their letters making this request Ponty replied that a postponement was not possible for legal reasons.[48] It should be remembered that 1910 was a year of serious economic and political crisis in Guinea. The collapse of wild rubber deprived the colony of a major source of wealth. French traders' resentment was focussed on the Lebanese community whose political attitudes were also suspected by Ponty and Guy. It is against this background of widespread anxiety and uncertainty that the fears relating to Alfa Yaya and his son Aguibu should be seen.[49]

In December 1910 Ponty was in Guinea, and Tierno Aliou was summoned to appear before the Governor-General and Guy in Kindia, but he refused. Just as Sheikh Ahmadu Bamba's refusal to pay his respects to the Governor had been interpreted as a sign of open revolt, so too was Tierno Aliou's action interpreted in the most sinister way possible.[50] For Marty, too, it represented a turning point: 'It is at this moment and at this moment only that I would place the abandon by Tierno Aliou of his traditional policy of friendship and collaboration with the French. The latter abandoned him and even let it be understood that they were about to deal with him very severely'.[51] Certainly from December events developed rapidly.

By chance Mariani, who had been chiefly responsible for sowing doubts about the loyalty of the *wali* of Goumba in 1909, was once again on a mission of inspection in the Futa Jallon and once again he painted a disturbing picture of the situation. Sensibly he recognised that one of the major problems was lack of contact between the French administration and their subjects: 'In general' he wrote, 'the population of the Fouta, indeed the population of Guinea hardly know us at all'.[52] That Mariani contributed to a better mutual understanding is doubtful. He was disturbed by the fact that his porters carried him from town to town singing the praises of the Prophet Mohammed.[53] On another occasion he argued that:

> In adopting the Muslim religion the Blacks of Guinea have in large measure renounced the amusements of their ancestors and since I left Kindia I have very rarely heard music being played ... Only exceptionally in the isolated hamlets do the Foulah still enjoy themselves and the youngsters take pleasure in disturbing the peace of the household with their joyous songs ... Above all it is the sound of the *muezzin* and the recitation of prayers which troubles the silence of the Fouta night.

Mariani was also distressed to learn how popular Samori still was after his stay in Kankan.[54] The following month he reported to Ponty that 'The action of the marabouts is seldom favourable to us and those amongst them who would like to help us in our efforts would gradually lose their prestige if they did so ... I do not see in the loyalty to us of which some give proof anything other than a desire to obtain a few advantages.[55]

Mariani, however, had an axe to grind. As Inspector of Public and Muslim Education he was a firm believer in the importance of French secular education and of the *médersa*. Just as his frequent polemics against the mission schools should be seen as part of the campaign for secular schools, so too should his tirades against the Muslim leaders of the Futa Jallon be seen as a means of highlighting the urgent need for a *médersa* in the Futa Jallon. The *médersa* was proposed as the only solution to a problem (i.e. the spread of Islam) which French negligence had already allowed to go too far. Having visited the *cercles* of Pita and Ditinn, Mariani concluded that 'Unable to eradicate Islam we should try to channel it, and the present moment would seem to be the most opportune to create a *médersa*'.[56] However, Ponty and Mariani could not agree on a suitable location for the new *médersa*, and the scheme was forgotten.[57]

Despite official misgivings Alfa Yaya returned to his native Guinea in December of 1910 and swore an oath of loyalty to France. In return he was accorded a pension and allowed to reside in Labé. At first the administration thought that the ex-King of Labé would not cause any trouble but when his son, Modi Aguibu, returned from exile at the end of the year Alfa Yaya's attitude appeared to change. In January he protested at not being reinstated as chief of Labé and he was suspected of getting in contact with leading marabouts and chiefs from neighbouring Sierra Leone and to be plotting against the French. So, early in February, Alfa Yaya together with his son Modi Aguibu and his counsellor, Umaru Kumba, were all arrested. Alfa Yaya was shortly afterwards sentenced to a ten-year prison sentence in exile. As Guy explained to Ponty, Alfa Yaya's return in 1910 was a major political event in the colony:

> His return preoccupied not only Alfa Yaya's family but also the aristocracy of the entire country, who anticipated it eagerly. The Foulahs saw in their ex-chief a power whom they could use as a counterweight to our authority. For his parents and friends he was a protector. The notables found in his return yet another element for their perpetual intrigues. The marabouts, despite taking care to disguise their opinions favoured him and it is certain that it is on them that Alfa Yaya's party would rely, in order to recover their sovereignty.[58]

Ponty reported to Paris that:

> Alfa Yaya, blinded by his religious fanaticism and his feudal mind learnt nothing from his contact with us in Dahomey . . . It is therefore of the highest political importance for us to eject from the Fouta Djallon all the militant elements liable to obstruct the work of emancipation that we are undertaking in this country. Given the nature of Islam in the Fouta, the excessive credulity and social nervousness of the Peuhl and the existence of links between Muslim groups from one end to the other of AOF, the presence of Alfa Yahia and his son Aguibou, not just in Guinea but even in AOF, would enable his partisans to maintain their secretive agitation . . . A moral embarrassment would continue to weigh down upon the populations who are quite willing to rally to our cause if we protect them against their credulity.[59]

Thus the peculiar logic of the French vision of the civilising mission spiced up with more general anxieties about the international situation, particularly the course of events in Morocco, was leading to a situation in which conflict between the French and the former ruling élite of the Futa Jallon would soon be inevitable.

Soon after Alfa Yaya and Aguibu were exiled for the second time, M. Pherivong, the Inspector General of the Colonies who also happened to be in Guinea on a mission, published a lengthy report containing his views on French policy in the past towards Alfa Yaya and the marabouts.[60] Pherivong went back to Bastié's murder describing how French suspicions came to light on Tierno Aliou. He criticised Liotard for not having instructed Bobichon to look specifically for the responsibility of religious elements in Bastié's murder – Bobichon, it will be recalled concluded that the murder was an isolated act of religious fanaticism and not part of an orchestrated campaign against the French. Luckily, according to M. Pherivong, Mariani was in the area at the time and he could not believe that the murder was a simple act of fanaticism. Mariani pointed the finger at the ageing *wali* of Goumba. Seemingly innocent actions now took on a sinister light. It was recalled that shortly before the murder, Tierno Aliou had asked for permission for armed men to assemble in Goumba in order to go elephant hunting – permission which had readily been granted at the time – but it was now realised that the elephant hunt was a ruse, a cunning way of assembling armed men in order to attack the French. Tierno Aliou denounced Amadu Tijani, the man suspected of killing Bastié, but this again was simply in order to fool the French. Tierno Aliou was always the first to pay his taxes but he did so out of cunning not loyalty. He refused to go and pay his respects to the Governor-General in Kindia and through his disciples, who worked as interpreters and secretaries in the French administration, he was able to spy upon the French and keep one step ahead of their moves. Pherivong noted that 'If all the other *karamoko*s are of the same metal one can see with what dangerous men the administration, whose only auxiliaries are of dubious loyalty, has to deal'. The situation was exacerbated by the return of Alfa Yaya. Almost immediately he started organising the import of arms and soon fifty guns a day were reported to be pouring into Guinea from across the border with Upper Gambia in Senegal. The arms were hidden by the marabouts:

> who were said to have formed an association which was designed to combat the French influence, whose final demise had long been prophesied, and which would profit from the return of Alfa Yaya to realise its goal. Secret meetings called by emissaries from Touba were said to have been held as far away as Rio de Nunez to persuade the Muslims to fight. But they refused. All the documents agree on the fact that Guinea was being worked by Islamic propaganda.

Mariani, said Pherivong, explained how the marabout network functioned, but his warnings were not taken seriously until the return of Alfa Yaya in December 1910 and the appearance of fresh evidence of an Islamic conspiracy. Pherivong concluded therefore that the unrest of February 1911 was without doubt a continuation of the unrest of March 1909.

Guy wholeheartedly agreed with the conclusions of the Inspector and in the space made available for his comments on the report, he restated in the clearest and most unequivocal terms the way in which his administration viewed the situation in the Futa. It is worth quoting at length for it summarises many of the themes discussed so far in this chapter:

> Indeed [wrote Guy], it is not a question of isolated acts perpetrated by the members of the Foulah aristocracy who regret the disappearance of their former power, but rather it is an organised movement in which are involved all the *karamoko*s and the marabouts of the country, whose boundaries unfortunately are not just those of French Guinea . . . and if one wants to go back to the mysterious sources of this permanent conspiracy one should recognise the commands which the Muslim prophets receive from Mauritania and from even further afield, Morocco and Tibesti. The generosity we showed towards the *ouali* of Goumba at the time of Bastié's assassination has made this redoubtable and hypocritical chief into a powerful enemy who thinks to deal as an equal with the Governor-General, and consents, whilst biding his time before showing his true colours, to execute his orders on condition that he

doesn't have to enter into direct relations with him. Such a situation cannot carry on without giving the population of the Fouta Djallon . . . the impression that we are afraid of them and that we do not dare to act. Indeed, the population of the Fouta Djallon have never been easy to handle because they have never been made aware of our strength and they have never seen our soldiers. Our policy which since the beginning of our installation has consisted of obtaining their submission and getting them to pay taxes through the intermediary of a big chief, grossly overpaid for his services and assured that all his crimes would go unpunished, has been a disastrous policy. Acting thus we have gained time but there comes a time and that time is now when appetites reveal themselves and ambitions stir and when uprisings are prepared in the shadows.

I therefore believe that the Fouta should be occupied militarily, that the leaders of this movement should be arrested without weakness, and then when we have struck down the leaders that we should penetrate not just the country but the souls of the natives as well by means of the doctor, schoolteacher, roads and railways and finally by means of a more numerous and active administration than exists today in this almost unknown country. In doing so we will avoid the pain of having at a certain moment, perhaps not so far away, to repress a full-blooded revolt against our poorly understood and mistrusted authority.[61]

Recruitment of schoolteachers and doctors could only be increased slowly, but Guy was already poised to strike the first blow for the French Revolution in Guinea by arresting the chiefs of this 'permanent conspiracy' in the Futa Jallon. The time of pussyfooting with hypocritical marabouts was over, now there was going to be a bit of action.

On 7 March, Guy gave the following instructions to Captain Tallay of the Seventh Company of the Second Regiment of *tirailleurs*:

The Fouta Djallon is a mountainous area inhabited by natives of the Peuhl race, known under the name of Foulah in the colony. This population is Muslim and its religious faith, its hope in the definitive and imminent triumph of the laws of the prophet and, in consequence, their aversion – often even their hatred – for Whites who do not have the same beliefs, are all carefully nourished by numerous marabouts whose influence is sometimes considerable.

Since Alfa Yaya's return, Guy continued, the situation had progressively deteriorated to the point that it was now necessary to arrest the ringleaders, namely Karamoko Sankoun and Ba Gassama in Touba and Tierno Aliou, the *wali* of Goumba. From Guy's subsequent description of the *wali* it appeared that his health had improved dramatically, for this man who had recently been described as being on his deathbed was now portrayed as 'an alert old man who goes horseriding daily and who would be capable of riding fifty to sixty kilometres in one stretch if his safety depended on it'. On 22 March, Tallay was warned that the *wali* was surrounded by a force of 500 able-bodied men in the *missidi* which had been specially fortified in anticipation of an imminent attack and that, therefore, the greatest care should be taken in making the arrests. On 29 March on the eve of the planned arrest, there were three detachments of seventy-six, fifty-three and thirty-eight men camped around the *missidi* ready to make the arrest early the next day. However, the following morning Captain Tallay decided on impulse to arrest the *wali* using only a small force of men, but once inside the encampment he and twelve of his men were all killed. There was then a fierce three and a half hour battle between the rest of the Seventh Company and the defenders of the *missidi*. The battle was finally ended after a French sergeant 'showing heroic courage' set fire to the village which was completely destroyed. The French forces did not suffer any further casualties but over 300 of their opponents were killed.[62]

It is not certain that the *wali* was in the village at the time of the attack[63] but a price was immediately put on his head and Sussu chiefs were employed by Guy to help the French track down the *wali* and his followers.[64] Ponty sent Guy an extra company of *tirailleurs* to contribute to the show of strength and a police tour of the Futa Jallon.[65] However, Ponty emphasised to the Colonial Ministry that the importance of the incident should not be exaggerated and that it was due to clumsiness and lack of caution on the part of Captain Tallay. A few days later he again played down the incident. Although he did not think that it would have a serious repercussion it was nonetheless, he said, yet another example of the problem of religious fanaticism in West Africa:

> One must not forget that religious fanaticism pushed as far as the complete destruction of the personality puts in the hands of the marabouts men who obey them blindly and who are prepared, if ordered, to sacrifice themselves. Very fortunately the rivalry which exists between the religious chiefs forces them to act in isolation. There is no doubt that a suitable policy can win us the support of the least compromised. For if for the mass of the Foulahs only the religious question is at stake, for the marabouts it is really a question of ameliorating or at least of maintaining their material situation which has inevitably been affected by our domination. We can furthermore count on the devotion of the Soussou population, the enemies of the Foulah.

There should not have been any real danger of the Colonial Ministry forgetting the problem of religious fanaticism or the official explanation of why the marabouts were hostile to the French, for they were arguments that were regularly rehearsed at every available occasion.

In Guinea, however, the situation was more complicated than the description given to Paris by Ponty. The deaths of the two European officers, Captain Tallay and Lieutenant Bornand, deeply worried the European population of the colony. Guy, who arrived in Goumba in the middle of the battle, and who accompanied the corpses back to Conakry reported that at the station of Kindia 'All the European population . . . were waiting on the platform in order to show their solidarity in such painful circumstances'. The dead African *tirailleurs* were buried in Kindia but the bodies of the European officers were taken on for burial in Conakry where once again crowds of Europeans gathered to pay their respects.[66] However, European mourning soon acquired political overtones. On 15 April a Conakry-based paper published an editorial article under the title of 'The truth about the Fouta-Djallon affair'. Having stated that the 'Goumba massacre is merely a tragic episode in the Alpha Yaya affair, whose beginnings take us back five years', the article went on to comment on the succession of Lieutenant-Governors who had passed through the colony. Frezouls was praised for having exiled Alfa Yaya and for having laid the foundations of 'une Guinée saine, grande et prospère' but Roume, so the article ran, underestimated the 'Foulah peril', obstructed Frezouls so that 'the results of the personal policy of the Governor-General are so nefarious that five years later, all our Fouta is up in arms and the commerce of the colony brought to a standstill'. Frezouls' successor, Richard, was dismissed as a lackey of Roume. Poulet, the interim successor, did not have time to realise his good intentions and Liotard had been too hesitant towards Alfa Yaya and was partly responsible for the Goumba massacre. Guy was credited with having started well and acted against the Muslims with courage.[67] Guy was not, however, treated so kindly by two articles appearing in May in *Annales Coloniales* in which he was accused of having given Tallay last minute instructions to go unarmed into the *missidi* and so to a near-certain death.[68] Similar charges appeared the following month in another Paris-based weekly *La France d'Outre-Mer* in which, under the heading of 'The truth about the Goumba massacre: the balance sheet of a whimsical and arbitrary administration in French Guinea', it accused Guy, without actually ever naming him, of short-sightedness and of having been in complicity with Tierno Aliou. The accusations against Guy were peculiarly virulent and it called for Guy's removal.[69] The investigations into the 'Goumba affair' were causing embarrassment all round and everybody was looking hard for a scapegoat. Guy for his part was not without his supporters. The articles written in *Annales Coloniales* met with swift protest from, amongst others, the Conakry Comité union sportive, the members of the Cercle de Conakry, the Conakry Grand Orient, the Conakry Chamber of Commerce and from all the members of the Commission Municipale all of whom sent telegrams in defence of Guy.[70] Guy also counted Ponty, Pherivong, the Conakry paper *L'AOF* and August Terrier, chairman of the Comité de l'Afrique française, amongst his supporters and claimed that the campaign against him was being orchestrated by Poulet, Bobichon and the paper *Annales Coloniales*.[71] Guy's defence proved effective and towards the end of the year he was not only promoted but also awarded the Légion d'honneur, a sign which he took as final proof that his job was safe.[72]

The personal campaign against Guy is yet another factor which has to be included in the Goumba affair and serves as a reminder of the omnipresence of politics – both high and low. France and Islam are the two main protagonists in this study but both within 'France' and 'Islam' there were a multitude of conflicts.

Tierno Aliou, meanwhile, having fled to the neighbouring colony of Sierra Leone, was arrested by the British authorities in the second week of April and by the end of June all the extradition formalities had been accomplished so that the *wali* of Goumba could be brought to trial in Conakry.[73]

Concrete evidence against Tierno Aliou was lacking. A prisoner captured after the destruction of the *missidi* was reported to have been carrying a message written by Tierno Aliou urging the murder of Europeans, and, when pressed, the prisoner also admitted that Tierno Aliou had an efficient spy network based on loyal disciples in the employ of the French administration.[74] Such confessions seemed to confirm the conclusions reached in Pherivong's report in February. However, as in other attempts to prove the existence of an Islamic conspiracy, proofs were in short supply. Instead the French relied on innuendo, and chief amongst the basic suppositions behind French thinking was the belief that the Fulbe were not to be trusted. In his political report for the month of April the administrator of the *poste* of Touba wondered 'What goes on in their minds? One can never say – hypocritical and cunning they know how to hide their feelings'.[75] Sasias explained how he and all his predecessors had been taken in by Tierno Aliou's show of loyalty: 'With all the cunning of which a Foulah is capable he was able to fool the *commandants de cercles*, make himself appear harmless and so spread his influence throughout the region'. In retrospect Sasias could clearly see that the *wali* of Goumba's elephant hunt and his swift denunciation of the murderer of Bastié were mere ruses, and although Sasias was still surprised that the murderer, even when under interrogation, had never even indirectly implicated his old master in the crime, nonetheless he was now sure that the *wali* was 'the true instigator of Bastié's murder'.[76]

The other basic supposition in French thinking was that there was a widespread Islamic conspiracy generally and that specifically in the Futa Jallon Islam was peculiarly hostile to the French. Thus in the April report from Touba the administrator wrote that:

> The Foulah is in general very superstitious. They have a blind confidence in the *gris-gris* which are confected by the marabouts, who make a fortune from them. The influence of the marabout is limitless. For us he is an irreducible enemy whom we must put in a position where he cannot possibly do us any harm.[77]

Guy recalled the warnings he had been given by Ponty about the circulation of Mauritanian marabouts and the increasingly widespread dissemination of pamphlets in Arabic: 'The pamphlets are generally written in vague terms but all prophesy the arrival of an unknown *mahdi*, and for the natives of the Fouta Djallon this, as they were told each Friday in the mosques, could be no other than Tierno Aliou, the famous *ouali* of Goumba'.[78] An article in the newspaper *L'AOF* gave a melodramatic account of the events of 30 March for which the reader was given as 'general background information' the astonishing fact that 'The disciples of Cheikh Saad Bou form a vast brotherhood in West Africa. The hatred of the white man is the unique aim of their activities'. Tierno Aliou, the article continued, thanks to his spy network, knew all about the plans to arrest him and so he laid a carefully planned ambush. When Captain Tallay and his men entered the *missidi*, 'All the village shouts "Allah-ou-Akhbar" with great fervour; that's the war hymn . . . there is a precipitous rush onto the Whites; it's Holy War. The officers' bodies are mutilated, their mouths are stuffed with their cut-off sexual parts. The *tirailleurs* are also wounded horrendously'.[79]

Pherivong, still in the colony, reported to his superiors in the rue Oudinot that the recent events showed that it was no longer possible to deny the existence of an Islamic problem. He argued that the surest solution lay in the spread of the French language, 'the best method of combatting the activities of the marabouts about whom we are poorly informed since between them and us there is no contact except through interpreters who are their own pupils'.[80] Nowhere was the insecurity of the French more obvious than in their fears about having to rely on untrustworthy, even downright hostile, intermediaries. The role of interpreters in the Goumba affair was an important one: it counts little in the end whether or not the French were being spied upon – it was certainly very possible – what really counts is that they believed they were.

The Goumba affair reached its climax in the trial of Tierno Aliou in September in the Palais de Justice in Conakry. Unfortunately the only records available of the case are the press reports in the Conakry paper *L'AOF*.[81] As we have already seen this paper was much given to journalistic flourish, often at the expense of the truth. If it is not too heretical for an historian to say so, the 'truth' in this particular court case does not much matter, it is the atmosphere that counts. Thus we learn that at the opening of the trial: 'On the balcony of the Palais de Justice are the ladies, come to witness this spectacle. Despite the fact that it is morning, they are very well dressed. If the object of their curiosity was not so solemn, one could believe that one was at a revue or some sort of show'. In the next few days the prosecution based their case on the official reports from which we have already quoted. Mariani's reports, in particular, were of crucial importance. Sasias gave evidence that he had always distrusted Tierno Aliou saying that he had always considered him a stirrer. The judge consistently refused to accept evidence that pointed to the *wali*'s innocence. On the last day of the trial the courtroom was again full – 200 Europeans including sixty 'ladies' – had come to hear the verdict. The Chief Prosecutor summed up his case. 'He was' the paper reported, 'by turn, moving, ironical, biting and always eloquent. A merciless accuser, he put his long experience of criminal affairs at the service of the society which he represented and which he sought to defend'. M. Facciendi, the Counsel for the Defence and a young lawyer, 'put his case spendidly. He was as eloquent as one could hope for and right to the end, right to the very last minute, he put all his efforts into saving his client. He pleaded with an energetic desire to win and truly it required an unshakeable conviction on the part of the court for it not to be convinced'. Facciendi decried the press campaign against the Fulbe and the lack of positive proof against Tierno Aliou who had paid his taxes right up to 28 March. He had only been appointed as lawyer six days before the trial began and so, arguing that his client had acted in self-defence when he saw that a whole company of *tirailleurs* had been sent to arrest him, he demanded an acquittal. In order to dispel doubts about his loyalties, M. Facciendi ended by declaiming that 'I am not a lover of Negroes but a lover of justice for Negroes'. He pleaded in vain, and the *wali* was sentenced to death.

That the trial was a mockery is, of course, beyond doubt. It is rather pathetic to think of Tierno Aliou, a man in his eighties who had spent most of the latter part of his life as a loyal and dutiful French subject, being brought to trial in the pomp and splendour of the Palais de Justice for a crime which he may not have committed and without any chance of defending himself, for anything that he said or was said on his behalf simply would not have been believed, because, as everybody knew, the Fulbe were cunning schemers and not to be trusted. It is also shocking to realise the extent of the French 'overkill' during their counter-attack on the *missidi*, but such responses were common in this early colonial period.[82] What was perhaps less common was to stage a full-scale European-style trial in order to judge the accused whose guilt in the nature of things was a pre-established and known 'fact'. Why bother? Mock trials like sham elections clearly serve a basic function of providing at least an appearance of justice – or, as the case may be, democracy – which the conventions of 'civilisation' require to be preserved.

But the trial of the *wali* of Goumba was more than a mere exercise of cosmetic justice cooked up for metropolitan consumption; it was also an act of ritual. Just as the Europeans all came to the station platform in Kindia and in Conakry to meet the train carrying the bodies of the two dead officers, so too did they now flock to the Palais de Justice to see that justice was being done. But the justice was emphatically not the summary justice of the battlefield, but rather the elaborate and civilised affair of the French judicial system. One had to dress up for it, and it was a fitting spectacle for ladies. Lawyers pleaded their case eloquently and wittily – just like in France. The defendant – this curious *wali* of Goumba – played a suitably passive part, no unseemly outbursts or violent physical attacks on his captors; in short, he had been tamed. And whilst Europeans may have squabbled amongst themselves and used this incident to settle some old scores with their colleagues and compatriots, here in the courtroom they were all united in solidarity with the dead officers, in abhorrence of the Islamic peril and in a shared feeling of relief. The trial was homely and reassuring, but also quite exciting really. All in all not so very different from a good melodrama in a provincial theatre.

What then was the significance of the Goumba affair? Firstly it is perhaps the clearest example of how Ponty's *politique des races* could work in practice. Ponty's policy was based on the observation of profound inequalities in African societies, inequalities both between and within different ethnic groups. Such an observation was based on reality as few people today would seek to deny the existence of such inequalities in pre-colonial African societies. However, the inequalities were complicated inequalities[83] and it was these complications which Ponty and his colleagues tended to gloss over. Nowhere was this more evident than in their attitude to the *wali* of Goumba. The *wali*'s position in the Futa Jallon was very particular. He had quarrelled with the *almamy* of Timbo and was forced to move literally and metaphorically to the periphery of the Federation and found a new settlement away from the established political and religious centres. The following that he attracted was recruited from a wide assortment of social backgrounds including ex-slaves. The *wali*, himself, enjoyed excellent relations with the French for most of his life. However, the combined beliefs that the Futa Jallon was a feudal society and that the greatest obstacle to French progress in Africa was an alliance between feudal slave-owning chiefs and a religious caste more interested in its own temporal welfare than in ministering to the spiritual needs of its followers required a revision to be made of the portrait of the *wali*. Thus a man whose followers included many former slaves and who had quarrelled with the local chiefs and who was quite content with the French presence was now portrayed as somebody who inevitably was hostile to the French. Thus when Mariani began to sow doubts in the minds of the administration about the loyalty of the *wali*, conflict between him and the French became a self-fulfilling prophesy as the French, prisoners of their own republican rhetoric and blinded by their stereotypes of the Fulbe character, came more and more to suspect their erstwhile ally to the point of sending an entire armed company to arrest him. Given this treatment by a power whom he had loyally served for most of his life it is not surprising that the *wali* and his supporters attacked the soldiers sent to arrest him.

Secondly, the Goumba affair highlights the importance of stereotypes. In this Mariani's role was particularly important as it was he more than anybody else who, by playing on the stereotype of the Fulbe character, managed to discredit Tierno Aliou in the eyes of the French. In the end the stereotype proved more powerful than the empirical evidence, and Tierno Aliou was guilty of nothing so much as being a Fulbe marabout and all that that implied. We ourselves should be wary of type-casting the French. The French were divided amongst themselves and far from confident that their Gallic birthright would protect them against all misfortune. The deaths of Bastié, Tallay and Bornand were all unnerving experiences. Once again we have to include fear and insecurity in our description of the French psychological make-up. The good Republican liberator is clearly as inadequate as the double-dealing Fulbe.

Thirdly, it is important to note that much of French insecurity stemmed from the fact that the Futa Jallon had never been conquered and that its people had never been made aware of the reality of French force. The French always felt uneasy about their choice of intermediaries and suspected them constantly of plotting against them. It is significant that chief amongst Guy's proposals for policy reform in the Futa Jallon was a military occupation.

Fourthly, a lesson was learned from the episode, and there seems to have been a tacit admission from the French that they had overreacted. Marty's account of the whole affair is explicitly critical of the way in which both Tierno Aliou and the Jakhanke marabout, Karamoko Sankoun, were treated by the French. He ridiculed the attribution of ulterior motives to the *wali*'s slightest gesture and thought that the French had acted clumsily in the whole affair. The violence was unnecessary, he argued, because 'Right up to the eve of the conflict the relations and the attitude of the *ouali* have always born witness of his desire to return to his first loves ... There are numerous facts of all kinds which suggest that even at the start of 1911 this old man of eighty years desired at bottom only his own tranquility'. About Karamoko Sankoun he wondered 'By what chain of circumstances did one manage to make of this sympathetic marabout and conciliatory magistrate the deportee of Port Etienne?' French fears of a St Bartholomew Day massacre instigated by the marabouts were ' ... pure imagination. Through an unreasonable sentiment of fear one wanted to capture in one sweep of the net all the Islamic notables of the Fouta'. The French were unable to discover the huge arms caches whose existence had been reported so confidently before the Goumba affair.[84] To a certain extent the affair marked the end of a period in terms of French attitudes to Islam, a period characterised by exaggerated fears and belief in the 'permanent conspiracy' of Islam.

The *wali* of Goumba was the clearest victim of this understanding of Islam. Condemned to death by the judge in Conakry he died naturally of illness whilst awaiting execution on 3 April 1912. The French authorities felt cheated that he had escaped his punishment and were worried that the population of Guinea would interpret it as an indication either that the French did not dare execute him or that Allah had intervened to prevent the *wali* suffering the indignity of the guillotine.

Part III

French scholarship and the definition of *Islam noir*

Va dire au Gouverneur que nous lui obéissons. Que nous executerons ses ordres et que nous respecterons ses dépenses.

Et que nous n'opposerons pas aux oeuvres enterprises par lui, à ce qu'il nous commandera d'important ou de minime, ses moindres ordres seront obéis.

Je me confie à Dieu contre tous les maux du Siècle.

(Verses from the poem of Sheikh Sankoum of Tonba (Guinea), 'Sur la Puissance des Chrétiens', 1912. This is the translation from the original Arabic made by the French administrator Gilbert Vieillard who made a lifelong study of Fulbe custom and culture. This and other manuscripts which he collected can be found in the archives of IFAN, Fonds Vieillard.)

You are an intelligent fellow, and you will ask how a Polish adventurer, meaning Enver, and a collection of Jews and Gipsies should have got control of a proud race. The ordinary man will tell you that it was German organization backed up with German money and German arms. You will enquire again how, since Turkey is primarily a religious power, Islam has played so small a part in it all. The Sheikh-ul-Islam is neglected, and though the Kaiser proclaims a Holy War and calls himself Hadji Mohammed Guilliamo, and says the Hohenzollerns are descended from the Prophet, that seems to have fallen pretty flat. The ordinary man again will answer that Islam in Turkey is becoming a back number, and that Krupp guns are the new gods. Yet – I don't know. I do not quite believe in Islam becoming a back number. (John Buchan, *Greenmantle*, 1916.)

Introduction

After the fiasco of the Goumba affair both the French and – as Sheikh Sankoum's poem bears witness – the Fulbe appear to have gone in for some soul-searching. The third part of this study describes the first wave of considered intellectual reflection by the French about the nature of their presence in West Africa. By the First World War some administrators had already acquired considerable knowledge of indigenous societies and during the war years themselves this knowledge increased beyond all reasonable expectation as a result of research initiatives from within the colonial administration. Three men in particular were responsible for this burst of activity: François Clozel, Maurice Delafosse and Paul Marty. Although all three operated from within and for the benefit of the colonial system, all nonetheless contributed to a liberal understanding of African society which has been hugely influential amongst both European and African policy-makers. Within this liberal understanding Islam occupied a central position: largely as a result of the wartime scholarship of Clozel, Delafosse and Marty, the nature of Islam was redefined and accommodated within an understanding of African culture which emphasised the power of ethnically specific 'traditions' in shaping society. The French definition of *Islam noir* as a religion which was quite distinct from the type of Islam practised elsewhere in the Muslim world acquired a particular significance in the context of a war in which the enemy forces included the Ottoman Empire. The burden of colonial rule grew heavier as Africans were enrolled both directly and indirectly into supporting the allied war effort in western Europe and consequently the response of West African Muslims became a question of great concern. John Buchan would have been pleased to know that Islam was certainly not 'a back number' in French West Africa.

6

Scholar-administrators and the definition of *Islam noir*

The Futa Jallon was not the only area in which the French feared an Islamic rebellion in 1911. In March Clozel, the Lieutenant-Governor of Upper Senegal and Niger, telegrammed Ponty warning him of three marabouts recently returned from Mecca who were rumoured to be plotting against the French. Neither Ponty nor Clozel thought there was much substance to the rumours but, nonetheless both thought that in view of recent events in Futa Jallon it would be wise to take precautions. Ponty immediately wrote to the Governors of Senegal, Mauritania and Guinea informing them of the rumours and asking them to make discreet enquiries. He thought it necessary, however, to ask the Governors 'to moderate ... the zeal of certain administrators who might be tempted to make premature arrests whose only results would be to excite fanaticism and perhaps unleash local movements against us'.[1] In Senegal, recruitment for the Moroccan campaign and fears of a renewed Yellow Fever epidemic, made the authorities particularly apprehensive. In June, Cor, the Lieutenant-Governor, wrote to Ponty that 'Circumstances have never been as favourable for an Islamic rebellion as they now are in the colony. ... Those who watch from the side of Islam – and they are still numerous – are aware of the circumstances which would make it very difficult for us to repress troubles were they to occur'. Cor proposed to conduct an investigation into the state of Islam in the *cercles* of the Fleuve, Niani-Ouli and Upper Gambia. The investigations were to be made by two trustworthy 'native agents', Soce So and Bakhane Diop, chiefs of Diambour and Goe-Joal respectively, supervised by M. Brunot and M. Boinnassies, two of the very limited number of administrators whom Cor thought were competent in Islamic issues in the colony. Cor also increased the number of guards in the *cercles* where he most feared an Islamic uprising and made arrangements for an extra 1,496 rifles and 134,500 cartridges to be sent to these *cercles*. However, the enquiry which he commissioned revealed no trace of a plot, although it did show 'a certain effervescence in maraboutic *cercles*'. All in all Cor was confident that 'the severe repression of Goumba, had introduced a certain 'salutary fear in the maraboutic milieux'.[2]

94

In August Mariani reported rumours of a meeting of marabouts from all over AOF in N'Diawara on the right bank of the River Senegal to discuss a movement against the French. The rumours were, he admitted, impossible to verify but nonetheless he believed that 'The marabouts . . . are organising a silent conspiracy against us or else they are giving unsolicited, but false, information designed to mislead us in our research'.[3] In September, a Soninké marabout, Fode Ismaila, who had recently returned from Mecca, was exiled with four other marabouts and chiefs for having caused anti-French unrest by proclaiming to enthusiastic crowds the news that the French were about to withdraw.[4]

In the same month the Italians declared war on the Ottomans and invaded Cyrenaica. With vastly superior forces the Italians were able to inflict heavy losses on the Ottoman forces but their initial calculation that the Sanusiyya would not support the Ottomans proved wrong. Even after various treaties between the Italians and the Ottomans had been signed, the Sanusiyya continued to resist the European invaders and by using guerilla tactics were able to tie down the Italians with great effect.[5] The war was watched with great interest by the French authorities south of the Sahara. The interim Lieutenant-Governor of Upper Senegal and Niger was worried by the contents of correspondence from Tripoli which had been seized by the postal service of his colony:

> The general tone of these letters [he wrote] is of an exaggerated optimism. But the real danger lies above all in the accounts of the efforts made by the Faithful of all nationalities . . . to achieve unity against the Foreigner.[6]

Concern about developments in the Muslim world was sufficient to justify the creation in Paris in June of an Interministerial Commission on Muslim Affairs whose task it was 'To determine the means of our Muslim policy and to look for a solution to the problems common to different departments concerned with the Muslim question'.[7] In October the Colonial Ministry nominated three of its most senior officials – You, Marchand and Julien – to the Commission. One of its first policy documents stated that:

> Without doubt Islam with its moral precepts and its rudimentary social organisation constitutes a superior principle of civilisation for primitive peoples. But its doctrines, so simple in appearance contain some abstractions which the humble mentality of the recently converted Blacks and the uneducated Arabo–Berbers cannot assimilate. As a result the suggestions of the Islamic faith cause . . . a sentiment of religious exaltation that is always lively and which consequently make the handling of native Muslims singularly delicate. Explosions of fanaticism are always to be feared . . . It seems that African Islam is never stable.[8]

But what relevance had the Commission for West Africa? It would appear very little. The most consistent activity of the Commission was to publish a regular review of the Muslim press, copies of which were sent to Dakar where they were regularly left unread and are even today available in neat, dusty piles arranged in exact chronological order in the archives.[9] Unfortunately its neatness seems to be in inverse proportion to its value and interest, not only to the contemporary French administrator but also to the present researcher on Islam in West Africa. Increasingly Paris and Dakar came to have two very different perceptions of Islam. Although pan-Islamism did not disappear from the nightmares of administrators in West Africa, the more internationalist perspective of Paris gave way to a localised view which caused fewer anxieties. The shift in perspective did not, of course, take place overnight.

The localised view of Islam developed from a remarkable series of studies carried out between 1912 and 1921. These studies themselves developed from a series of government directives to local *commandants* to send in information to Dakar about Muslim notables and Qur'ānic schools. However, such requests, made initially in 1906, met with a mixed response. In 1911 Ponty complained that he had received very few of the personal files that Roume had asked for in 1906,[10] and so he repeated the demand in another strongly worded circular at the end of the year. He warned that Muslim agitators were making use of modern methods of propaganda such as the printing press and that the need to be informed about their activities was more urgent than ever.[11] In his instructions for his interim replacement Ponty described the circular as having created 'a central Muslim information service for all the colonies of the group' and he stressed that 'an essential condition' of France's successful action in AOF was finding 'a solution to the problems posed by the incontestable development ... of Coranic doctrines'.[12] It is from around this time that one can begin to talk of the existence of a special Muslim department in the federal administration, though it was not until 1913 that such a department was formally instituted as part of wider administrative changes.[13]

In 1912 Robert Arnaud, in his last year as chief adviser on Muslim affairs, published an account of French Muslim policy which can in some sense be seen as a bridge between a view of Islam obsessed with brotherhoods and conspiracies and a more pragmatic understanding. Unlike his 1906 book this work is concerned with the whole of West Africa and not just Mauritania. Perhaps this explains why the tone of the book is much more patronising and paternalist. The African Muslim, we learn on the first page 'is still like a child who has just learnt his catechism'.[14] Nonetheless he could still be a nuisance, and Arnaud proceeded to give a summary of the Islamic rebellions – major and minor – that had taken place since 1905.[15] Arnaud, like Ponty, saw conversion to Islam as a social issue: in the case of the Wolof population of the Senegambia, he argued that the original Islamisation had been 'A veritable social revolution ... the opposition of the proletarian caste to the aristocracy, a class struggle', but that since then Islam had been assimilated by the aristocracy who had made it the hand-tool of their own political supremacy.[16] Arnaud therefore whole-heartedly endorsed Ponty's commitment to religious neutrality and his *politique des races*. His main fear about Islam was that:

> The Black in becoming a Mahommetan has less admiration for us since he knows that knowledge and wealth come from God. He has even a feeling of the superiority which God gives to the believer over the infidel. He believes that our paradise, created by our own effort is of this transitory world whereas he will enjoy his, created by prayer, throughout eternity.[17]

The Sufi brotherhoods were no longer seen as the powerful and well-organised institutions that he had portrayed them as in 1906. Indeed he even suggested that the French exaggerated the xenophobic tendencies of the Sanusiyya. Arnaud specifically rejected the idea of following the Algerian example of providing financial support for the mosques.[18] More importance was attached to the *grands marabouts* who were to become the focus of French Islamic policy during and after the First World War.[19] Arnaud concluded that France should ensure that 'Islam should never be anything other than a religious belief'[20] and that 'Still half confused with fetishism, Islam must not evolve in the sense of Turko–Egyptian nationalism nor in the political traditions of Muslim states, but in the sense of French ideas'.[21]

It would be exaggerating to claim that this series of articles amounted to a major shift in perception from, say, the 1906 book. Nevertheless, it was clearly influenced by Ponty's thinking on the relationship between Islam, a 'feudal' aristocracy and slavery. This view was shared by most other contemporaries, including Clozel, Delafosse and Marty, and it is with these three scholar-administrators that this chapter is concerned.

THE SCHOLAR-ADMINISTRATORS AND ISLAM

Clozel

Marie-François Joseph Clozel was born in 1860 in the Ardèche.[22] In 1881–82 he did his military service with the First Regiment of Zouaves (the mixed Franco–Algerian troops) in Algeria where he also worked between 1885 and 1886 as an interpreter in the Native Hygiene Service. In 1892 he was a member of the Maistre mission which explored Central Africa between the Congo and the Niger and the following year he himself led an ethnographic mission in Adamawa and Chad. In 1896 he was posted to the Ivory Coast where he remained for ten years.

He arrived in the Ivory Coast at a time when the military were being forced to withdraw by a coalition of interests between the Treasury Department in Paris and local traders, anxious to increase trade with the prosperous Baule region.[23] In contrast to the military view, the civilian administration under the governorship of Louis Gustave Binger preferred the Muslim Dyula traders to the animist populations of the colony, and this preference was reflected in the writing of both Binger and Clozel. In order to rule the colony without soldiers it was decided, as in the Futa Jallon, to make use of existing social structures but, unlike in the Futa, a serious attempt was made to understand the customs and institutions of the indigenous population. Early in 1901 Clozel, now the interim Lieutenant-Governor of the colony, issued a circular to the local administrators requesting ethnographic details, especially details of local customs relating to legal procedures. The circular and its replies were published in a 600-page volume the following year under the title of *Les Coutumes indigènes de la Côte d'Ivoire*.[24] It was in his introduction to this volume that Clozel spoke most positively of Islam:

> [Europeans] will obtain faster and more satisfying results from the Muslims than from the Pagans because their very religion, their special but undeniable civilisation makes them less distant than the fetishists and more able to understand what it is that we require of them. . . . Binger, in the course of his great journey in the Niger Bend, seems also to have experienced on his arrival in Kong the same feeling of relief and well-being that I myself felt when, as part of the Maistre mission, we arrived in Muslim Adamaoua after eleven months of travel amongst pagan peoples.[25]

Clozel reserved especially warm words for the Dyula for, as traders 'They consider as the greatest of goods peace and the security of the roads . . . and so they willingly accept the foreign authority which assures them these advantages'.[26] He concluded with a plea for a less prejudiced view of African society based on deeper understanding which would permit good and efficient government.[27] Pride of place amongst the ethnographic studies went to Delafosse's work on the Baule. It has recently been argued that the quality of this work led to 'a premature sophistication' of French under-standing of the Baule: 'Once [administrators] had read Delafosse's writings on Baule history and customs and memorised a few key words from his published vocabulary lists they felt sufficiently introduced to the Baule to handle administrative affairs with confidence'.[28] The author of these comments goes on to show how in the context of a rapidly changing economic system (Baule prosperity was based on the trade in slaves, rubber and palm oil, all of which suffered greatly in the 1900s) this confidence was misplaced. More interesting for our purposes is the fact that such studies changed people's perception of the 'primitiveness' of animist cultures. Clozel himself was the most obvious case of such a change, to the extent that one may almost speak of his 'discovery' of animism as a coherent and well-structured system of beliefs and institutions. Certainly by the time that he moved on to take charge of Upper Senegal and Niger in 1908, he had acquired great respect for traditional African religion and, at the same time, had lost his early admiration for Islam.

In Upper Senegal and Niger, Clozel again emphasised the role of the Dyula traders as the most effective agents of Islamisation, but he now saw their role in a less positive light describing the trader as 'a sort of religious travelling representative who earns his way to heaven by paying for it handsomely on earth'. The suppression of the slave trade had, he said, destroyed the basis of their economic wealth and consequently they were anxiously to take their revenge on the French.[29] But above all he was struck by the influence of ancestral beliefs on African Islam:

> The fetishist convert in uttering the ritual formula does not acquire the mentality of the Arab or Berber. His psychic constitution is in no way upset by this fact. The survival of local superstitions, belief in spirits and in an order of ideas, customs 'and traditions which are often contrary to the rules of the Coran show that the man has made a gesture only, that he has given up nothing of his personality. Sudanic Islam seems to be profoundly stained with fetishism. It is a mixed religion, the product of two different original beliefs.[30]

One of the most striking aspects of Clozel's character was his bookishness. There is no doubt that he was a man of great learning and of great commitment to learning. He appears to have had little time for the military with whom he clashed in both the Ivory Coast and the Sudan.[31] Typical of his intellectual approach was a letter to Ponty in October 1909 in which he reported that 'Islam is losing ground amongst the arable farmers but is expanding slightly amongst the pastoralists'. This fitted in well with Renan's theory on the origins of monotheism amongst Semitic peoples which Clozel summarized thus:

> The nomad, constantly aware of the immensity of his surroundings, is naturally carried towards contemplation and meditation which give birth in his uncultured spirit . . . to the idea of a divine power, the unique dispenser of laws . . . and sovereign mistress of human destinies . . . The arable farmer, constantly bent over the nourishing soil whose inexhaustable fecundity . . . has for infinite generations assured him the good fortune of being able to live without either fatigue or constraint of any kind, naturally envisages his future destiny in a comfortable and agreeable light entirely lacking in metaphysical speculation. His present divinity and faith are contained in this natural world which feeds him, which supplies all his needs and whose magnificence and mysterious power . . . are sufficient for his spiritual aspirations.

The ownership of slaves, he went on to argue, in freeing the African from the obligation of manual labour on the soil encouraged Islam through allowing more time for contemplation of the eternal and universal verities of life. Thus Clozel arrived at the formula: 'Islam has always prospered and continued to prosper in countries ravaged by slavery and in towns inhabited by non-farming elements of the black population'.[32] Whereas the initial argument about the relationship of monotheism to the type of life-style commands respect and although there was a close relationship between Islam and slavery, the attempt to relate these facts to hard and fast rules about slavery and Islam appears contrived. Yet the belief in an intimate and almost exclusive link between Islam and slavery was one of the corner-stones of French Islamic policy at this time.

Clozel made a serious effort to document the precise state of Islam in his colony. In August 1911 he issued a circular to the local administrators asking them each to make an annual report on the Islamic situation in their *cercle*.[33] The circular contained a long preamble in which Clozel outlined his belief of how the French conquest had altered the religious balance in the colony:

> Fetishist society, deprived of its chiefs and no longer able to exclude the Muslim element from its bosom has been without defence against ... the marabouts and Dioulas who, using sweetness and persuasion and often presenting themselves as our auxiliaries, have ... gradually obtained results which have been as successful as those of the savage conquering prophets.

In contemporary West African society there was, he suggested, a new solidarity between the Muslim Fulbe, Tukolor and Soninke:

> Thus it is certain that not only rivalries between Muslims of all nationalities will die down but that also a Muslim nationality that transcends all ethnic differences will one day constitute itself. The religious ideal will cement all the diverse groups which in the past were separate. One can thus state that we are witnessing on the one hand the breakdown of fetishist society and on the other the concentration of Muslim forces which are profiting from the social transformation resulting from the French conquest.

This conquest had been made easy by the very divisions along ethnic and religious lines which were now in danger of disappearing. 'We have, therefore' he wrote, 'a primordial interest ourselves in maintaining these divisions, the religious ones at least, and *in opposing the invasive Islam with a strong centralised and self-conscious fetishism. This concept is . . . the pivot of the native policy of our colony.*' Clozel then proceeded to a distinction between Muslims and animists which was to be heard frequently over the next few years:

> Everywhere the fetishists appear to us as submitted, devoted and open without any malicious thoughts about the fertile influences of our civilisation. One should note that these excellent dispositions have been fortified by the liberation of captives from which animists have greatly profited. Islam, by contrast, shows itself to be unjustifiably reserved . . . and if we have sometimes found amongst its votaries loyal and convinced partisans, how many on the other hand have borne a sneaking grudge against us, considering us as infidels who must be suffered until they can get their revenge?

In order to prevent the breakdown of animist society Clozel reminded his local administrators of the importance of using local customary law in preference to Muslim law:

> You will be aware of how much our subjects of non-Muslim status (*de statut coutumier*) are attached to their ancestral traditions. Having studied them, *you also know how logical, just and respectable these traditions are.* . . . These customs are the corner-stones of fetishism and it is around them that we should group the scattered elements of this society which is in danger of falling apart.

However, the task did not end there: 'At the same time as we build up the defences of fetishism against the Muslim contamination we should ensure that we can follow, day by day, the developments of Islam'. So in view of recent events in the Futa Jallon, Clozel proposed to create 'a Muslim police force' which would be able to force local chiefs to declare the names of all the marabouts, imams and *karamokos* resident in their areas and which, through a network of informants, would be able to spy on the activities of the Muslim leaders.[34]

The following year Clozel received a flood of reports in response to the circular. Most of the reports contained little more than repetitions of ethnic and religious stereotypes, padded out with tables and statistics of doubtful value. Others were more interesting. In the *cercle* of Ségou the *commandant* claimed to have made extensive tours in the bush and to have held many 'palavers' with local chiefs whom he exhorted to remain faithful to their traditional customs, providing that these were not contrary to civilisation. One of his local agents was proving invaluable, he said, because, as he would write in Arabic, he was able to write down conversations before he forgot them – an interesting comment on the general standard of agents, perhaps.[35]

Clozel's most comprehensive statement on Islam and what French policies towards it should be is contained in his 'Lettre de Korbous' published in 1913 and which Delafosse later described as 'perhaps the best summary of Muslim policy ever made'.[36] Clozel repeated the arguments about the need to protect animism from Islam whose followers in any case, he claimed, accounted for a mere fifth of the total of the Sudan. He did not deny that conversion to Islam represented 'a real progress' for animists but he said that 'Once this first step has been taken the people become less willing to take the second step'.[37] However, the originality of the account lay in his attempt to define Islam by ethnic group, and most of his article was taken up with a consideration of the different ethnic types of Islam: the Wolof community in the Sudan was proud and religious and a potential threat, the Soninké and the Fulbe, despite their fanaticism, could easily be bought off. Education would rid the Songhay and the Moors of their fanaticism, and Clozel believed that the best hope of winning the allegiance of the warlike Tuareg was to recruit them into the French army.[38] Clozel's work clearly bore the stamp of an ethnologist. It was, of course, also in keeping with the underlying principles of Ponty's *politique des races*.

As something of an intellectual it is not surprising that Clozel took a keen interest in education. Indeed, it was he who was chosen to undertake the mission to Algeria in 1906 to study the working of the *médersa*s. Although he had then reported in favour of applying the *médersa* system south of the Sahara, within a few years he had become much more sceptical about their value in Black African society. He was worried that they might give new life to a religion which he hoped had lost much of its earlier vitality. He now argued that all the French should seek to do was to 'channel' Islamic belief. He was accordingly in favour of creating a *médersa* in Timbuktu which, with a curriculum that allotted a large place for French, would, he hoped, help to win over the Songhay population.[39] He stressed, however, that the *médersa* should not try to emulate the Algerian model. When Mariani, inspecting the new *médersa*, argued that not enough attention was being given to training Muslims for administrative functions Clozel was incensed:

> I protest against this tendency [he wrote to the Governor-General] which is all too common amongst our administrators raised in Algeria, of assimilating the races and institutions of the Sudan to those which they have got to know in our great colony in North Africa. There is absolutely no a priori reason for such a comparison. We should simply try and give our Nigerian [*sic*] population the institutions which suit them without worrying ourselves about those that exist in Algeria or Tunisia. If I have not chosen to make the Tombouctou *médersa* into a nursery for administrators it is because I believe that in the Sudan, unlike in Algeria, we are not under the obligation to create administrative openings for an entirely Muslim population.... I believe we have done enough for Islam – perhaps too much – in creating the *médersa* at Djenné and that it would be both pointless and dangerous to open a similar institution in Tombouctou. My aim, uniquely political, has been to control indirectly the action of the native teachers of Tombouctou and to create a place for French influence in the intellectual education of the young pupils.... In a word my concern was political and not pedagogical.[40]

Delafosse

Maurice Delafosse was born in 1870 in a small town in the middle of France.[41] At the age of eighteen he entered a seminary but, realising that he had no vocation, he left after nine months in order to study medicine. As a student in Paris he was introduced into colonial circles and began to think about a teaching career in Senegal. To this end he started to attend Arabic lessons with Octave Houdas, one of the most respected of French orientalists and whose daughter Delafosse was later to marry. As his Arabic interests increasingly dominated his medical studies, Delafosse came into contact with the work of Cardinal Lavigerie, who had recently founded a quasi-monastic anti-slavery society – L'Institut des frères armés du Sahara – which was intended to complement the work of French troops in the Sahara.[42] The Institut was to be based in one of the oases on the caravan trade routes and, using arms if necessary, would free any slaves carried by caravans stopping in the oasis. Delafosse was impressed by the idea and was one of the first volunteers when he joined up in the winter of 1890–1891. However, the Institut was a disappointment for him: the romantic vision of freeing slaves in far-flung oases was unfulfilled as the young volunteers were simply used, it seems, as gardeners and domestics for the full-time missionaries. Within a year Delafosse had left the Institut and started his military service as a *zouave* in Biskra. His military career, however, was brought to a premature end through illness.

In September 1892 he returned to his studies at the Ecole des langues orientales where he specialised in Hausa, still with a view to teaching in Senegal. However, in 1894 Binger, whom he had got to know in Paris, offered him a post as a Native Affairs Officer in the newly created colony of the Ivory Coast. It was here that Delafosse struck up his partnership with Clozel and where he conducted his first serious ethnological research.

It is interesting and important to note the link between the anti-slavery movement and ethnology. Charles Monteil, another of the early group of ethnologists who worked alongside Clozel and Delafosse in the Ivory Coast and the Sudan, cited an article published in 1913 in *L'Afrique Libre*, a French anti-slavery journal, in which it was argued that Europeans would be incapable of contributing towards the emancipation of slaves in Africa unless they had a thorough understanding of African custom and tradition.[43] The link between the anti-slavery movement and ethnology is personified in Delafosse, a member of the French Anti-Slavery Committee and one of the most respected and influential of the early ethnologists.

After Clozel left the Ivory Coast Delafosse quarrelled with the new Governor, Angoulvant, who supported the military in their wish to deal with unrest amongst the Baule by force of arms. Delafosse left the colony to join Clozel in the Sudan. He did not stay long there and by the end of 1908 he was back in Paris where he was given charge of a course at the Ecole coloniale on 'African Languages and Culture' – a course which he taught until the war. Shortly before his return to France Delafosse lost his faith. He wrote to his wife: 'I am not a hypocrite and I would hate to pretend to practise a religion in whose divine character my reason forbids me to believe'.[44] In the next two years he published three short articles on the subject of Islam in which his own personal religious neutrality and a certain disillusion with the French colonial effort were apparent. In the first and most interesting of the articles he argued that Islam was a better influence on Black Africa than either Christianity or 'Europeanisation' and that France was no more threatened by Muslims than by animists as both were equally unenthusiastic about the French presence.[45] He argued that Islam in West Africa was almost always the product of a mixture between traditional religions and orthodox Islam and that the Sufi brotherhoods were much less powerful and less organised in West Africa than in the Maghreb.[46]

However, Delafosse's principle publication whilst he was in France was his three-volume account of the country, people, languages, history and civilisation of the colony of Upper Senegal and Niger.[47] The work was suggested by Clozel who had laid the foundations with a circular in January 1909 (reprinted in the introduction to the work) outlining to his administrators a proposed study of indigenous customary law. Delafosse based his work on personal observation, conversation and correspondence with like-minded administrators – notably Gaden (who devoted his life's work to a study of the Fulbe) and Monteil – and a truly impressive amount of reading as the nine-page bibliography at the end of volume three testifies. The originality of the work lay in the fact that it should have been written at all, for the idea that it was actually possible to fill three volumes on the *culture* and *history* of such an area was in the early twentieth century a revolutionary one. The manifesto of the book is contained in the last section on 'Civilisation':

> If by 'civilisation' one understands the state of social, moral and material culture attained by the great nations of Europe and America, it is certain that one is forced to consider the natives of the Sudan as not being members of what is commonly called 'the civilised world'. But if one gives to the word 'civilisation' its true meaning, that is if one understands by this word the present state of culture of any society or nation, if, in other words, one speaks not of 'the civilisation' but of 'civilisations' . . . one is forced to admit that although they have a social state that is very different from ours, the inhabitants of the Sudan nonetheless have themselves civilisations which are worth the trouble of studying and describing. They are constructed by a group of customs which although only transmitted by tradition have an effect on the life of the people as considerable as our customs augmented by our laws have on our life.

Although these customs varied in detail from village to village nonetheless, said Delafosse, 'the guiding principles of customary law are the same'.[48] Delafosse applied the same argument to religion as he attempted to show that for all the local variations, 'animism' constituted a coherent religion in its own right and one which was practised throughout Africa:

> In reality the non-Muslim Blacks have a true religion, which is in general quite complicated, presenting itself in many different aspects despite a common source in which fetishism proper, that is to say the confidence accorded to amulets, forms only one superficial part without actually forming part of the *religious* belief.[49]

> Most of the natives of West Africa, probably even all of them, believe in the existence of a unique God, God the creator, which they are not far from considering as a pure spirit, to which in any case they never give an anthropomorphic character but which they often confuse . . . with the sky.[50]

> The Black believes that in all natural phenomena and in all living beings there exists a spiritual power, a dynamic spirit . . . which can exist by itself. From this is reached the religion of the spirits, personifying the natural forces, and that of the spirits of the dead, spirits that have been liberated by the death of their temporary human receptacle. To each of these genii or spirits the Black accords both reason and passion.[51]

The strength and universality of this system of animist belief together with the strength of local social systems embodied in the local civilisations were such, Delafosse argued, that pure Islamic beliefs and institutions were rare in West Africa:

> Whatever may be the number of our Sudanese subjects converted to Islam and practising the religion of Mohammed . . . it is very rare that the native Muslims have adopted Coranic law, at least in its entirety. In Islamism proper, religion and law hold together, both deriving either from the Coran or from the *hadith*. But when people other than Arabs convert to the Muslim religion, be they in Asia, Europe or in Africa, they by no means always adopt the Muslim code which in many cases clashes with secular customs and a social or economic state at odds with the prescriptions of Coranic law. . . . As a result

the official Muslim code ... is of very restricted use and in order to apply it
with discernment it is necessary to know the principles of native customary law
with which the spirit of the Muslim regions of this colony are strongly impreg-
nated.[52]

In his final section on Islam, Delafosse repeated the essential arguments
contained in his earlier articles. He did not see that there was any particular
reason to be either an Islamophile or an Islamophobe. Although Islam had
put an end to some of the worst excesses of some animist societies and was a
good barrier against alcoholism it was not, he suggested, a greatly superior
social or political influence than animism. In his final paragraph he summed
up his arguments and briefly stated his own vision of the future:

In my opinion Islam in the Sudan should be regarded as neither good nor evil
... I would say that in our political interests it is sometimes preferable,
especially at the beginning of an occupation of a country to deal with Muslims
rather than with animists, and that in any case the Islamisation of our subjects
would be less serious than their Christianisation. But I would add that from a
purely objective point of view and considering only the interest and future of
the native races, even though from this angle too Islamisation is preferable to
Christianisation, the best solution would be for the Sudanese population to
limit themselves to perfecting the local religions. and, perhaps, in the end that
would be the best solution for everybody.[53]

This benevolently paternalist and rather Voltairean vision of everybody cultivating his own religion was to be dealt a severe blow by the war in which
Delafosse was to fall foul, both of the authorities in Paris (who were for the
first time unashamedly and unequivocally decided upon extracting from
West Africa every available resource both human and material) and of a
Senegalese Christian and Europeanised élite, equally anxious to use the war
as a lever on the French with which to attain better recognition and representation not as Senegalese, still less as Wolof or Lebu, but as Frenchmen.

However, the intellectual strength of the arguments contained in *Haut-
Sénégal et Niger* was sufficient to ensure that they survived the vicissitudes of
war. Written at a time of personal spiritual crisis and disillusion with the
colonial establishment,[54] it was a remarkable book which implicitly raised
many of the doubts about the 'civilising mission' that were later to be raised
explicitly by Delafosse amongst others. In the immediate context in which
it is discussed here its importance lies in the added weight it gave to the view
that non-Muslim societies deserved greater respect than they often received
and that Muslim societies themselves owed as much, if not more, to pre-
Islamic custom as to either the Qur'ān or the *hadith*.

Marty

Paul Marty was born in 1882 in Boufarik, a small village outside Algiers.[55]
At the age of nineteen he volunteered for a four-year commission in the
zouaves. He soon started training as an interpreter and was posted to the

105

Native Affairs Bureau in Tunis where he remained until 1907. The following year he was sent to Casablanca which had recently been occupied by the French and from 1909 to 1911 he was on a detachment to the Foreign Ministry to help and advise on Moroccan issues. In September 1912 he was attached to the Colonial Ministry and was sent to Dakar to advise the Lieutenant-General on Muslim affairs. He remained in AOF until 1921 during which time he was promoted to the top rank of military interpreters and made a chevalier of the légion d'honneur. After AOF, he returned to Morocco where he was made Director of the Muslim College of Fez (1922–5) before joining the Native Affairs Department in Rabat of which he became the head in 1930. He was actively involved in the controversial Berber *dâhir*[56] which sought to apply Berber rather than Muslim law to the Moroccan Berbers. In 1935 he was posted to Tunisia where he joined the High Command of the Tunisian troops. Three years later he died in the military hospital in Tunis. For someone whose origins appeared to have been humble and whose schooling was modest his career was an impressive one. It was above all his Dakar posting which established his reputation.

It is perhaps surprising that such an impressive military career has not been more widely celebrated, and although no one who has worked on Islam in West Africa has failed to acknowledge their debt to the pioneering work of Marty, the man himself appears anonymous. Little is known of him beyond the official description on his military record card of a man 1.80 metres tall, with grey eyes, large nose and mouth and a high forehead.

Around the time that Marty arrived in Dakar, Ponty was adding the finishing touches to his Muslim policy. In January 1913 he reminded the local administrators of the order given in December 1911 to send files on marabouts to Dakar:

> It is impossible [he wrote] to exercise a real surveillance of Islam, to follow its development and, if necessary, to take suitable preventive action, if one does not have an effectively organised information service. More than in other Muslim countries, Islam in West Africa takes on the form of anthropolatry. Superficially it is still the religion of Allah but above all it is the cult of maraboutism. Consequently ... the political surveillance of Islam primarily involves the surveillance of Muslim personalities. These people are not numerous and are very well known. It is easy, but delicate, to get information on their family, ethnic and religious origins.[57]

In a circular on 'Native policy' in April, Ponty restated the 'liberal principles' which dominated his *politique des races* and emphasised that in his view 'the surest factor of stability amongst the Blacks lies in a combination of their material progress, justice, thoughtful generosity, well-wishing firmness and, to use an expression which I like, of *apprivoisement*'.[58] In August he reviewed his achievements and summarised his future concerns. The circulars of 26 December 1911 and 15 January 1913 had, he said, established the need for an index of Muslim personalities but he added:

Today a larger and more complicated task is necessary. It is our duty to study the Muslim society of our colonies in West Africa in the minutest detail. It is a study which demands almost a scientific method. It presupposes special studies, a previous documentation and a serious knowledge of the sociological laws of Islam which the great Orientalists of France and of Europe have now virtually succeeded in establishing ... [The study] will seem very attractive to many because of the scientific interest attached to it. But above all it is interesting for political and administrative reasons. It is almost impossible to administer an Islamic people wisely, if one does not understand its religious faith, its judicial system and its social organisation which are all intimately connected and are strongly influenced by the Coran and the prophetic tradition. It is this understanding of native society which, alone, will enable a peaceful and profound action on the minds of the people. It is, therefore, in this study ... that we will find the surest bases and the most suitable directions for our Muslim policy.[59]

From these circulars we should emphasise three main themes. The first is the importance that was attached to acquiring more knowledge of Islam, an indication both of the shortcomings of Arnaud's earlier contribution and of the increasing awareness of the extent to which the 'scientist' could contribute to the work of the 'Practical Man'. The second theme is the emphasis placed on the need to achieve security through means other than force, a message which had long been dear to ministerial accountants in Paris and whose importance had been underlined by the Goumba affair. Thirdly, they show how the administration had arrived at the conclusion that they should direct their policy at individuals rather than the invisible forces of society, preparing the way for what has been described as 'the co-option of the Saints'.[60]

In September 1913 the departments of the federal administration were reorganised by administrative decree and, for the first time, the existence of a Service des affaires musulmanes was officially and explicitly recognised. Its duties included the centralisation of information on Islam, the translation of Arabic documents and the study of Islamic developments. Paul Marty was, of course, in charge.[61] Although Marty's obligations were varied – soon after his arrival he was consulted on Muslim burial rites by the head doctor of the colonial hospital in Dakar who was anxious to ensure that Muslim soldiers who had failed to survive his treatment were at least buried properly[62] – there were in 1913 three issues on which he had to report as soon as possible. The issues were those of education, the Mauritanian conquest and the Mourides.

Education

Education was a major administrative preoccupation, and Marty was expected to address himself immediately to the question of what type of education was best suited for Muslims. In September he wrote to the appropriate administrations in Algeria and Tunisia for information on the systems adopted in those two countries[63] but in his report to Ponty in

107

November it was clear that he did not believe the North African model was suitable for Senegal. He introduced his report with an account of the marabouts who taught in the Qur'ānic schools of which there were, according to official figures, 1,385 in Senegal at the end of 1912. Although he admitted that some marabouts taught out of piety he argued that their main objective was to recruit children to work in their fields or, if they were urban traders, to open a school as proof of their religious zeal and thus attract favourable publicity using the schools, said Marty as 'a sort of religious advertisement'. The general level of scholarship was very poor, and there were serious language problems. Blacks, he claimed, could only pronounce fifteen of the thirty-eight letters of the Arabic alphabet with the result that 'If truly as the purists maintain Allah can only understand Arabic – and well pronounced Arabic at that – the prayers of the Senegalese marabouts certainly do not rise up to his throne'. The pupils having finished their education at the age of thirteen then went on to learn a trade and to forget most of what they had learned. For Marty this was a point in their favour: 'The Coranic schools' he wrote, 'do not create any *déclassés*'. He then went on to criticise past French policy to the schools, reserving particularly harsh words for the decrees of 1903 and 1906 which he castigated as 'too severe. . . . Rules which produce the opposite of the desired effect . . . which up-end all customs, traditions and wishes of the natives. They seem to hinder the natives arbitrarily without any advantage to our administration'. He listed all the proposals suggested by Cor and Risson for the reform of Qur'ānic schools, explaining why for the most part the reforms were unworkable. There was, he said, a need to respect tradition and so:

> To forbid children to work for their marabout amounts to the same as wanting to abolish the school altogether. As for the begging of the children, it is in general discreet, it amuses the local people, doesn't annoy anyone and benefits the children as much as the marabout and constitutes a rather interesting aspect of local civilisation.

The only restriction with which Marty was in favour was to deny Qur'ānic schools access to animist regions.

Marty argued that although the French should make certain improvements in the standard of education and that they should attempt to bypass the use of Arabic by transcribing native languages into the Latin alphabet they should not attempt to do much else besides:

> The Coranic school such as it functions is riddled with faults of all kinds, no one denies it. It is a purely religious and purely mechanical education which has no effect on the intellectual development of the time. . . . But one must acknowledge that this Coranic education system does not cause any political danger . . . and has no bad repercussion on public tranquility. It would, therefore, be impolitic to upset this institution which satisfies those who use it or to remedy its unfortunate social consequences by opposing it with French schools, burdened with all sorts of privileges, which restrict the freedom of the Coranic school.[64]

The report was interesting on several counts. It showed how quickly Marty adapted to his new environment, and whilst one may object to his heavily patronising tone and his insistence on the racial reasons for the intellectual inferiority – as he saw it – of the Blacks as opposed to Arabs one should also applaud his willingness to recognise Qur'ānic schools as an integral part of Senegalese society which met an identifiable need of the local people. The begging of *talibés* continues even to this day to be a very contentious issue in Senegal, and objections to the system are understandable, but Marty was correct to set it in its wider social context, emphasising that the custom was part of a way of life, 'a rather interesting aspect of local civilisation'. Such an attitude was a radical one – and undoubtedly raised a few eyebrows at the time.[65]

In the same year the Djenné *médersa* was closed down. In his annual report the local *commandant* stated that initial hopes that the *médersa* would 'purify' Islam had been dashed:

> In our *médersa* it is . . . ignorance that we cultivate. . . . In the future we shall do without the help of the marabouts and we shall work not actually against them but at least independently of them. The creation of the *médersa* seemed to bestow Islam with official recognition and protection. Religion will now be a private affair. It will rest in the field of conscience. Until the day comes when we can tame it, Islam will be a form of opposition to our domination.[66]

Whilst Marty would never have suggested that France should actually do without the help of the marabouts he did agree that the Djenné *médersa* had been a failure. In 1917 he reflected that:

> It is an accepted fact that *médersa*s are an error in Black Africa. The veneer of Islam and Arabic that cover this faith . . . is extremely superficial. Except for a few scholars whose intellectual achievements are quite impressive total ignorance dominates everywhere. Most of the teachers don't even know the elementary catechism to say the simple prayers correctly. The result is perhaps deplorable from an Islamic point of view but it is excellent from the French point of view. Perfectly ignorant, the natives have never been able to understand the reason for the struggle of Islam against Christianity . . . The purely Islamic danger has never been an issue in the Sudan amongst the Blacks . . . It has required the solidly thick skulls of our young Blacks to resist such an education.[67]

The smugly patronising tone of these comments was very typical of European writing on Black Africa. 'Perfect ignorance' and 'solidly thick skulls' conjure up a host of European clichés about Africa. They also defined the limits of colonial thinking, and it is within these limits that we must understand Marty, a man of great talent but nonetheless a soldier and a scholar of his time. It is interesting to note his willingness to preserve 'the perfect ignorance of the natives' which he regarded as an asset rather than a liability to the French. Such a view contrasts with the philosophy behind the *médersa*s when they were introduced as a means, it was hoped, of educating the Muslim élite and of inculcating them with a better understanding of the modern world. It was also a view that was wholly at odds with the rhetoric of the 'civilising mission' – but nobody seemed to notice.

Mauritania

The second question to which Marty addressed himself was that of Mauritania. It will be recalled that after the death of Coppolani, official backing was given to occupy the region of Adrar. However, even after this was achieved under General Gouraud in 1909, the French were still unable to exercise serious control over their main enemy, Sheikh Ma el-Ainin and his son, el-Hiba, whose operational base in the Seguiet el-Hamra threatened French positions both in Morocco and in Mauritania. In 1910, Ma el-Ainin was said to have claimed a right to the Moroccan throne and in May he visited Marrakesh, but the French prevented him from continuing on to Fez as he had intended. Soon after his return to his *zawiya* in Tiznit he died at the age of seventy-nine.[68] However, his son el-Hiba took up the challenge and succeeded in mounting effective resistance against the French just at the time when the French were establishing their Protectorate over Morocco. On 10 January 1913 his men ambushed and annihilated almost an entire detachment of the *meharists* at Liboirat, 175 kilometres north-west of Atar. Lieutenant-Colonel Mouret, the Governor of the colony, described it as the most serious trouble ever experienced in Mauritania and argued that only a concerted action from French forces in Morocco and Mauritania would be capable of defeating el-Hiba.[69]

Marty, who had been actively involved in the French occupation of Morocco prior to moving to Dakar, laid more stress on a Mauritania-oriented policy. There were, he said, two possible ways of dealing with el-Hiba. The first possibility was a military campaign, but this Marty rejected for practical and financial reasons and fears of political objections from Paris and from Spain. The second possibility was to adopt a diplomatic approach using the influence of the elderly and pro-French Sheikh Saad Bu over his young nephew el-Hiba. Marty argued that el-Hiba would welcome a settlement with the French and proposed conceding him the command of Seguiet el-Hamra. Marty realised that Mouret preferred to work with the warrior Emir of Adrar, Ould Deïda, but he stressed that Sheikh Saad Bu was more influential and more amenable than the Emir. He further denied that using Saad Bu in this way would make him too powerful. The Sheikh was an old man with no likely successor and any power he did obtain, argued Marty, would serve the French as a useful balance to the growing prestige of the (admittedly ultra-loyal) Sheikh Sidia.[70]

By December Marty thought the submission of el-Hiba was 'imminent' and along with Lyautey in Morocco he urged the need for a coherent French policy towards him. Both Marty and Lyautey agreed on the need to make concessions to el-Hiba. However, Marty added that making el-Hiba responsible for an area approximately the same as Seguiet el-Hamra was only an interim aim and, in words that could have been lifted straight from

Coppolani, he said that 'The true, the only aim of the present policy, it is perhaps cynical to say so, is to provoke anarchy in order to have peace in our territory.'[71]

The Mourides

The Mouride question was indirectly related to the Mauritanian questions but, more fundamentally, it concerned the much broader issue of French perceptions of Islam in Black Africa. The Mouride brotherhood is probably the best known of all the West African brotherhoods and it is not the purpose of this study to describe in great detail what has already been described and analysed many times before, sometimes more pertinently and eloquently than others, in the vast literature devoted to the brotherhood of Serigne Ahmadu Bamba, the *borom* of Touba. Suffice it to say that following the French defeat in 1866 of Lat Dior, the *damel* (king) of the Senegambian state of Walo, Ahmadu Bamba, a marabout who had been at the *damel*'s court, returned to his native village of M'Backé. Here he soon began to attract a large following as large numbers of leaderless men from Lat Dior's defeated army looked increasingly to the marabouts for leadership and inspiration. Ahmadu Bamba's popularity with the *ceddo*, the slave soldiers who made up the bulk of Lat Dior's army, greatly concerned the local authorities in M'Backé and within two years Ahmadu Bamba was forced to move. In 1888 he founded a new village, Darou Salem, not far from M'Backé.[72] A year later, in March 1889, his name appeared for the first time in official correspondence when the Department of Political Affairs wrote to the administrator of Kayor that they were worried by rumours that 'a marabout called Amadou Bamba' had settled between Baol and Kayor and that he was attracting a large following. The administrator, Angot, was asked to make discreet enquiries. In April, Angot reported that:

> In the course of my mission I have made enquiries in several places about the activities of the marabout Amadou Bamba. Everywhere ... I've heard only good about him. He is a pious and tranquil man whose only fault is that he takes on a lot of good-for-nothings as pupil marabouts and if these people aren't watched closely they will gradually cause trouble.[73]

Angot was the first of several Frenchmen who thought that reports of Ahmadu Bamba's fanaticism were much exaggerated but who were nonetheless worried by his popularity amongst those that were considered to be the less desirable elements of society.

It was about this time too that Ahmadu Bamba, who had been initiated into the Qadiriyya, began to receive visions and to develop the specific doctrines which distinguished his teaching from that of other Qadiri marabouts. For the rest of his life Bamba continued to produce an impressive quantity of religious poems, the form in which most of his doctrinal work was written.[74] In the meantime, his following continued to increase. Local chiefs, who had become increasingly anxious, found it easy

111

to persuade the French that more direct action was needed to be taken against Bamba who, they claimed, was preaching Holy War against the Europeans. Of all the local chiefs only one, Samba Laobe, the chief of Jollof, was not upset by Bamba's influence. In July 1895 M. Leclerc, the administrator of the *cercle* of St Louis, reported that Ahmadu Bamba had held a meeting attended by 700 men, many of whom were former followers of Lat Dior:

> I do not know [he said], the exact words of his speeches but it is certain, as anybody who knows the prudence of Amadou Bamba will know, that nothing reprehensible was spoken by him. But it is no less certain that in the evening whilst the marabout was talking in his hut . . . his *talibés* circulated from group to group giving instructions for an uprising later in the year.[75]

The following month the same M. Leclerc warned that:

> All the old followers of the Damel, all the *tiédos* who lived only through war and pillage and whom the present administration has reduced to poverty have grouped around the *mahdi* marabout, the destroyer of the white man . . . If Amadou Bamba is cunning and protests his devotion to the French cause, his *talibés* are less circumspect and openly proclaim him *mahdi* in the middle of St. Louis. Add to these bands of discontented *tiedos* the band of fanatics who always follow these preachers of Holy War and you can judge the size of the movement which could explode at a sign from Amadou Bamba.

Leclerc thought that it was unlikely that Bamba would try anything before the end of the hot season and so he thought that the French had time to prevent unrest by exiling Ahmadu Bamba to Gabon. This was also what the chiefs wanted to see.[76] The Director of Political Affairs was worried that if the French did not act against Bamba they would be guilty of what Faidherbe, in connection with French attitudes to Mamadu Lamine, had called 'excessive tolerance'.[77] Accordingly in September, despite a lack of concrete evidence, the Conseil privé exiled Bamba to Gabon. Samba Laobe was replaced as chief of Jollof by Bouna N'Diaye, a very young man but the product of a good 'French' education in the Ecole des otages in St Louis and of the Alaoui college in Tunis.[78]

Bamba's reputation was enormously enhanced by his period of exile in Gabon (1895–1902). When, after the intervention on his behalf of the Senegalese deputy, Carpot, Ahmadu Bamba returned to Senegal late in 1902 he was greeted by huge crowds, all the more enthusiastic as a result of the widespread belief that he had been released through a miraculous divine intervention. The French authorities, especially M. Allys, the administrator of the *cercle* of Tivaouane, were worried. Allys went to the extent of employing his most trusted secret agent, Omar Niang, to infiltrate Bamba's following by posing as a would-be *talibé* and provided him with 300 francs to offer to Ahmadu Bamba as the customary present of a *talibé* to his marabout.[79] In May 1903 Bamba refused to appear before the French Governor in St Louis. In June he was arrested again and exiled to Souet el-Ma in Mauritania, the camp of Sheikh Sidia, where the French hoped the tolerance and loyalty of Sheikh Sidia would rub off on his disciple. In 1907 Bamba was allowed to return to Senegal but he was kept under administrative surveillance in the village of Cheyen in the Jollof region. A secret agent sent a daily report to St Louis with details of visitors (and their presents) to his residence.[80]

Despite the fact that in 1910 Ahmadu Bamba issued a *fetwa* justifying obedience to the French, the authorities remained suspicious. In his instructions to his interim successor, Ponty summed up the basis of French fears about Bamba:

> It seems as if it is in our oldest colony of the group that Islam manifests itself in the most mystic form to such a degree that we have to ask ourselves if this deviation which the Mourides have imprinted on the great and rigid traditions of the true faith will not finally create a sort of politico-religious association in which religious interests will merely be a pretext for exploiting the ignorant masses. That the followers of the sect rely entirely on their cheikh for the direction of their earthly life and for guarantees of their future one, it matters little to us. But we cannot turn our eyes from the repercussion of a form of propaganda which concerns equally our political, administrative and social actions. *It is undeniable that for the Mouride our authority scarcely exists* and that in matters concerning his disciples it is often the Cheikh who intervenes and decides for them. Finally . . . one cannot disguise the fact that if the sect develops it will greatly disturb the economic life of Senegal. Under the cover of religion a part of the public fortune is removed from the colony each year.[81]

Apart from the role played by the chiefs in bringing Ahmadu Bamba to the attention of the authorities and lobbying for his banishment, French action against him was motivated by two main concerns. One was political and concerned the fear that, in the words of Coppolani, Sufi brotherhoods could form 'a state within a state'. In the case of the Mourides the fear was perfectly justified as the bonds of allegiance that are strong between any *talibé* and his sheikh were – and still are – peculiarly strong as Mouride doctrine emphasised the absolute submission of the *talibé*. The second base was economic. We have already seen the objections raised about the alms-collecting tours of Sheikh Saad Bu and similar objections were also raised about the gifts given to Ahmadu Bamba by a stream of visitors to his residence in Souet el-Ma and Cheyen. Such fears were particularly acute in view of the fact that the vast majority of Bamba's disciples came from the area in which groundnuts were grown. Groundnut production in Senegal was expanding rapidly[82] and Mouride leaders took an active part in its development. In particular, Sheikh Ibra Fall, a former *ceddo* who had in 1886 attached himself to Ahmadu Bamba pledging eternal and absolute devotion to the Sheikh and who was later described by Marty as 'the Minister of Economic Affairs' for the Mourides,[83] was quick to see the economic potential of using his own devoted following – mostly ex-*ceddo* like himself – for groundnut farming. By 1912 he was said to have 1,000 *talibés* working for him producing an annual income estimated at nearly

113

50,000 francs.[84] Thus Ponty had good reason to fear the economic might of the Mourides.

However, in the course of the next two years the French came to realise that neither the political nor the economic strength of the Mourides need be detrimental to their authority, that indeed, on the contrary, to continue regarding Ahmadu Bamba and his followers as enemies would be both unwise and dangerous. Signs of a change of heart were evident in Ponty's comments on proposals made by M. Theveniaut, the administrator of Baol, for imprisoning Ahmadu Bamba and his brother Sheikh Anta who was also widely regarded as a malevolent schemer.[85] Ponty argued that:

> Our policy towards the Islamised native should make use of skill and tact rather than severity ... Furthermore, we should not forget that Amadou Bamba is a pupil of Sheikh Sidia, the most venerated chief of the country of the Moors. *Cheikh Sidia was the pivot of my predecessor's policy and also of my own action in Mauritania.* The Mouride sect was started in Senegal by Amadou Bamba. The word 'mourid' properly means 'discipline of the faith'. That is to say that Amadou Bamba is still under the authority of Cheikh Sidia, the most devoted artisan of our influence beyond Senegal. How would our double-faced policy appear to Cheikh Sidia? On the one hand, favouring his influence we make use of his great authority whilst on the other we are persecuting his own pupils.... That would be to play a double game from which we risk being ourselves the victims. It would be to adopt a policy which the present incidents are in no way sufficient to justify.

When dealing with Islam, Ponty warned against following the narrow instincts of local *commandants*, as he argued that action should be taken within the framework of French Islamic policy in AOF and in North Africa. So when Theveniaut wanted to imprison Sheikh Anta immediately before even a judicial enquiry was made Ponty warned against such haste: 'Whatever the result of the enquiry I will decide in good time what measures seem to me to be suited to avoiding a recurrence of a new *ouali* of Goumba affair'.[86] This letter provides an excellent insight into how Ponty's perceptions and priorities were changing. It clearly shows the importance of Sheikh Sidia and his family in French calculations, and this was one of the great constants of French policy through from Coppolani to the post-Second World War era.[87] Sheikh Sidia's role was particularly important at a time when the Mauritanian and Moroccan issues were at the forefront of French preoccupations. Secondly it is further evidence that the *wali* of Goumba affair came as a real shock to senior French administrators, and Ponty's warning about the narrow-mindedness of local administrators is interesting too in this respect.

Cor, the Lieutenant-Governor of Senegal to whom Ponty's comments were addressed, was not convinced and continued to provide Ponty with evidence of what he saw as maraboutic fanaticism. Ponty, however, was dismissive:

> I have not been particularly struck by the fanaticism with which you believe the writings of Amadou Bamba to be filled. They do not seem to me to

114

indicate a more obviously hostile character than most of the writings of this genre . . . We should not be unduly alarmed.

Ponty did, however, share Cor's doubts about the wisdom of using Ahmadu Bamba to help in recruitment for the Moroccan campaign, for both feared that this would give added weight to his prestige and authority. Recruitment and tax-collection were to be entrusted to political chiefs only.[88] Such then were the limits of French action in 1912. As we shall see the administration would soon, under the pressure of war, embark on a more opportunist policy, as Ahmadu Bamba was to become in his own right a pillar of French policy in Senegal.

That the French felt more confident to make use of him in the war was in large part due to the report made by Marty on the Mourides in 1913.[89] Marty produced the report very rapidly. It is not clear when he started, but by August 1913 the typescript was in the hands of Le Chatelier, the editor of the *Revue du Monde Musulman*, through whom all of Marty's work in West Africa was published.[90] The speed with which the report was made is reflected in the brisk and administrative style which was characteristic of all of Marty's studies. Marty relied heavily on local archives and it is not surprising to find that he repeated the official version of events leading up to the first and second exile of Ahmadu Bamba. In later years Marty became more critical of his sources. However, in the account of these early years of French contact with the Mouride leader, Marty's most original contribution was to argue that Ahmadu Bamba should never have been allowed back from Gabon for whilst he was away there was a period of 'perfect tranquility' in the colony.[91] The book was intended as an administrative report and it proceeded from a consideration of the Mouride personalities in the various *cercles* of Senegal to a discussion of the doctrine of Ahmadu Bamba through to a more general consideration of its relation to indigenous judicial, social and economic customs and institutions. The report was relatively short (136 pages) with a further twenty pages of appendices.

One of Marty's strengths as a writer was an ability to write excellent character sketches of which a professional biographer would not have been ashamed. His descriptions of the leading personalities of the Mouride brotherhood are as lively as any that have ever been drawn since. Sheikh Anta was portrayed as a cynical politician who had used his family position to build up contacts with the most important businessmen and politicians of the colony:

> One cannot deny [wrote Marty] that this 'Minister of Foreign Affairs' as he is called, has acquired . . . a very practical way of dealing with situations. He is certainly not bothered by scruples of hindering his brother's religious mission. Cheikh Anta, it is easy to see, has not believed in this mission for a long time. Mouridism provides him with excellent personal opportunities. (p. 20)

Sheikh Ibra Fall, whom Marty described as 'a veritable black Potin' (after Felix Potin, the founder of a chain of groceries in France), was also portrayed as an astute businessman despite his superficial appearance of madness:

> Ibra Fall has an unfortunate physique which does not help him. With his nervous tics and his wild laughter, a sort of *delirium tremens* with which he is afflicted, one would be tempted to take him for a simpleton. However one should remember that he was one of the first disciples of Amadou Bamba at a time when no one suspected the future importance of the Serigine, and this shows a certain flair on his part. Since then he has devoted himself, tenaciously and intelligently, to the increase of his material wealth. He owns houses in St Louis and in Dakar, and has concessions in Thies, Diourbel, Ndaule and Kebemer. He has set up commerce houses at several trading posts and gets his disciples and wives to manage them. Commerce does not take up all his time. Under the supervision of one of his disciples he also gets his followers to cultivate enormous fields of groundnuts, millet and various other grains, and he himself skilfully takes care of their retail. (p. 28)

Ahmadu Bamba was the only person to emerge without a strong character – a reflection perhaps of the fact that he was a reclusive holy man lacking the penchant for political and economic activity in which his family and followers seemed to revel.

However, the most important aspect of the book was the way in which it contributed to a fundamental change in the understanding of Islam in Senegal. The main theme of the report was that 'Mouridism' was a bastardised form of Islam: '*une sorte de religion nouvelle née de l'Islam . . . en plein vagabondage islamique . . . l'islam à l'usage des Ouloffs*' (pp. 42–3). Marty showed how in doctrinal, judicial and economic habits Mourides differed from 'orthodox' Islamic teaching:

> The black mentality [he wrote] is completely incapable of bearing the metaphysical concepts of the Oriental semites and the ecstatic digressions of the Soufis. These scenes are nothing other than an act of common prayer, soon followed by dances, choreographed mimes and bamboulas of which the Blacks are so fond. (p. 53)
> As Islam distances itself from its cradle . . . as races and conditions change, it becomes increasingly deformed. Islamic confessions, be they Malaysian or Chinese, Berber or Negro, are no more than vulgar *contrefaçons* of the religion and state of the sublime Coran. (pp. 123–4)

Marty believed that Bamba had been guided by 'the invisible hand' of Wolof custom and that this had proved a more potent force than the original Islamic doctrine (p. 120).

Marty, therefore, argued that the Mourides should not be assimilated in French minds to the Islam of the Arab world. This meant, for example, that there was no point in using *Sidi Khalil* as a legal textbook in Senegal, however cheap and convenient it may have been. (This was something of a 'hobby-horse' for Marty who devoted four pages to the subject in his report and mentioned it also in his correspondence with local administrations.) Instead, Marty urged native tribunals to make more use of Wolof customary law (pp. 90–3). It also meant that the Mourides – along with most other West African Muslims – were immune from pan-Islamism. Marty said that stories of Mouride connections with the Ottomans or even el-Hiba were 'much exaggerated' (pp. 113–15).

He did not suggest that the Mourides represented no danger at all. Indeed he emphasised that there were local dangers and that, whilst observing the strictest religious neutrality, the French should exercise a close watch over the activities of the Mourides and be prepared, in the event of crimes 'to act repressively, immediately and vigorously' (p. 130). The administration should make use of family disputes in order to keep a balance of power (p. 133). As for Ahmadu Bamba himself, Marty believed that he had renounced his former ambitions and that he was probably sincere in his protestations of loyalty (p. 137).

It is clear that Marty's argument that Mouridism was deeply influenced by Wolof custom was not an original one. Right from the start of the development of the brotherhood, the administration was aware of the way in which the old elements of Wolof society – especially the *ceddo* – were being reconstructed in the Mouride brotherhood. Both Clozel and Delafosse had argued that African Islam was heavily influenced by local traditions, that there were as many different types of Islam in West Africa as there were ethnic groups. Clozel, in particular, had emphasised the importance of local traditions and had urged the use of customary law by Native Tribunals. Ponty, too, was sympathetic to this line of argument. What Marty had done was to document a specific example of 'African Islam' with a thoroughness that was unique in the writing that until then existed on the subject. For the first time ever the French administration was starting to develop an official line on what Islam in AOF actually amounted to. With the publication of Marty's report the era of French doubts and uncertainties about Islam in Africa was drawing towards a close. In the next decade – a decade which included the First World War – Marty continued to document in minute detail the state of Islam in AOF and the next chapter will examine more closely his contribution to scholarship against the background of the war in Europe.

7

The First World War

The outbreak of war in Europe in August 1914 and, more particularly, the break-off of diplomatic relations with the Ottoman Empire on 1 November inevitably caused great apprehension amongst the French administration. Clozel was the most anxious of all the administrators and asked for permission for special emergency powers, including the declaration of a state of siege, in order to deal with troublesome marabouts in the Sudan. Ponty, however, thought that such powers were unnecessary.[1] He assured Paris that most African Muslims were not interested in the fate of the Ottoman Empire and in any case looked to the Moroccan Sherif rather than the Sultan of Turkey for ultimate spiritual guidance.[2] The Governor-General went on to issue specific instructions to the local administrations of AOF: malicious rumours were to be suppressed and the traditional friendship between France and Islam was to be exalted throughout AOF. The successes of the French army (at this stage just beginning to recover from the initial German push into northern France) were to be likewise glorified. Nonetheless a careful watch on the marabouts was to be maintained, and a strict censorship of the post was to be enforced.[3]

French anxieties were not confined to fear of Muslim unrest. The Liberian Christian prophet, Harris, and his followers who had for some time been active in the Ivory Coast, was seen as posing a very similar sort of threat as Ahmadu Bamba. The administration admitted that Harris himself appeared loyal and calm but feared that his less restrained disciples might cause trouble. In view of the reduced European personnel in the colony, the Governor of the Ivory Coast thought it would be wise to persuade Harris to return to Liberia.[4] But clearly the German–Ottoman alliance made the question of Muslim loyalty one of the most immediate administrative preoccupations, and both French and British minds were set to work on finding a Muslim card of their own with which to trump the German's Ottoman ace. In the Arabian peninsula, the Levant and in the shadowy streets of Constantinople this search was, quite literally, the stuff of which

118

novels are made. Richard Hannay and the weird 'Companions of the Rosy Hours' doing battle with the agents of 'Hadji Mohammed Guillamo' was thrilling stuff – whichever side of the English Channel one was on.[5] But in French West Africa there was to be little scope for such daredevil adventure.

Just as fears in metropolitan France that the Socialists would oppose the war were quickly dispelled, so too in AOF were anxieties about Muslim resistance in the name of the Ottoman Sultan quickly proved to be without foundation. Within a very short space of time Muslim leaders from all over AOF were inundating the Governor-General with assurances of loyalty. Ponty telegrammed the Colonial Ministry in November to say that 'The most reassuring news about the attitudes of the Muslim populations is reaching me from all over the colonies'. The situation in Mauritania was particularly promising as there was a virtually unanimous denunciation of the Ottoman Sultan.[6] Almost without exception Muslim notables from all over AOF wrote addresses and poems in praise of France and in condemnation of the Ottomans and the Germans. These writings were collected and published in two issues of the *Revue du Monde Musulman*. Sheikh Sidia was one of the first to declare his loyalty:

> Through the penetration of French power into the countries of the Toucouleurs, the Moors and the Blacks, God, the generous, the merciful, the savant and the sage has revealed incalculable advantages that we never knew before. The abandon by the tribes of the instruments of war, the abolition of acts of oppression inherited from our ancestors, the repression of pillage and death sentences ... France has also developed justice and security in the countries of all their sedentary and nomadic subjects. She has sunk abundant wells ... She has introduced capable doctors to the natives, rich and poor ... We ask God to consolidate ... this power and to protect it against all enemies.[7]

The leaders of the Senegalese Tijaniyya all showed their devotion to the French cause. El-Hajj Abdullah Niasse declared in Kaolack:

> We have loyal sentiments and pure affection for our glorious French nation which is the most powerful of all the European nations because of its justice. Why shouldn't we like France? It is she who has made us progress from barbarity and savagery towards the light of civilisation. When she raised her Tricoleur flag in our country we were without a leader. We lived in anarchy and were cutting each other's throats. We enslaved children and committed acts of brigandage on the roads. Fear and anxiety were widespread throughout our country. The French government in taking possession of Senegal has punished the guilty and helped the oppressed until there were no brigands or thieves left in the country.[8]

El-Hajj Malick Sy, who said prayers for a French victory every Friday, gave this message to his *talibés*: 'Know, oh Muslims, ... that we must live on good terms with the French government and pray that God accords it peace and victory. For its happiness is our happiness. He who denies it is like the man who cuts his throat with his own hand'.[9] The address of the notables of Timbuktu gave a rather more legalistic reason for their refusal to respect or follow the Ottoman example in the war:

> We have learned that the Turkish Sultan has embraced the cause of Germany against France. We condemn this act for we are attached to France and we will always be the enemies of those who declare war ... Furthermore, the Turkish Sultan does not know us. He is not our chief. He is a usurper. Nor did our ancestors have any relationship with him. They knew only the Sultan of Morocco. ... We are faithful to God, His Prophet and the Cherif of Mecca. This man is our only legitimate chief according to the witnesses of the *hadith*.[10]

This reference to the sole legitimacy of the Sherif of Mecca could not, however, have been altogether welcome. For the Ottoman alliance with Germany raised doubts once again in French minds about where the ultimate authority in the Islamic world lay. As we have seen Marty, Delafosse and Clozel had already done much to emphasise the particularity of African Islam and thus redress the universalist image of Islam that was the order of the day at the turn of the century. Nonetheless, the French administration, including Marty, were not at the end of 1914 absolutely confident that African Muslims would not at some stage follow the orders of a foreign Islamic authority. The Interministerial Commission on Islam decided that the French would be unwise to get involved in the issue of authority and obedience in the Muslim world. The Colonial Ministry reported to Ponty in December:

> The Commission expressed its opinion that as much as possible we should keep away from questions of obedience in Islamic matters. It would be ... doubtful that we could achieve the desired aim if we appeared to recognise a claim to Mahometan orthodoxy from one of the elements who claim spiritual authority in Islam. ... It does not in any way appear desirable to spread in Muslim circles the notion of rallying around a religious centre. Our Islamised natives of AOF are for the most part ignorant about the questions of the khalifate or the imamate and we can only benefit from maintaining this state of ignorance.[11]

Soon after the rupture of diplomatic relations with the Ottomans the French authorities in North Africa decided to forbid Muslims to go on the pilgrimage in order to lessen the possibility of pan-Islamic agitation in their colonies. The Colonial Minister wrote to Ponty to tell him of this decision and to urge him to do the same. The ban should, he stressed, be issued in such a way:

> so as not to provoke unflattering comments or to upset the religious sentiment of the Muslims. It would perhaps be impolitic to stop the pilgrimage through a formal decree at a time when such a measure would appear to be motivated by fear of letting our subjects have contact with the Turkish Empire. But the local administration could advise against departure for the pilgrimage by arguing that the boats normally used to transport the pilgrims have been

requisitioned by the belligerent powers and that, therefore, the pilgrims run the risk of waiting indefinitely at the ports without ever having the opportunity to embark.[12]

The following year similar instructions were given. The Allies were helped in their task of dissuasion by a *fetwa* issued by the Grand Mufti of Egypt which strongly advised Muslims not to go on the pilgrimage. However, in both 1914 and 1915 Ponty reported that there were in any case no requests from would-be pilgrims for permission to leave AOF.[13]

The pilgrimage question became much more interesting the following year when the Sherif of Mecca, supported by the Arab tribes of the west and central Arabian peninsula, proclaimed his independence from the Ottoman Empire. In June 1916 the Colonial Minister wrote to Angoulvant, the interim Governor-General, with news of the Reuters' report carrying details of the Sherif's proclamation. Angoulvant was asked to give wide publicity to the proclamation taking care not to mention the part played by the Allies in the Arab revolt or the fact that the information came from Reuters rather than France's own information sources and finally to emphasise that the Sultan of Constantinople no longer had the authority to act in the name of Islam. Angoulvant then issued these instructions in a circular to the colonies of AOF. The interim Lieutenant-Governor of Niger thought that the news was splendid and suggested celebrating the independence with extra festivities on 14 July which he thought would be a symbolic manifestation of the union between France and Islam. Angoulvant, however, was not impressed with the idea which he thought would prove hard to square with the official line on the independence of the independent Sherif of Mecca.[14] More serious thoughts on the implications of the proclamation of independence came from the Foreign Ministries in Paris and London who both, for separate reasons, thought it wise on reflection not to give wide publicity to the proclamation and so decided against a formal publication of its contents. In London the Foreign Office was reported to be worried about the repercussions of the news in India, whereas the French were anxious not to encourage the idea of Muslim unity.[15]

The decision was taken instead to send copies of the proclamation to selected Muslim leaders in French colonies. From AOF the following were selected: Sheikh Sidia from Mauritania; el-Hajj Malick Sy, the leader of the Tivaouane Tijaniyya in Senegal; el-Hajj Sliman from Agades;[16] Karamoko Dalen, a Fulbe Tijani from Timbo in the Futa Jallon who had, according to Marty, been Bokar Biro's *éminence grise* and who now helped the French with carrying out censuses, collecting local information and organising vaccinations;[17] Abdullabba Ahmed Baba, a *Chorfa* and *qadi* of Timbuktu;[18] Imam Mohammed ben Essoyuti, also of Timbuktu, who had formed part of the delegation of Timbuktu notables who had approached the Moroccan Sultan, Mawlay Hassan, in vain for help against the French, but who in 1911 was appointed by Clozel as a teacher in the *médersa* of Timbuktu;[19] and finally Imam Mohammed Kunandi Timitie from

Bondoukou in the Ivory Coast, the *almamy* of the town's principal mosque who had a long record of pro-French activity.[20]

At the beginning of August it was also decided – in Paris – that the French should send an official mission of pilgrims from French colonies in North and West Africa. The mission was due to catch a boat from Marseilles on the 1 September leaving very little time for the AOF authorities first to select a representative and then to send him on to Marseilles. The metropole would bear the cost of the mission from Marseilles onwards but AOF was expected to pay the boat fare from Dakar to Marseilles. Angoulvant was not enthusiastic. He replied to the Colonial Minister that there were only two Muslim notables, Sheikh Sidia and el-Hajj Malick Sy, who lived close enough to Dakar to be able to catch the boat on time, but Angoulvant doubted that el-Hajj Malick Sy who was old and nearly blind would agree on such a voyage and he felt that the presence of Sheikh Sidia in Mauritania was too important. He also feared that the sudden disappearance of the two men would cause confusion and might be seen as a deportation. He regretted, therefore, that AOF could not participate in the mission at such short notice. However, the Colonial Minister quickly replied that the mission had been postponed by two weeks and wondered if that might not be enough time to find a representative, not necessarily a marabout, he added, but any good Muslim, although in view of the possibility that he would miss the Marseilles boat and would have to travel to Alexandria by himself it would help if he could speak French. Perhaps, he suggested, a good loyal Senegalese chief?[21]

Angoulvant wrote to the Lieutenant-Governor of Senegal asking him if he could think of a suitable candidate and suggested himself the *qadi* of St Louis or Bouna N'Diaye, the chief of Jollof. Six days later there was still no reply from the Senegalese Lieutenant-Governor so Angoulvant wrote again, adding the somewhat loaded question: 'Do you see any inconvenience from the point of view of our Islamic policy in sending to the Cherif of Mecca delegates who, even though chosen from outside the circle of influential marabouts, might return from their voyage with a tendency to unify the diverse Islamic groups which exist at the moment?' Angoulvant wrote to his superiors in Paris to explain the delay and to express his own misgivings about the project:

> Without talking of the risk of torpedoes and of tendentious rumours that the delegates might pick up and be unable to interpret properly, it is to be feared that they will bring back cherifian directives from Mecca intended to unify the present diverse groups of AOF, the multiplicity and contrary tendencies of which make it easy for us at the moment to restrict and to supervise Islam, whereas anything which favours unification inevitably creates a danger for us.[22]

Neither the Colonial Minister nor the Lieutenant-Governor of Senegal were, however, unduly worried by these thoughts. From Paris, Angoulvant received a swift explanation of the official motives behind the mission:

> It is not a question of either seeking to strengthen the Muslim faith of our
> subject peoples or of involving ourselves in Islamic controversies and internal
> dissensions but rather of elevating the prestige of the Cherif, whose attitudes
> coincide with the interests of the Allies. . . . The mission is being sent by and in
> the name of the French Government in the well-considered interests of the
> nation. The mission should therefore be made up of political personalities
> who are devoted to our cause in preference to religious chiefs.

The Lieutenant-Governor of Senegal, seeing no objections to the mission,
selected Abdou Kane, a jurist from Kaolack who had been nominated for,
but had not received, the Légion d'honneur several years before. Since the
outbreak of the war he had helped with recruitment amongst the Tukolor
and so, having been selected to go to Mecca, he was nominated again for the
Légion d'honneur which he was duly awarded towards the end of August
1916. On the 24 August he left Dakar for Marseilles in a first-class cabin and
with a personal cook provided courtesy of the AOF government.[23]

The mission was reported to have been a great success. Lieutenant-
Colonel Bremond, who accompanied the pilgrims told Briand, the French
Prime Minister and also Foreign Minister, that the Algerian representatives
gave proof of their French mentality and expected to get the vote after the
war as a reward for their sacrifices, that the Tunisians were Turcophile and
the least co-operative of the group, whilst the Moroccans had 'a good
attitude although a bit simplistic'. As for Abdou Kane – 'this good old man
with the finesse of a peasant' – Bremond reported that he had become
increasingly pro-French as the journey had continued and was struck by the
lack of racism on the part of the French officers with whom he ate at the
same table.[24] The Colonial Minister rewarded Abdou Kane with another
honorific title.[25] The following year the Quai d'Orsay insisted that there
should be more 'French' pilgrims in order to avoid the impression that
Germany still controlled the Mediterranean. Such an impression would, it
was feared, weaken the French bargaining position with the King of Hedjaz
at a time when a powerful lobby in Paris was already staking its territorial
claims in the Levant. However, the French were not prepared to pay for the
pilgrimage as they had done the previous year unless there were not enough
pilgrims able to pay for themselves.[26]

The caliphate question highlighted the dilemma that characterised much
of French thinking on Islam. On the one hand, as we have seen, frequent
claims were made that France was a *Muslim* power[27] and, of course, it was
true that the French colonies contained many Muslims. But, on the other
hand, France, unlike Britain, did not control any of the great world centres
of Islam. The degree of French obsession with and suspicion of Islam that
continued right up until decolonisation cannot be adequately explained
without reference to this fact.

General Lyautey was particularly sensitive about this issue. As news of
the Sherif of Mecca's proclamation reached him, he wrote to the Foreign
Minister with a long account of his views. His main theme was the

desirability of the French sponsoring an alternative western caliphate that would act as a balance to the eastern caliphate of Mecca which, he believed, was tinted with pan-Islamic sentiments and was in the hands of the British. If the French upheld the idea of a single caliphate, he argued that they would put themselves at the mercy of the British, reliant upon their good will in order to participate in decision-making. Furthermore, he argued:

> Even if we were always to encounter loyalty from our ally and all its agents we would still have to reckon with their clumsiness. The *quant-à-soi* of the English, their disdain for natives, their confidence in the all-mightiness of Great Britain serve them ill for handling the moral forces of Islam ... It is all the more important to recognise the clumsiness of the English when one compares it to the skill we possess in such matters. Thanks to the universalist character of the French genius and an experience of Islam we have at our disposal personnel who offer both a vocation and an infinitely superior suitability ... I am aware of the fact that in religion as in any political affair we have an interest in dividing rather than unifying. But it is not a question of knowing whether the religious unity of French Islam is good or bad but rather of knowing whether this unity isn't the only guarantee against a greater evil, namely the unity of all Islam, including our own, under the primacy of a foreign or enemy chief. It is also a question of whether within the limits of our African possessions the religious unity under a khalifate docile to our wishes ... isn't the surest guarantee against dangerous excitation, notably against the actions of brotherhoods who are involved in all insurrections.

Lyautey, therefore, proposed backing the claims of the Moroccan Sultan for spiritual suzerainty in north-west Africa, excluding Tunisia for which he preferred to recognise the Ottoman Sultan rather than the Caliph of Mecca. The idea of opposing the Caliph of Mecca with a strongly backed Moroccan Caliph was not an original one. Felix Gaillard, the Secretary-General of the Sherifian government, had used a very similar argument early in 1915 but it is interesting to see it put forward so strongly by Lyautey.[28]

However, to a certain extent this debate was of academic interest only in AOF where for some time increasing emphasis was being placed on the particularity of African Islam, a particularity that was so strong that African Islam was barely recognisable as 'orthodox' Islam. Marty for example had described the Mourides as being *'en pleine vagabondage islamique'*.[29] In addition to the spiritual heresy of African Islam there was, according to this same belief, an ethnic heterodoxy which made the idea of a unity of African Islam almost a contradiction in terms. So when in January 1916 the Colonial Ministry proposed as part of a package deal to reward Muslim loyalty, which included a mosque and a special hospital for Muslims in Paris,[30] to elect some Muslim representatives on to the Interministerial Commission on Muslim Affairs, Clozel's response was both swift and predictable:

> Our Muslim populations understand and apply their Muslim faith only in the form of affiliation to maraboutic groups. These groups almost always correspond to ethnic collectivities. One can state as a principle that West Africa is

like a chess-board where religious chapels and ethnic groups almost always coincide and where as a result maraboutic jealousies and polemics have attached themselves to the secular rivalries of peoples and races. This extreme division of *Islam noir* has been up until now the main factor in our policy. It is because of it that our action has been easy and effective. It is thanks to this that neither before nor since the outbreak of war have we had to fear any general uprising. . . . It is because of this that all local incidents can be dealt with quickly and have no repercussion. . . . Should I myself attempt to bring together in one electoral college all the *serignes*, *alfas* and *karamokos* . . . to elect a Muslim counsellor? Will I myself be the artisan of a *rapprochement* of people who do not know each other and who are jealous of one another? Will I myself prepare the way for an agitator or simply an adventurer who will use Islam as his electoral springboard and perhaps even cause a pan-Islamic action? It is out of the question. For in this mosaic of peoples and brotherhoods no attempt at unification . . . should be risked. Such an action would amount to organising ourselves the Muslim dream and creating the lever which has always eluded the leaders of Holy War, to succeed in a general uprising of West African Islam. To ask us to prepare with our own hands the means of our eventual ruin seems to me to exceed all the limits of possible madness.

Clozel proposed nominating four men to represent some of the major strands of West African Islam – Sheikh Sidia, Aymin Seck (the *qadi* of St Louis), Ahmed Baba and Tierno Ibrahim Dalen – but if the Colonial Minister insisted on only one representative then Clozel would choose the last of the four mentioned.[31]

The Colonial Minister did not appear to insist and the scheme to co-opt West African Muslims onto the Interministerial Commission was, like many other such schemes of the time, stillborn. Instead Clozel himself sanctioned the creation within AOF of a Consultative Committee on Muslim Affairs to be composed of the heads of the Department of Civil Affairs, the Department of Muslim Affairs, the Military cabinet and selected Muslim notables of AOF. In all twenty Muslims were nominated, including Sheikh Sidia, Sheikh Saad Bu, Serigne Ahmadu Bamba, el-Hajj Malick Sy and Karamoko Dalen.[32] However, the Committee met with the disapproval of at least one local administration. The Lieutenant-Governor of Guinea feared that it would provide an alternative system of advancement for Muslims and would therefore undermine the colony's means of patronage. The scheme did not in any case have a very illustrious history and it too quickly faded into oblivion.[33]

So what then was the reality of French policy towards Islam during the First World War? The grandiose schemes of official missions to Mecca apart, the humdrum of everyday dealings was mundane and apparently undemanding. One task consisted of censorship, overall supervision of which was entrusted to Marty. In January 1915 Antonetti, the Lieutenant-Governor of Senegal, reported that Syrians were selling colour prints of the Italian and German royal families, the Sultan of Turkey and other political subjects which he feared 'might have a bad effect on the mentality of our natives'.[34] But Ponty assured the Minister of Colonies that there was little to worry about on that score as AOF had an efficient system of censorship. For example, a history book written by Enver Pacha on the Turko–Italian war which had been ordered by several Syrians before the war would, he said, be confiscated as soon as the order arrived.[35]

In 1917 Delafosse, in his capacity as Head of the Department of Civil Affairs, drew up a circular banning the *Revue du Maghreb* which he had been told by the Minister of Colonies was an instrument of German propaganda. Delafosse instructed the Head of Customs to allow Franco–Arabic dictionaries but to confiscate German printed editions of the Qur'ān and a French textbook, *L'Histoire moderne*, which had been published before the war and contained pictures of the Kaiser alongside portraits of allied heads of state.[36] The French, of course, countered with their own propaganda and produced posters of their own showing portraits of the President of the Republic and various military chiefs.[37]

THE DEVELOPMENT OF SCHOLARSHIP

Apart from such vigilance there was no real alarm about Muslim loyalty once the initial shock of war itself was over. Indeed, it is interesting to reflect that it was precisely during the period of the war that Marty did the bulk of his research and writing on Islam. A period that one might have expected to be intellectually barren turned out paradoxically to be the time when research on all aspects of African culture actually flourished as it had never done before.

In part this was due to the influence of Clozel who was delegated Governor-General following Ponty's death in June 1915. As we have seen Clozel was a scholarly person and as Governor-General he continued to support scholarly activity. In 1915 he founded the Comité des études historiques et scientifiques de l'AOF. The Comité, which published a regular *Bulletin*, had the specific aim of fostering scientific research in which Africans were also encouraged to participate. Clozel was to be its president, and Delafosse and Dr Bouet its two Vice-Presidents. For the last two years of the war Delafosse also occupied a senior position in the Dakar administration. On the invitation of his patron, Clozel, he was made head of the Department of Civil Affairs (SAC) early in 1916. Clozel had to work hard to secure the post for Delafosse, whose articles under the pseudonym 'Broussard' in the *Dépêche Coloniale* attacking Blaise Diagne and his party, known as the Jeunes Sénégalais, had earned him some powerful enemies in high places in Paris. Diagne was a central figure in France's recruitment campaign in AOF, and the rue Oudinot was anxious to retain his services. Clozel had to threaten to resign before Delafosse was finally appointed. Clozel himself, who had never actually been nominated as Governor-General but only 'delegated' for the duration of the war, was sacked in May 1917 as a result of differences with the rue Oudinot over recruitment. He was replaced by the 'technocrat', Angoulvant, who had 'pacified' the Ivory Coast and who was more sympathetic to military demands than were either Clozel or Delafosse. Although Delafosse survived Clozel's removal from office, his career nonetheless suffered and he never obtained the promotion that he desired to become Lieutenant-Governor of a colony in West Africa.[38] Marty, the good soldier, appeared never to have got involved in the colonial politics of the war period.

The scholarly triumvirate of Clozel, Delafosse and Marty, which held the stage for much, if not all, of the war was an impressive one by any standards. As a result of its presence the war period was a far richer one in terms of research and publications than one would have expected.

Marty was the most prodigious of the wartime scribblers. *L'Islam en Mauretanie et Sénégal* (1915–16), *L'Islam en Guinée* (1917–20) and *L'Emirat des Trarzas* (1917–18) all appeared in wartime volumes of the *Revue du Monde Musulman* (RMM). In collaboration with Colonel Mangeot he wrote in 1918 a study of the Tuareg of the Niger Bend which was published in the *Bulletin du Comité des Etudes Historiques et Scientifiques de l'AOF* (1918). The first volume of *Etudes sur l'islam et les tribus du Soudan* appeared in volume thirty-seven of the 1918–19 edition of the *RMM*, and the other three volumes appeared shortly afterwards in a separate collection. *Les Bracknas*, a study of the other main political grouping in southern Mauritania to complement his earlier work on the Trarza, was published in volume forty-two of the *RMM* in 1920. In 1921 he wrote a study of Islam in Niger which was not published until 1930–1[39]. The years 1922 and 1925 saw the publication respectively of his work on the Ivory Coast and Dahomey. In addition there were a number of other minor articles of lesser importance. With such a large corpus of writing it is not easy to generalise beyond certain basic statements. All the studies were essentially administrative and followed broadly similar layouts – an introduction to the history of the region and description of the main Muslim personalities followed by an analysis of the importance of Islam in the social, political and economic life of the indigenous population. They were also very specific either to one area or to one ethnic group, but between them they covered all the territories of AOF. Despite the variety of subjects it is still possible to identify certain key themes in Marty's description of Islam.

Marty's belief that the Mourides were a Muslim heresy was one which he extended to most other West African Muslims. In an article written in 1914 on the subject of the role of amulets in Senegalese society he declared 'Here in West Africa Islam is not so much an adaption of persons and of characters but rather a deformation of doctrines'.[40] This judgement was not, however, rigorously applied to all Muslims in AOF. For example, Marty argued that the Muslim Mande population of the Ivory Coast were 'strictly orthodox as far as the rites are concerned, more orthodox even than in North Africa'. The Mande, he said, did not practise saint worship and prayed directly to

God.[41] An exception was also made for the Moors who were regarded as extremely orthodox Muslims and very accomplished scholars to boot: 'One must not forget that in the Trarza we find ourselves in the presence of intelligent and well-educated people who resemble Europeans on many points'.[42] The Muslim communities of Timbuktu, Djenné and Nioro – all traditional centres of Islamic scholarship – were similarly respected by Marty who made no attempt to deny their orthodoxy or, indeed, their relations with the wider Islamic world.[43] Marty also acknowledged the scholarship of el-Hajj Malick Sy, 'the most educated marabout in Senegal'.[44]

But such recognitions were exceptions. Writing on the subject of Sheikh Bu Kunta, an unscrupulous Moorish marabout who exploited his family origins to earn his living near Tivaouane in Senegal, Marty declared that 'The Moorish–Arabic mentality of Bou Kounta and the experience of a life spanning three-quarters of a century caused him to see in the blacks nothing more than birds good for eating'.[45] Although the paternalist Marty did not approve of Bu Kunta's attitude to the Blacks he nonetheless shared the belief in the low intellect of the black races. This was very clear in Marty's attitudes to education, and was also reflected in his belief in the fundamentally different nature of 'African Islam' as opposed to 'Arab Islam'. In May 1915 Marty was asked to give his opinion on the wisdom of distributing in AOF a pamphlet prepared by the British giving an account of the rupture of relations with Turkey. He considered that:

> Our black countries are scarcely Islamised and are not in the least up to date with the current events in the Orient. Since the beginning of the war our policy has been to maintain the Blacks in this happy state of mind and we have abstained from all communications that might change this state of affairs.

Marty agreed, however, to give copies of the document to 'a few black marabouts and a larger number of Moorish marabouts'.[46]

Marty continued Ponty's crusade against the use of Arabic in the administration. At the end of 1918 the Lieutenant-Governor of Senegal decided to include a compulsory oral and written examination in Arabic for all interpreters. Marty considered this to be,

> an affront to the Muslim policy inaugurated in 1908 by M. Ponty and methodically followed since then by all the Governor-Generals. It is a clear backward step which, moreover, is in keeping with the tradition of the Senegalese administration which since Faidherbe has practised a constant policy of Islamophilia and which has endeavoured to Arabise and Islamise populations which were almost all still fetishist in 1850. The Governor-General has eliminated Arabic, the vehicle of Islam, from all official institutions in AOF. To reinstate it officially and obligatorily in the interpreters' exam is to work towards Islamising in a short space of time the corps of Senegalese interpreters and to transform them into marabouts who will be much more loyal to local pontiffs than to the order of the administrator. It would also result in eliminating numbers of young fetishists, Christian or

religiously independent young Senegalese who have not learned, and who have no need to learn, Arabic and the principles of the Muslim faith. It would obviously favour Arabic to the detriment of French, and the marabout to the detriment of the schoolteacher.[47]

Marty was in this case particularly strident in his criticism and uncharacteristically melodramatic in his warnings – but the use of Arabic was, like the use of *Sidi Khalil*, something he felt strongly about. It is interesting to see Marty's views on the pro-Islamic tendencies of the Senegalese administration as these views seem to fly in the face of fact. As Marty himself had so well described, the conversion of the Wolof to Islam was caused by a process much more complicated than the simple use of Muslim intermediaries by the French. It might also be said that neither Cor nor Guy, two recent Lieutenant-Governors of Senegal, were noted for their love of Islam. Still the belief that the French were themselves mostly responsible for the development of Islam in Senegal was a strong one, another stereotype that proved itself to be a hardy perennial.

The reason why Marty felt that 'African Islam' was fundamentally different from 'Arabic Islam' was that Marty – like Clozel and Delafosse – believed that the indigenous pre-Islamic customs and traditions were a more powerful influence than the doctrines contained in the Qur'ān, *hadith*, etc. French knowledge of indigenous customs derived principally from studies commissioned for legal purposes, that is studies that were intended to provide French administrators with a corpus of customary law that was more suitable than either the Code Napoléon or the *sharia*. At least a third of each of Marty's books was devoted to the question of customary laws and the influence of Islam upon them (and vice versa). Marty argued that:

> Pure Muslim law has never governed the Senegalese communities. They have always retained their judicial customs, which are more or less coloured by Islam, sometimes only very slightly. So it is not to the Coran or to the law of Islamic authors that one should refer in order to judge questions of civil law concerning our Islamised subjects.[48]

In his study of the region of Kayes, Marty stated that the population of 75,000 comprised one-third fetishists, one-third lapsed Muslims and one-third 'Islamised . . . in the sense that one understands it in West Africa, that is to say coloured by Islam but above all anxious to pass themselves off as Muslims'.[49] Marty's comments on the Islam of the Bozo – a group of fishermen and boatmen on the Niger near Mopti – are revealing:

> In African Islam so superficial as it is the Bozo seem to hold the record, but despite everything one cannot really laugh because their faith, although unenlightened, seems nonetheless to be strong and active. They also suffer from the need to believe and seem to be tending towards a more complete Islam. It is hardly necessary to add that the influence of Islam in their judicial institutions as well as in their social customs is almost nil. They are well able in their minds to amalgamate belief in the new religion and respect for all their

129

former beliefs – *tana*, magic practices, witchcraft, supernatural therapy etc. –
which are similar to Bambara customs.[50]

In these two quotes we can see examples of Marty's cynical attitude to
Islamic conversion. Africans became Muslims out of snobbery, 'to pass
themselves off as Muslims' or because 'they suffer from a need to believe'.
Another reason for conversion which Marty offered with reference to
traders was one of sheer practicality. For example, in the Ivory Coast Islam
was confined mainly to the Muslim *dyula* (traders) who, said Marty,
prospered handsomely under the umbrella of the *pax gallica*. Wherever the
dyula went they did not neglect to say their prayers for,

> This simple yet grandiose religion practised by almost all the Blacks coming
> from the North, apart from its intrinsically seductive qualities, established
> itself as a veritable necessity, as an obligatory passport for native fetishists
> desirous in their turn of trading with the cities of the Sudan which have been
> described to them in marvellous terms. These fetishists leaving for the north,
> therefore make their *salaam* but without great conviction, motivated by more
> or less the same reasons as those which decide a traveller [in Europe] to
> become a member of a 'touring club'.[51]

Although there is an acknowledged connection between long distance trade
and Islam, Marty's dry humour – one of his strengths as a writer –
nonetheless betrays a superior and dismissive attitude towards African
Islam.

So, if as Marty said, it was scarcely worth repeating that in most cases
African Islam was heavily influenced by pre-Islamic customs and traditions,
what then in Marty's eyes were the relative merits of Islam and animism?
The answer is not entirely clear. An interesting insight into Marty's overall
view of religion in general in Africa can be gleaned from some handwritten
notes made by M. Deharain, keeper of the library of the Institut de France
and secretary of the *Journal des Savants*, who had a long conversation with
Marty about religion in Africa some time in 1921. Unfortunately the notes
are barely legible but it seems that Marty likened Islam to a wolf and
fetishism to a lamb. Although the notes do not explicitly ascribe the role of
shepherd to the Christian missions, the implication is nonetheless there for
it was suggested that the missions represented the best chance of keeping
the lamb safe from the wolf.[52] Marty certainly believed that the animist
societies required some sort of protection from Islam. The only restriction
that Marty believed necessary for Muslim Qur'ānic teachers, for example,
was that they should not be allowed to teach in animist areas. In an essay on
Islam in Casamance, Marty again emphasised the importance of keeping
Muslims away from the animists:

> In the aspect of our Muslim policy in West Africa which concerns the fetishist
> peoples there is an extremely delicate role to play. It is necessary that we
> safeguard this interesting and prolific Diola people, great growers of rice and
> industrious workers ... from all Islamic influnce. With the Sereres, whom

they greatly resemble, they constitute two ethnic unities, the only two of importance who are left to us in Senegal on whom we can count to carry our civilising effort.[53]

Marty had been very impressed with the success of the Liberian Christian prophet, William Harris, in the Ivory Coast. In an area, the Gulf of Guinea, which he described as 'the paradise of magic',[54] Marty was astounded at the success of Harris in converting the animists to Christianity and at the same time encouraging them to work more and to drink less alcohol.[55] Harrism was, he said:

An almost unbelievable religious fact which has upturned all the ideas which we had about the primitive and rustic black societies of the coast and which along with our occupation will be the most considerable political and social event in ten centuries of history past, present and future of the Ivory Coast.[56]

However, the war interrupted the Harris experiment, and the authorities, worried by 'a multitude of imitators [of Harris], a scattering of little prophets of Yessas (Jesus) and sons of God, who show much less tact and disinterest than their master or model', 'invited' Harris to leave the colony.[57] Harris' success was thought to be surprising because it was widely believed that the sedentary forest dwellers were incapable of conceptualising a single and unique God. In his study on Dahomey, Marty extended the lesson of the Ivory Coast experience to the Fon and Yoruba, two animist ethnic groups with a strong social structure who were both nonetheless, according to Marty, 'on the threshold of a religious crisis' and before long were likely to convert, depending on mission activity and government policy, either to Islam or to Christianity. Marty warned that 'One must underline strongly the fact that here, as elsewhere, our confessional neutrality is a great advantage to Islamic proselytism'.[58] Taken together with other evidence such as the wolf and lamb analogies, this last warning about the dangers of religious neutrality would seem to suggest that Marty was more in favour of mission activity than were either Arnaud or Ponty.

However, it would be an oversimplification to argue that Marty held to a simple and dogmatic belief in the inherent wickedness of Islam and the innocence and perfectibility of animism. For, like all his contemporaries, Marty was struck by the 'superiority' of Islamic over animist society. The same Diola population, whom he had lauded for their industry and willingness to associate themselves with the French civilising mission, were also described as having retained along with the other animist groups of Basse-Casamance 'the most extremely barbarous customs' and he proceeded to catalogue an impressive list of vices which were compounded by the fact that 'No *commandement* exists, neither great nor medium.... This scattering of authority makes administration almost impossible'. It was for these reasons, said Marty, that the French had in the past preferred to make use of the minority Muslim Mandinka community as chiefs and intermediaries.[59]

In the Ivory Coast Marty spoke of the way in which Qur'ānic education improved indigenous society:

> However rudimentary the education given by marabouts may be, however absurd its methods often are ... it still nonetheless represents a sort of development of the brain, an obligation for the native spirit to rid itself of its congenital torpor and laziness, an attempt at intellectual labour. It gives a rudiment of general knowledge which enables the Black to a certain extent to rise above his milieu, teaching him to glimpse and conceive a mentality which is different from their own and, since it is Arabic, different from ours as well, it is true, but one which is certainly superior to the ambiance in which they vegetate. Finally, through desire to go to Paradise and through fear of going to Hell and respect of God it inculcates them with a primitive, but healthy and realistic morality. It has become a commonplace to affirm that Islam constitutes a certain progress in the primitive mentality of the Blacks. There is no doubt about it.[60]

Marty also argued that women were better off in Islamic society than in an animist one. In the region of Djenné and Macina Marty wrote that:

> The situation of women is certainly better amongst the Islamised population of the Niger valley than amongst the fetishist societies. Islam gives her a certain personality, thanks to which she can acquire, possess and sell [material goods] ... to a certain extent govern her own life and, above all else, she may pray. The fetishist women, similar to the woman of pagan antiquity, takes no part in religion ... and if she is reasonably free physically to come and go as she pleases she is not by any means her own mistress.[61]

Although Marty admitted that some Muslims obstructed the physical liberty of women by imposing the veil, the preference for Islam is nonetheless clear. In view of the fact that the position of women in society was regarded by some contemporaries as the touchstone of civilisation, such a belief contained a more general comment on the relative merits of animist and Islamic societies than just the specific issue of the position of women in society might suggest.

The final theme running through Marty's books that we shall consider concerns the importance attached to personalities in his studies. As a brief glance at any of his published works will quickly show, a large proportion is taken up with lists and character sketches of the main Muslim figures. The biographical bias of Marty's work was justified by at least two considerations. The first applied more particularly to the nomadic and semi-nomadic people of the Saharan fringes. As we saw in the study of Coppolani's attempt to win over the clerical tribes of Mauritania, personal diplomacy was, in the absence of a strong military commitment, one of the few tools of conquest available to the French. This was true also of French relations with other societies similar to the Moors and to whose conquest the French were at best only reluctantly committed. Diplomacy was complicated by, amongst other things, the intense factionalism that characterised many of the societies involved. Much of Marty's work on these societies is simply concerned with suggesting possible chiefs. In the case of the Trarza where the French protégé, Emir Ahmet Salum, had had no successor following his assassination in 1905, Marty argued that since 1910, when the emirate had been restored, French rule and French policy had been to create 'a protectorate regime ... to free the local authorites of the worries of the internal administration of the tribes ... We aimed at getting the Moors to administer the Moors, but *à la française*, that is to say with precision and without depradation'.[62]

Marty attempted also to provide guidelines to help French administrators through what he called 'the *maquis* of Muslim law'[63] and to warn them of:

> the astuteness and perfidy of the Moor, and especially of certain maraboutic tribes. ... An administrator who arrives from Black Africa and who has never had to deal with such intrigue is far from being able to imagine such a state of mind and ends up by allowing himself to be duped by this structure of apparent simplicity and the honeyed and well-turned speeches of the Moors. Let us not forget that the Moors are white.[64]

What were the qualities that Marty emphasised as being the hallmarks of a good chief? Marty respected birth and for this reason tolerated the laziness of Eli Mahmud, the chief of the Mechdouf, whose main interest in life it seemed was in drinking calabashes of tea and milk in his tent.[65] But it was clear, nonetheless, that Marty's preferences lay with Mokhtar ould Mohammed Mahmud, the second of Eli Mahmud's brothers. He was, said Marty:

> a fine man, cunning and energetic. He has always shown proof of a certain independence and even in the beginning of an undisguised hostility towards us. He is certainly the most intelligent and also perhaps the most warlike of the family ... His personality should hold our attention, and I would be inclined to see him as the best of the candidates for the emirate from our point of view.[66]

Elsewhere Marty again made it clear that he did not necessarily hold someone's past against him. Thus the chief of the Labat tribe in Brackna, who as a young man had fought an intermittent campaign against the French before finally submitting in 1909, was described as an excellent chief:

> This young and intelligent bandit of yesteryear understood that he had to come closer to the French in order to restore his tribe. So he came to live at Aleg at the beginning of 1912 and for a few months attended lessons at school. Then ... he studied for a year in the *médersa* of St Louis and for four years in Boutilimit. Today he speaks and writes French reasonably well. He is an excellent chief who bears himself well.[67]

Another chief of whom Marty warmly approved was Salah ould Rachid Abd el-Oualibouh, a marabout chief of the warrior Awlad Nacer. Marty said that he was one of the most influential Moorish chiefs of the western Sahel: 'He is an intelligent man, learned and very sympathetic. As *cadi* of the Oulad Nacer he exercises a great authority over these querulous nomads. Many strangers come to obtain judgements and *fetwa* from him.

His tent is a little nomadic *zawiya* where thirty-odd men and young people improve themselves in higher learning.'[68]

Other chiefs were criticised for a variety of shortcomings: Sheikh Mohammed Djeddou of the Jouman tribe was described as being 'more stupid than his camels',[69] Torad ould Sheikh Hadrami, Mohammed Fadel's grandson and nominal chief of the Ahel Taleb Mokhtar, was suspected for having made too noisy a denunciation of Ma el-Ainin and el-Hiba, his uncle and cousin respectively, and for scorning *'le menu peuple'*.[70] Sheikh Fall, a former porter at the masonic lodge in St Louis, who had risen from humble origins, was sacked from his administrative post for corruption.[71]

The second justification for paying so much attention to biographical detail was that Marty believed African Islam was governed by personalities. In Senegal he said that:

> To be a Muslim is to obey the orders of one's marabout and to earn through one's gifts and devotion a share in the merits of the saintly man. The study of the Islamised world is thus almost uniquely a study of maraboutic personalities.[72]

The idea of studying personalities was not, of course, a new one. After all, Roume's 1906 circular was specifically intended to create a register of marabouts, but it was Marty and the added urgency of war that translated administrative intentions into reality. In doing so not only did he contribute hugely to the official understanding of *Islam noir* but he identified a broader range of Muslim allies than hitherto the French had considered using. Marty was enthusiastic about the results of the close collaboration with Sheikh Sidia:

> Such a complete accord between the French authority and one of the representatives of Moorish Islam ... represents one of the most brilliant aspects of the French government in West Africa for Sheikh Sidia is not afraid of compromising himself at our sides. Nothing could better illustrate the leading principle of this policy: the channelling and utilisation of Islam in *Muslim country*. This utilisation involves nothing more than amicable collaboration.[73]

The 'amicable collaboration' between the French and Sheikh Sidia had, of course, existed for some time but it was until the First World War a fairly unique relationship. However, by the end of the war the French had cast their net much wider in their search for Muslim allies. El-Hajj Malick Sy became one of Marty's favourite Senegalese marabouts. Marty wrote that:

> In this country where one has to be wary of Tidjianisme which through its Omarien and Toucouleur branch has only ever showed itself as one of our most irreducible enemies, one is pleasantly surprised to see that this Ouloff branch, under the inspiration of its chief, has nothing but sympathetic sentiments and acts of devotion towards us.[74]

El-Hajj Malick Sy's pro-French sentiments preceded Marty's arrival in the colony, but it was Marty who did most to publicise them. The case of Ahmadu Bamba was particularly striking; although he remained under surveillance throughout the war, the French were prepared to make use of him for recruitment to an extent that would have been inconceivable beforehand. Marty was also prepared to criticise former attitudes to particular Muslim personalities, and the most obvious of such cases was his criticism of the French treatment of the *wali* of Goumba and the Jakhanke community in Touba.

His willingness to recognise the pro-French tendencies of many marabouts and to criticise past actions was an important corrective to the wilder theories of a militantly xenophobic Islam. Fuelled by resentment of Lebanese and Moroccan traders (not all of whom were Muslims!), some sections of the European community in West Africa were still obsessed by the Muslim threat. An article in the *AOF-Echo* – a newspaper owned by Conakry traders – declared in October 1916 that:

> All the Muslims of our colonies are entirely hostile to all 'Europeanisation'.... Certain of their books, besides the Coran, speak of Europeans ... with the greatest scorn 'dogs and sons of dogs, pork eaters, uncircumcised, etc....' whose race should be destroyed.[75]

Such attitudes died hard and it is doubtful that any amount of scholarship would have succeeded in reducing them to extinction. The newspaper article is cited as a reminder that attitudes towards Islam remained heterogeneous. Whilst the focus of this study is on shifting trends of perception, one should not ignore the constancy of a number of gut prejudices in relation to Islam.

Marty could not hope to destroy such prejudices but he did make it less likely that senior administrators would share them. It is not possible, unfortunately, to know how widely read his work was. In April 1917 Ernest Leroux, who published all of his major studies, offered the Governor-General 167 copies of *L'Islam au Sénégal* for 1,500 francs. I have found no record that this offer was ever taken up, but it is interesting to note that three months later the Governor-General, Van Vollenhoven, suggested to the Governor of Senegal that each *cercle* should have two copies of the book.[76] As Van Vollenhoven recognised, Marty's studies were excellent guides for administrators who possessed little knowledge of Islam. They were written clearly and simply. Although there is at least one reference to Durkheim – in *L'Islam en Côte d'Ivoire*, the most theoretical of all his studies[77] – Marty did not on the whole indulge in intellectual speculation in the way that Clozel was prone to do. His studies were empirical, based on personal observation, conversation with Muslims and French experts and on a selective use of local monographs. He would also send local administrators a series of very specific questions concerning aspects of Muslim life and culture in their *cercles*. For example, the *commandant de cercle* of Odienne in the Ivory Coast was asked nine questions about local Muslim culture. A measure of the preciseness of the questions can be gauged from the fact that of the nine questions, four related to hairstyles, beards, moustaches and tattoos.[78] Marty's general conclusions and his message were likewise clear and simple: Islam in Africa should not be assimilated to Arab Islam for it was strongly coloured by the indigenous pre-Islamic culture and traditions of the various ethnic groups. The French should not encourage Islam through the use of Arabic or Qur'ānic law, and animist communities should be offered some sort of protection from Muslim intrusion. Within Muslim areas, where the French had nothing serious to fear from Islam, the French task was principally of forging alliances with Muslim leaders. Marty was clearly not a particularly original scholar but he was much more thorough than any of his predecessors had been, and therein lies his strength and value, not only for his contemporaries but also for subsequent generations of scholars of Islam in Africa.

Part IV

1920–1940: The French stake in *Islam noir*

J'ai eu à administrer au cours de ma carrière des tribus algériennes et des peuplades noires. Je dois reconnaître que j'ai rancontré beaucoup plus de gens compréhensifs chez les noirs que chez les berbères. Les nigeriens acceptent, l'africain du nord refuse. (R. Randau and F. Abdelkader, *Les Compagnons du jardin*, 1933.)

Introduction

Advertisements appearing in the monthly journal *L'Afrique Française* remained virtually unchanged in the first twenty years of the journal's existence: champagne with corks for tropical climates, special tents and pills to cure constipation (and worse) were all constant features of the curious epoch of French colonialism in the first two decades of the twentieth century. However, by the early 1920s the tents and pills had made way for banks, theodolites and drawing boards. (The champagne, however, survived.) This change clearly reflected the increasing popularity of the idea of *La mise en valeur des colonies* associated particularly with the post-war Minister of Colonies, Albert Sarraut. The use of colonial soldiers during the First World War had indicated the economic potential of the colonies, and the financial ruin and social hardship which France experienced immediately after the war gave added urgency to the need to exploit the economic potential of her overseas Empire. The war had helped France both to understand and to define her colonial mission – and the itinerant adventurer with his tents and pills was transformed as a result into the rather more permanent figure of draughtsman and engineer planning the rational exploitation of Africa's wealth.[1]

During the 1920s the development of new and improved transport systems helped to integrate the colonies to the metropole. Airplanes flew between Dakar and Algiers at least as early as 1920 and in 1927 there was the first direct crossing by air between Africa and South America. Air travel reduced not just the isolation of empire but also the risks and hazards of tropical climates: in June 1922 an administrator bitten by a rabid dog in Bamako was flown in less than twelve hours to Dakar for hospital treatment.[2]

In many ways it must have seemed that the colonies were about to embark on a glorious new era of economic development.

However, other changes had to be taken into consideration. The First World War had been fought by the Allies in a spirit of mutual distrust and it was only their shared hostility to Germany which prevented the alliance from breaking up. Once Germany had been defeated it took several years before the need to restore financial stability and to rebuild the European economies brought the Allies into a semblance of agreement. In the mean time they fell apart over the share-out of the spoils of victory with Anglo–French squabbles over the division of the Ottoman Empire and a much more serious disagreement between the French, British and Americans over German reparations. France, which had suffered in the war more than any of the Allies, claimed huge reparations from Germany. 'L'Allemagne paiera' was the single answer from Frenchmen of all walks of life to their country's economic problems. As it became obvious through the series of conferences held in the early 1920s to determine the extent and nature of German reparations that Germany would not and could not pay for all the damage sustained by France during the war, an accusing finger was pointed by French nationalists, led by Poincaré, at an Anglo–Saxon conspiracy against France.[3] One of the effects of these tensions was to heighten French sensitivity to international criticism, but particularly American criticism, of French colonial practices. For example, an article in *L'Afrique Française* in 1930 attacked countries without colonies (i.e. the United States), who were unaware of the 'psychological or material realities of the native populations', but who used the League of Nations to criticise colonial powers.[4]

Suspicion of Anglo–Saxon intrigue was, however, greatly exceeded by fear of Bolshevism. The Russian October Revolution had introduced a new factor into the political calculations of Western Europe. The success of the Bolshevik Revolution caused European governments to fear for their ability to preserve the *status quo* not only in Europe but also in the colonies. Although Marxist theory towards pre-capitalist societies was somewhat unclear, nonetheless the beliefs in the internationalism of the Revolution and in the notion that imperialism represented the highest form of capitalism were sufficiently strong for the Bolshevik government to make a muddled offer of support to the peoples of Africa and Asia. The Second Congress of the Comintern in July 1920 discussed the issues of nationalism and colonialism and was attended by delegates from India, Turkey, Persia, China and Korea. At the instigation of the Turkish delegates the commission charged with considering the colonial question specifically insisted on the need to pursue the struggle *against* pan-Islamism. However, later the same year the First Congress of Peoples of the East which met in Baku decided to make a greater appeal to the tradition of Islam and declared a *jihad* against capitalism. Another development in 1920 which signalled the Bolshevik interest in the 'Orient' was the foundation of an Institute of Oriental Studies which, along with the Communist University of Toilers of the East and the Scientific Society of Russian Orientalists (both founded in 1921), was intended to train people for political activity in Asia.[5] Thus within three years of coming to power the Bolshevik regime was actively courting the support of its neighbours who were ruled by colonial powers.

The possibility of an alliance between the Bolsheviks and the Muslim subjects of colonial powers was made all the more real by the growing force of nationalism throughout the British and French colonies. Nationalism was, of course, by no means a post-war invention but it is clear that the war had altered the position of the colonial nations in the world sphere and that the political experience gained by African and Asian soldiers, combined with the spirit of Wilsonian rhetoric, had contributed to an increase in nationalist activity throughout the world. The rise of nationalism in India, Egypt, Tunisia, Algeria and Morocco is well documented and does not need to be described here. It came as no surprise to either French or British governments that increasing nationalist demands were made. Successive French governments recognised France's need to repay her colonial populations for the sacrifices made during the war. Millerand, elected as Prime Minister in the autumn of 1920, stated that:

> Our Algeria, our countries of the Protectorate and our colonies whose admirable growth attests to the genius and tenacity of Republican men of state have paid fully and in all kinds their debt to the metropole. The metropole will in its turn recognise what she owes them and will associate them ever more closely in her political and moral life.[6]

Colonialists who spent much of their life physically isolated from the metropole had always been sensitive to domestic criticism of their activity. Whereas before the war such criticism had been largely (but not exclusively) based on the cost of imperial expansion, after the war criticism of colonialism acquired a sharper political edge as socialist and communist intellectuals, artists and politicians championed the cause of African nationalists. In 1921, Réné Maran, a West Indian and former French colonial administrator, was awarded France's most prestigious literary prize – *Le Prix Goncourt* – for his novel, *Bataouala*. The novel is set in a French colony in central Africa and is heavily critical of the violence involved in the 'civilising mission' of colonialism. In his preface Maran cited a Hindu poet's view of 'civilisation': 'You build your Kingdom on corpses. Whatever you may wish, whatever you will do, you will die away in untruth (*tu te meurs dans le mensonge*)'. In the course of the novel Maran turns traditional African 'vices' into 'virtues' and accuses Whites amongst other things of hypocrisy, prudery and impotence. Today the novel may strike the reader as merely an exotic catalogue of sensationalist and racist clichés but in 1921 it represented a sharp departure from mainstream colonial novels. The award of *Le Prix Goncourt* outraged the editorial committee of *L'Afrique Française* who cited Maran as an alarming example of what could happen if education for colonial populations was not restricted to French, elementary science and artisanal training. Any more advanced education would not, they said, create French citizens but:

> ... vainglorious, *déclassés* and rootless peoples who lose their native qualities and acquire only the vices of their educators. It is through this system that we have created such people as Réné Maran and that one fine day a novel appears like *Bataouala* which is very mediocre from a literary point of view, infantile in

> conception and unjust and pernicious in its tendencies. It needed only a handful of idiotic *littérateurs* who know of Africa nothing more than the jazz band and negro art to recommend to everybody this work as the finest *French* novel of the year.[7]

However, Maran was not to remain out of favour with the colonial establishment for long. In 1934 his novel *Le Livre de la brousse*, which in many ways was very similar to *Batouala*,[8] was given a very different review in *L'Afrique Française*. The reviewer, Robert Delavignette, who had been taught by Delafosse and who was the rising star of the French colonial administration, wrote enthusiastically that the book was a 'masterpiece' and that the central character, Kossi, was the most realistic portrait of a pre-colonial African that had ever been made.[9] That Maran was accepted into the colonial establishment reflects the influence which men such as Delafosse had on developing what may be called the colonial consciousness of the 1920s and 1930s. The creation of an Institute of Ethnology in the Sorbonne in 1927 and the creation in London of the International African Institute, with its journal *Africa*, were measures of both the increasing sophistication of Europeans' perception of Africa and of the realisation by colonial powers of the need to show greater method in their colonial administration. Yet 'Science' and the 'Practical Man' – to borrow again the characters of the Malinowski/Mitchell debate in the pages of *Africa* in 1929[10] – sometimes proved unhappy bedfellows, despite the fact that 'Science' wooed the 'Practical Man' with tales of her cost effectiveness!

The need to exploit the economic potential of the colonies had long been the principal justification for the expenditure on the colonial army. Reading general accounts of the colonial era in West Africa it is easy to gain the impression that the role of the army had come to an end by the 1920s but, whilst it is obviously true that the era of grand colonial conquest belonged to the late nineteenth century, it should not be imagined that the 1920s saw no military action. Neither Morocco nor Mauritania were finally 'pacified' until the mid-1930s. The colonies, even in years so close in memory to the European battlefields of the Great War, were still an arena in which military glory could be gained and paraded: in 1921 two colonial soldiers – Lyautey and Gallieni – were promoted to the rank of Field Marshal, and the fact that Gallieni's promotion was posthumous does not detract from the fact that of the seven Frenchmen ever to be made Field Marshal, four were colonials.[11] The close identity between the colonies and the military remained strong.

This brief and impressionistic survey of some of the main themes that run through the two decades that we shall cover in the last three chapters of this book serves to indicate the complexities and paradoxes of the inter-war years. Many of the themes are old ones: the need to exploit the economic potential of the colonies, resentment of international conspiracies, fears of nationalist movements, the increasing sophistication of European knowledge of Africa and the eternal presence of soldiers are all very familiar. However, they were almost all given a new twist: economic development was to be undertaken not so much in the brave new world of technological development but in the climate of economic retrenchment associated with the Depression;[12] conspiracy was not the conspiracy of exotic sultans but of former comrades-in-arms; nationalism was made much more frightening after the October Revolution and, although Europeans were coming to know more about Africa, Africa itself was changing.[13]

8

Post-war attitudes to Islam

As far as French attitudes towards Islam were concerned there was one major thread of continuity with the pre-war situation: Paul Marty remained in Dakar until 1921. At one stage it seemed as though he was to be posted to Lebanon, but this project was abandoned at the last minute. On learning of this change of plan Marty wrote: 'I am delighted and am packing my cases with joy to return to my dear Moors and Blacks in A.O.F'.[1] One of the people with whom Marty had become acquainted in the course of his research into West African Islam was the colourful figure of Sheikh Ibra Fall. In October 1921, Sheikh Ibra Fall came to Dakar to profess both his and his master Serigne Ahmadu Bamba's continued loyalty to the *mère patrie* and to show their respect to the new Governor-General, Merlin. He had been meaning to do this for a long time, but he explained that:

> My visit has always been delayed on account of the fact that that noble pha-lange of good old Africans who brought us up in the love of France and who guided us in our dealings with our white and enlightened chiefs have now almost all disappeared and have made way for unscrupulous politicians in whom we can have no confidence.[2]

Whilst Sheikh Ibra Fall's regrets about the passing of the era of 'good old Africans' should be taken with a pinch of salt, it was certainly true nonetheless that the key personalities in France's Islamic strategy were all approaching the end of their lives: el-Hajj Malick Sy died in 1922, Sheikh Sidia in 1924 and Ahmadu Bamba in 1927. As a result of these deaths the French administration was forced to look for new intermediaries to act on their behalf. But the passing of the 'good old Africans' can be taken to mean no more than the demise of a few personalities, for it suggests also the changing political climate associated with the emergence of mass politics in Senegal.

Delafosse, another link with the pre-war past, was acutely aware of the need to accommodate these changes. In the last year of the war he wrote a series of articles in *Dépêche Coloniale* in which he argued that Africans needed to be given more authority:

> After all the natives of Africa did not ask us to come. Since we have come, sometimes in spite of them and always without at least consulting them, and since we are going to stay it is important that in front of the people who observe us and who compete with us and in front of posterity who will judge us, that we should be able to justify our presence here and to show that in coming here we had other interests than in filling our pockets and then leaving.[3]

Angoulvant, who did not often see eye to eye with Delafosse, agreed that the war had created an entirely new situation and that it had upset the comfortable predictions in the gradual evolution of African society. Angoulvant argued that the French would have to be more careful to recruit colonial administrative personnel equipped to meet the new situation.[4] However, whilst some improvements continued to be made in the training of administrators in Paris, hopes of either a much larger or a more suitably qualified administration fell foul of economic recession.[5]

The intellectual response to the general sense of the need for change was to reaffirm the underlying thesis of the earlier work of Clozel, Delafosse and Marty that the French should base their administration on ethnic and religious particularism. It is particularly interesting to follow Delafosse's development in these years. Delafosse's criticism of colonial policies and practices became increasingly explicit. In 1921 he wrote that:

> In no case can I see as the motive for our colonial expansion in Africa the real and reasoned desire to contribute to the happiness of the populations whom we went to subjugate. That is only an excuse that we can give ourselves after the event, it was never our design. In effect we feel the need to excuse or at least to justify acts which ... on our part have consisted of dispossessing peoples of their independence for the profit of our country.[6]

This level of soul-searching does not appear to have spread throughout the colonial establishment and should be seen in the context of the immediate aftermath of the war.[7] However, even if the rue Oudinot did not change overnight into a ministry of repentant imperialists, an evolution in the way in which African society was regarded was nonetheless underway. For central to Delafosse's argument was his conviction, expressed before the war in *Haut-Sénégal et Niger*, that African civilisation deserved respect and that this had to be the starting point for any successful 'native policy'. This assertion was to be repeated in various guises and in several different contexts throughout the inter-war years: it was an argument which was attractive both to radicals, anxious to emphasise the value of African culture, and to conservatives, fearful of what might replace the traditional virtues of 'primitive' society.[8]

By African society Delafosse meant not only pre-colonial but also, in many cases, pre-Islamic society. The argument that animism constituted a much more systematic and sophisticated mode of belief than was usually credited had, of course, been advanced before the war, and in a sense it is as much the timing as the content of the post-war rehearsal of this argument that is of interest. Delafosse argued that official statistics overestimated the number of Muslims in AOF and that 'negroes' were inherently hostile towards Islam for three main reasons: firstly, he suggested that 'The collectivism of Blacks naturally estranges them from Islam. The Black's notion of hierarchy turns Islam ... into a religion that is good for the great and noble, but not for the mass of proletarians'; secondly he argued that Africans could not accept and could not afford the time to study a religion which did not include the earth, sky, rain, rivers and other natural elements in its cosmology; and, finally, that animism was a deep-rooted religion which corresponded entirely with the needs of Africans.[9] Delafosse explained any recent conversion to Islam in terms of French preference for Muslim intermediaries.[10] He admitted that he was deeply worried by the possible effects of conversion to Islam both on indigenous society and on French rule in Africa.[11]

Delafosse summed up his misgivings about Islam in his preface to a book written by Jules Brévié, Director of the Department of Political and Administrative Affairs in Dakar, *L'Islamisme contre 'naturisme' au Soudan français: essai de psychologie politique coloniale* (Paris, 1923).[12] Delafosse explained that:

> It is not at all my intention, nor that of M. Brévié, to organise a new crusade against Islam for which on the contrary both I and he have great sympathy. We merely believe that the lessons of the past and of the present have shown us that the Muslim civilisation meets neither the aspirations nor the needs of black societies, and that these societies possess a civilisation of their own which suits them better than any other because it is the logical product of their natural evolution and that it is as much in their interest as it is in our own to let this indigenous civilisation continue and achieve its development in the direction given to it by nature and determined by circumstances.[13]

This heavily deterministic view of African religious practice suggests that to the innate humanism which characterised the three volumes of *Haut-Sénégal et Niger*, Delafosse had added a large dose of Durkheimian sociology.

This latter influence is even more apparent in the main text of *L'Islamisme contre 'naturisme'* with its long passages from Levy Bruhl's *Les Fonctions mentales dans les sociétés inférieures* (Paris, 1910). Brévié's first chapters outlined his belief in the universality of his 'naturist' model of religious belief and civil administrative structure amongst primitive peoples of the world, past and present:

> Primitive collectivities ... all appear to be conceived on the same model and to obey a superior command. Within the great human orchestra they seem to play a part to which it is forbidden for them to add the slightest original note. The impulse of this collective determinism is so strong that they seem devoid of personality.[14]

146

Brévié's 'great human orchestra' follows a Hobbesian conductor:

> The history of societies is no more in sum than the struggle of the social instinct which tends to draw men together against the egoistic and anarchic tendency of the individual. When man has understood the advantages that the collectivity can bring to his preservation and well-being, he accepts his participation without either recrimination or regret.[15]

This stage is the 'naturist' system of social organisation which Brévié defined as:

> A collection of prescriptions and prohibitions born of collective and generally mystic representations by which the social instinct reacts against the egoism of the individual and obliges him to co-operate in the developments of the collectivity.[16]

Brévié then went on to describe Sudanese Islam. He deplored the confusion, which he said dated back to Faidherbe, of Islam north and south of the Sahara and denied the applicability of the Algerian model to the Sudan. In the Sudan, Islam had had great difficulty in overcoming what he called the 'impermeability of religion based on national and ethnic character'. What success it had had, he claimed, was solely due to conquest.[17]

Whatever the reason for it, Brévié had some dramatic words about the effects of conversion to Islam on the individual African:

> The infantile gaiety, the exuberance and the *joie de vivre* which are the hallmark of the fetichist give way to a profound sadness, an overwhelming seriousness, a lack of sexual appetite . . . The eye is dull, the brain empty, the gestures become mechanical and the body moves only as if in a hypnotic sleep broken only by painful awakenings when in the course of the repeated prostrations the head . . . strikes the ground over violently.[18]
>
> We have spoken of the physical and moral tribulations of the new convert and we have found part of the cause in the sadness, and perhaps, the disappointment which he experiences in substituting for his own dear beliefs a religion in which his native sensibility cannot be satisfied. But this explains only his despondency and his profound exhaustion, not the access of anger and the sudden movements which reveal the desire in his troubled soul to execute some action pleasing to God and thus acquire the right to the celestial delights. It is these new morbid manifestations which complete the diagnosis of individual fanaticism. The subject then assumes disgust for his previous life and avoids his fellows with whom contact is for him odious and sometimes painful. He walks, bent under the weight of a nagging obsession, his fevered fingers telling his beads. As if chewing in his sleep he constantly mouths his prayer *La illah ill'Allah* which he repeats at first with a stubborn wish and then mechanically in the torpor of his vacant brain . . .[19]

Brévié then listed the five pillars of the faith and various Muslim institutions such as the Sufi orders and Qur'ānic schools. None were portrayed in a particularly flattering manner.

The third part of Brévié's book covered French policies towards 'naturism' and Islam. Brévié made it clear that he considered that Islam had thrown down the gauntlet to the French: 'West Africa is a closed field in which the Arab civilisation is challenging French influence for the moral conquest of some twelve million naturists'.[20] After a false start in an Islamic policy which was based on the Algerian experience, the French, led by Clozel, had embarked, Brévié noted approvingly, on a more sensible course which emphasised the importance of secular education given in African languages. The purpose of such education was to 'reveal to this powerful, but dumb, people of Africa their own strength and to give them the means of expressing their own thought'.[21] Factory work was also suggested as an important part of the curriculum as a means of inculcating Africans with work discipline[22] – a measure, perhaps, of how flexible the notion of specific ethnic education could be!

L'Islamisme contre 'naturisme' is a curious book on several counts and deserves to be taken seriously not the least because Delafosse wrote the preface and Brévié was to become the longest serving and most influential of the inter-war Governor-Generals. Brévié clearly belongs to the 'bookish' tradition of Governor-Generals in AOF[23] and it is obvious from reading this book that he was a man of considerable learning. However, the really striking feature of the book is the deterministic theories used to explain 'naturist' society. Clozel had argued that 'animism' deserved respect but he had done so on the basis of close observations of societies in the Ivory Coast. Brévié's account of 'naturism' was also based on the first-hand observations of both the author and his fellow administrators, but these were all tied into the sweeping generalisations of Levy Bruhl about the 'pre-logical thought' of 'primitive' societies. Levy Bruhl, whose work was published in the journal *Annales Sociologiques* that had been founded by Durkheim, based his theories on a wide and somewhat indiscriminate range of accounts of 'primitive' life throughout the world, though chiefly from Australia and South Africa.[24] In Brévié's book, 'naturism' was portrayed as a powerful and entirely systematic mode of belief – and as such it should be treated by us with suspicion.[25] Brévié's account of Islam is more straightforward, founded as it seems to have been on a profound dislike of the religion. No reference was made to Marty, and instead Brévié quoted extensively from the local reports on Islam commissioned in 1911. Quite apart from the fact that these reports were already ten years out of date, it should be remembered that the standard was very variable and they cannot be taken as a reliable source. However, what is perhaps more interesting to note is that having described 'naturism' as the natural religion of the Sudanese Africans who are 'impervious' to all other religions, Brévié went on to talk of the challenge thrown down by Arabic civilisation for control of West African souls. If what Brévié had written about 'naturism' was true, then the Arabic challenge should not have been a serious one. Yet clearly Brévié was not entirely convinced by his own arguments. Here again we come back to the element of uncertainty that characterised so much of French writing on Islam in West Africa in the early twentieth century.

This uncertainty is particularly clear in the work of Delafosse, who was more concerned about Islam at this time than he had ever been since his flirtation with Lavigerie. In his preface to Brévié's book he stated that 'Amongst African Blacks Islamisation is synonymous with social breakdown'.[26] This was the most serious accusation that Delafosse could level against Islam and represents something of a shift from his earlier position in which Islam's place in African society was seen as less disruptive. It was a serious accusation on at least two counts. Firstly, there can be no doubting Delafosse's intense personal commitment to the idea of indigenous African *civilisations*. His commitment was a form of what might be dubbed 'radical paternalism', and it is interesting to see the important part he played in the Ligue de la défense de la race nègre, an organisation founded in 1927 which drew on studies of African art and history to affirm the existence of African civilisation as an alternative to the model of French civilisation. Although the Ligue was a metropolitan and mainly white organisation, it was to be of importance in shaping the distinctive cultural nationalism of francophone Africa in the 1940s and 1950s.[27] Thus, in Delafosse's personal terms, if Islam was a destructive agent in these African civilisations, then that was a very serious criticism indeed. Secondly, and more generally, one did not have to be as sincere an admirer of African civilisation as Delafosse was in order to have regrets about its breakdown. For the preservation of the old order – whatever that was – was widely regarded as the best safeguard against nationalist political disorder. Delafosse was very concerned about the development of pan-Africanism and he wrote angrily about American policy in Liberia which he believed encouraged it.[28] He also admitted to being concerned by pan-Islamism which, he said, was something that had never worried him unduly before. However, he believed that it should now be taken seriously because of 'The new situation throughout the Muslim world created as a result of European, but above all English policy in the Orient. This has encouraged amongst Mahometans of all races and nationalities a complex sentiment in which nationalism ... predominates over the purely religious idea'.[29]

It should be remembered that across the Sahara in Morocco similar arguments about the 'foreignness' of Islam were being advanced in respect of the Berbers. From 1914 until the early 1930s French policy in Morocco was based largely on the premise that the Berbers should be isolated as much as possible from Arab Muslim influences and that the French should take care not to encourage Islam by instituting legal and educational systems which were based on the Muslim faith. More attention was to be paid instead to the preservation of indigenous Berber laws and traditions. Paul Marty, during his time in Morocco, was one of the most enthusiastic supporters of this 'politique Berbère' which culminated disastrously in the Berber *dâhir* of 1931.[30] Delafosse's arguments should then be taken in the context of their day for it was the spectre of nationalism more than anything else which seems to have caused his views on Islam to have become so hostile.

THE PORTO NOVO INCIDENTS OF 1923

Apart from the Four Communes of Senegal, the colony in AOF where political life was most advanced and where fears of nationalism seemed justified was Dahomey, and in particular Porto Novo on the coast close to the Nigerian border.

Since the mid-eighteenth century the town of Porto Novo had been an important Yoruba slaving post both during the era of the Oyo empire and after its decline.[31] It accommodated itself well to the move to legitimate trade in the early nineteenth century with its economy now based on palm oil. Competition between British and French merchants for this trade on the Bight of Benin led to increasing European involvement in local politics and rivalries along the coast. Various treaties were signed with local chiefs but it was not until the Anglo–French treaties of 1889 and 1890 that the spheres of influence were finally delimited. The 1890s were dominated firstly by the French military campaign against Behanzin, King of Abomey, and then by the French exploration and subjugation of the interior. In an administrative reorganisation of the colony in 1896 the old kingdoms, including Porto Novo, were classed as 'protectorates' and retained their traditional chiefs.

The two main ethnic groups in Porto Novo – the Fon and Yoruba – were almost entirely animist but there were also Christian and Muslim communities. Mission activity in Dahomey was remarkably cosmopolitan: French, British and German missions, Catholic and Protestant, were all active in the late nineteenth century. In addition Dahomey's links, through the slave trade, with Brazil had led to the establishment of a Brazilian community made up initially of traders but later predominantly of Creoles – a group which included freed slaves. The Creoles followed several different religious beliefs. Many of the freed slaves had reverted to traditional beliefs but there were also substantial numbers of Christians and Muslims amongst them. One of the oddities of Porto Novo was that many of its leading Muslim families still bore the Catholic–Brazilian names of their former owners. There was also a small indigenous Muslim community. The final point to note in this brief introduction to the history of Porto Novo is that the royal house was divided into two rival branches, Dé Hakpan and Dé Méssé, and succession was supposed to alternate between the two branches.

From this brief survey it can be seen that the potential for political intrigue in Porto Novo was enormous: a divided royal house ruling in a notional protectorate close to the border of a foreign colony and presiding over an urban community comprising a relatively large number of mission-educated Creoles and freed slaves, but which also included indigenous

150

animists, Christians (Catholic and Protestant) and Muslims, were all ingredients calculated to ensure that political life in Porto Novo was never dull!

In 1908 King Toffa from the Méssé branch of the royal house died but the Hakpan candidate, Sohingbé, was not made king as the French suspected him of intriguing with the neighbouring British.[32] Instead, Toffa's son, Adjikji, became king and Sohingbé moved across the border to Nigeria. The following year the imam of the principal mosque in Porto Novo, el-Hajj Moutarou, died. The mosque had been built in about 1885 and even before its completion there had been disputes about who should be imam as both the Creoles and the indigenous Muslims, led respectively by Paraiso and Mouteirou, had their own favoured candidates. El-Hajj Moutarou, who had been elected imam in 1899, had, however, managed to reconcile both camps and his death, following so soon after the controversy surrounding the royal succession, was a blow to political stability in the kingdom. Moutarou was replaced by a Creole candidate, Bissirou. However, in 1913 both Bissirou and the King, Adjikji, died. Sohingbé's name was again put forward for the royal succession and again it was looked over in favour of another of Toffa's sons, Agoba. Trouble ensued and Sohingbé was arrested only to be released shortly afterwards. Another Creole was chosen as imam but he appears to have at least attempted to keep a balance between the two communities – so much so that he was accused by the Creole Muslims of being anti-Creole. In addition to the disputes over the royal succession and the choice of imam there was a third quarrel concerning the construction of a new mosque after the French decided to demolish the old mosque in 1910 – partly because of complaints about the noise of the *muezzin* from some nearby European trading houses but also because of wider plans for the reconstruction of Porto Novo's European quarter. The French donated 5,000 francs towards the construction of a new mosque and another Creole Muslim, Gonzalo Lopez, was put in charge of the fund-raising in order to complete the building. However, by November 1912, after being accused of embezzlement, the Lopez–Paraiso group had run out of money. The indigenous Muslims, the Mouteirou group, took over control, but they were hardly any more successful, and their money ran out after only six weeks. The Lopez–Paraiso partnership took over again but by July 1914 their money had again run out before the minarets were built or the walls plastered. Such then was the situation in Porto Novo at the start of the war.

During the war Paraiso identified himself very strongly with the French and was duly awarded the Légion d'honneur in 1919.[33] The Mouteirou group, on the other hand, were equivocal in their loyalty to France. They accused Paraiso of being a lax Muslim and made much of the fact that he had allowed his son to become a Catholic. In August 1916 over 100 Mouteirou Muslims staged a demonstration in Porto Novo in which they waved British flags. Marty considered that although the demonstration was not 'subversive' it was nonetheless in 'bad taste'.[34]

The French were much weakened in Dahomey during the war and the local élites were able to enjoy considerable power. In 1917 a Senegalese Creole lawyer, Germain Crespin, who had family ties with Blaise Diagne, succeeded on behalf of a Dahomean pressure group, led by a local plantation owner, Toualou Quenum, in getting the Lieutenant-Governor of the colony, Charles Noufflard, removed from office.[35]

At some stage during the war a branch of the North African Comité franco–musulman was founded in Dahomey and although little seems to be known about the Dahomean group it appears to have had good connections with France for in October 1919 the Minister of Colonies was questioned by a Dr Doizy, the *député* for the Ardennes, concerning the Comité's accusations of colonial abuses in Dahomey. The Comité accused the local administration, in general, of brutal recruitment practices during the war and the Governor, Fourn, and one of his officers, in particular, of speculation on the Porto Novo market, by requisitioning food which they subsequently resold at inflated prices. Fourn was asked about these accusations and denied them all categorically. He added that he was surprised to note that the accusations and complaints came from a Muslim group as he had expected the Muslims to be thoroughly pleased by his gesture the previous year of awarding Paraiso the Légion d'honneur. If this latter protestation was an innocent one it reveals a remarkable ignorance of the state of Muslim politics in his colony.[36]

In June 1920 the imam of the mosque died. Immediately both groups resumed their campaigns on behalf of their candidates and in July the King announced that the Paraiso candidate, Lawani, had been chosen. A few months later the French decided to halt construction of the mosque, which had been restarted after the war, as animosity between the two Muslim groups had grown ever more bitter.[37] At the same time Marty was sent to investigate and he arrived early the following year. Marty met all the leaders and reported pessimistically that 'Five long days of palavers permit me to conclude that there is total stalemate and no solution'. However, he noted that as long as the mosque remained unfinished the problem was lessened as both groups simply held Friday prayers in a mosque of their choice. Marty therefore suggested that the best solution would be to allow both groups to build their own mosques as this arrangement had appeared to work well in settling differences between different Muslim groups in Lagos. Marty noted that the Paraiso group was not very numerous and that the life-style of its members was not typical of most African Muslims. The leaders of the Mouteirou group, on the other hand, he said were 'incontestably in the African tradition', by which he meant they were illiterate. Marty, nonetheless, regretted the fact that the only French connections of this group were with 'indigenophile Associations in Paris'.[38]

The situation seems to have remained much the same throughout 1921 and 1922. Governor Fourn reported gloomily to Dakar in April 1922 that:

In Porto Novo the two Muslim parties – one full of devotion to the French cause and the other aiming to entangle the whole of the Muslim church with the sincere but imprudent support of the Comité franco–musulman – are continuing their internecine struggle. The apparent reasons for the struggle are religious ones such as the nomination of the new imam and the condition of attendance at the principal mosque, but fundamentally the struggles are intended to support certain elements of disorder.[39]

Early in 1923 the government announced its intention to increase the capitation tax in Porto Novo, and immediately there were demonstrations. On 12 February groups claiming to represent the Ligue des droits de l'homme[40] and the Comité franco–musulman made a public protest in Porto Novo and on the following day there were calls for strikes. On 18 February the police were sent in to break up a meeting, but the arrrest of the leaders provoked a further and much larger demonstration in which the demonstrators besieged the town hall. Fourn decided to use the army to free the town hall and at the same time requested more troops and permission to declare a state of siege. Governor-General Merlin agreed to send more troops but was reluctant to declare a state of siege for fear of adverse reactions in France. Fourn replied that the situation was getting worse all the time and explained that he did not believe that the ostensible pretext for the demonstrations, the tax increases, was the real reason for the revolt: 'In reality' he wrote, 'the agitations are due to the actions of subversive milieux whose propaganda is being followed by the Colonial Ministry'. Three days later, suitably impressed with the urgency of the situation, Merlin gave in to Fourn's request and on 26 February he declared a state of siege.[41]

In the rue Oudinot, however, the Colonial Minister, Sarraut, was far from happy about the measures taken and thought that Fourn's description of the agitators was much too vague. Merlin informed Sarraut that although the dock-workers in Cotonou had now gone on strike, the situation was under control. Extra troops from Togo had been sent for and he expected these to be in Porto Novo in ten days. The reinforcements had been called for on the basis of the principle that 'the show of imposing force makes it unnecessary to use force'. Merlin agreed with Fourn's diagnosis of the troubles and dismissed claims that tax increases and hardships caused by recruitment were responsible. Rather, he wrote, the real reasons lay firstly in the succession dispute and Sohingbé's continuing scheming and secondly, and 'more deeply', in the fact that since 1892 the population of Porto Novo had been treated with 'excessive sweetness and have never had to accept the firm discipline which follows a conquest'. Until they were forced to realise that the French had the means to enforce obedience, their 'undisciplined and rebellious character' made unrest more or less inevitable.[42] Early in March the local Administrative Affairs Inspector reinforced Merlin's comments and added that both local and international trouble-makers were at work. Amongst the indigenous agitators he singled out the Mouteirou group of Muslims:

153

> The Muslims seem to form an elite in the country. Consequently their number has increased greatly and many attach themselves to the Muslim Party for no other reason than to distinguish themselves from the crowd.... These newcomers have not wasted any time in founding a veritable political party. Finding the first generation Muslims too subservient to the French authority they took the first opportunity to separate from them. The Muslims of Porto Novo are today divided into two main groups – the old Muslims, reasonable men, concerned about their religion and respectful of the established order – and the Young Muslims, restless, rebellious and more preoccupied with political action which they hope will lead to the acquisition of material advantages, than they are with religious beliefs.

The Inspector also claimed that the Dahomean section of the Comité franco-musulman had been founded with neither the permission of the local authorities nor with the blessing of the North African secretary of the Comité. The rebellious elements had all exploited, he said, the visit to Porto Novo of a delegate of the Conseil supérieur des colonies to stage demonstrations in order to embarrass the government.[43]

By this stage Sarraut was satisfied that the unrest was serious and that international agitators were involved. He was particularly concerned by evidence from Nigeria of the international Communist connections of Dahomey's political activists, particularly Louis Hunkanrin.[44] At the beginning of the year the Colonial Ministry had circulated a note with details of Bolshevist propaganda in the colonies. *Izvestia* of 22 November 1921 had carried an article stating that:

> The most violent blow to the international bourgeoisie will be delivered when a liberation movement ignites among the blacks, a tenth of whom live in America. Such a movement will not only affect capitalist America it will also reach England and France in Africa, where we have to propagate Bolshevism through the channel of American negroes.[45]

And, indeed, it was not long before the Porto Novo incidents were splashed across the headlines of the French Communist party paper, *L'Humanité*. Early in March the Comité franco–musulman had sent a telegram to Carpot, an influential Créole lawyer in Dakar, denouncing police brutality against demonstrators protesting against tax increases. The text of the telegram was published a month later in *L'Humanité* which commented:

> Here are the beauties of French civilisation in Dahomey, in a colony whose population is distinguished by its great faculty for assimilation! And, moreover, everywhere else it's the same story. The working class of the metropole must struggle to relieve the oppression and the misery with which these unfortunate people have to struggle. Only Communism will assure the emancipation of Blacks, just as much slaves of capital as workers of the white race.[46]

However, by the time this exhortation was being read by French workers in the working-class suburbs of Paris, the struggle in Porto Novo was already over. The troops of Togo arrived in Cotonou on 11 March and a combined administrative and military action, first in the town of Porto Novo and then in the other subdivisions of the *cercle* had led to an immediate payment of the capitation tax. Fourteen men considered as the principal agitators were in prison awaiting trial, and, in addition, Fourn requested permission to intern Sohingbé and Hunkanrin.[47] In the course of April the agitators were all sentenced to varying lengths of imprisonment in Mauritania, Niger and Sudan. Fourn related the details of how, through a system of different postal addresses, Hunkanrin and his comrades had kept in touch with Communists in Paris and concluded that it was el-Hajj Mouteirou who had played the leading role: 'Even though it is impossible to give material proofs of his participation in recent events, his previous conduct, his state of mind and his close connections with the principal agitators all point to him as one of their best confederates'. One could be forgiven for thinking this was hardly conclusive proof! Whatever the rights and wrongs of the French analysis of events, by the end of July the administration felt confident enough to lift the state of siege.[48]

A week after the article in *L'Humanité* Delafosse gave his reaction to the Porto Novo incidents in an article in *Dépêche Coloniale*. He argued that the unrest could be explained firstly by the proximity of Porto Novo to Lagos where a spirit of unrest was 'constantly fuelled by the excitations of a few chestnut-coloured [i.e. of mixed race] lawyers' and where the impression of the existence of autonomous African states caused 'brains, exalted by a hasty education, to form notions of independence too vague to be healthy'. Secondly, and this disturbed him greatly, Delafosse suspected the activities of philanthropic organisations in France who went out of their way, he claimed, to discover abuses in the colonial system:

> The wind which will unleash the tempest in Africa often blows from the metropole. It is a very small wind, I know, because the great majority of the native population is imbued with a solid good sense ... But all the same one should not forget that little streams sometimes create great rivers.[49]

It is an interesting comment on the nature of francophone nationalism that Delafosse, here mixing metaphors in a virulent denunciation of nationalism, should nonetheless have been a major influence in the development of nationalist thought in francophone Africa.

THE ANDRÉ MISSION

Amongst all the correspondence between Cotonou and Dakar there came an instruction from the Governor-General on 5 April to ask Captain André, who had just been appointed as the Governor-General's chief adviser on Islamic affairs, to make a study of Islam in Dahomey.[50] Five days later the report was on its way to Dakar – a sign that Marty's successor was to be another fast and industrious worker. In reality, however, Marty and André had little in common. It is not at all clear from the archives exactly when

155

André appeared in Dakar. The first sign of his presence in West Africa was a report to the Governor-General dated 5 January on 'The present tendencies of Islam and practical measures for keeping Islamic propaganda under surveillance'.[51] His qualifications for writing this report were questionable for although he had published several studies on Cilicia and on the Berbers, the only evidence that he knew anything about Islam in West Africa comes from a few pages in his two-volume study of *L'Islam et les races* (Paris, 1922) – which was a survey of contemporary Islam throughout the world in which he demonstrated that all the upheavals in the Islamic world stemmed from the difficulties for settled societies of adopting the laws of Islam which had been created by and for nomads. His few pages on Islam in sub-Saharan Africa[52] appear to have been based on two books only – O. Meynier's *L'Afrique noire* (Paris, 1911) and Delafosse's *Les Noirs de l'Afrique* (Paris, 1922). In both *L'Islam et les races* and his subsequent report, it is clear that André's interest lay more in attempting to understand and document the broad sweeps of history rather than the minutiae of Islamic practices and institutions in West Africa.

André argued in his report to the Governor-General in January that events throughout the world since 1913 showed that Islam in itself was incapable of uniting Muslims against European powers. Nevertheless, and this was a familiar caveat, exterior forces could exploit Islam to the disadvantage of the colonial powers. André regretted the impact of President Wilson's Fourteen Points but he singled out the Russians as the major disruptive influence in the world:

> The Russians, who come from a country which is much more Asiatic than European, have adopted the old German ambitions, but with much surer methods, as a result both of their personal intimacy with the oriental soul and of the presence amongst them of educated and astute Muslims such as the Turco–Mongols.... At the instigation of Berlin the men of Moscow are attempting to cause difficulties all over the world for both the British and the French.

In keeping with his country's interest in the Levant, André went on to argue that as long as France held Syria, a barrier between East and West, then AOF was reasonably safe. However, the situation was complicated in West Africa by the influence of Garveyism which, he claimed, the British in their anxiety to recruit African regiments with which to replace untrustworthy Hindus in India, were making little or no effort to stop. Both 'xenophobic Islam' and Garveyism had to be closely watched for both were 'possible means of political emancipation or resistance for Blacks against European supremacy'. André concluded by urging the French authorities in West Africa both to continue with the studies undertaken by Marty and to create what he called 'listening posts' at strategic places in AOF so that the administration should never be caught by a surprise attack from Islam – or any other anti-European force.[53]

By now the themes of this report should seem familiar enough. Islam, such as it existed, was not a threat but care needed to be taken to prevent third parties from disturbing the present tranquility of relations between the French administration and their Muslim subjects. André also more than hinted that the administration would do well to employ him as an additional safeguard against Islamic unrest – yet another instance of how career-building and colonial policy-making were inextricably linked. André was duly rewarded, and in March an Intelligence and Muslim Affairs Department, with André in charge, was attached to the Federal Political Affairs Office in Dakar.[54] Quite how this department differed from the Service des affaires musulmanes is difficult to say. Its brief was contained in Articles II and III of the *arrêté* and was almost identical to that of its predecessor instituted in 1913 and reconfirmed as recently as July 1920.[55]

Eleven days after the *arrêté* 'creating' the Service des affaires musulmanes in Dakar had been signed, André reported to the Governor-General on the activities of the office in the first quarter of 1923. This long report rehearsed many of the points that André had made in January and included a strongly worded and even longer attack on the work of the 'Germano–Bolsheviks'. It was to counter such forces that the Service des affaires musulmanes had been created and André reported that since it had been inaugurated it had investigated the Arab press received in AOF, British recruitment, Garveyism and pan-Islamism. André said that he was not unduly worried by signs of a revival of *mahdi*sm across the border in Sokoto at the tomb of 'the great Toucouleur conqueror Othman Fodie' for, like his predecessor Arnaud, André adopted a fatalistic attitude towards *mahdi*sm, 'the endemic sickness of Islam, the boil which can burst anywhere at any time'. Later in the same report he argued that the prevalence of *mahdi*sm in AOF was a sign that Africans could lay as good claim as any others to be true Muslims. It is interesting to note André's ignorance of the ethnic origin of Usuman dan Fodio, one of the key figures in the development of Islam in West Africa, and this ignorance was typical of the cavalier attitude to detail which characterised much of his writing on Islam. André's preoccupation was rather with the world forces that had come into play since the war: 'The problem is a world one and in Black Africa a drama is being enacted which is the same one that is being played out in the Ruhr and in the Orient'. The Service des affaires musulmanes, with its staff of a typist, an interpreter, an Arabic writer and André himself, all crammed into one office of the Direction des affaires politiques et administratives, was a part of this world drama and its modest role, said André, citing the decidedly unglamorous words of Gallieni, was 'to know which dog has urinated in which corner'.[56]

One of the first scenes of the world drama which André was called upon to investigate was, of course, the Porto Novo Affair. In view of the speed with which the report was produced, it is not surprising that André's analysis added little to the facts that were already known. Bearing in mind too his interest in world-wide trends, it is equally not surprising that he focused on the international aspects of the Porto Novo incidents:

> It would not be exaggerated to hypothesise after studying the events of Porto Novo that the propaganda which is delivered from Moscow via Paris and Ankara could well have completed the circle in Lower Dahomey. We have just witnessed the Communists at work and from an Islamic point of view the following incident should be reported: thirteen kilometres east of Porto Novo on the British frontier is the customs post of Meridjonou. The French brigadier there has reported that the native customs officer who has now moved to Ouidah pronounced the following prophecies: 'The Whites won't be commanding you much longer, arm yourselves, be patient and await the order that will come from Mecca.

André concluded:

> Muslims tend to create a world-wide Islamic milieu and to form states within states. This accounts for the complexity of the Dahomean problem for besides the local rivalries . . . the situation is such that any dissident movement allies itself to world-wide movements. We already have Communism and pan-Islamism and now we have Africanism. Such questions go beyond Dahomey and even AOF. Local measures can be taken but they cannot prevent the continuation of outside propaganda. General decisions must be taken in the metropole to develop the sort of policies which are necessary to deal with the trouble that has arisen throughout the world as a result of the Great War.[57]

It should be recognised that international forces were at play in Porto Novo. The Comité franco–musulman for example, showed itself able to mobilise political opinion in France, and to this extent André and other commentators were quite right to argue that the world was changing. However, it is impossible to avoid the conclusion that 'Germano–Bolshevism', or whatever one chose to call the new world force, was also an excellent scapegoat, and it is particularly remarkable in the case of Dahomey how local causes of unrest were apparently never investigated although initially Sarraut, the Minister of Colonies, had thought that these were the main reasons for the unrest.[58]

In this tendency to prefer analyses of local unrest which laid the blame on international trouble-makers, André and the other administrators involved in the Porto Novo incidents were following a well-worn tradition that continues to this day . A more interesting aspect of the Porto Novo events was the way in which the Muslim community was divided so rigidly, in French minds, into two distinct camps: one moderate and pro-French, the other fanatical and anti-French. That the Muslim community of Porto Novo was divided and that it had been divided for a considerable period of time there seems little doubt. But what were originally fluid divisions and alliances had been frozen by French decisions consistently to support one group against the other. Given the complexity of Porto-Novoian politics as a whole and the wider political options available in Porto Novo as a result of its proximity to the Nigerian border, it is not surprising that the Monteirou group acted in the way it did, for the French left them little choice. In the past internal rivalries in Porto Novo appeared to have been resolved, however anarchically, by the alternating kingship but this mechanism was destroyed in the early colonial period when the Dé Hakpan line was repeatedly overlooked in favour of the Dé Méssé candidates. Marty understood the nature of local politics better than most, and his tolerance of the apparently pro-British tendencies of the Monteirou group together with his prescription of a policy of 'live and let live' as the only one likely to ensure a minimum of peace in what he admitted was a particularly intense rivalry, are further signs of the maturity of his judgement and of his understanding of West African politics. It was a maturity that very clearly was not shared by André or indeed by many others of his contemporaries. As we shall see in the next chapter the characteristic political calculation made by the French in their dealings with Islam was one of extreme simplicity: Muslims were either pro-French or they were not.

André left Dahomey in April and crossed the border to Nigeria where he intended to investigate the way in which the British organised their intelligence service. He was not put off by acting-Governor Cameron's assertion that the British had no such organisation; the British, he reported, employed a number of different officials varying from Residents to Touring Officers disguised as members of scientific and ethnological missions, to maintain an intelligence service that was 'infinitely supple'. André's visit coincided with increasing British concern about *mahdi*sm in northern Nigeria. Palmer, the Resident of Bornu, claimed to have discovered the existence of a *mahdi*st plot and had arrested a certain Mallam Said who was said to be in correspondence with Abdu Rahman, the son of the Sudanese *mahdi*. Mallam Said was detained and subsequently deported to Cameroun for twenty years. André was pleased to note that 'This time the English have acted the part of policeman in our favour'.[59]

André's mission continued back into AOF through Niger and Upper Volta. In Niger, André reported that there was widespread expectation that the *mahdi* would come three months after the close of Ramadan. The local Tijaniyya and Qadiriyya, he claimed, were on the best of terms and equally enthusiastic about the imminent coming of the *mahdi*. André went on to explain:

> Let us note that in the east of AOF the Tidjania chiefs are the descendants of one of our strongest enemies, the Peuhl Cheikh Oumar and that they have taken refuge in Nigeria, and that the Qadriya chiefs are equally the inheritors of the great Peuhl conqueror Othman dan Fodie and have been dispossessed of their paternal empire by the English and the French. It is therefore not in the least surprising that these inheritors of ancient bitterness are disposed to listen to bad and xenophobic advice.[60]

Although on this occasion André managed to get Usuman dan Fodio's ethnic origins correct he failed with the Tukolor al-Hajj Umar Tall, here described simply as a Fulbe. But quite apart from such points of detail,

159

André's comments reveal an exceptional ignorance of basic facts of West African history. Whilst it was true that al-Hajj Umar Tall's mid-nineteenth-century empire was destroyed by the colonial intervention, the same could not be said of the Sokoto caliphate of Usuman dan Fodio of which the basic administrative structure was preserved rather than destroyed by the British authorities. The loyalty of the northern emirs of northern Nigeria to the colonial authority has already been noted in the context of the Satiru revolt of 1906 and the situation was essentially the same in 1923. However, such matters were of no concern to André for by now he was hard on the trail of the *mahdi*. On his way from Niamey to Bamako in June, André summarised the situation:

> The descendant of the Qadria *mahdi* of Omdurman is trying to reorganise the active and xenophobic party of his fathers. The British authorities have uncovered this attempt but the would-be *mahdi* has tried and is still trying to win to his cause the descendants of the great conquering families of West Africa who have been dispossessed of their power by the English and the French.[61]

In Bobo Dioulasso in Upper Volta, André claimed that Martin, the local *commandant de cercle*, had reported that Islamic agitation was one of the factors which, along with exposure to xenophobic propaganda in Europe, explained the restlessness of the 7,000 *anciens tirailleurs* in the colony and which had resulted in massive exoduses to the Gold Coast. However, on reading this account of his conversation Martin was surprised to see these views imputed to him. He wrote to the Lieutenant-Governor of the colony to complain that he had been misrepresented. Martin's version was that he had said that animism was a much more powerful influence than Islam amongst the *anciens tirailleurs*, of whom in any case there were only 4,000 and not 7,000 as André had claimed. Furthermore, Martin had made no reference to massive exoduses to the Gold Coast but instead had told André of more limited movements to the Ivory Coast.[62] If Martin is to be believed, then these were major distortions on André's part and constitute a severe indictment of André's professional credibility. André left Upper Volta with his usual recommendations for organising an intelligence service and claimed (again how plausibly one cannot tell) that all the *commandants de cercle* were in favour of writing a monthly intelligence bulletin.[63]

Following André's warnings about the likelihood of the appearance of a *mahdi*, the Governor of Niger instructed one of the colony's administrators, M. Chatelain, to make an investigation. Chatelain spent several weeks in Nigeria and Niger trying to find further evidence of preparations for a *mahdi*st revolt. He reported that 'Neither the local *commandants* with whom I have been in touch nor the native chiefs who I have asked to make declarations, nor the English authorities in Katsina and Kano nor even myself have unearthed the slightest evidence of preparation for a revolt or the least symptom of unrest. . . . In all the regions through which I have travelled . . . the population are absolutely calm'. Nor was Chatelain impressed with the accuracy of André's account of British attitudes towards Islam. He did not believe that 'the English authorities attach a special importance to Islamic affairs'. Chatelain found no evidence of any military preparations in either Katsina or Kano to counter a *mahdi*st revolt and explained the reason for the British calmness:

> It must be said that the large protectorates shelter the English from many surprises. The emirs of the Muslim provinces would doubtless think twice before following commands given by anybody from the Orient ... As for the possibility of a popular movement prepared without knowledge of the sultans, it is unimagineable as through the actions of the twin police forces of the English authorities and the emirs ... the slightest beginning of agitation would immediately be surprised, and without doubt repressed.[64]

Chatelain was able to back up his arguments with a much more thorough and detailed knowledge of local personalities than André had been capable of doing. He showed that the Umarien section of Sokoto led by Maradi, the grandson of al-Hajj Umar and nephew of the Emir of Sokoto, had no interest in rebelling against either the British or the French, whatever these powers might have done to his forefathers.

Meanwhile André was coming to the end of his six-month mission throughout AOF and Nigeria. André concluded that apart from Mauritania (which he had not visited), AOF had lost its former 'creative faculty' in the matters of Islam and that now the main foyers of Islam were in British territories. The British, he said, were very worried by 'Qadirism ... the brotherhood of the great Toucouleur conqueror Othman dan Fodie' and had placed three companies of the Nigeria Regiment on stand-by to deal with any problems. André's thoroughly confusing discussion of the Tijaniyya moved rapidly to a survey of the Khalwatiyya in Asia Minor and the Sudanese Sayeed Abd el-Rahman el-Mahdi. André urged particular vigilance in the ports of Dahomey, Gold Coast and Nigeria and hoped that the British and French would continue their willingness to co-operate 'against the common enemies of the Orient'.[65]

However, the Governor-General's confidence in André's ability was severely shaken by Chatelain's report on the situation in Nigeria and Niger. He sent a copy of the report to Paris along with a note of the conclusions he had drawn up:

> Captain André, whose competence I do not deny, envisages Muslim affairs under a rather special light. He has a tendency to consider the different manifestations of the Islamic doctrine in profoundly Muslim countries and then extend and generalise the effects that these might have. He seems to lose sight of the fact that in this part of Black Africa the religious question is not the same as in countries which for a long time have been entirely ruled by Coranic law.... I would like to add that Captain André appears to deny our administration any competence in these matters and I have had to disabuse him of this belief. We have very well informed administrators who have been familiar with Islam for a long time and who ... follow with vigilance the evolution of our subjects, their tendencies and their aspirations and who draw

appropriate, practical and sensible conclusions from their judicious observations.[66]

The Minister of Colonies agreed that Chatelain was the more reliable judge of Islamic matters in AOF and that his report 'reduced to their just proportions incidents which Captain André in his imperfect understanding of Islam in AOF has unconsciously exaggerated'. However, the Minister warned that in the future the administration could not be so confident that Muslims in West Africa would be untouched by developments in the Arab world as in an era of better communications and improved educational standards contact within the Muslim community was bound to increase.[67]

All in all André did not emerge very favourably from his six-month mission as he seems to have antagonised a large number of colonial administrators. His name disappears from the archives around this time but the reason for this was probably not so much that he had been retired in disgrace but rather that he was preparing his notes for a book that he published the following year, *L'Islam noir: contribution à l'étude des confréries religieuses islamiques en Afrique occidentale*. That he was not entirely out of favour is suggested by the fact that Governor-General Carde agreed to write the preface for the book. The book itself rehearsed all the arguments that André had made during his mission (and, incidentally, repeated his confusion about Usuman dan Fodio who appeared as a Fulbe on page twenty-two and as a Tukolor on page twenty-three). André's most important argument concerned the growing internationalisation of Islam:

> Muslim questions, like most other political and economic questions of the present time, cannot be followed within the narrow frame-work of a colony, nor even a group of colonies. The growing importance of communications, increasing frequency of travel and the development of education are all abolishing the old frontiers.[68]

These were opinions which accorded well with the Minister of Colonies' opinions expressed in his letter to Carde who, it seems from his preface to André's book, was also of a like mind. André's actual description of *Islam noir* was divided into discussions of the various Sufi orders. The chapters were short and unremarkable with the exception of the chapter devoted to the Ahmadiyya, an order which originated in Pakistan and which had just started to gain a foothold in West Africa.[69] With fifteen pages it was the longest chapter in the book, even though by any account the order itself was probably the least typical form of Islam in West Africa. It was of interest to André, however, because having arrived on the West African coast with Indian traders it epitomised the new internationalism of Islam. It was a brotherhood of the sea-routes *par excellence*, and André believed it was a sign of things to come. Furthermore, the order's origins in the Indian sub-continent gave André an excuse to introduce Gandhi, Indian nationalism and the Non-Cooperation Movement into his discussion of African Islam.[70]

With the publication of *L'Islam noir* André ended his brief encounter with West African Islam. His departure from West Africa seems as mysterious as his arrival but it appears that he went on to have a successful military career, rising to the rank of General. It is interesting to see in 1952 that he was still publishing works on global studies of Islam in a changing world.[71] His failure to come to grips with West African Islam does not seem to have done his career any harm at all.

9

The French stake in Islam

André does not appear to have had any successor as advisor on Islamic affairs to the Governor-General until 1943 when Henri Martin, the first of a succession of graduates from the Centre des hautes études d'administration musulmane (CHEAM) was appointed to the newly created Bureau des affaires musulmanes in Dakar.[1] Indeed, on the whole, the French administration in Dakar during the 1920s and 1930s saw less cause for alarm in Islam than they had done in previous eras. The same could not be said of the Colonial Ministry in Paris which watched events in the Middle East with considerable apprehension. The optimism of Paris' hopes for an alliance with Turkey soon gave way to traditional fears about nationalism. In October 1923 the Colonial Minister wrote to Governor-General Carde in Dakar with a warning about nationalism in the Middle East:

> The Muslim world such as it has appeared throughout the centuries with its rigid fanaticism, its theocratic basis, its explosion of *mahdi*sm, its cult of saints and the influence of religious congregations seems to be wanting henceforward to evolve towards new destinies under the impulsion of a superficially secular ruling class.
>
> The leaders of the neo-nationalism have perfected the theory of pan-Islamism. They have used it to give a sense of direction to the vaguely formulated wishes for a renaissance in Islam as a reaction against Western domination.

He reminded Carde that the first ever meeting of Muslim delegates from all over the world was to take place in March to discuss the caliphate. He noted that although 'the conservatism of our African subjects keeps them outside the neo-Muslim movement', nonetheless the French could not be confident that this would always be true and he urged Carde to organise a central intelligence service. Carde copied the Minister's letter to the other colonies of AOF, all of whom replied that there was no cause for alarm but promised to make immediate enquiries.[2]

Nonetheless Carde insisted again on the importance of keeping influential marabouts and Arab traders under surveillance.[3] In February 1925 the Colonial Minister asked Carde whether or not AOF should send official

164

delegates to take part in the elections for a new caliph but Carde replied, predictably, that there was no point in this suggestion as Muslims in AOF were not interested in the election. However, Muslims were free to go privately if they so wished.[4] This sort of correspondence between Paris, Dakar and the colonies of AOF falls into a common pattern and, for all the talk of 'neo-nationalism' and 'neo-Islam', it was really no different to the correspondence during the war about the wisdom of sending African delegates to the Interministerial Commission on Muslim affairs.

Although fears of nationalism were genuine and, as the Porto Novo incidents and André's career demonstrate, a source of considerable anxiety to the French administration in Dakar, one should not exaggerate them. For throughout the years covered in this study fears about the development of Islam in the Middle East were always counterbalanced by the belief in the innate docility of Africans. Indeed, so confident were the French in the loyalty of African Muslims that the *tirailleurs sénégalais* were specifically recommended as the best troops to use in other Muslim countries.[5]

However, by the late 1920s the French had progressed from complacency towards an active realisation that they had acquired a considerable stake in Islam in AOF, a stake which was both economic and political and which was so important that it had to be carefully protected. It was difficult to date precisely the realisation of the existence of this community of interest between the French and the Sufi brotherhoods (for that was where the French stake was invested) but it became most obvious at the deaths of such people as el-Hajj Malick Sy, Sheikh Sidia and Ahmadu Bamba. Their deaths gave the French the chance to try and fragment their respective followings and divide the various Sufi orders into their component parts. However, the reverse of this policy was followed and the 1920s and 1930s witnessed instead an unprecedented degree of French intervention in the internal affairs of the Sufi orders in order to maintain a strong and unified command.

L'ENTENTE CORDIALE I: THE MOURIDES AND THE FRENCH

The doubts held by the French at the start of the war about Muslim loyalty were, as we have seen, soon dispelled. Attitudes towards the Mourides in particular were transformed, and the 1920s saw the start of the symbiotic relationship between the state and the Mouride brotherhood that has survived by and large to this day. The 'Rapport politique' for Senegal in 1925 noted the continued respect shown by all the religious leaders towards the French state and commented on Sheikh Ahmadu Bamba's request for permission to build a mosque in Touba:

> Monsieur, the administrator of Baol . . . has pointed out that this construction project . . . will help to attract and to fix a large number of natives in the region of Touba whose commerce and agriculture is just beginning to grow but whose population is insufficient. As a result of their work habits which are

165

> encouraged in the *talibés* by the Mouride cheikhs [these natives] will contribute to the economic development of this part of Diourbel.[6]

Permission to build the mosque was duly given at the end of April 1926. Around this time Ahmadu Bamba contributed 500,000 francs to a fund designed to help stabilise the French franc. This was a huge amount of money for an individual African and amounted to a quarter of what the whole of the Senegalese colony had been asked (but refused) to donate as a 'voluntary contribution'.[7]

The economic potential of the Mourides was by now far too tempting for the French. The 'Rapport politique' of 1926 acknowledged Bamba's contribution of 500,000 francs and continued:

> Although it is possible to regret the fact that we have allowed this Mouride power to establish itself because it might one day be a source of difficulties, it must be admitted that from an economic point of view the action of the Mourides has contributed enormously to the development of agricultural production in the region of Baol. This beneficial action is clearly a serious counterbalance to the possibility of future difficulties.[8]

By this time it was clear that Ahmadu Bamba did not have long to live and that there would be several possible contenders for his successor. The French believed that they had to decide between a policy of encouraging divisions within the brotherhood and of choosing a successor of whose loyalty they could be confident and who could be expected to maintain 'all the members of the brotherhood in the strictest discipline towards our authority'.[9]

They chose the second policy, and Ahmadu Bamba's eldest son, Mamadou Moustapha M'Backé, became the *Khalife* of the Mourides. The French backed him heavily against challenges to his leadership. With over one hundred files on Mouride marabouts in a special Mouride dossier,[10] the French were particularly well-informed about the brotherhood and felt very confident about intervening in its political struggles. In his annual report for 1928 the Lieutenant-Governor of Senegal stressed the importance of this fact and contrasted it with the lack of knowledge and understanding of the animist societies of Senegal:

> The influence of the chiefs of the Mouride sect is characterised by the fact that it is exercised in the open and in accordance with the representatives of the administration. The same is not true of the fetishists about whom we know nothing at all – neither about their rites and customs nor about their chiefs – for with a few rare exceptions the fetish priest has nothing in common with the village or canton chief. And it is because we have never been able to identify the true leaders of men and thus penetrate the mysteries of the different sects that in Casamance we have never touched the soul of the Diolas, Floups and Balantes who are as foreign to us now as they were when we first met them.[11]

Although the Mourides were probably the closest observed of all the various groupings in AOF, the same contrast between French knowledge of Muslim societies and ignorance of animist societies applied elsewhere. It

166

was a contrast that applied in the days of Faidherbe and it is interesting to see it being restated here as late as 1928.

The most serious challenge to Mamadou Moustapha M'Backé's leadership came from Sheikh Anta. Sheikh Anta had been discounted by the French as a possible successor to Ahmadu Bamba because it was felt that he was too much of a modern businessman to be trusted. Relations between Anta and the French worsened in the late 1920s. By July 1929 opposition to Sheikh Anta was a clearly stated policy as the following incident shows. Whilst on leave in Paris, Governor-General Carde heard that the *commandant de cercle* of Diourbel had given permission to Sheikh Anta to keep a piece of land which he had seized illegally. Carde wrote to his interim that he would be furious if this story was true: 'I have a policy and nobody . . . has the right not to follow it exactly. I forbid anybody to grant Sheikh Anta, who is my avowed enemy, a concession of land which he intends to use for speculation'. The Lieutenant-Governor of Senegal immediately instigated an investigation into the behaviour of the *commandant* of Diourbel from which it emerged that the *commandant*, faithful to Carde's policy, was doing all in his power to obstruct Sheikh Anta. He believed that the stories that had reached Carde had been spread by Sheikh Anta himself in order to discredit the new administration. Sheikh Anta was reported to be attempting to extricate himself from an obligation to pay 1.2 million francs towards the construction of the new mosque in Touba.[12] In February 1930 he was arrested and imprisoned for infringing emigration regulations on a recent trip ot Gambia[13] and he was kept under surveillance outside Senegal for the next three years. In July 1932 M. Cruel, a schoolteacher in Aix-en-Provence, whose link with Sheikh Anta is not clear in the sources, approached the Minister of Colonies asking for Sheikh Anta's release. The authorities in Dakar were, however, adamant in their opposition to such a move. The Service de sûreté in Dakar discovered that Cruel's action was merely the first part in an orchestrated campaign (by unnamed anti-colonial pressure groups) in France and in Senegal and alerted the Governor of Senegal who took steps to ensure that circulars and petitions on behalf of Sheikh Anta in the metropole did not reach the colonies.[14] In July 1933 the administration in Dakar still insisted that Sheikh Anta should not be allowed to return to Senegal. Groundnut prices had fallen sharply between 1931 and 1932 and this had resulted in a drastic cutback in production so that exports standing at 450,000 tonnes in 1931 had sunk to 190,000 in 1932. The administration, acutely aware of Senegal's total dependence on groundnuts, were anxious to increase production to nearer 500,000 tonnes and in order to do this, in the face of understandable peasant scepticism about the point of growing groundnuts at all, the administration was dependent on the co-operation of the Mouride leadership. To allow Sheikh Anta back to Senegal would risk alienating Mamadou Moustapha 'whose help' it was noted in July 1933 'is assured and which in the present circumstances is indispensable'.[15]

167

Another component in the complex relationships between Mamadou M'Backé, his uncle Sheikh Anta and the state were the political allegiances of the two Mouride protagonists. The *Khalife* backed, and was in turn backed by, Blaise Diagne whose arch rival, Galandou Diouf, had close links with Sheikh Anta. A measure of the significance of these alignments is shown in the fact that the release of Sheikh Anta did not come until Galandou Diouf was elected as Deputy for Senegal. The intrigue, corruption and vigour of Senegalese political life – which makes it read like an episode of Trollope in the tropics – has been fully chronicled by others[16] and little can be added to this story here. In 1939 Mamadou Moustapha M'Backé patched up his quarrel with Sheikh Anta. A special celebration was organised in Darou Mousty to which the *Khalife* travelled in a convoy of four cars. Sheikh Anta, for his part, travelled in a car that had been sold to him by Galandou Diouf for 45,000 francs[17] – another small illustration of the interplay between politics, religion and commerce that has made Senegal a favoured hunting ground for political scientists!

It was not just the politicians who were attracted to the Mourides' money. In 1926 the funds available for the construction of the new mosque in Touba ran to several million francs.[18] However, within months much of this money had found its way into other people's pockets, principally those of M. Tallerie, the administrator of Thies who had been charged with supervising the financing of the mosque. According to Balla M'Backé's bank statements, 916,529 francs were paid into Tallerie's account between the end of August 1926 and the beginning of February 1927. M. Brumauld, another French official, received 153,500 francs and, on Tallerie's instructions, Galandou Diouf was paid 70,000 francs.[19] The embezzlement was soon discovered, and the subsequent investigation showed that Tallerie had been tempted as a result of the illness of his wife in Senegal. He had intended to make a quick fortune out of the Mourides and then to return to France with his wife. Brumauld claimed that he had been tricked by Tallerie who had said that the authorities had approved all the payments.[20] This incident was another illustration of the extent to which the Mourides had imposed themselves upon the Senegalese political scene.

The relationships which variously tied the Mouride leadership to their peasant constituency, to the Senegalese urban élite and to the colonial state were now of such complexity that French perceptions of the brotherhood had increasingly little to do with religion. In January 1930 the *commandant de cercle* of Baol noted approvingly that since Ahmadu Bamba's death 'the general spirit of the sect is becoming less mystical, less fanatical and the sect is slowly but surely developing into a mutual aid religious association with economic aims'. As far as the French were concerned, the *commandant* argued, the brotherhood was 'a considerable economic force which the administration should use to spread new forms of cultivation and to develop the southern part of Djolloff and the north of Sine-Saloum'.[21] The French countenanced what has been described as 'le grand rush Mouride' to new lands in the interior.[22] The expansion of Mouride cultivation (concentrated mainly in the two periods from 1934–7 and 1942–5) brought them into conflict with the Fulbe who lived in the areas claimed by the Mourides, and fights were common. Although the administration deplored and sometimes punished the violence, no action was taken to prevent the displacement of the Fulbe. For example, in June 1936 a fight occurred between the Mourides and the Fulbe over some land which the Fulbe were cultivating. The Mourides were held responsible for causing the violence, their action was immediately disowned by Mamadou Moustapha M'Backé and their local leader was imprisoned for two months. However, their legal right to cultivate the land was upheld.[23]

Some doubts were raised about the degree of French support for and reliance upon the Mourides, but even dissenters agreed that in practice the French had little choice.[24] On the whole the administration was confident that its close relationship with the Mouride leadership was sufficient to ensure that French interests would not be overlooked. A CHEAM monograph, written in 1948 but based on the author's experiences in Senegal between 1936 and 1938, suggests that some of the administrators also believed in certain positive virtues of the brotherhood. Captain Chansard recalled that:

> One felt that there existed among the Mourides a solid organisation, which was accepted by all, a well-defined hierarchy and obedience to orders given by both religious and administrative chiefs, and an ardour for labour which one seldom came across elsewhere. In the villages the Mouride 'squares' were distinguished by their cleanliness, their prettiness even, with their yards and borders swept and tidy, their well-maintained and carefully cultivated fields.
>
> At the time of assemblies the men led by their chiefs presented themselves in an orderly and silent fashion, disciplined, *correcte*, robust in their appearance and having in no way the appearance of people reduced to servitude, on the contrary they showed a certain pride. They were clean and adequately dressed. The same was not true of the Serers and in certain other villages where there were no Mourides.[25]

These virtues of order and discipline, which recommended themselves so strongly to the intensely hierarchical structure of colonial administration, were the ones that the French had always been looking for in the Sufi brotherhoods of sub-Saharan Africa. They were the same virtues that Coppolani had argued would make the task of administering Muslim territories so simple but which, as we have seen, in practice often proved illusory. In this respect the history of French relations with the Mourides represented an undoubted success story for an Islamic policy *à la Coppolani*. But the Mourides were a special case.

L'ENTENTE CORDIALE II: THE TIJANIYYA AND THE FRENCH

French relations with the Tijaniyya, a brotherhood whose following, unlike that of the Mourides, was spread throughout West and, of course, North Africa were rather more complex. It will be recalled that the French conflict

169

with al-Hajj Umar Tall in the mid-nineteenth century had left the French
with a firm belief in the fanatical and militant nature of Tijani doctrine. This
was generally contrasted with the tolerant and peaceful nature of the
Qadriyya.[26] However, in the early twentieth century the French stereotypes
of the Tijaniyya had been substantially revised, mainly because of the
excellent relations between the French and el-Hajj Malick Sy, the leading
Tijani marabout in Senegal. The most dramatic example in the change in
Franco–Tijani relations emerged in the inter-war years in the person of
Seydou Nourou Tall, the grandson of al-Hajj Umar Tall.

After the French conquest of the Futa Toro the leadership of the
Umarian Tijaniyya was divided in its response to the French. Some moved
east to Sokoto and beyond in order to escape from the French completely,
and others stayed. Of those who stayed some – notably al-Hajj Umar's son,
Aguibu – allied themselves with the colonial power whilst others retreated
into a reclusive life of contemplation.[27] It was in these years that Seydou
Nourou Tall grew up. He received a traditional education studying with
Tijani marabouts in Khayes, Boghe and, finally, St Louis.[28] In St Louis he
established close relations with el-Hajj Malick Sy, cementing the relationship by marrying one of Malick Sy's daughters. From an early stage it seems
that Seydou Nourou Tall followed his father-in-law's example of cultivating
friendly relations with the French. However, he does not initially appear to
have met with much success. Marty, for example, dismissed him as someone
who 'exercises absolutely no influence in Senegal and who tries through his
tours and journeys to give his *baraka* sufficient prestige to allow him to live
comfortably'.[29] During the war Seydou Nourou Tall joined the army and
returned an officer.

His career did not take off properly until the death of el-Hajj Malick Sy in
1922. It was in this year that the French administration began to use him as
an ambassador of French civilisation and international trouble-shooter. The
transformation of the nonentity described by Marty into one of the most
important figures in West Africa was a dramatic one. More research is
needed before we can know exactly how this transformation came about.
The archival sources, such as they are, are not very helpful. A collection of
documents in the Federal Archives in Dakar nonetheless provides an
interesting testimony both to the wide-ranging nature of Seydou Nourou
Tall's tasks and the extent of French appreciation of his work. In 1938 de
Coppet, the Governor-General, arranged for a collection of several
hundred letters and reports about Seydou Nourou Tall written by various
administrators between 1923 and 1938 to be retyped and bound together in
book-form and offered to the *grand marabout* as a present. Without
exception the reports and letters sung the highest praise of this loyal servant
of France. The collection contains letters from all over AOF, and even some
parts of AEF, praising Seydou Nourou Tall for actions which ranged from
encouraging cultivation of cash crops and higher standards of personal
hygiene to adjudicating in local disputes and urging loyalty to France. The

essence of French satisfaction was summed up by the Governor of Mauritania, Brunot, in 1935:

> It is moving to think that the grandson of the greatest of our enemies is the greatest of our friends. When I told him that my father, under Faidherbe, had taken part in all the battles against his grandfather his face lit up with joy, doubtless at the thought of the great work that we have achieved in this our common country.[30]

The collection is indeed a remarkable one. The itinerary of Seydou Nourou Tall it reveals was an exhausting one that must have made him the best travelled man – French or African – in West Africa. The fact that he was frequently sent on missions to non-Muslim countries did not escape criticism. For example, M. Cau, an administrator in Senegal for ten years, drew up some notes for use in training administrators on Islam in Senegal in which he argued that the Dakar authorities had made excessive use of Seydou Nourou Tall and that by sending him to non-Muslim countries they were encouraging the spread of Islam.[31] However, the symbolism of al-Hajj Umar's grandson appearing as the most enthusiastic of French supporters was understandably too tempting for the French. What Frenchman could have resisted giving as wide publicity as possible to an African who could outdo the French themselves in his awareness of the glory of the civilising mission? On Bastille Day 1939 Seydou Nourou Tall broadcast to the whole of AOF:

> Today is the opportunity for we overseas Frenchmen to affirm our attachment to the mother-country which unceasingly introduces more happiness and well-being among its coloured children. The French Republic which has won its liberty and brought it to the rest of the world has liberated ourselves from disease, poverty, servitude and cruel traditions which prevented Black Africa from flourishing ...
>
> My ancestors fought against France and as a child I followed them until the day I realised that France not only came to the native with her hand held out in friendship but that she also knew how to bend over towards him, not to exploit him but to comfort him and make him aware of his dignity as a man, respectful of his legitimate traditions and beliefs ... Whatever the circumstances, France, our country, will find African populations prepared for all eventualities even to the supreme sacrifice.[32]

Seydou Nourou Tall cannot be dismissed as an unthinking stooge of the French. In terms of Islamic doctrine his response to colonial rule was a perfectly acceptable position which had already been taken by many other Muslim leaders in colonised countries. However, it was by no means the only possible response and other Tijani marabouts adopted a different strategy. Of the alternative strategies open to all Muslims the possibility of withdrawing from political life altogether and attempting to restrict contact with the colonising power to a minimum was more common than outright hostility. However, such a strategy was not an easy one to pursue successfully as the career of Sheikh Hamallah, a Tijani marabout from Nioro

171

illustrates. Sheikh Hamallah was one of the most controversial figures in West Africa between the wars, and over the years the facts of his life have been obscured behind the slurs and myths of both his detractors and his followers. Recent scholarship has done much, however, to uncover the reality.[33]

Sheikh Hamallah was born in 1886 of a Moorish father and a Fulbe mother. In the course of his education he acquired a reputation for learning and pietism. The environment in which he grew up was a tense one in which the French having successfully destroyed the Umarian hegemony were unable to replace it with a comparable power. The fragmented Tijani leadership was incapable of preventing the recently Islamicised Bambara of the region around Nioro from reverting to their traditional religious beliefs. Nevertheless, Nioro remained one of the principal Islamic centres of West Africa. Marty described it as 'the boulevard of African Islam in the region of Upper Senegal' and ranked it with Djenné and Timbuktu in terms of the vigour of Islamic life and the influence through the network of *dyula* merchants that it had on surrounding areas.[34]

Around the turn of the century an Algerian Tijani marabout called al-Akhdar appeared in Nioro. According to the Hamallist versions he had been sent by the Caliph of the Tlemcen *zawiya* in Algeria to identify a successor as caliph who would also be capable of reviving the Tijaniyya south of the Sahara. Sheikh Hamallah, it was claimed, was the person revealed to him through a number of esoteric signs as being the person who had been chosen to lead the Tijaniyya. This version, however, is contested by other Tijani leaders who do not recognise the legitimacy of al-Akhdar's mission and who consequently reject the claim of Hamallah's followers that Hamallah was the Caliph of the Tijaniyya.[35] What is clear is that al-Akhdar preached a purified form of Tijani doctrine whose most distinctive feature, though scarcely the most important, was the practice of repeating one of the Tijani prayers known as 'The Jewel of Perfection' eleven times instead of the usual twelve. Sheikh Hamallah adopted the practice of repeating the prayer eleven times, and as a result of this all his followers were frequently referred to in the colonial literature as 'Tidjania onze grains' (after the number of prayer beads on the Muslim rosary) as opposed to the supposedly orthodox 'Tidjania douze grains'. The awe with which the authorities were to view the practice of repeating the prayer eleven times was in many respects every bit as superstitious and mysterious as the respect of the West African Muslim for the esoteric sciences of his marabout!

By 1910 Sheikh Hamallah had begun to attract a significant following. At the same time local Tijani leaders became increasingly suspicious and fearful of Hamallah's growing reputation and, in an atmosphere marked by a serious drought in 1913, relations between Hamallah – or more particularly his followers – on the one hand and the old guard of the Tijani leadership on the other, were tense.[36] Nonetheless there is little indication that at this stage the French were unduly concerned by Hamallah. Marty's account published in 1920 recognised the importance of Sheikh Hamallah but it did not suggest that he was a danger:

> [He] is the most curious figure in Nioro and one of the leading Muslim personalities of the Sahelian–Moorish borders. At the moment he is no more than a bubbling spring but a spring which one can see from the growing force of its current, the virtue which everybody attributes to its waters and the convergence of neighbouring streams, will become a great river.[37]

This picturesque metaphor hardly suggests the extreme hostility with which Hamallah was later to be regarded. Marty continued:

> Cheikh Hamallah is above all a mystic and it is upon this that his reputation is based . . . His attitude to us is correct but reserved and he only comes to the office of the *cercle* if he is formally called to do so. It seems that with a bit of skill we could co-opt him very quickly.[38]

Marty noted that his influence was already very great with the Moors of Nioro and that he also had some Moorish followers in the region of Kayes and some Soninke followers in villages some way away from Nioro. Marty acknowledged that Hamallah had some powerful local enemies but stressed that he had not got involved in any of the various intrigues caused by this enmity. Finally, Marty was pleased to note that the Moors who were in his obedience were the ones who were 'the most docile to our orders'.[39]

However, not for the first time Marty's balanced and perceptive judgement was ignored and within five years of the publication of Marty's report Hamallah had been transformed in French eyes into a sinister fanatic: the 'bubbling spring' had been badly poisoned. This transformation can in part be explained by the death of el-Hajj Malick Sy in 1922 which removed a moderating influence from the authorities in Dakar.[40] But the major factor appears to have been the accusation that Hamallah was implicated in a series of violent disputes in 1923 and 1924. The violence was investigated by a French administrator, Descemet, and it was his report which more than anything else seems to have sealed Hamallah's fate. It is interesting to note that as late as May 1925 the Governor of Sudan, Brévié, made no mention of Hamallah's supposed role in the violence of the previous two years. In his report to the Governor-General on the state of Islam in the colony Brévié simply noted that:

> In Nioro, a marabout, Cherif Hamala, living as an ascetic and distributing almost all of the numerous presents which are given to him as alms, is trying to regroup the Tidjania and is using the eleven bead rosary as the rallying sign.[41]

Yet by the end of the year Hamallah had been arrested and sentenced to ten years' exile in Mauritania.

Descemet's report was undoubtedly a major factor in this transformation. The report was a damning one and concluded that although Hamallah was not personally involved in anti-French agitation, he had done nothing to prevent it. Descemet described Hamallah as 'a sly and hypocritical enemy of the French colonial regime'.[42] The case has many parallels with the *wali* of Goumba: Hamallah like the *wali* in his later life, attempted to restrict his relations with the French to a minimum and was the victim, as was the *wali*, of a campaign of insinuation inspired in part by other Africans but championed by a French administrator, with Descemet playing the part that Mariani had done in the Futa Jallon. However, it would be a mistake to ascribe Hamallah's punishment entirely to individual caprice, for the international situation must also be taken into account.

Hamallah was exiled to Mederdra in Mauritania but the continuation of disturbances associated with Hamallah's followers convinced the authorities that he was still able to exert an anti-French influence. It must be remembered that the French were still engaged in the military conquest of Mauritania and that vast areas in the north of the country were beyond their control. In addition across the Sahara in Morocco they were facing fierce resistance. Towards the end of the 1920s there were growing signs of impatience in the French administration at their lack of progress in Mauritania. In September 1928 Governor-General Carde noted with regret that French policy of trying to win the submission of the northern nomads through peaceful means had failed to achieve anything. This policy was associated in particular with Lieutenant-Governor Gaden, and Carde claimed that it had outlived its usefulness. He quoted from a recent book written by a French officer in Mauritania: 'Why delude ourselves with the vain hope of leading dissidents to submit voluntarily when they are secure and out of our reach?'[43] Henceforward, Carde urged that allies should be made to show positive proof of their loyalty and that enemies should be strictly punished. Gaden and his supporters were ousted in a change of regime in Mauritania and were replaced by hardliners led in St Louis by Lieutenant-Governor Chazal and, in command of the army in Adrar, Commandant Dufour who was noted for his 'energetic temperament' – a military euphemism for his thirst for battle. However, Dufour's lack of courtesy to just about everybody earned him hostility in Dakar and Mauritania, and he was soon replaced.[44] One of the most embarrassing incidents to the French, which highlighted their weakness in the area, occurred in 1928 when two French airmen who had had to make a forced landing in the desert were taken hostage by anti-French Moors. The French sent a negotiating team (which included the Emir of Trarza) and were forced to make concessions to their enemies in order to secure the release of the two pilots, Reine and Serre. Carde's worries were twofold: locally in Mauritania he had been forced to admit the weakness of the French position but he could not risk a military expedition for fear of a hostile reaction in the metropolitan press which by and large agreed with Gaden that the conquest of Mauritania was not worth the loss of French lives – especially civilians like the two pilots. This delicate situation was reflected in the ambiguous nature of Carde's 'Note' on French policy in Mauritania from which we have quoted above, in which although Carde clearly did not approve of Gaden's reluctance to fight he was unable to condone the 'energetic' policy of Dufour. However, what is more directly relevant to the discussion here is that Sheikh Hamallah was included in the list of twenty prisoners whose release was demanded by the Moors in exchange for releasing the two French hostages.[45] This particular demand was not, of course, met by the French, and Hamallah remained their prisoner. This incident is an important reminder of the political context within which French attitudes to Hamallah must be understood. The fact that Hamallah's name was now so explicitly linked to forces resisting the French in Mauritania (and in southern Morocco) was bound to convince the French that they were right to see Hamallah not as an other-worldly ascetic, but as a dedicated opponent to French colonial rule.[46] It is important to emphasise this aspect of a corrective to the impression in Traoré's account that French hostility to Hamallah was founded on the personal animosities of certain influential French administrators. For the French – not a collection of individuals but rather a colonial power with strategic interests on both sides of the Sahara – had reason to fear Hamallah who was as much the victim of the dictates of imperial strategy as he was of the slurs and innuendoes of individuals, both French and African.

The next major event connected with Hamallah occurred towards the end of 1928 when disturbances and fighting broke out in the region of Kaedi in Mauritania. The central figure in these events appears to have been a Soninké disciple of Hamallah called Yacoub Sylla. Yacoub Sylla was said to have exacerbated already existing divisions within the Tijani community of Kaedi by, amongst other things, ordering women to adopt a Moorish style of dress, to give away their gold jewelry and to make public confessions of their adultery – all of which led to a great deal of bitterness, not to mention a dramatic fall in the local price for gold. The *commandant* ordered everybody to follow the 'orthodox' Tijani prayer formula and forbade Yacoub Sylla to return to the area. He further noted that 'The credulity of the Sarakoles is well known and it is necessary to shelter them from the charlatans of Islam'.[47] However, tension remained high and in December 1929 and February 1930 violence broke out. On the latter occasion the French opened fire on a crowd of Yacoub Sylla's supporters killing between thirty-five and eighty people. The official report blamed the deaths on the Hamallists who were described as constituting a phenomenon of 'a collective and mystical madness'.[48]

Although it was admitted that no direct blame could be attached to Hamallah himself, it was nonetheless decided that he should be sent further away from Mauritania to spend the remaining years of his exile in Adzopé in the Ivory Coast. In March 1930 Carde issued a circular note on the subject of the Tijaniyya in AOF. He recalled the division between what he called the xenophobic and anti-French Moroccan branch of the order and a more tolerant Algerian branch. He reminded his administration that it was the Moroccan branch that had spread to the colonies of AOF, and continued:

> This historical insight indicates that the Tidjanisme practised in the colonies of the group [i.e. AOF] is impregnated with a xenophobic political character and that, transposed unchanged, the Moroccan doctrine inevitably presents the fanatical and anti-French aspect which characterised the teaching of el-Hadj Omar and his son Ahmadou Cheikou.
>
> The loyal attitude of the majority of the leading cheikhs of local Tidjanisme ... naturally reassures us. However, one should not lose sight of the fact that beyond these cheikhs who are personally won over to us, other cheikhs, or even simple *moqaddem*, may suddenly appear who are more attached to the cause of religion than to our own.

Movements of reformist Tijani (and Carde cited in this context the example of Aly Yoro Diaw in Dagana in 1908) always, he said, attracted the youngest and most troublesome elements of society. 'Cherif Hamallah's success can only be understood in the light of these considerations' and he continued:

> The question is one of psychological rather than truly doctrinal causes. The action of the reformist marabout was quickly appreciated because it revealed the sectarianism that is latent in the minds of all Tidjani and because it offered an opportunity for the surviving disciples of the Toucouleur Prophet to come out of their disenchanted retirement. The significance of his propaganda was above all that it rallied the latent opposition forces of Islam.... The eleven-beaded rosary threatened to become the rallying sign of Muslim xenophobia.[49]

With this warning to all the colonies of AOF, Hammallah was firmly implanted in French minds as a dangerous enemy and henceforward administrators were expected to keep a close look-out for that outward sign of Islamic resistance – the eleven-beaded rosary. The fear expressed in Carde's circular that Hamallah might be capable of playing the same role that al-Hajj Umar had played in the Futa Toro some seventy years before was particularly significant, for it was the experience of the resistance led by Umar which more than anything else coloured subsequent French attitudes towards Islam in the early twentieth century.

In 1933 the French claimed to have uncovered a 'veritable conspiracy' centred on Yacoub Sylla's brother, Fode Sylla, in the *cercle* of Koutiala in Sudan. Brévié, the Governor-General, reported to Paris that Fode Sylla had proclaimed himself *mahdi* and had preached that the French would be powerless against Africans in an imminent war. By chance an African *garde de cercle* overheard a discussion about the war which he reported to the *commandant*. An enquiry was instituted and, in the course of April and May, Fode Sylla, and thirteen of his followers were arrested and given prison sentences varying from ten to twenty years. Brévié reported that the plan had been to massacre Europeans on the night of the *Tabaski* (the feast of *al-Kabir*) on 6 April and that in view of the fanaticism involved it was likely that 'the worst and most odious crimes *would have been perpetrated*'.[50] However, the seriousness of this conspiracy and, indeed, of the anti-French nature of the Hamallists in general was not universally accepted. Beyries, a future Governor of Mauritania, argued that:

> The 'way' of Cherif Hama Allah is no more xenophobic than any other Muslim mystic 'way'. Circumstances must lend themselves in order to make these 'ways' into machines to combat Europeans ... The conspiracy is reduced simply to the speech of some fanatics whose importance has been greatly exaggerated.[51]

Nonetheless, such a view was a minority one.

Meanwhile Hamallah was finishing his sentence in the Ivory Coast. The administrator of the *cercle* in which he was kept reported in March 1935 that 'Since [Hamallah] arrived in Adzopé he has made no conciliatory advance which would allow us to believe that he has modified his sentiments'. Because of this he recommended that Hamallah should be made to serve the full length of his sentence and not be granted any remission – even though he would have been glad to expel from Adzopé a person whom he called 'a living example to the native of opposition to the French cause'. Brévié agreed with this judgement and reported to Paris that, like the Bourbon court, in exile Hamallah 'had learnt nothing and forgotten nothing'.[52]

Hamallah returned to Nioro after serving out his full ten-year sentence in January 1936. On his return he adopted the practice of abridging his prayers, an option that was open to Muslims only when they were travelling, felt threatened or were at war. The significance of this act was not lost on either fellow Muslims or on the French administration. Hamallah's presence in Nioro attracted large numbers of visitors who returned to their homes also abridging their prayers. This new development worried the French. In an influential report on the spread of this practice in the region of Adrar, Lieutenant Long, a French military interpreter in Mauritania, argued that the shortened prayer was of 'exceptional seriousness' and proceeded to spell out for French benefit its significance in Islamic doctrine. Lieutenant Long warned that the greatest danger to the French lay in localised unrest in which the Hamallists could be expected to gain new martyrs for their cause. He regretted that in Adrar, where at least twenty-five leading Moors had recently returned from visiting Hamallah, the French could not count on any marabouts of sufficient stature to counter Hamallah's influence and he argued that France's best hope lay in 'buying off' the local chiefs and making them 'prisoners of honour'.[53]

The use of the shortened prayer worried the French greatly. In February 1937 de Coppet, the new Governor-General, circulated details of Long's report, adding that:

> The verses on which the 'abbreviators' based themselves must be considered as manifestly bearing the sign of combatant Islam and one is justified in fearing that these people will gradually acquire a somewhat anti-French orientation in the course of the exercise of their religious practices.

177

De Coppet stressed furthermore that Hamallah was ultimately responsible for all that his followers did:

> Even if he does not himself go so far as to indulge in specifically criminal activity that would justify a sanction, he makes use of indirect means, which superficially bear the marks of detachment and disdain but which are carefully thought out and adapted to achieve the required aim. This silent aggression not only may encourage the 'differentiated' Tidjaniyans – who are already too inclined towards ecstatic excitation and xenophobic reactions – to show disaffection to the protecting nation but also it bears within itself the seeds of discord and sharp doctrinal quarrels between Muslims themselves.

All administrators were consequently urged to keep a close watch for the appearance of the abbreviated prayer formula.[54] This message was repeated in a further circular issued in September:

> The use of exceptional formulas reserved 'in case of alert' is all the more serious because the writings and especially the poetry which are of a xenophobic nature and which are being circulated clandestinely by the followers of 'Hammalism' leave little doubt about the underlying intention of the leader of this religious movement.

De Coppet agreed with the analysis of the Governor of Mauritania which linked the popularity of Hamallism with the aspirations of the poorer and disadvantaged elements of society. He also agreed with the Governor's conclusion that although this made the French more sympathetic to Hamallism 'There can be no question of encouraging the movement for to do so would alienate the followers of the old Islam'. For de Coppet, who owed his position to the election of the Popular Front Government in France, the association of the Hamallists with the poorer elements of society placed him in an ideological dilemma. He did not want to be seen to be persecuting a religious movement which might be labelled as 'progressive' in metropolitan circles but neither was he prepared to give the movement total freedom. The dilemma was resolved by distinguishing between the 'justifiable aspirations of the poor' and the selfish political and material ambitions of their leaders. The French task then was to intercede in order to protect the poor from their 'bad shepherds' – language and sentiment that was entirely in keeping with the colonial policy of the Popular Front. The administration were to try and persuade the mainstream Tijani to be more tolerant and understanding of the desires of 'the humble mass of the dispossessed'. The attack on the 'bad shepherds', however, was to be firm and comprehensive, and de Coppet went on to list a number of measures that could be used against Hamallism. On a psychological level, first of all, the aura of ascetic and other-worldly mysticism surrounding Hamallah was to be destroyed by broadcasting stories of how Hamallah had mocked and mistreated elderly marabouts; doubts about the theological soundness of Hamallah's doctrine were to be encouraged (and de Coppet noted with some satisfaction that in 1937, for the first time in twenty-five years, numerous leading Qadiri and 'orthodox' Tijani mara-bouts had made tours in Mauritania to collect *ziara* and had all taken the opportunity to preach against Hamallah); and lastly the French could themselves make use of superstition and fear: 'The counter propaganda of the old brotherhoods could even take place at time of drought, local famines, plagues of locust and other calamities when public opinion is alert and anxious to know the hidden reasons for the bad luck that has temporarily hit them'. On the more conventional level of police action, de Coppet reminded his administrators that the legislation already existed which would enable them to punish speeches and the sale of books and pamphlets which denigrated the French with prison sentences of up to two years and to punish the more serious crime of conspiracy and organising against the French with prison sentences of up to twenty years.[55]

It seemed for a while as if the 'counter offensive' of the established marabouts was to be successful. In September 1937 Seydou Nourou Tall persuaded Hamallah that he need fear nothing from the French and that, therefore, he should revert to the normal prayer formula. However, this brief reconciliation between the two branches of the Tijaniyya was short-lived and broke down in the tension which quickly resurfaced between Hamallah and his supporters on the one hand and the 'establishment' Tijani on the other.[56] Hamallah was unable to prevent further violence from breaking out in 1938 in the region of Nioro. His eldest son, in particular, was humiliated by a hostile Moorish tribe and resolved to exact his revenge. According to Traoré, he made clandestine preparations against his enemies swearing his allies to secrecy, even from his father. His efforts culminated in a bloody battle in the village of Mouchgag in 1940. Hamallah protested his innocence of these events and condemned the violence used by the followers of his son. The Vichy authorities were convinced, however, that he was implicated and he was arrested in June 1941 along with several hundred of his followers who were all sent to prison camps in AOF. Inevitably, perhaps, given the way in which Islamic unrest was always regarded as being in part at least caused by enemies of metropolitan France, it was suspected that a Free French agent, a certain M. Montezer, who had arrived in West Africa shortly before the war and who had published a small handbook on Islam, had had a part in the violence.[57] Hamallah himself was deported to Algeria and thence to France where he died of pneumonia in the military hospital of Montluçon in January 1943.[58]

Hamallah was the victim of the narrowness of the French vision of Islam. Throughout the period discussed in this book but particularly during the 1920s and 1930s, the French divided Muslims into two categories: those who *actively* supported the French and those who did not. This narrowness of vision was compounded by the essentially ahistorical understanding of African society which characterised almost all colonial thinking on colonised societies. The French arrived in West Africa at a specific juncture in the development of West African societies and believed that 'the Africa' they had encountered was the product of an unchanging past, a 'primitive' society that had not changed in centuries. Hamallah was forced into this ideological straitjacket: he inevitably revived memories of al-Hajj Umar and, in the end, the French were never able to believe that he did not cherish exactly the same ambitions as the Tukolor leader. This misconception was encouraged by the representatives of *le vieil Islam* whom de Coppet was not prepared to alienate. For the authority of the old guard depended to a large extent on the trick which the colonial authorities had played with history. The 'orthodox' Tijani leaders and the *ulema* of Nioro had a vested interest in reminding the authorities that the leopard (i.e. reformist Islam) can never change his spots, and Hamallah paid the price. It is these sorts of factors, along with the sort of strategic interests which we have described above, that must be taken into account if the degree of French hostility to Hamallah is to be properly understood. Even so, the French probably would have been prepared to call off their campaign against Hamallah had he been willing to intervene *actively* in all areas of life on behalf of the French, but this, for his own deeply held religious convictions, he was not prepared to do.[59] A CHEAM monograph written in 1941 detailed the French reasoning:

> Cherif Hamallah is more than an important religious personality, he is also a political force as a result of the enormous influence and obedience which he commands. Therefore, we can at least reproach him for not having used this influence to stop the exactions and brutalities of his disciples, who are generally at the origin of these quarrels: *il a laissé faire, voilà pourquoi sa responsabilité est lourde.*[60]

The experiences of the relations between the French, the Mourides and the Tijaniyya in the 1920s and 1930s show some interesting similarities. (It should be said that some of the following comments apply equally to the experience of the Muslim communities in Porto Novo.)

The first comment to be made is that the French intervened very directly in the internal affairs of the brotherhoods, and this was a policy which contrasted with the pre-war consensus according to which the French ought to have remained as aloof as possible from internal disputes. The reasons for this change of policy towards intervention were firstly that, after the work of Marty and the continued build-up of files on Muslim individuals, the French were much better informed about Muslim politics and, therefore, more confident of their ability to intervene successfully and, secondly, that increasingly they now had vested interests in certain sections of the Muslim community. The most striking example of this vested interest was their economic stake in the Mourides but equally they had a substantial political stake in Seydou Nourou Tall. By the 1920s the French had made very real political and economic investments which they were naturally very anxious to safeguard. Thus when these investments were threatened either directly, as in the case of Sheikh Anta, or indirectly, as in the case of Hamallah, the French were obliged to intervene.

The second general comment is that the French were now seen to be anxious to preserve the monolithic structure of the Sufi brotherhood in West Africa whereas before the war the conventional wisdom was that French interests were best served by a policy of 'divide and rule' based on encouraging religious and ethnic particularism.

The third and final comment concerns the fossilisation of French relations with the brotherhoods. Before the war relations between the French and the Mourides, for example, were very fluid – so fluid in fact that the French policy shifted from a position of outright hostility to one of cautious support. The same was true to a lesser extent of the Tijaniyya. However, in the 1920s and 1930s the French stake in the two brotherhoods was such that not only could the French not challenge the brotherhoods but also they could not afford to let anyone else challenge them either. There were, in these terms, only two possible positions – either for or against the officially sponsored leadership. Two factors, however, were able to qualify these rigid divisions and categories: elections and the influence of the metropolitan press. Sheikh Anta would not have been rehabilitated were it not for the fact that the Senegalese voters of the Four Communes elected Galandou Diouf. Likewise all administrators had to keep half an eye open to the possibility of adverse comments in the metropolitan press.

The metropolitan factor was an increasingly important one in the inter-war period though its precise importance is not easy to quantify. There were a number of different pressure groups who took an interest in colonial affairs of which the most significant were the Union intercoloniale (f. 1921), Ligue de la défense de la race nègre (f. 1926) and the Ligue contre l'oppression coloniale et l'impérialisme (f. 1927, President, Albert Einstein). In addition both the Communists (PCF) and the Socialists (SFIO) together with their respective trade-union allies were broadly anti-colonialist in their orientation, though the nature of their anti-colonialism requires some comment. Until 1936 the PCF followed the Moscow line in denouncing colonialism itself, whereas the SFIO denounced only the abuses of colonialism and not the system. The PCF moved towards the position of the SFIO as it became clear that priority should be given to opposing the rise of fascism in Europe. Individuals, such as André Gide, were sometimes able to bring conditions in the French colonies to the attention of the French public. It is, however, very difficult to gauge the effect of the various types of anti-colonial activity on public opinion. The inter-war years were after all the years in which the 'colonial idea' achieved its greatest popularity with the French, and it would probably be more realistic to emphasise the *lack* of interest shown by the political parties in criticising colonialism and in campaigning on behalf of France's colonial subjects. In any case little attention was paid to Black Africa in comparison to North Africa and Indo-China. So, in describing the metropolitan factor as it affected West Africa's Muslim population, we must recognise the fact that some West Africans were able to get access to politicians and to newspapers but that

181

the avenues for doing so were rather haphazard and that the effectiveness of the various groups and individuals who lobbied on their behalf was very uncertain.[61]

The willingness of the French to intervene in Muslim affairs is a useful corrective to the notion that the inter-war years marked a shift towards 'indirect rule' or in French terms a policy of 'association'. Such labels serve little purpose in aiding our understanding of the mechanics of colonial rule and were, in any case, designed chiefly for metropolitan consumption to win support for budget allocations in the Chamber of Deputies or the House of Parliament. In the next chapter we shall discuss another form of interventionism associated with a very particular era in French history, the Popular Front (1936–8).

10

The 'rediscovery' of Islam

By the 1930s the French had identified their stake in Islam and were prepared to go to considerable lengths to protect it. Such a policy had been made possible by the gradual evolution of a consensus within the French administration regarding the nature of Islam itself: namely a religion which bore little resemblance to the 'orthodox' model of the Arab world but which was much closer to the pre-Islamic traditional African beliefs and which was held together almost solely through the agency of the Sufi brotherhoods. This understanding of Islam was shared by all but a few mavericks who were convinced of the innate fanaticism of the Muslim faith. It was an understanding which was undoubtedly patronising but which was also immensely reassuring to the French administration.

There were, however, some signs in the late 1930s that the consensus was being at least questioned if not seriously challenged. The early focus of the questioning was the Mauritanian administration of de Coppet and Beyries and with de Coppet's promotion to Governor-General he brought with him some new ideas and initiatives concerning Franco–Islamic relations. De Coppet was not unfortunately in power for enough time for us to draw very firm conclusions about how seriously he challenged prevailing ideas on Islam. Furthermore, the declaration of war in Europe in 1939 and the advent of the Vichy regime in Dakar in 1940 heralded such abrupt changes that it is doubly difficult to place de Coppet in his correct context.

THE REVIVAL OF THE *MÉDERSA* IDEA

Amongst a series of educational reforms introduced in 1924[1] was a specific provision for the inclusion of Qur'ānic education within the overall structure. The Decree of 1 May 1924 gave Lieutenant-Governors of Islamised colonies the authority (providing they had the Governor-General's approval) to establish *médersa*s whose 'essential aim is to establish a point of contact between literate Muslims and our administrators by the training of interpreters, judges and secretaries of native tribunals'.

In view of some of the misgivings expressed before the war about the benefits of the *médersa* system it is perhaps not surprising that there was no rush of Lieutenant-Governors eager to take advantage of the new law. Indeed, it was not until 1930 that the first *médersa* was established as a result of it. Conditions for admission to the Boutilimit *médersa*, established by Chazals, the Lieutenant-Governor of Mauritania, made it plain that entry was to be limited to the sons of the nobility.[2] Clearly the confusion between the *médersa* and the Ecole des fils des chefs, which had been evident in the early history of the St Louis *médersa*, had still to be resolved.[3]

The old formula for a *médersa* of a school which provided education in a vaguely Islamic idiom for sons of chiefs appealed to the authorities. In 1932 Brévié wrote to the Lieutenant-Governor of Sudan urging him to establish an institution along the lines of the Boutilimit *médersa* that would contribute effectively to the training of the *commandement indigène* of the Moors and Tuaregs of Sudan. The Lieutenant-Governor obliged with a *médersa* at Timbedra in the Hodh region. The first year's report explained that the local administrator had been firm with the chiefs in getting them to send their sons to the *médersa*. The problem of recruitment thus dealt with, the staff were now seeking to teach their young Moorish charges the elementary rules both of hygiene and of football and to get them used as soon as possible to eating from individual plates.[4] The following year it was reported that great care was being taken to provide good food for the pupils so that 'Parents could never cite the mediocrity of the food given to their children as an excuse to refuse to entrust them to us'. Despite this very French consideration, recruitment of sons of important chiefs was a problem and the author of the annual report, M. Assomption, the head of the Education Department of the Sudan, was forced to conclude that 'true chiefs were very rare in the Sahel'. He further believed that the senior Moorish teacher, Mohammed Moctar Dicko, the brother of the chief of the Awlad Nacer (and 'our only collaborator amongst the Moorish race'), was purposely obstructing the French. The Senegalese teacher, Ahmadou Ba, however, was reported to be honest and hard-working. Assomption proposed replacing Mohammed Dicko with the wife of the French director of the *médersa*, Mme. Follenfant. She would, he said, not only be able to supervise catering and laundry, but would also be able to provide for the younger boarders 'a point of affection and devotion of which women alone are capable'.[5]

Assomption appeared to have applied criteria which were more suited to a provincial French boarding school than to a training-school for future chiefs and civil servants in West Africa. His assertion, too, that Mohammed Moctar Dicko was the 'only' Moorish collaborator either betrays an appalling ignorance of France's position in Mauritania and Sudan or, perhaps, suggests a more general dislike of the non-black indigenous population. Without any further evidence, however, one should reserve judgement on his qualifications to inspect the *médersa*.

In any case it is clear that other administrators did not share the generally negative view of the *médersa* which is suggested in Assomption's report. The Lieutenant-Governor of Sudan considered establishing a similar institution in Bamba, a town some 150 miles east of Timbuktu on the Niger Bend, to cater for the colony's Tuareg population, but considered it unlikely that the success of the Timbedra *médersa* could be repeated because of 'the profound difference which separates Arab and Berber mentalities'. The Tuareg, he said, had no taste for intellectual work and most of them 'have not yet abandoned hope of seeing us leave their country and of resuming their life of pillage and plunder'. Previous attempts, he noted, to recruit Tuareg pupils to French schools had led to 'a dangerous restiveness'.[6]

The creation of a *médersa* in Atar (Mauritania) in January 1936 suggested that the administration was now convinced that the *médersa*s had a vital role to play in their recruitment and training of a *commandement indigène*.[7] The issue was very much at the forefront of the administration's thinking in the 1930s. Brévié, as Governor-General, had argued that special attention should be given to the training of traditional chiefs who should be integrated more fully into the administrative structure.[8] It was not an original argument – Ponty and Carde, for example, had both argued in this way – but it does seem to have been applied with greater conviction and sophistication by Brévié.[9] It is in the context of French policies towards chiefs rather than towards Islam that the *médersa* programme in the years 1924 to 1936 should be judged.

By 1936, however, there were signs of a shift in emphasis. Article 2 of the 'Décision' creating the Atar *médersa*, for example, stipulated that the *médersa* had two functions: firstly 'to ensure the maintenance of classical Arab culture in Upper Mauritania' and, secondly 'to train an indigenous élite, educated by contact with us'.[10] The order in which these two functions were listed is instructive in itself but it is the idea that *médersa*s should be servants of Arab culture that deserves special attention. It was one of the first signs that the French believed that the *médersa* should revert to its pre-colonial role as a centre of Islamic scholarship. Although the Atar *médersa* was reserved exclusively for sons of chiefs and notables (Article 3) it made no provision for teaching French. This gap was soon spotted and commented upon by Brévié who wrote to the Governor of Mauritania, de Coppet, urging the inclusion of French in the curriculum. De Coppet replied that neither he nor his Inspector of Native Affairs, Beyries, were in favour of this as they both believed that the overtly 'French' nature of the education provided in previous *médersa*s was the main obstacle to recruitment of pupils. Furthermore, de Coppet argued, because French control of the northern reaches of Mauritania was still not completely assured (el-Hiba's submission, it should be remembered, had taken place in 1935), the Atar *médersa* should be used as a way of encouraging the loyalty and confidence of the *grands nomades* of the north. De Coppet did not rule out the eventual inclusion of French but stressed that this would have to be postponed until France's position was more secure. Brévié agreed to this postponement only on condition that it should be for a maximum of two years after which French was to become obligatory regardless of any other considerations.[11]

This controversy is evidence of the fact that the received wisdom of men such as Clozel, Delafosse and Brévié regarding Islam, its place in West African society and French attitudes towards it was being abandoned. Just as Clozel and Delafosse could be said to have 'discovered' animism in the Ivory Coast at the turn of the century so too could it be said that de Coppet and Beyries had 'rediscovered' Islam in Mauritania in the 1930s. Islam appears in their writing to be a much grander and more dignified religion than is suggested by Clozel, Delafosse and Brévié. It is a view which seems closer to the nineteenth-century romantics than the sociologically inspired views of several of the commentators discussed in this study.

In September 1936 de Coppet was promoted to Governor-General and was thus able to encourage his administration to show greater respect towards Islam. Of course respect for the leaders of the principal brotherhoods was nothing new, but the originality of de Coppet's policy lay in the importance he attached to other senior personalities of the Islamic community – notably the *qadis* and imams. One of the most characteristic aspects of this policy was expressed in a circular to all the colonies of AOF in February 1937:

> On the occasion of *Tabaski* I would ask all *cercles* to transmit the good wishes of the Governor-General to the whole of the Muslim population and to give them assurances of our favourable attention. Please organise a reception for Muslim notables at your government houses and expound further on these sentiments.[12]

These instructions were carried out throughout AOF and appear to have created a very favourable impression amongst the Muslim population. The Governor of Senegal, Lefebvre, held a reception for St Louis' Muslim dignitaries who, he reported to de Coppet, had been very appreciative of the gesture: 'It is the first time, I was told, that the administration through an official action has associated itself with the intimate life of Muslim society, and the impression produced was profound'.[13] The imam of the principal mosque of Abidjan wrote personally to de Coppet with words of praise and thanks for the fact that 'For the first time we have recorded such an act from a Governor-General'.[14] De Coppet himself held a reception at his residence for Dakar's Muslim dignitaries at which the imam of the principal mosque of Dakar, al-Hajj Moustapha Diop, made a speech of considerable interest:

> All the inhabitants of Senegal rejoice in the arrival in their country ... of the Governor, M. de Coppet after the natives have endured suffering, poverty and fatigue. May Allah protect the supreme chief against calamities, may He preserve him against misfortune. Muslims should be content to have in him a

Governor whose like cannot be found anywhere in the world. His good policy has been proved by the preparations for our splendid celebration on our very important day. [De Coppet and his advisers] were all in full dress, wearing very expensive clothes to go to the place of prayer and were surrounded by cavalrymen to show publicly . . . the honour which they attach to Islam and to those who practise this religion.[15]

The President of the recently founded Fraternité-musulmane – a Dakar-based organisation of black Senegalese Muslims which, according to official sources, aimed to restore Islam to its former purity but which was also pro-French and had sided with the authorities against Hamallah[16] – wrote to M. Perrin, *député* for Nievre, to ask him to draw de Coppet's action to the attention of the Colonial Minister, Marius Moutet.[17]

At first sight many of these speeches and letters seem no different from, for example, the effusive declarations of loyalty to France during the First World War, but to see them as no more than this would be to underestimate the impact of de Coppet's gesture. All accounts of Muslim reactions report that Muslims were struck by the *novelty* of the action. Al-Hajj Moustapha Diop's speech also contains veiled criticism of previous administrations implicitly held responsible for the hardships of previous years.

De Coppet followed the official celebrations of *Tabaski* with another gesture of goodwill towards Muslims in the form of a donation of 1,000 francs to the Muslims of St Louis at the time of the *Mawlud* festival celebrating the birth of the Prophet. The money was distributed by Seydou Nourou Tall to the chiefs of the five districts of the town and the donation appears to have been gratefully received.[18] In January 1938 Abd el-Kader Diagne, a member of the Fraternité musulmane, suggested that de Coppet donate three sheep to the imams of the three principal mosques of Dakar, St Louis and Kaolack in time for the forthcoming *Tabaski* celebration. De Coppet noted in the margin 'Excellent idea! How much does a first-class sheep cost? Send the necessary money, charged to my personal account, to the three imams'. Lefèbvre reported that the price of a good sheep in Kaolack was 125 francs, 200 francs in Dakar and 250 francs in St Louis. De Coppet replied to Abd el-Kader Diagne thanking him for the suggestion and explaining that he had arranged for the sheep to be donated. He would not, he explained, be in Dakar himself during *Tabaski* as he would be on tour in Sudan, but he assured Diagne that he would take part in the celebrations there.[19] The following year neither the interim Governor-General, de Boisson, nor the new Governor of Senegal, Ponzio, attended the *Tabaski* celebrations. In 1940, although the Governor-General did not himself attend, the administration was strongly represented at the celebrations at which the *Grand Imam* prayed for French victory over the impious Germans. French participation in the celebrations ceased under the Vichy regime but in 1944 *Tabaski* was an occasion of great pomp and splendour as the Governor-General rode in procession to the mosque.[20]

There were, of course, sound political arguments for de Coppet's gestures. The French stake in Islam required protection not just from other Muslims (such as Hamallah) but also from politicians (such as Galandou Diouf). It is interesting to note that one of the main motives behind de Coppet's apparently most generous gesture of all – the sponsorship of the construction of a new principal mosque in Dakar – was decided upon partly in order to pre-empt Galandou Diouf. In March 1937 de Coppet wrote to the Colonial Minister that Galandou Diouf had suggested the need for a new and larger mosque for Dakar and that he thought it would be an excellent piece of propaganda if the French government could appear to have spontaneously developed the same idea. De Coppet's argument was approved and in February the following year in a ceremony of great pomp he and Sheikh Alwali Cherif, a grandson of Sheikh Sidia, laid the first stone of the new mosque in a symbolic act of Franco–Muslim solidarity. Most of the speakers at the ceremony were appropriately fulsome in their praise for de Coppet. One exception was Wagane Diouf, a deputy mayor of Dakar who thanked all the initiators of the scheme – including M. Goux the mayor of·Dakar and Galandou Diouf. According to intelligence reports of the day's events, 'The evocation of [Goux and Diouf] provoked whispers and protests that were noticed by everybody. The speech was not applauded'.[21]

De Coppet clearly thought that the ceremony had been a success and made personal arrangements for an article on it to be published in the metropolitan press. Writing informally to the Director of the Agence économique de l'AOF in Paris he said:

> You know the importance which I attach to Islamic questions and I believe that AOF has not always been given the place it deserves in the Muslim world. In connection with this I want you to know that next year I would like you to present me personally, in my role as Governor-General of AOF, to the Feast of *Aïd el-Kébir* which takes place at the Paris mosque.[22]

De Coppet's gesture was no doubt a sincere one, the wish to outdo Galandou Diouf notwithstanding. Other examples of his keenness that Islam should be respected can be seen in the following examples.

The first concerns the construction of another mosque, this time in Kaolack. In March 1937 el-Hajj Ibrahim Niasse wrote to de Coppet requesting help in the construction of a new mosque in Kaolack and suggested specifically that special rates might be charged for the transport of building materials. The head of de Coppet's cabinet noted that 'From a political point of view it would be useful if we could give satisfaction'. However, the Inspector of Public Works, to whom the request was passed, refused on the grounds that a similar request for help in the construction of a church in Bobo Dioulasso had been turned down. De Coppet was not impressed with this excuse:

> One cannot liken the construction of a mosque, which meets the needs of the majority of the population of a Muslim town like Kaolack, with a church destined to be frequented mainly by Europeans and a small number of newly converted natives.

The Dakar–Niger Railway Company was consequently instructed to give reduced rates, and by February 1938 the mosque was finished. El-Hajj Oumar Kane, Ibrahim Niasse's representative in Dakar thanked de Coppet for arranging the fifty per cent reduction in freight charges and invited him to the opening ceremony. De Coppet declined the invitation but offered reduced party rates on the railway for any Muslim who wanted to travel from Dakar to the ceremony at which the Governor-General was to be represented by the *commandant* of Sine-Saloum.[23]

The second example was somewhat different, but it also involved el-Hajj Oumar Kane. In July 1938 de Coppet received a letter from the Muslim residents of the avenue El-Hadj Malick Sy complaining about the lack of respect shown by the patrons of the Café de la Patrie to their mosque situated next to the café. They claimed that patrons of the café urinated against the wall of the mosque and asked if it would be possible to rent the premises which the café occupied for use as a hostel for Muslims. De Coppet immediately replied to the leader of the Muslims – el-Hajj Oumar Kane – that he would order greater respect to be shown to the mosque and would see what he could do about their request to lease the building. At the same time he wrote to the administrator of Dakar with orders to ensure that holy places were respected and requested more information on this particular case. The administrator replied that the whole street had an unpleasant smell as a result of its proximity to a refuse site and that he believed the mosque was relatively respected and that the Muslims were complaining mainly because of the sale of alcohol on the premises. Whatever the truth, no further action seems to have been taken.[24]

A further insight into de Coppet's concern that Islam should be respected can be gleaned from his scheme to include a *médersa* in the plans for the new Dakar mosque.[25] The *médersa*, it was stressed, was to be paid for by the French in order, on the one hand, to guard against begging and unqualified teachers and, on the other hand, to ensure better French control. The education was intended to fulfil at least four functions: (i) to 'purify' *Islam noir* and 'give new life to its rites'; (ii) to fight against superstition and magic; (iii) within the framework of the Qur'ān to improve the condition of women and children; and (iv) to train 'literate and erudite' teachers. However, there were serious doubts amongst the upper echelons of the educational administration about the wisdom of creating such an institution. The Deputy Inspector argued that those graduates whom the administration could not employ as interpreters and court assessors would probably turn to Qur'ānic education as a means of earning their living. He argued that they would be able to do this very successfully as a result of the prestige they would gain from holding a diploma from the *médersa*. The Inspector feared that a thriving and dynamic system of Qur'ānic education would be a very serious challenge to French secular schooling and, consequently, he was far from happy about the proposed *médersa*.[26]

De Coppet believed that the *médersa* had a wider role than the training of administrators and interpreters:

> A Muslim intellectual *foyer* will help to maintain West African Islam in its present mood which renders it much more malleable and open to our administrative action than in any other region with a Coranic influence.

Specifically he thought that a *médersa* would help greatly in combatting Hamallism:

> I believe that the sly dealings of Cherif Hamallah like those of his present followers and those of his possible future imitators, will be much easier to overcome and to neutralise the day when the élite of our Muslim subjects have tangible proof of the sympathy of the colonising nation which will be seen to be as active on behalf of its own religion as it is on behalf of any other religion which does not offend either the principles of public order or our sentiments of humanity.

De Coppet believed that the problem of employment for graduates of the *médersa* had been exaggerated by the Inspector and he requested permission to make an immediate start on the building.[27] The immediate support for the project was not, however, forthcoming and with de Coppet's departure in 1938 the scheme lost its chief advocate.

In all these cases it is clear that de Coppet had to overcome misgivings and open hostility from senior administrators in order to fulfil his policy of being seen to help Muslims. In case it should be felt that he had transformed the state overnight into a gravy train for Muslims it should be noted that several requests for assistance were refused.[28] Equally it should also be noted that in two of the cases examined above an important Islamic personality was involved, namely Ibrahim Niasse. Niasse was the head of a major branch of the Tijaniyya and although at this stage his influence was not as great as it was to become – he was very soon to be recognised by the North African Tijani as the *khalife* of the West African Tijaniyya and had close relations with Muslim leaders in the Gold Coast and Nigeria – nonetheless by 1936/7 he was unquestionably a very important figure, and de Coppet was wise to treat him well.

Relations between de Coppet and Ibrahim Niasse had been greatly improved after, with French assistance, Niasse had made the pilgrimage not just to Mecca but also to various Tijani shrines in North Africa during the *hajj* of 1937.[29] De Coppet saw Niasse's fulsome praise for the French organisation of the *hajj* as vindication of his policy. He quoted large sections of the letter which Niasse wrote to him on his return from the *hajj* in a circular to the governors of AOF. Of particular interest in Niasse's letter was a suggestion for a possible reform or modification of Qur'ānic education. Niasse wrote:

> I regret that too large a proportion of our Muslim population make no effort to understand our moral duties and as a result acquire the skills which would enable us to contribute to the revival of the country. Of these skills the most neglected but also the most important, are those concerned with agriculture.

> I would therefore like to see the creation of *médersas* where the Muslim
> child will learn the Coran, Muslim duties, to speak and write Arabic and then
> also a manual skill which will enable him to earn his living.[30]

This was a very significant proposal and one which ran counter to all the
earlier beliefs in the hostility of Muslims towards a westernised form of
Qur'ānic education. It is probably best understood in the context of the
changing economic and labour situation in Senegal during the 1930s, a
decade which witnessed increased migrant labour together with urban
growth and unemployment.[31] It can perhaps be seen as Niasse's alternative
to Mouride expansion into new uncultivated land.

De Coppet was very sympathetic to the suggestion and asked for
comments from the Governors of individual colonies. The response was
mixed. The Governors of both Guinea and the Ivory Coast were enthusiastic, the Governor of Dahomey thought the suggestion 'irrelevant' to
Dahomey's population and Beyries, now the interim Governor of Mauritania, thought it – no doubt wisely – 'inappropriate' in view of the Moorish
caste system in which artisans occupied the lowest rank.[32] The Governor of
Niger, however, was pleased to note that at last 'something was being done'
against 'the state of neglect in which we have left the Muslim schools'. He
compared French policy unfavourably with British policy in Nigeria where
he particularly admired the recently created secondary college in Zaria at
which teaching was conducted not just in English but also in Hausa. In
Niger he said that he and his administration were making an effort to ensure
that, with the approval of the marabouts, manual skills and agriculture
would be taught to the 4,000 or more children attending the colony's 1,350
Qur'ānic schools.[33]

However, there is no evidence of any further action towards a reform of
Qur'ānic education along the lines proposed by Niasse. Niasse's proposal
coincided with another debate concerning the reform of Qur'ānic education, but the proposed reforms were of an altogether different nature. In
January 1937 de Coppet was sent a major report carried out by M. Kleinschmidt on the condition of Muslim education in Senegal. The report was
very critical both of the begging by *talibés* and of the low level of academic
achievement within the schools. It concluded that some system of control to
ensure a higher standard of teaching was necessary. The Deputy Inspector
of Education was broadly sympathetic. According to the most recent (1933)
statistics available, he said that in Senegal there were 8,981 Qur'ānic schools
attended by 65,416 pupils. However, none of the schools visited by the
Inspectorate merited, he said, the name of 'school': 'The teaching which is
given there lacks any form of method and creates by its monotony this
universal laziness of spirit which the pupils bring with them later to the
public school'. However, he was less sure than Kleinschmidt had been that
any controls other than a restriction of the hours in which the school could
open were possible.[34] Geismar, de Coppet's interim as Governor-General,
sent copies of the Kleinschmidt report and the Deputy Inspector's assess-

191

ment of it to the Governors of Senegal, Niger, Sudan, Guinea, Mauritania and to the administrator of Dakar and asked for their comments on this 'particularly delicate' question. He suggested that they also read Marty's earlier report on Qur'ānic education in Senegal. When the various Governors had all replied de Coppet reported back in turn to his superiors in Paris. It is perhaps not surprising that he was very firmly against any form of control, an opinion which it seems was shared by all the Governors with the exception of the Governor of Senegal and the administrator of Dakar. De Coppet argued that Marty's verdict on previous attempts at legislation was still valid and that the French should continue to make an effort to understand Qur'ānic education – including such activities as begging – from a Muslim rather than from a European perspective. He quoted the reply of the Governor of Sudan:

> Muslim education exists in conditions which do not appear to require any intervention on our part. Its very nature, its aims, the calm in which it is carried out, the paternal action of the schoolmasters and the docility of the pupils – all suggest that the Coranic school still meets certain needs which touch the very heart of native societies. It would be very dangerous in the present state of evolution of our subjects to prejudice the satisfaction of these needs, even if this were done with the best of intentions.

The only exception which de Coppet was prepared to make was to consider stricter control of the hygiene of Dakar's schools – but he stressed that this too required a sense of pragmatism and an awareness of political priorities.[35]

De Coppet's obvious wish to be seen to be according Islam official respect and his reluctance to transform Qur'ānic education into a disguised form of French education should be recognised as an original contribution to the development of French policy towards Islam. Both as Lieutenant-Governor of Mauritania and as Governor-General of AOF de Coppet showed clear signs of departure from the near consensus of the previous twenty-five years according to which the faith of African Muslims was thought to be closer to the precepts of some undefined 'traditional' 'African' cosmology than to the doctrines revealed in the Qur'ān and in the *hadith*. However, the 'novelty' of de Coppet's contribution requires qualification. In the previous chapter we saw how his behaviour towards Hamallah belonged very clearly to a tradition of support for the 'establishment' leaders of the brotherhoods, a tradition which goes back to the about-turn in French attitudes to Serigne Ahmadu Bamba in 1912. De Coppet was as anxious to preserve the monolithic structures of the brotherhoods as any of his predecessors had been. Sheikh Seydou Nourou Tall, as can be seen from his exhausting itinerary was one of the leading figures in de Coppet's Islamic strategy, and Ibrahim Niasse was clearly able to make his voice heard in the Governor-General's palace.

Another aspect of continuity in de Coppet's administration was the surveillance and censorship of Arabic literature. The Central Intelligence

Bureau (Service central de sûreté et de renseignements généraux) was increasingly active and vigilant. The fact that it surveyed all forms of political activity should not be allowed to hide the fact that a lot of its time was taken up in surveying Arabic literature. The staff of the Bureau increased steadily from eighty-seven in 1933 to 115 in 1938.[36] In 1936 its officers seized 503 Arabic periodicals and advised that a further 2,040 were 'dubious'; in 1937 these figures were respectively 124 and 1,056 and in 1938, 384 and 4,730. Particular attention was being paid to the Lebanese and Syrians for whom stricter immigration controls were introduced in 1938. The effectiveness of the controls – immigrants were required to make a larger money payment and to provide extra documentation – can be seen in the dramatic drop in arrivals from the Levant: 1,936 in 1937 to 979 in 1938. In both years over a thousand were deported.

The concern of the authorities probably stemmed more from Arab nationalism than from Islamic unrest: for example, two of the publications banned in 1938 were banned because they carried poems glorifying the Arab revolt in Palestine. However, French sensitivity to this issue was founded as much on the fear that it would encourage non-Arab Muslims to challenge colonial authority as on the restlessness it caused amongst the Levantine population of AOF.

In short, the colonial state during the years of the Popular Front was growing increasingly vigilant over its subjects of whom more than 50,000 by the end of 1938 were the subject of files in the archives of the Intelligence Bureau. In two years alone – 1936 and 1937 – a further 10,000 files were added.[37] Such statistics and the knowledge of de Coppet's attitude to Sheikh Hamallah serve to qualify any temptation to portray de Coppet as simply a benevolent and liberally-minded paternalist.

Nonetheless, the fact that de Coppet had conventional responsibilities as the most senior colonial administrator in the Federation to ensure law and order should not blind us to the evidence that he was prepared to go along new and untested paths. Furthermore, although it is clear that the Popular Front government was broadly 'reformist' or 'progressive', in colonial policy – witness the Blum–Violette proposals in Algeria – it seems that the initiative for de Coppet's Muslim policy in AOF came from himself and from the impression of Islam that he had gained in Mauritania.

Something of a paradox, De Coppet would probably have been quite at ease with the later ambiguities and uncertainties of official French thinking that were to become so evident in the concept of the Union française of the 1950s.

11

Epilogue 1940–1960

The last two decades of French colonial rule in West Africa witnessed rapid and dramatic constitutional changes. These changes, however, were a reflection of the turbulence of metropolitan politics and had little to do with the situation in West Africa itself.

In June 1940 metropolitan France capitulated to the German invasion forces. In North and West Africa the administrations hesitated before electing to recognise the legitimacy of the Vichy government; a decision which was motivated partly by a desire to maintain the integrity of the French Empire and partly to ensure that there would be no German invasion of the colonies. If the French Empire in north-west Africa was an Empire which 'definitely would not strike back',[1] the same was not true of equatorial Africa where the Governor of Chad, Felix Eboué, the first black governor of a French colony, declared himself for de Gaulle and the exiled Free French government. The other colonies of AEF all followed suit with the exception of Gabon whose pro-Vichy administration had to be removed by force. The Allied invasion of North Africa in 1942 was the signal for a change of heart by the administration in Dakar which now declared its loyalty to the French government in Algiers. As the war drew to an end it became apparent that France would have to make wide-ranging reforms in the colonies in recognition of the hardships that the colonies had endured and the contribution they had made to salvaging national pride in the wake of the metropolitan collapse in 1940. De Gaulle acknowledged this need in his speech at the Brazzaville conference in 1944 in which he promised to give the colonies a greater measure of autonomy, to abolish the *indigénat* and to provide more funds for social and economic development.

The constitution of the Fourth Republic, approved in 1946, gave AOF a greater degree of direct representation through elected deputies in Paris and also established local territorial assemblies in each colony together with a Federal Assembly sitting in Dakar. Although numbers participating in the elections to the various assemblies were relatively small, political debate in AOF was very lively, and, as it became increasingly obvious that the prize for the winners was likely to be control over an independent state, elections were fiercely contested. The 'politicians' were overwhelmingly drawn from the urban western-educated élites of AOF, and, as their demands were seen to be increasingly at odds with the wishes of the administration, the French attempted to court the more conservative rural constituencies through the agency of the traditional chiefs.[2]

However, the tensions within AOF were as nothing compared to the divisions within the Fourth Republic in Paris as successive governments showed themselves quite incapable of coping with the problems of post-war reconstruction and still less capable of dealing with the crises in Indo–China, Morocco, Tunisia and, above all, Algeria. The *Loi cadre* of 1956 was designed to defuse the growing crisis in the colonies by granting a greater degree of autonomy to individual territories. However, in Algeria the reform succeeded only in antagonising settlers and nationalists alike whilst in West Africa its main effect was to balkanise the Federation to the concern of West Africa's federally minded politicians. 'Balkanisation' was accelerated further after the Gaullist coup in Algiers in May 1958 which finally brought down the Fourth Republic. The constitution of the Fifth Republic gave individual territories the opportunity to be associated as autonomous administrations within the newly named French Community. Whatever his initial calculations may have been, de Gaulle seems quickly to have realised, however, that the price for maintaining French sovereignty in the overseas Empire was a heavy one and he made no attempt to stand in the way when the West African colonies chose to become independent in a series of votes in 1960.

Our knowledge of the last two decades of French rule in West Africa is far from complete, and as new archival material becomes available there is much scope for future research. However, it does seem clear that during these years of rapid political developments there was a constant dualism in official French attitudes to the colonies; that rarely had the white man spoken with so forked a tongue. On the one hand concessions were being made all the time to the demands of the new political classes, whilst on the other hand a concerted effort was being made to shore up the position of France's traditional friends. For example, in July 1948 the family of Sheikh Sidia was voted an annual allowance of 500,000 francs CFA which was justified by Governor Beyries of Mauritania in the following terms:

> We should demonstrate that we are all the more generous with regard to the *Ahel* Cheikh Sidia [i.e. the people (family) of Sheikh Sidia] because the number of distinguished personalities on whom France can count for support is not great. Our generosity will not surprise any loyal Muslim in AOF; rather it will show in a concrete manner that we can still today, as we have always done in the past, recognise the service of those who have kept faith with us.[3]

Amongst these traditional friends the Muslim allies occupied a particularly important place, especially as France became enmeshed in war with Muslim Algeria. As a result, France's Muslim policy of the 1920s and 1930s survived through the process of decolonisation, and the rigid and unimaginative

195

distinctions between Muslims deemed to be either friendly or hostile to France remained almost entirely unchanged. This was particularly obvious in the case of the Hamalliyya which continued to be vilified in French administrative writing. For example, one report in 1955 described them as the 'shock troops of the RDA' (Rassemblement démocratique africaine), as the author of the report argued that the wish of the RDA 'to liberate Africa from European rule' coincided with the 'xenophobic aspirations of the Hamallists'.[4] This static conception of Franco–Islamic relations during the colonial period probably also contributed to the pattern of highly personalised and innately conservative relationships which have characterised Franco–African relations since 1960.

One area of research which need not wait for the opening up of government archives is a systematic study of the huge corpus of writing on Islam produced by students and teachers at the Centre des hautes études d'administration musulmane (CHEAM) which was founded in 1936 to provide specialist in-service training for military and civilian administrators in the French colonies. (In 1958 it was renamed Centre des hautes études administratives sur l'Afrique et l'Asie modernes.) From a very brief preliminary survey of the *CHEAM* monographs it is clear that the bulk of the monographs dealing with West African Islamic issues were concerned with the societies on the southern fringes of the Sahara, and this no doubt is a measure of the predominant interest in North Africa. Although the writings reflected contemporary administrative preoccupations, such as Hamallism,[5] their cumulative effect in retrospect was to add more flesh to the bones of *Islam noir* as they reinforced the image of an orthodoxically suspect religion which was heavily influenced by pre-Islamic custom and which was dominated by the marabouts of the Sufi brotherhoods. The one modification which they added to official understanding of Islam was perhaps to reinforce suspicions that the clerical castes in the southern Saharan areas had taken the French for a ride in posing as men of peace harassed by the warrior aristocracies of the desert edge.

One of the most striking developments in attitudes towards Islam during these years was the way in which a radical critique of West African Islam emerged from within the Muslim community that was in many respects the same as the views held by the administration. Most of the Muslim societies of West Africa in the twentieth century were themselves products of earlier 'reform' movements, but as the reformers had become the establishment they inevitably became open to charges of corruption and slackness in doctrine. The French administration, not surprisingly, noted this evolution with satisfaction and drew considerable comfort from it. However, for numbers of Muslims – particularly those who had made the pilgrimage to Mecca or had been educated at the Egyptian university of al-Azhar – it was a cause of concern, sadness and anger.

The post-war reformists are often referred to as 'Wahhabi' (after the Saudi Arabian Wahhabiya). However, in West Africa this term (which was first used by the French administration as a term of abuse) is most usefully regarded as no more than a convenient label to designate a certain type of reform movement. J.-L. Triaud[6] has identified four principal characteristics of the West African Wahhabi: (i) 'a symbolic rupture with the majority of the Muslim community' through the use of special outward signs, the formation of associations and through worship at separate places of prayer; (ii) 'a refusal of all forms of popular piety' (including consultation of marabouts and the cult of saints); (iii) 'an exclusive reference to the Qur'ān and the Sunna of the Prophet linked with a marked distrust of all jurisprudence'; and (iv) 'a vehement opposition to brotherhoods … considered as innovatory and heretical sects'. Triaud suggests that the Wahhabi were recruited mainly from urban Muslims who suffered 'a double exclusion' both from French culture and from that of the Islamic establishment. It was a movement which has had (and still has) particular appeal for urban traders, and with its stress on the value of education and hard work it has sometimes been described as an essentially bourgeois movement.[7]

The origins of the post-war movement can be found in the increased number of pilgrims from the 1930s and the return to West Africa of graduates of al-Azhar.[8] For Africans making the costly pilgrimage or seeking to finance their studies at al-Azhar, life was made easier by the development both in Saudi Arabia and Egypt of various organisations which catered specially for their needs. In Medina and Riyadh, for example, there were a number of African teachers whose schools were particularly popular with black pilgrims whose stay in the Holy Places, in the days before the package deal pilgrimages, was often a prolonged one as pilgrims came not merely to visit the holy shrines of Islam but to complete their religious education. In Egypt the *Subban al-Muslimin* (the 'Society of Young Muslims'), founded in 1927, provided financial aid for African students at al-Azhar. The examples of piety, learning and charity set by these various individuals and institutions could easily be contrasted with the Muslim establishment of AOF which had grown rich on its collaboration with the colonial authorities and its encouragement of superstitious practices.

In Sudan the Wahhabiya was introduced by four al-Azhar graduates who returned to West Africa towards the end of the war. In 1946 they made an official request to the administration for permission to open a *médersa* in Bamako but the French, fearing 'the political connections [the graduates] might have kept with Arab countries',[9] refused permission. When, after long discussions, which had raised public awareness of the religious issues involved, the *médersa* eventually opened in 1949, it was an immediate success and soon had a roll of 400 students. In the same year a Subbanu society based on the model of the Egyptian *Subban al-Muslimin* was formed in Bamako. Meetings of the society were very serious and orderly and laid great emphasis on the explanation of Islamic doctrine. The society was

197

particularly popular with the Dyula traders of Bamako and it was largely through their trading network that by 1956 a further twenty branches of the Subbanu society had been created throughout West Africa. However, the French authorities soon regretted their decision to allow the foundation of the Subbanu *médersa* and in 1951 closed it down on the pretext that it was causing divisions within the Muslim community as there had been a number of incidents arising from the non-payment of fees. These incidents had achieved a certain local notoriety and were even the subject of a popular song distributed on a 78 r.p.m. recording. However, it is clear that the administration's principal concern was that the Subbanu school was taking students away not only from French schools but also from 'traditional' Qur'ānic ones as well.

In 1953 a branch of the reformist organisation, L'Union culturelle musulmane (UCM), was founded in Bamako, Article 3 of the founding statutes of the UCM stated that; 'The aim of the association is to combat through appropriate means the scandalous exploitation of charlatans, the fanaticism and the superstitions; in a word to purify Islam by ridding it of all corrupting influences and practices'.[10] The hostility towards the Sufi brotherhoods declared so explicitly in the founding charter of the UCM (and, incidentally, in language which closely resembled that of the colonial Islamicists) was a direct challenge not only to the Islamic 'establishment', but also to the colonial authorities who had invested so heavily in that establishment. Inevitably in a time of growing political activity the message of the UCM soon acquired political overtones even though it was forced very soon to moderate its anti-marabout position. The establishment of a federal organisation of the UCM in Dakar 1957 was motivated by a wish common to all Muslim reform movements to maintain the widest possible Islamic community. Thus by its very nature the UCM was opposed to the 'balkanisation' of the West African Federation and this in itself had certain political implications. However, the UCM was also undoubtedly pro-Arab in orientation and it identified strongly with Arab nationalist movements, particularly in Algeria.[11] The federal instincts of the reformists together with their nationalist, anti-colonial sympathies made them the natural allies of the RDA which campaigned as a radical pan-African party.[12] In May 1957 the French administration in Sudan (Mali), worried by the links between the RDA and the reformists, encouraged 'traditionalist' Muslims to go on the rampage in the Wahhabi district of Bamako, destroying and looting hundreds of Wahhabi properties.[13]

French opposition to the Wahhabi UCM need cause no surprise. The Wahhabi with their Arabian links were bound to inspire fears of anti-western pan-Islamism, particularly in the context of the Algerian war and the rise of Nasser in Egypt. Furthermore, the French perceived the movement to be socially disruptive in exactly the same way as they had done with the Hamallists. Finally, the Wahhabi were a direct threat to the French Muslim allies whose goodwill the French were as anxious as ever to maintain. There was in this sense nothing new about French reactions to the reformers whose integration into the post-colonial states of West Africa remains problematic.

The case of French relations with the Mouride brotherhood in Senegal is another instance of continuity in policy.[14] In July 1945 the *Khalife-Général* of the brotherhood, Mamadou Moustapha, died, and the brotherhood was once again thrown into a succession dispute. Before his death Moustapha had recognised his eldest son, Sheikh M'Backé, as his rightful successor. The French, however, suspecting Sheikh M'Backé of being hostile to the administration and of fostering pan-Arab and Senegalese nationalist sympathies, were not inclined to see him accede to the most powerful position in the brotherhood. Instead they announced that Falilou, Moustapha's eldest surviving brother, was to be the new *Khalife-Général*. This had the effect of splitting the brotherhood as Sheikh M'Backé refused to recognise the legitimacy of his uncle's succession and declared that he himself was the only rightful heir. For the next few years the French administration and Sheikh M'Backé were engaged in a trial of strength. In an attempt to defuse the rivalry within the brotherhood the French proposed the creation of a Conseil d'administration mouride (1947–52) in which all factions were represented. However, by 1952 Falilou, with his administrative backing, was powerful enough to exclude Sheikh M'Backé from the Council. The exclusion not only rendered the Council meaningless but it also emphasised the fact that Falilou's position was now secure. The fact that Falilou was now secure as *Khalife-Général* owed everything to the French policy of being prepared to get heavily involved in the internal affairs of the brotherhood and to give full support to the individuals they had identified as their allies.

Rivalries within the brotherhood acquired a wider political significance in exactly the same way as they had done before the war but with the extension of the franchise, the political role of the brotherhood was hugely increased. The reason for this was simply that the Mourides, along with the other brotherhoods, provided the politicians with access to the rural voters who now made up the majority of the Senegalese electorate. In post-war Senegal the two main political protagonists were the Catholic, Léopold Senghor, leader of the Bloc démocratique sénégalais, and the Muslim, Lamine Guèye, leader of the Senegalese branch of the Metropolitan Socialist Party, Section français de l'internationale ouvrière, (SFIO). Senghor's political skills ensured that his Catholicism was never a serious handicap in winning Muslim votes, With characteristic astuteness he allied with Falilou from the start of the Mouride succession dispute, and the support he enjoyed in turn from the Mouride leadership undoubtedly helped his electoral performances in 1951 and 1952. Lamine Guèye, on the other hand, backed the wrong horse in Sheikh M'Backé and found in addition that his westernised upbringing and manner made it very difficult for him to play the Muslim card with any great conviction or success. The rural Senegalese electorate was much more impressed by Senghor's promises to raise the price of groundnuts than by Lamine Guèye's appeal to partisan religious emotions. Lamine Guèye succeeded also in offending Seydou Nourou Tall who, after alleging that he had been publicly insulted by the SFIO, put the Union générale des originaires de la vallée du fleuve at the disposal of the Bloc democratique sénégalais (BDS) in 1951. Thus, the leading Muslim politician in Senegalese politics found himself disturbingly at odds with the most powerful Muslim leaders of the country. However, Lamine Guèye's relationship with the Senegalese brotherhoods, improved following his *rapprochement* with Senghor in 1957, and the healing of this political rift also helped to bring about a reconciliation within the leadership of the Mouride brotherhood between Falilou and Sheikh M'Backé. Although the Sufi leaders were undoubtedly hugely influential, particularly at a time when the majority of the electorate were unfamiliar with the political process, it would be a mistake to imagine that they simply 'delivered' votes to their political allies. Their relationship with the Senegalese politicians was similar to their relationship with the French administration: that is one based on an exchange of services and mutual respect. It is a relationship which has scarcely changed in the post-colonial era.

One possible modification to the narrow and exclusive relationship between the French administration and the Muslim leaders might have resulted from plans, which were never properly developed and certainly never implemented, to form a new administrative unit covering the whole of the French Sahara. This proposal was motivated by French concern to secure the oil resources of the Sahara (the first comercial well came on a stream in January 1958) and to continue to use the desert for atomic tests (the first French atomic bomb was exploded in Reggane in January 1960). Such a move would have required the French administration to increase its network of alliances to include the nomadic groups who until now had been the principal victims of colonial rule, Evidence of willingness to do this is very scanty particularly as archival records are not yet generally available. However, the comments of Captain Cardaire in April 1956 are suggestive. Speaking of a secret mission to Colomb Bechion in the Adrar, Cardaire, who at the time was head of Muslim intelligence in Bamako, wrote: 'I am afraid that Dakar will get rid of me for stupid financial reasons. But this is precisely the moment when we should forge an intimate and durable liaison between the south [of Algeria] and AOF. . . . AOF is not Dakar – when will we understand that? – and Islam in AOF is not Abdullah ould Cheikh Sidiya or Seydou Nourou Tall'.[15] The frustration behind Cardaire's remarks is obvious and suggests that West African administrations were reluctant to depart from their traditional pattern of Dakar-based alliances in order to pursue wider strategic interests. However, without further research it would be foolish to make too much of Cardaire's remarks. Perhaps it would be sufficient to note that French diplomacy in the Sahara during the 1950s is a subject in itself that is worthy of further study.

These years of momentous changes in West Africa were not accompanied by a corresponding evolution in the way in which the French administration thought about its colonial subjects. Even the liberal scholarship of the Institut fondamental sur l'Afrique noire, founded in 1936, was rooted in the traditions established by Clozel and Delafosse. The image of an Africa secure in the timeless and unchanging cultures of its component ethnic groups found its way too into the distinctive cultural nationalism of francophone Africa. To a very considerable extent, both the French and the African leaders approached political independence with ideas about the nature of African society which had been developed in the first two decades of the century.

12

Conclusion

The combined processes of the gathering and utilisation of information about the communities of Africa has been a neglected aspect of colonial rule which deserves further study. In focussing specifically on French attitudes and policies towards Islam in West Africa, I have described the evolution of a particular view of Islam which itself was part and parcel of a wider view of African society generally.

I have argued that the various experiences of the nineteenth century, both in West Africa and also in Algeria, formed the prelude to the emergence of a distinctive perception of and policy towards Islam. These experiences combined to produce a somewhat contradictory picture of Islam: the fiercest adversaries of French military imperialism had been Muslim leaders, but it was with an army comprising large numbers of Muslim soldiers that the forces of al-Hajj Umar and Samori Ture had eventually been defeated; Mgr. Lavigerie emphasised the relationship between slavery and Islam, yet Louis-Gustave Binger doubted that the unemployed of metropolitan France were as well treated as the house slaves of African Muslims; and, finally, the scholars in Algeria had warned of well-organised secret Islamic brotherhoods but, south of the Sahara, Le Chatelier, one of France's foremost experts on Islam, argued that such organisations were the product of French imagination. What then in French eyes were the essential features of African Islam? At the turn of the century you paid your money and took your choice.

Although many of these contradictory views persisted throughout the colonial period, I have suggested that there was nonetheless a recognisable evolution of thought towards a consensus view of Islam. Furthermore, this evolution can only be understood by taking into account the cultural and intellectual environment of early twentieth-century France as well as by looking closely at the specific circumstances of colonial scholarship and policies in West Africa. Intellectual and political developments are seen to have been inextricably linked with the evolution of thought and policy.

The second phase in this evolutionary process took place in the years between the end of military conquest and the start of the First World War.

They were years in which conspiracy theories dominated both domestic French politics and international diplomacy. French understanding of Islam was still muddled and veered from the views associated with the Algerian school of thought, which emphasised the structure and organisation of Islam, to views on the other hand which stressed the irrational, unpredictable and intrinsically 'untameable' nature of African Islam. Whilst the Algerian theorists hoped that control of Islam offered France the key to cheap and efficient domination of the whole of north-west Africa, others feared that basing French administration on the foundation of Islam was a futile and even dangerous policy. When Xavier Coppolani, one of the leading spokesmen for the Algerian school, was himself killed by a Muslim opponent the latter view came to dominate French thinking and, at a time of widespread millenarian expectations amongst African Muslims, the French were particularly fearful of *mahdi*st activity. In addition, the Muslim leaders – the marabouts – were seen by the French as being the allies of a slave-owning 'feudal' aristocracy which used religion as a pretext for exploiting the rest of society. The image of the marabout was further worsened by its association in the minds of some Frenchmen with that of the metropolitan clergy and, with anti-clericalism being one of the fiercest of political passions in France, this was a particularly unfortunate association. In these circumstances Islam presented itself as the major obstacle to the advancement of French 'civilisation' and to the imposition of French rule.

The third part of this study describes how during the years from around the start of the First World War to around 1920 the French came to revise their understanding not just of Islam but of African society generally. The influence of ethnology and later also of Durkheimian sociology led to a radical reappraisal of the relative merits of Islam and animism in West Africa: animism hitherto despised for its 'primitive' and its localised nature, its superstitions and its lack of either a written doctrine or any other easily discernible moral code was now seen by some as a relatively rational and sophisticated system of universalist beliefs which responded well to the needs of African societies. Islam, by contrast, was seen increasingly as an alien and disruptive force from which animist societies required some protection. These views were associated in particular with François Clozel and Maurice Delafosse. However, it was the work of a third scholar-administrator – Paul Marty – which above all contributed to a change in the official understanding of African Islam. In his multi-volume study of Islam in AOF, Marty described a religion which was distinguished by its wholesale adoption of pre-Islamic African customs. Marty was not in the least hostile to this 'distortion' – as he saw it – of Islamic doctrine: on the contrary, he suggested that African Islam – *Islam noir* – was a relatively docile and, from the French point of view, harmless religion. He demonstrated how the French could benefit from a more tolerant attitude towards its leaders and through his very thorough documentation of personalities, of legal practices and of the history of Islam in West Africa he succeeded in painting a very detailed and coherent picture of Islam that has dominated informed European perceptions at least until the 1960s.

The fourth and final part of the study describes what I have called the French stake in Islam. During the 1920s and the 1930s, the French developed very strong alliances with certain leaders of the Muslim community on whom the French had become reliant for a range of economic and political services. Relationships between the French and the Muslim leaders became fossilised and there was decreasing scope for flexibility in the choice of allies. The initiative for these alliances came as much from the Muslims themselves as it did from the French, for the French could in their turn offer important services to their Muslim allies – including protection against challenges to their leadership from within the Muslim community. This pattern of mutual support between the French authorities and the Muslim establishment appears to have been much the same whether in coastal Dahomey with its minority Muslim population or in the predominantly Muslim societies of the Sahel. Furthermore, it was a pattern that not only lasted through to the end of the colonial era but which also can be seen in most of the independent states of West Africa.

The development of this relationship between colonial authorities and Muslim subjects together with the theoretical assumptions on which it was based were central features of the colonial experience in French West Africa. The very different fates of Tierno Aliou, the blind old *wali* of Goumba, on one extreme and of Seydou Nourou Tall, the jetsetting grandson of al-Hajj Umar Tall, on the other, were largely determined by the way in which the French authorities understood Islam. Colonial 'realities', – the burning huts of the *missidi* in Goumba, the bulging files of the Service des affaires musulmanes, the pomp and ceremony of the foundation celebrations for the new mosque in Dakar – all these demand an understanding of the way in which colonial governments thought about the people they ruled.

Notes

1 Introduction

1 The first such mission was led by A. Le Chatelier in 1898.

2 Quellien, *La Politique musulmane*; Carles, *La France et l'islam*.

3 The literature on *jihad* is enormous. Last, 'Reform movements in West Africa', is the best introduction to the subject and provides the most comprehensive survey of recent scholarship. I am grateful to Dr Last for allowing me to read this chapter before publication. Robinson, *Holy War* is not only the fullest account of the Umarian *jihad* but also gives a stimulating overview of the series of Fulbe *jihad*s. Martin, *Muslim Brotherhoods* is another excellent introductory text.

4 See M. Johnson, 'The economic foundations of an Islamic theocracy – the case of Masina', *JAH*, XVII (4), 1976, 481–95; M. Klein, 'Social and economic factors in the Muslim revolution of the Senegambia', *JAH*, XVII (3), 1972, 419–40; Sanneh, 'The origins of clericalism', pp. 49–72; Sanneh, *The Jakhanke*; Stewart, 'Southern Saharan scholarship', pp. 73–93; Stewart, *Islam and Social Order in Mauretania*; Willis, 'The Torodbe clerisy', pp. 195–212.

5 See, for example, Lovejoy, *Transformations in Slavery*.

6 Klein, *Islam and Imperialism in Senegal*; C. A. Quinn, *Mandingo Kingdoms of the Senegambia: Traditionalism, Islam and Colonial Expansion*, Evanston, 1972; Robinson, *Chiefs and Clerics*; Traoré, 'Contribution à l'étude de l'islam'.

7 Senegal is the favourite hunting-ground for political scientists. See, for example, O'Brien, *Mourides*; *Saints and Politicians*; Coulon, *Le Marabout et le Prince*.

8 See, for example, F. Dumont, *La Pensée religieuse d'Amadou Bamba*, Dakar/Abidjan, 1975.

9 See, E. Isichei, *A History of Nigeria*, London, 1983, for a recent example of such an approach.

10 The debate about social control in nineteenth-century Britain raises important questions about the nature of authority and obedience which are interesting to apply to the colonial situation. Two critiques of the concept of social control written from very different perspectives are particularly instructive: F. M. L. Thompson, 'Social control in Victorian Britain', *Economic History Review*, XXIV (2), 1981, 189–208; G. Stedman Jones, *Languages of Class: Studies in English Working Class History, 1832–1982*, Cambridge, 1983, ch. 2, 'Class expression versus social control? A critique of recent trends in the social history of "leisure" '.

11 According to M. Delafosse, 'L'Ecole coloniale', *RCBCAF*, III, 1914, 137–46.

12 See, for example, Curtin, *The Image of Africa*; Cohen, *The French Encounter with Africans*; Waardenburg, *L'Islam dans le miroir de l'occident*; Djait, *L'Europe et l'islam*; Said, *Orientalism*; Rodinson, *Fascination de l'islam*.

13 Rodinson, *Fascination de l'islam*, p. 15.
14 Said, *Orientalism*.
15 *Ibid.* p. 70.
16 P. Burke, *Popular Culture in Early Modern Europe*, London, 1979, ch. 1, 'The discovery of the past'. I am grateful to J. Iliffe for suggesting this reference.
17 Cited in S. Lukes, *Emile Durkheim: His Life and Work*, Harmondsworth, 1973, p. 896.
18 See, *Africa*, II, 1929; III, 1930, for Malinowski's and Mitchell's articles.
19 Buell, *The Native Problem*, vol. II, p. 93.
20 Clarke, *West Africa and Islam*, pp. 189–90.
21 See Reberioux, *La République radicale?*, for general background.
22 See C. Andrew, *Secret Service. The Making of the British Intelligence Community*, London, 1985, ch. 2, 'Spies and spy scares', for evidence that elaborate conspiracy theories flourished on both sides of the channel.

Part I Introduction

1 Ly-Tall and Robinson, 'The Western Sudan', pp. 351–8, is the best summary of the early history of the colonial occupation of Senegambia.
2 Webb, Jr., 'The trade in gum Arabic', pp. 149–68.
3 Barrows, 'The merchants and general Faidherbe', pp. 236–88.
4 Last, 'Reform movements in West Africa' and Robinson, *Holy War*, provide the most stimulating and informative overviews of the *jihad* movements.
5 Cited in Ly-Tall and Robinson, 'The Western Sudan', p. 361.
6 Robinson, *Holy War*, pp. 141–3.
7 Kanya Forstner, *The Conquest of the Western Sudan*, is the classic account of the French military conquest.

2 French Islamic policy in Senegal and Algeria

1 See Ly-Tall and Robinson, 'The Western Sudan', pp. 342–80, for the best summary of French imperialism in West Africa in the second half of the nineteenth century.
2 Bouche, 'L'Ecole française', pp. 218–35; Jones 'The Catholic mission', pp. 321–40. See also, ANSOM, Sénégal et Dépendances (S et D) X, 3 quat, Commissaire de la Marine, 'Rapport à M. le Gouverneur', 16 December 1836; Gov. p.i. Sénégal to Ministre de la Marines et Colonies, 10 January 1837.
3 ANSOM S et D X 51, Gov. Sénégal to Min. Marines et Colonies, 18 October 1852; 'Commission superieur des études' to Gov. Sénégal, 12 December 1854.
4 ANSOM S et D X 15 *bis*, Gov. Sénégal to Min. Marines et Colonies, 11 April 1856; see also, L. C. Barrows, 'Faidherbe's Islamic Policy in Senegal, 1845–64', *French Colonial Studies*, 1977, 34–53.
5 ANSOM S et D X 15 *bis*, M. Barbieu to Directeur des Colonies, 23 May 1856.
6 ANSOM S et D X 15 *bis*, Min. Marines et Colonies to Gov. Sénégal, 11 October 1857.
7 Ly-Tall and Robinson, 'The Western Sudan'.
8 Schnapper, 'Les Tribunaux musulmans', pp. 90–128, is an excellent account of the operation of Muslim law in colonial Senegal. I am grateful to Jean-Louis Triaud (Paris VII) for the reference.
9 ANSOM S et D VIII 4 *bis*, Gov. Sénégal to Min. Marines et Colonies, 12 October 1832.
10 ANSOM S et D VIII 4 *bis*, Gov. Sénégal to Min. Marines et Colonies, 16 October 1848; same to same, 25 October 1848.
11 ANSOM S et D VIII 14 *bis*, Faidherbe to Min. Marines et Colonies, 13 September 1856; Directeur des Colonies to Min. Marines et Colonies, 5 March 1857; Faidherbe to Min. Marines et Colonies, 10 March 1857; decree 20 May 1857.

12 ANSOM S et D VIII 23 *bis*, 'Petition', 28 April 1865; Chef du Service Judiciaire to Gov. Sénégal, 22 February 1866.
13 ANSOM S et D VIII 23 *bis*, Gov. Sénégal to Min. Marines et Colonies, 26 February 1866.
14 Ly-Tall and Robinson, 'The Western Sudan'; Kanya Forstner, *The Conquest of the Western Sudan*; Klein, *Islam and Imperialism in Senegal*.
15 ANSOM 8, Chef du Service Judiciaire, 'Rapport', 22 June 1888.
16 ANSOM 8, 'Procès verbal de la commission chargée de l'étude de la réorganisation de la justice musulmane', 1 April 1889.
17 G. Hardy, *Histoire sociale de la colonisation française*, Paris, 1953, p. 108.
18 Cited in Pasquier, 'L'influence de l'expérience algérienne', p. 274.
19 The following paragraphs are based on Julien, *Algérie contemporaine* and M. Morsy, *North Africa 1800–1900*, London, 1984.
20 Cited in Julien, *Algérie contemporaine*.
21 *Ibid.* pp. 330–37.
22 *Ibid.* p. 341. See also Ageron, *Les Algériens musulmans*, vol. I, pp. 131–4, for decline of *bureaux arabes*.
23 V. Monteil, 'Les Bureaux arabes au Maghreb (1833–1961)', *Esprit*, Nov. 1961, 575–600.
24 The classic account is in Ageron, *Les Algériens musulmans*, vol. I, part I, 'Vae Victis'.
25 Ageron, *Les Algériens musulmans*, part IV, 'Le Mythe kabyle'; Ageron, *Politiques coloniales*, part II, 'Mythes et politiques coloniales françaises'.
26 Cited in Prost, *Les Missions des Pères Blancs*, p. 5.
27 See Renault, *Lavigerie, l'esclavage africain*. The Lavigerie quotation is from vol. II, p. 369.
28 Ageron, *Les Algériens musulmans*, pp. 397–428.
29 The background is best described in Ageron, *Les Algériens musulmans*, vol. I, part I, 'Vae Victis'.
30 ANSOM Afrique IV 37a, Gov.-Gen. Algeria to Govs. Sénégal, Soudan, Côte d'Ivoire, Guinée, n.d.; replies dated Jan. 1894.
31 Rinn, *Marabouts et Khouan*.
32 *Ibid.* p. 116.
33 There is no single reliable biography of Coppolani. His friend and colleague, Robert Arnaud, writing under the pseudonym of Robert Randau, wrote the fullest biography in 1939, *Un Corse d'Algérie chez les hommes bleus: Xavier Coppolani, le pacificateur*, much of which had already been published in a barely fictionalised form in his novel *Les Explorateurs roman de la grande brousse*, Paris, n.d. There are a number of other shorter works most of which draw heavily upon Arnaud's account but which also include some personal memoirs: 'D'Otton Loyewski, 'Coppolani et la Mauritanie' pp. 1–69; Désiré Vuillemin, 'Coppolani en Mauritanie', pp. 291–342; J.-F. Maurel, *Xavier Coppolani: son oeuvre*, St Louis, 1955.
34 Ageron is particularly dismissive of the conclusions reached in the book which he describes as 'un constat de non lieu.... La conclusion a été écrite d'avance', *Les Algériens musulmans*, pp. 514–15.
35 Depont and Coppolani, *Les Confréries religeuses*, pp. xiii–xiv.
36 *Ibid.* pp. 107–20, especially p. 110.
37 *Ibid.* p. 121.
38 See below, ch. 5.
39 Depont and Coppolani, *Les Confréries religieuses*, p. 182.
40 *Ibid.* pp. 169, 191, 192.
41 *Ibid.* pp. 176–7, 263–5.
42 *Ibid.* p. 175.
43 Rebérioux, *La République radicale?* provides an excellent summary of the political upheavals of these years.

Part II Introduction

1 See Kanya Forstner, *The Conquest of the Western Sudan*.
2 Newbury, 'The formation of the Government-General', pp. 111–28. See also, Harrison, Ingawa and Martin,' The establishment of colonial rule in West Africa' pp. 487–547.
3 Kanya Forstner, *The Conquest of the Western Sudan*, pp. 249–50.
4 See, Ageron, *Les Algériens musulmans*, vol. I, part I, 'Vae Victis'.

3 The fear of Islam

1 On developments in the Islamic world, see A. Hourani, *Arabic Thought in the Liberal Age*, Oxford, 1962 and on European uncertainties, see Rodinson, *La Fascination de l'islam*, ch. 8.
2 See editorial of first issue of *Moslem World*, 1911, and a series of articles in *International Missionary Review*, 1912, on 'The vital forces of Islam and Christianity', for insights into mission attitudes towards Islam during these years.
3 *RMM*, 1911 and see Le Chatelier's justification for this issue in *RMM*, 1912.
4 Becker's article, 'Ist der İslam eine Gefahr für unsere Kolonien?' appeared in French translation as *L'Islam et la colonisation de l'Afrique*, Paris, 1910.
5 See H. Brunschwig, *Mythes et réalités de l'impérialisme colonial français, 1871–1914*, Paris, 1960; R. Girardet, *L'Idée coloniale en France de 1871 à 1962*, Paris, 1971 and Ageron, *Les Algériens musulmans*.
6 The following paragraph is based on Terasse, *Histoire du Maroc*, which gives a blow-by-blow account of the Moroccan crisis. C.-A. Julien, *Le Maroc face aux impérialismes*, Paris, 1978 is a good introduction to more recent scholarship.
7 Le Chatelier, *L'Islam dans l'Afrique occidentale*, p. 8.
8 Le Chatelier, 'Politique musulmane', pp. 61–2.
9 See the author's comments in his introduction to *L'Islam dans l'Afrique occidentale*.
10 *Ibid.* pp. 10–11.
11 *Ibid.* p. 12.
12 *Ibid.* pp. 163, 259.
13 *Ibid.* p. 313.
14 *Ibid.* p. 348 (emphasis added).
15 Dr Barot, *Guide pratique*.
16 *Ibid.* pp. 316–17.
17 H. Brunschwig, 'Louis Gustave Binger' in L. Gann and P. Duignan (eds.), *African Proconsuls*, New York, 1978.
18 Binger, *Esclavage*.
19 Binger, *Péril*.
20 See, C. M. Andrew, P. Grupp and A. S. Kanya Forstner, 'Le Mouvement colonial français et ses principales personalités (1890–1914)', *RFHOM*, LXII (229), 1975. On the Mission laïque see below, p. 61.
21 Binger, *Péril*, p. 55.
22 Kanya Forstner, *The Conquest of the Western Sudan*, ch. 9.
23 ANSOM Soudan 1/9a, M. Audeod to Commt Region Nord, 15 September 1898; same to same, 27 October 1898.
24 ANSOM Soudan 1/9e, 'Rapport politique du 31 Décembre'.
25 ANSOM Soudan 1/9e, Lt.-Gov. Soudan to Commt Region Nord et Nord-Est, 19 December 1898.
26 Randau, *Corse d'Algérie*, pp. 27–8; Maurel, *Xavier Coppolani*, p. 23. It seems that M. Hanoteaux, the Foreign Minister, disliked Coppolani.
27 ANSOM AP 1420/1, Coppolani, 'Rapport d'ensemble sur ma mission au Soudan français', p. 14.

28 *Ibid.* p. 18.
29 IF Fonds Terrier no. 5984, Arnaud to 'Mon Capitaine', 8 May 1899.
30 The verse is Swift's from 'On Poetry' cited in Curtin, *Image of Africa*, p. 198.
31 IF Fonds Terrier no. 5900, Henrys to Terrier, 27 July 1899.
32 Randau, *Corse d'Algérie*, p. 30. See also, ANSOM AP 1420/1, Coppolani, 'Rapport . . .', in which Coppolani wrote 'Quels que soient les sentiments de pitié qui peuvent nous animer à l'égard de la race noire du Sénégal et du Soudan, quels que soient nos efforts pour la sortir de l'état d'asservissement où elle est plongée depuis des siècles, il faudra plusiers générations avant de l'élèver au niveau des peuples libres. Pour sa vitalité elle-même, il lui faut une maître. Le Maure le demeurera encore longtemps'.
33 The first schemes for the railway were drawn up as early as the 1840s. See, G.-M. Désiré Vuillemin, 'Les Premiers Projets du transaharien et l'Afrique du Nord', *Revue de l'Histoire Maghrébine*, 1977, 107–21.
34 Governor-General Ballay stated bluntly: 'Une action en pays maures ne peut rien apporter'. Cited in Désiré Vuillemin, 'Coppolani en Mauritanie', p. 300.
35 ANSOM AP 1420/1, Directeur Affaires d'Afrique to Min. Colonies, 27 December 1899.
36 Randau, *Corse d'Algérie*, p. 74.
37 See ANSOM AOF III/4–9 for details of Blanchet mission.
38 ANSOM AP 1420/1, Coppolani, 'L'Organisation politique et administrative des pays maures de notre empire du nord-ouest africain', 12 June 1901.
39 The recommendation is contained at the end of the report of 12 June 1901.
40 ANSOM Mauretanie IV/1, Coppolani, 'Rapport présenté à la commission interministerielle du nord-ouest africain', 14 October 1901.
41 The best account of the Moorish social structure is contained in Stewart, *Islam and the Social Order in Mauritania*, ch. 3.
42 *Ibid.*, pp. 95–6.
43 ANSOM Mauretanie IV/I, Coppolani, 'Rapport . . .', 14 October 1901.
44 Members of its committee included Binger, Bourgeois, Hanoteaux, Houdas, Jonnart, Leroy-Beaulieu and Poincaré.
45 Editorial *Revue Franco-Musulmane et Saharienne*, I, 1902.
46 This calculation is based on information given in Marty, *Trarzas*, chs. 6, 7.
47 ANS 1 D 221, Gen. Houry (Commt Supérieur des Troupes en AOF) instructions to Lt. Delaplane, 3 March 1902; Delaplane to Houry, 13 April 1902.
48 ANSOM AP 1420/1, Gov.-Gen. AOF to Min. Colonies, 16 May 1903.
49 For a more detailed account of events between mid-1902 and 1904, see Harrison, 'French attitudes', pp. 99–110.
50 ANSOM Mauretanie IV/I, Coppolani, 'Rapport à M. le Gov.-Gen. sur l'administration du Tagant', 1 July 1904; ANS 9 G 20, Gov.-Gen. AOF to Min. Colonies, July 1904.
51 ANSOM AP 1407, Coppolani to Gov.-Gen. AOF, Dec. 1904.
52 All the biographies of Coppolani have a blow-by-blow account of the circumstances of his death – all of which are based on Arnaud's eye-witness account in *Corse d'Algérie*, pp. 155–85. See also files in ANS 1 D 224 for the official accounts.
53 Frèrejean cited in Désiré Vuillemin, *Contribution*, p. 293.
54 G.-M. Désiré Vuillemin, 'Notes sur les origines des pelotons méharistes du Mauretanie', *Revue d'Histoire des colonies*, 1958, 53–60.
55 At the turn of the century the Fadeliyya were enjoying 'une grande vogue' according to J. Cuoq, *Les Musulmans en Afrique*, Paris, 1975, p. 135.
56 ANS 9 G 21, Lt.-Gov. Sénégal to Gov.-Gen. AOF, 6 February 1905.
57 ANS 9 G 21, Jacques to L.-Gov. Sénégal, 7 February 1905.
58 ANS 9 G 21, Gov.-Gen. AOF to Adam (Commissaire adjoint Mauretanie), 8 February 1905; Gov.-Gen. AOF to Lt.-Gov. Sénégal, 8 February 1905.
59 ANS 9 G 21, Lt.-Gov. Sénégal to Gov.-Gen. AOF, 7 February 1906.

60 See Harrison, 'French attitudes', pp. 136–8.
61 ANS 19 G 1, Gov.-Gen. AOF circular, 10 February 1906.
62 ANSOM AOF III/3, Gov.-Gen. AOF to Arnaud, 21 March 1906.
63 Biographical details are taken from Arnaud's c.v. in ANSOM, rue Oudinot. I am grateful to the archivists for allowing me to see copies of extracts of the c.v.
64 IF Fonds Terrier, Arnaud to Terrier, 18 May 1907. In this letter Arnaud stated that the need to avenge Coppolani's death was top of his list of reasons why the conquest of Mauritania should be pursued.
65 These details are taken from R. Randau's *Isabelle Eberhardt*, Paris, 1945,. For Algerian background see Ageron, *Les Algériens musulmans*, vol. I, part I, 'Vae Victis'. See also R. Kabbani (ed.), *The Passionate Nomad: the Diary of Isabelle Eberhardt*, London, 1987.
66 For a full bibliography of Arnaud's writing, see C. Harrison, 'Bad monks and Frenchmen: a literary view of Islam in West Africa', unpublished seminar paper, SOAS African History Seminar, 2 November 1983.
67 For the 'philosophy' behind this school, see, for example, R. Randau, 'L'Ecrivain colonial au colonies', *Le Grande Revue*, Feb. 1926; E. Pujarniscle, 'La Littérature coloniale et ses difficultiés', *Le Grande Revue*, Dec. 1921, Jan.–Feb. 1922; J. Pommer, 'Le Mouvement littéraire française de l'Algérie', *Le Grande Revue*, June 1923; R. Lebel, *L'Afrique occidentale dans la littérature française depuis 1870*, Paris, 1925, chs. 3, 4. See also Randau's prefaces to his three novels *Les Colons*, Paris, 1907, *Les Explorateurs*, Paris, n.d., and *L'Aventure sur le Niger*, Paris, n.d.
68 R. Arnaud, *Précis de politique musulmane*, vol. I, *Les Maures de la rive droite*, Algiers, 1906, pp. 24–5.
69 *Ibid.* pp. 113–15.
70 *Ibid.* p. 119 (emphasis added).
71 ANS 11 G 4, Lt.-Gov. HSN (Haut-Sénégal et Niger) to Gov.-Gen. AOF, 26 March 1906. See also Adeleye, *Power and Diplomacy*, pp. 322–5 and Marty, 'L'Islam et les tribus du Niger', p. 350. 'La cause de tout le mal, le marabout pélerin Sahibou, était un petit homme aveugle.... Très adroit, malgré son cécité, possédant le don de la ventriloquie il avait tout ce qu'il fallait pour persuader à ses naifs coreligionnaires en faisant parler devant eux un arbre, un sandale, un Coran que c'était la parole de Dieu lui-même qu'ils entendaient. Et il annonçait ainsi l'extermination des Blancs, l'apparition subite d'une armée de vrai croyants.'
72 Adeleye, *Power and Diplomacy*, pp. 321–5.
73 ANSOM AP 193/3, Gov.-Gen. AOF to Min. Colonies, 26 March 1905.
74 The following were arrested on 30 March 1906: Ahmadu, Sultan of Zinder; Kaigama and Mosterama, both *chefs de province*; Mallam Gapto, described as a 'marabout intime' of the Sultan; Cherif Hattin, the Sultan's Arab interpreter; Tchaikafada, a former *chef de province*; Mamadu Chetima, 'marabout' of the Sultan; Mallam Yoro, a trader from Zinder; and Ali, interpreter of the *cercle*. For these details and Gadel's full report on events see ANS 11 G 5, Chef de Bataillon, Gadel to Lt.-Gov. HSN, 5 April 1906.
75 ANS 11 G 5, Gadel to Lt.-Col. Commt Région du Niger, 8 May, 1906.
76 ANS 11 G 5, 'Rapport de Capt. Lefebvre, Commt le cercle de Zinder sur les agissements du Sultan de Zinder et de ses complices en Mars 1906'. The other 250 pieces of evidence are also filed in 11 G 5.
77 ANS 11 G 4, 'Rapport à M. le Gov.-Gen. de l'AOF sur les mobiles islamiques des troubles de Janvier à Mars 1906 dans le Territore Militaire du Niger', 22 November 1906.
78 R. Randau, *Les Meneurs des hommes*, Paris, 1931, p. 28.
79 ANS 11 G 5, Lt.-Col. Lamolle, Commt Territoire Militaire du Niger to Lt.-Gov. HSN 6 January 1907; Marty, 'L'Islam et les tribus du Niger', p. 397; Baier, *Economic History*, pp. 97, 101.
80 ANS 11 G 4, Min. Colonies to Gov.-Gen. AOF, 24 April 1906.

81 ANS 11 G 4, Lt.-Gov. HSN to Lt.-Col. Lamolle, 7 May 1906.
82 The letter is filed in IC Fr. 378 (Levé).
83 Marks, *Reluctant Rebellion*, pp. 144–5.
84 See Baier, *Economic History*, chs. 4, 5.
85 Wesley, Johnson, 'William Ponty and Republican paternalism', p. 127. The following paragraph is based on this article.
86 See Lovejoy, *Transformations in Slavery*, for best summary of the nature and position of slavery in West African society.
87 See Klein and Roberts, 'Banamba slave exodus' and Lovejoy, *Transformations in Slavery*, ch. 11.
88 ANS 19 G 1, Gov.-Gen. AOF circular, 22 September 1909.
89 ANS 15 G 103, Gov.-Gen. AOF to Lt.-Gov. HSN, Aug. 1911.
90 ANS J 91, Gov.-Gen. AOF to Directeur Ecole normale de St Louis, 20 November 1906. Only three of the eighteen candidates had achieved above average marks for translation from Arabic to French.
91 ANS J 86, Mariani to Gov.-Gen. AOF, 2 April 1910.
92 ANS M 241, Gov.-Gen. AOF circular, 8 May 1911.
93 ANS 19 G 4, Gov.-Gen. AOF circular, 16 February 1908; replies of Lt.-Govs. to Gov.-Gen. AOF: Guinée, 11 March 1908, Côte d'Ivoire, 16 March 1908, Dahomey, 23 March 1908, Sénégal, 31 March 1908.
94 ANSOM AP 907 *bis*/1 contains all relevant correspondence.
95 ANS 19 G 1, Lt.-Gov. Guinée to Gov.-Gen. AOF, 19 September 1911; Gov.-Gen. AOF to Lt.-Gov. Guinée, 14 October 1911.
96 ANS 19 G 1, Lt.-Gov. HSN to Gov.-Gen. AOF, 14 December 1911; Gov.-Gen. AOF to Lt.-Gov. HSN, 25 January 1912.
97 ANSOM AP 1054/2, 'Mission Depont: émigration syrienne et les syriens en AOF', 28 August 1920.
98 On Levantine traders in Guinea, see 'Les Undésirables de l'AOF', *BCAF*, June 1911. On Levantines in Senegal, see R. Cruise O'Brien, *White Society in Black Africa. The French of Senegal*, London, 1972, pp. 42, 49–54.
99 ANS 19 G 5, Lt.-Gov. Côte d'Ivoire to Gov.-Gen. AOF, 7 August 1911; Gov.-Gen. AOF to Lt.-Gov. Sénégal, 24 August 1911; Lt.-Gov. Sénégal to Gov.-Gen. AOF, 14 October 1911; Gov.-Gen. AOF to Lt.-Gov. Côte d'Ivoire, 31 October 1911.
100 See, for example, ANSOM Sénégal 1/97, Gov.-Gen. p.i. AOF to Min. Colonies, 'Rapport sur la situation politique au Sénégal, 2ème trimestre, 1906'. The report regretted that gifts worth 10,000 frances had been given to Ahmadu Bamba.
101 ANS 15 G 3, Lt. Gov. HSN to Gov. Gen. AOF, 16 May 1906.
102 ANS 5 G 63, 'Côte d'Ivoire: rapport politique, 4ème trimestre, 1905'. See also Triaud, 'La Question musulmane en Côte d'Ivoire', pp. 542–71, for an analysis of French concerns about Islam in a predominantly animist society.
103 ANS 5 G 63, Benquey to Lt.-Gov. I, Côte d'Ivoire, 20 October 1907.
104 ANOM AP 145/2, 'Procès verbal de la séance du 29 Décembre 1908 de la commission permanente du Conseil de Gouvernement de l'AOF'.
105 ANSOM Sénégal IV/132, 'Carnet journalier' written by Henri Chessé, the *administrateur* of the *cercle* of Dagana, is the fullest account of the event. See also letters of Lt.-Gov. p.i. Sénégal to Gov.-Gen. AOF, 16 March 1908, 26 March 1908 and of Commissaire du Gov.-Gen. en Mauretanie to Gov.-Gen. AOF, 16 March 1908. See also ANS 2 G 8 (36), 'Rapport mensuel: Dagana', Feb. and March, which refers to locusts and drought. ANS 13 G 116, Commissaire du Gov.-Gen. en Mauretanie, 21 March 1908, reports that followers of Aly Yoro were poor.
106 ANSOM Soudan I/2, 'Haut-Sénégal et Niger: rapport politique, 1ème trimestre, 1908'. See also Arnaud, 'L'Islam et la politique musulmane française', p. 7.

107 See below, p. 74.
108 Marty, *Etudes sur l'islam et les tribus du Soudan*, vol. I, pp. 100–13; ANSOM AP 145/2, Lt.-Gov. p.i. HSN, 'Rapport au conseil de gouvernment', 20 June 1910.
109 ANS 15 G 103, Gov.-Gen. AOF to Lt.-Gov. HSN, Sept. 1911.
110 ANS 19 G 1, Gov.-Gen. AOF circular, 26 December 1911 (emphasis added).

4 Education policy and Islam

1 See Zeldin, *France 1848–1945: Intellect and Pride*, ch. 4, for a survey of the importance of education in French society.
2 Bouche, *L'Enseignement*, vol. II, pp. 500–1. See also her article, 'L'Ecole française', pp. 218–35.
3 Hardy, *Une Conquête morale*, p. iii.
4 Dubois, *Notre Beau Niger*, p. 208.
5 Bouche, *L'Enseignement*, vol. II, pp. 704–47.
6 ANS J 86, Lt. Gov. Sénégal to Gov.-Gen. AOF, 29 July 1907.
7 See below, ch. 6.
8 For his c.v. see Bouche, *L'Enseignement*, vol. II, p. 718fn.
9 ANS J 11, Mairot to Gov.-Gen. AOF, n.d.
10 ANS 17 6 33, Lt.-Gov. HSN to Gov.-Gen. AOF, 30 January 1904; same to same, 9 September 1904.
11 ANSOM Soudan 1/2 *bis*, Ponty, 'Note sur la colonie du Haut-Sénégal et Niger', 25 June, 1905.
12 ANS 11 J, Mairot to Gov.-Gen. AOF, n.d.
13 See conclusion to Depont and Coppolani, *Les Confréries religieuses* and ANS J 91, Coppolani, 'Note . . . au sujet de l'enseignement à donner aux indigènes musulmans'.
14 A. Mairot, 'Etude sur les écoles coraniques de l'Aof', *JOAOF*, 22 July 1905, pp. 371–5.
15 ANS J 10, Inspecteur de l'enseignement, 'Statistiques relatives à l'enseignement', 5 May 1907 . . . 'Quelle que soit l'importance des sacrifices budgetaires et quel que puissent être le dévouement et l'activité des maîtres, il n'est malheureusement pas possible de reçevoir dans les écoles publiques tous les enfants qui ont atteint l'âge de scolarité'.
16 For good summary of issues see, Reberioux, *Le République radicale?*, pp. 65–71.
17 ANS 17 G 33, Min. Colonies to Gov.-Gen. AOF, 15 April 1905; Gov.-Gen. AOF to Min. Colonies, n.d.; Gov.-Gen. AOF circular, June 1905.
18 The main qualifications related to the lack of funds available for carrying out surveys of Church property and the need to continue support for the charitable mission institutions such as the orphanages and the dispensaries. In 1905 the colony paid 47,200 francs in salaries for the Christian clergy plus 4,625 francs to the Muslim *Tamsir* of St Louis. The *Tamsir*, unlike the priests, was to retain his stipend as he was considered to be more of a judge than a priest. ANS 4 E 2, Lt.-Gov. Sénégal to Gov.-Gen. AOF, March 1906.
19 ANS 4 E 2, Lt.-Gov. Sénégal to Gov.-Gen. AOF.
20 ANS 17 G 35, Gov.-Gen. AOF to Min. Colonies, 26 May 1906.
21 Maze, *La Collaboration scolaire*, pp. 151–2.
22 Prost, *Les Missions des Pères Blancs*, p. 79.
23 Cited in Audoin and Daniel, *L'Islam en Haute Volta*, p. 87.
24 This paragraph is based on Burrows, 'Les Origines de la Mission laïque', pp. 35–7. I am grateful to Dr C. Andrew for this reference.
25 Mairot report, 22 June 1905, *JOAOF*, 1905.
26 ANS J 86, 'Arrêté accordant des subventions aux professeurs libres d'arabe qui enseignent le français dans les écoles', 12 June 1906. This was reissued 22 June 1907. See also Bouche, *L'Enseignement*, vol. II, p. 725.
27 ANS J 93, Gov.-Gen. AOF to Lt.-Gov. Sénégal, 22 August 1910.

28 ANS J 91 contains Combe's and Clozel's reports.
29 ANS J 94, 'Arrêté', 4 July 1906.
30 ANSOM Soudan I/11, 'Rapport politique AOF, 2ème trimestre, 1906'.
31 ANS J 94, Lt.-Gov. AOF, 11 May 1907.
32 ANSOM Soudan X/7, Inspecteur Enseignement Musulman to Gov.-Gen. AOF, Jan. 1908.
33 ANS J 92, Lt.-Gov. Sénégal to Gov.-Gen. AOF, April 1906.
34 ANS J 91, Gov.-Gen. AOF to Directeur de l'Ecole normale à St Louis, 26 November 1906.
35 ANS J 92, Inspecteur Enseignement Musulman to Gov.-Gen. AOF, 10 November 1906.
36 ANS J 93, 'Enseignement français: curriculum de la *médersa* de St Louis', 1906.
37 ANS J 92, 'Arrêté . . . réorganisation de la *médersa* de St Louis', 28 October 1909; Bouche, *L'Enseignement*, vol. II, pp. 741–2.
38 ANS J 92, Inspecteur Enseignement Musulman to Gov.-Gen. AOF, 19 April 1910.
39 *Ibid.*
40 ANS J 12, Inspecteur Enseignement Musulman, 'Note sur l'enseignement musulman en Guinée française', 20 April 1907.
41 One of the most common Muslim 'types' encountered in the novels of Randau, for example, is such an enlightened, French-educated Muslim whose hallmark is a subscription to the *Revue des Deux Mondes* – and, of course, an intimate acquaintance with the complete works of Robert Randau!
42 ANSOM Soudan X/7, Inspecteur Enseignement Musulman to Gov.-Gen. AOF, 15 January 1908.
43 ANS J 86, Inspecteur Enseignement Musulman to Gov.-Gen. AOF, 24 April 1910.
44 *Ibid.*
45 ANS J 93, Gov.-Gen. AOF to Lt.-Gov. Sénégal, 22 August 1910; same to same, 6 October 1910; Lt.-Gov. Sénégal to Gov.-Gen. AOF, 24 October 1910; Gov.-Gen. circular, 'Emplois dans les services publics à réserver aux indigènes anciens élèves des écoles officielles', 31 October 1910.
46 See Combe's report on the *médersas* (in ANS J 91) and above p. 31 for perspectives on France as a Muslim power. It is interesting to note that this political identification with Islam had a spiritual equivalent in the work of France's leading 'Orientalist', Louis Massignon. Massignon, a Catholic mystic who identified very strongly with Islamic mysticism, regarded it as a French duty to help Muslims rediscover their traditional culture. Such an intense personal association with Islam – or at least a certain view of Islam – seems to be a peculiarly French tradition. Few British Islamicists, for example, have been able to match the personal commitments of scholars such as Massignon, Rodinson, Berque, Monteil and Giraudy, the last two of whom have converted to Islam. On Massignon, see Waardenburg, *L'Islam dans le miroir de l'occident*. See also Said's comment, 'It became France's obligation . . . to defend Muslim traditional culture, the rule of their dynastic life, and the patrimony of believers', *Orientalism*, p. 271.
47 ANS O 85, Gov.-Gen. AOF Circular, 18 April 1907.
48 ANS J 86, Lt.-Gov. Sénégal to Gov.-Gen. AOF, 6 May 1911. This letter included the Seck and Zanetacci report.

5 French Islamic policy in crisis: the Futa Jallon, 1909–1912

1 See Diallo, *Institutions politiques*, pp. 27–35; Marty, *L'Islam en Guinée* pp. 2–6; Y. Person 'The Atlantic coast and the southern Savannahs, 1800–1880' in J. F. Ajayi and M. Crowder (eds.), *History of West Africa*, London, 1974, vol. II, pp. 262–307; Sanneh, *The Jakhanke*; J. Suret-Canale, 'Touba, Holy Place of Islam' in C. Allen and R. W. Johnson (eds.), *African Perspectives*, Cambridge, 1970, pp. 53–82. An excellent summary of the origins and history of the Futa state is to be had in Robinson, *Holy War*.
2 *Almamy* is a derivation of the Arabic *al-imam*, the leader of prayer.

3 Diallo, *Institutions politiques*, pp. 35–55; Marty, *L'Islam en Guinée*, p. 21; Robinson, *Holy War*, p. 53.

4 For history 1888–97, see Diallo, *Institutions politiques*; Marty, *Guinée*; Arcin, *Histoire de la Guinée française*; W. McGowan, 'Foula resistance to French expansion into the Futa Jallon, 1889–96', *JAH*, 1981, 245–61. For an account of French relations with Bokar Biro see ANSOM Guinée IV/6, Gen. Boilevé, Chargé de l'Expédition des Affaires Militaires, to Min. Colonies, 17 January 1897.

5 Sanneh, 'Tcherno Aliou', pp. 73–102.

6 ANSOM Guinée IV/6, Gov.-Gen. AOF to Min. Colonies, 18 February 1897.

7 Marty *L'Islam en Guinée*, p. 41.

8 *Ibid.* p. 22.

9 Suret-Canale, 'Un Aspect de la politique coloniale française en Guinée', pp. 13–19; R. Cornevin, 'Alfa Yaya Diallo fut-il un héros national de Guinée ou l'innocente victime d'un règlement de compte entre gouverneurs?', *RFHOM*, 1970, pp. 288–96.

10 ANS 7 G 95, Billault, Commt de Labé to Lt.-Gov. Guinée, 26 April 1905.

11 Marty, *L'Islam en Guinée*, pp. 41–4.

12 ANS 7 G 96, Frezouls to Gov.-Gen. AOF, 25 October 1905; same to same, 31 October 1905; Gov.-Gen. AOF to Min. Colonies, 28 November 1905; Marty, *L'Islam en Guinée*, p. 44.

13 ANSOM Guinée IV/6, Cousturier margin note in De Beeckman to Cousturier, 9 November 1896.

14 Marty, *L'Islam en Guinée*, p. 22.

15 Caillié, *Voyage*, vol. I, p. 269.

16 Cf. ANSOM AP/170/3, N. Duchène, 'Rapport à la commission extra-parlementaire et administrative pour la protection et sauvegarde des populations indigènes'. This classification went from: i) Berbers and Arabs of white origin; ii) Peuhl – 'semitic traces'; iii) Hausa, Songhay, Wolof and Soninké – 'destined for better things'; iv) Mandingos, Bambara, Malinke, Soussou, Agni, Nagos – 'although retaining the crudeness of the primitive customs, distinguish themselves by their relative intelligence and energy'; v) Serer, Dioula, Balanke, Habe – 'a state of primitive savagery'. See also Tauxier, *Le Noir*, which likewise has five categories. At the bottom the 'Primitives – or the relatively Primitive, for the absolute Primitives . . . where are they to be found?'; then the 'Inferior pre-Mandingos' – the losers, defeated because of their lack of social and political organisation; then the 'Superior pre-Mandingos'; then the 'Mande-mandingo'; and finally, at the top, the Foulahs.

17 Barot, *Guide pratique*, p. 330.

18 Ita, 'Frobenius', pp. 673–88.

19 Tauxier, *Le Noir*, pp. 191–2.

20 Arcin, *Histoire de Guinée*, pp. 98–9.

21 IFAN Fonds Vieillard (F-D) 30, M. Maillet, 'Monographie du cercle de Timbo', 1908.

22 ANS 7 G 68, Guebhard to Commt de la Région du Fouta-Djallon, 15 July 1903.

23 Dupuch, 'Essai sur l'emprise religieuse', pp. 291–2; see also M. P. Delmond, 'Un aspect de l'islam peuhl: Dori', *CHEAM* (R), 1103, 1947, in which the author argued that the contemplative nature of the Fulbe was similar to that of the Bedouin.

24 Capt. Normand, 'Notes sur la Guinée française', *RCBCAF*, 1902, 146.

25 Machat, *Les Rivières du Sud* pp. 293–4; on respectability see also Caillié's description in *Voyage*, vol. I, pp. 268–9.

26 Rouget, *La Guinée*, p. 172.

27 On Tierno Ibrahim, see Marty *L'Islam en Guinée*, pp. 64–5.

28 ANSOM Guinée IV/6, Noirot to Lt.-Gov. Guinée, 26 May 1899.

29 ANS 17 G 35, Lt.-Gov. Guinée to Gov.-Gen. AOF, 30 June 1900. In two months in 1900 there were about 4,000 deserters from the workforce for the railway, whose supervisors

were accused of great brutality in their methods. See J. Magolte, 'Le chemin de fer de Konakry au Niger', *FRHOM* 1968, 37–105.

30 ANS 7 G 68, Lt.-Gov. circular, 'Renseignements concernant le mouvement musulman', n.d.; replies from *commandants* dated June and July 1903.

31 Marty, *'L'Islam en Guinée*, p. 77; ANSOM Guinée IV/9, 'Rapport Pherivong', 1911.

32 ANSOM Guinée IV/9, 'Rapport Bobichon', 16 June 1909.

33 Marty, *L'Islam en Guinée*, pp. 69–77. The following paragraph is based on this account.

34 Sanneh, 'Tcherno Aliou', p. 75; Marty, *L'Islam en Guinée*, pp. 57–60.

35 Sanneh, 'Tcherno Aliou', pp. 96–7.

36 *Missidi* in Fufulde means a place of prayer. Cf. IFAN Fonds Vieillard, 'Monographie du cercle de Timbo', 1908: '*missidi* . . . une unité religieuse'; IFAN Fonds Vieillard (F-D) 12; Vieillard notes, '. . . Marga c'est là où on mange. . . . C'est le marga qui est le lieu de nourriture, la *missidi* c'est la lieu de dévotion enver Dieu'.

37 ANS 7 G 86, Mariani to Commt Kindia, 20 March 1909.

38 ANS 7 G 86, Mariani to Commt Kindia, 21 March 1909; Mariani to Lt.-Gov. Guinée, 10 April 1909; same to same, 22 April 1909; see also 7 G 69, Mariani to Ponty, 23 May 1909.

39 ANS 7 G 86, Bobichon, 'Rapport sur la mission politique dans la Fouta-Djallon', 16 June 1909.

40 ANS 7 G 69, Mariani to Gov.-Gen. AOF, 28 July 1909; Mariani, 'Notes sur l'islam en AOF. Les marabouts du cercle de Kindia', 30 July 1909.

41 ANS 7 G 86, Fournier, 'Note pour M. le Gov.-Gen. de l'AOF', 15 September 1909; Ponty to Lt.-Gov. Guinée, 25 September 1909. For a discussion of slavery in the Futa Jallon, see Sanneh, *Jakhanke*, chs. 6, 9 and Suret-Canale, 'Touba', pp. 64–6. Touba's population fell by several thousand as a result of slave exoduses in the first decade of the century.

42 ANS 7 G 69, 'Rapport politique, mois d'Avril, cercle Mamou, 1910'.

43 ANS 7 G 99, Gov.-Gen. AOF to Lt.-Gov. Guinée, 17 October 1910.

44 ANSOM 5 PA, Gov.-Gen. AOF to Lt.-Gov. Guinée, 1 November 1910.

45 Marty, *L'Islam en Guinée*, p. 79.

46 ANSOM 5 PA, Sasias to Lt.-Gov. Guinée, 14 January 1910.

47 Verdat, 'Le Ouali de Goumba', pp. 33–5.

48 See correspondence in ANS 7 G 97.

49 On wild rubber, see Mark, 'Economic and religious change among the Diola of Boulof (Casamence)', pp. 81–90. On attitudes to Lebanese, see O. Goerg 'Echanges, réseaux, marchés', p. 525.

50 ANSOM Guinée IV/6, Pherivong, 'Rapport . . .'.

51 Marty, *L'Islam en Guinée*, p. 81.

52 ANS J 12, 'Rapport de M. l'Inspecteur sur les cercles de Ditinn et Pita', 8 December 1910.

53 ANS 7 G 69, 'Extrait d'un rapport de M. Mariani en mission en Guinée', 21 November 1910.

54 ANS J 12, 'Rapport de M. l'Inspecteur sur Kouroussa . . .', 19 January 1911.

55 ANS J 91, Mariani to Gov. AOF, 10 February 1911.

56 ANS J 12, Mariani, 'Rapport sur les cercles de Dittin et Pita', 8 December 1910.

57 ANS 7 G 69, Fournier, 'Note pour M. le Gov.-Gen.', 4 August 1910; Ponty to Lt.-Gov. Guinée, 25 August 1909; 'Note pour M. le Chef du Cabinet du Gov.-Gen.', March 1910. Mariani wanted the *médersa* in Labé, but Ponty and Fournier favoured the Jakhanke centre of Touba whose scholarly atmosphere they compared to the medieval Sorbonne.

58 ANSOM 5 PA, Guy to Ponty, 21 January 1911. See also Marty, *L'Islam en Guinée*, pp. 49–51.

59 ANS 7 G 97, Ponty to Min. Colonies, 7 April 1911.

60 ANS 4 G 12, 'Rapport . . . concernant la situation politique de la Guinée à l'époque du 25 Février 1911'.

215

61 ANS 4 G 12, 'Rapport Pherivong . . . suite donnée à la verification par le Gouverneur Guy', 26 February 1911.
62 ANS 1 D 174, 'Rapport d'ensemble établi par le Capitaine Lanssu de l'Infanterie Coloniale à la suite de l'affaire de Goumba, le 30 March 1911', contains a detailed account of the military proceedings, including copies of all Guy's instructions. See ANSOM Guinée IV/9, Guy to Ponty, for 'heroic courage' and description of battle.
63 Verdat, 'Le Ouali de Goumba'.
64 ANS 1 D 174, 'Rapport d'ensemble . . . Chef de Bataillon, Boin', 18 July 1911, for details of police tour. The report argued in favour of a policy of divide and rule and supporting younger chiefs against older ones.
65 ANSOM Guinée IV/9, Ponty to Min. Colonies, 31 March 1911; and same to same, 7 April 1911.
66 ANSOM Guinée IV/9, Guy to Ponty, 1 April 1911.
67 ANSOM Guinée IV/9 contains collection of newspaper cuttings, including 'L'AOF: l'echo de la côte occidentale de l'Afrique', 15 April 1911. The article was written by the paper's editor, L. Ternaux.
68 ANSOM 5 PA, *Annales Coloniales*, 12 May 1911; 19 May 1911.
69 ANSOM Guinée IV/9, *France d'Outre-Mer*, 13 June 1911; 20 June 1911.
70 Telegrams in ANSOM 6 PA.
71 IF Terrier 5900, Guy to Terrier, 5 June 1911; 30 October 1911. See also ANSOM Guinée IV/9, Ponty to Min. Colonies, 11 July 1911, for defence of Guy against the accusations from the military.
72 IF Terrier 5900, Guy to Terrier, 30 October 1911.
73 ANSOM Guinée IV/9, Ponty to Min. Colonies, 11 April 1911; same to same, 29 June 1911.
74 ANSOM 5 PA, Commt cercle Ditinn to Guy, 3 April 1911.
75 ANS 7 G 99, 'Rapport politique, cercle Kade, poste de Touba', April 1911.
76 ANSOM 5 PA, 'Rapport de M. le Commt de cercle de Kindia sur les évènements qui se sont produits dans le Goumba Foulah . . . ', 15 May 1911.
77 ANS 7 G 99, 'Rapport politique, cercle Kade, poste de Touba', April 1911.
78 ANSOM 5 PA, Guy to Gov.-Gen. AOF, 8 June 1911.
79 ANS 7 G 99, 'Reconstruction inédite du massacre de Goumba', *L'A.O.F.*, 27 May 1911, also gives the following casualty figures: French losses 15, Fulbe losses 1,028.
80 ANSOM Guinée IV/9, Pherivong to Min. Colonies, 14 June 1911.
81 The fact that the newspaper accounts are the sole source is confirmed by Verdat, 'Le Ouali de Goumba', p. 60. Verdat was a former archivist and presumably had free access to archives. The following account is based on newspaper reports 20 September 1911 – 30 September 1911 which can be found in ANS 7 G 99 and in ANSOM Guinée IV/9.
82 See for example, Weiskel, *Baule Resistance and Collaboration* on French suppression of Baule revolt in Ivory Coast, and J. Iliffe, *A Modern History of Tanganyika*, Cambridge, 1979.
83 See F. Cooper, 'The problem of slavery', pp. 103–25; Klein and Roberts, 'Banamba slave exodus'.
84 Marty, *L'Islam en Guinée*, pp. 86, 117.

6 Scholar-administrators and the definition of *Islam noir*

1 ANS 13 G 67, Lt.-Gov. HSN to Gov.-Gen. AOF, 31 May 1911; Gov.-Gen. AOF to Lt.-Govs. Sénégal, Guinée, Mauretanie, 31 May 1911.
2 ANS 13 G 67, Lt. Gov. HSN to Gov.-Gen. AOF, 11 June 1911; same to same, 19 July 1911.
3 ANS 9 G 28, Mariani to Gov.-Gen. AOF, 27 August 1911.
4 ANS 9 G 28, Colombani (Res, Guidimaka) to Commissaire du Gov.-Gen. en Mauretanie, 7 September 1911; Commission permanente en conseil to Gov.-Gen. AOF, 29 September 1911; arrêté, 30 September 1911.

5 See Evans-Pritchard, *The Sanusi*, ch. 5, 'The first Italian–Sanusi war'.

6 ANS 19 G 4, Lt.-Gov. p. i, HSN to Gov.-Gen. AOF, 23 March 1912.

7 ANSOM AP 913/1, Decree, 25 June 1911.

8 ANSOM AP 913/7, 'Note sur la politique musulmane et la Commission interministérielle des affaires musulmanes', n.d.

9 The reviews are filed in ANS 9 G. For a more enthusiastic attitude to the commission see F. Chautemps, 'La commission des affairs musulmanes' in *L'Action*, 16 January 1912, a copy of which is filed in IF Fonds Terrier 5917.

10 ANS 15 G 103, Gov.-Gen. AOF to Lt.-Gov. HSN, Sept. 1911.

11 ANS 19 G 1, Ponty circular, 26 December 1911.

12 ANS 17 G 39, Ponty to Gov.-Gen. p. i, AOF, December 1912.

13 See below, p. 107.

14 Arnaud, 'L'Islam et la politique musulmane française'.

15 *Ibid.* pp. 5–8.

16 *Ibid.* p. 9.

17 *Ibid.* p. 121.

18 *Ibid.* p. 150.

19 *Ibid.* pp. 117–19.

20 *Ibid.* p. 144.

21 *Ibid.* pp. 144–9.

22 I am grateful to the archivists in the rue Oudinot for showing me a copy of Clozel's official c.v. on which the following paragraph is based.

23 Weiskel, *Baule*, ch. 3.

24 Clozel and Villamur (eds.), *Les Coutumes indigènes*.

25 *Ibid.* p. 41.

26 *Ibid.* p. 46.

27 *Ibid.* pp. 68–72.

28 Weiskel, *Baule*, p. 152n.

29 ANS 15 G 103, Clozel, 'Note sur l'état social des indigènes et sur la situation présente de l'islam au Soudan français', 1908. It is interesting to contrast Clozel's attitude to slavery in the French Sudan with his earlier more indulgent view of the same institution in the animist Ivory Coast where he was above all concerned to maintain good relations with the (slave-owning) Baule chiefs. See Weiskel, *Baule*, p. 151.

30 ANS 15 G 103, Clozel, 'Note sur l'état social . . .'.

31 See IF Fonds Terrier, Clozel to Terrier, 22 April 1911, for Clozel's criticism of the military. The issue is also dealt with in Weiskel, *Baule*, pp. 152–6.

32 ANS 15 G 103, Clozel to Gov.-Gen. AOF, 1 October 1909.

33 ANS 15 G 103, 'Circulaire au sujet de la politique musulmane dans le Haut-Sénégal et Niger', 12 August 1911.

34 *Ibid.* (emphasis added).

35 Replies are filed in ANS 15 G 103.

36 Clozel, 'Lettre de Korbous', pp. 60–2, 106–9, 149–52, 182–5. Delafosse writing in *BCAF*, 1918, 81.

37 Clozel, 'Lettre de Korbous', p. 61.

38 *Ibid.* pp. 106–9, 149–52.

39 ANS J 94, Clozel to Gov.-Gen. AOF, 14 October 1910.

40 ANS J 94, Mariani, 'Rapport . . . sur la *médersa* de Tombouctou', March 1911; Clozel to Gov.-Gen. AOF, 14 May 1911; Mariani to Gov.-Gen. AOF, 10 November 1911.

41 The best account of Delafosse's career is his daughter's biography: Delafosse, *Maurice Delafosse*. Except where otherwise indicated biographical detail is taken from this source.

42 See Renault, *Lavigerie*, pp. 388–409. The order was a controversial one, chiefly because the brothers carried firearms. Cambon thought that they should be confined to areas where France was already firmly in control. The Radical press in France was hostile: for example,

the newspaper *Lyons Républicain* wrote 'N'écoutons pas trop M. Lavigerie et ne nous brouillons pas trop avec Allah', cited in Renault, *Lavigerie*, p. 398.

43 Monteil, *Les Khassonké*, p. 8.
44 Delafosse letter 23 May 1909, cited in Delafosse, *Maurice Delafosse*, p. 270.
45 Delafosse, 'L'Etat actuel de l'islam', pp. 32–54.
46 Delafosse, 'Le Clergé musulman', pp. 177–206; 'Les Confréries musulmanes', pp. 81–90.
47 Delafosse, *Haut-Sénégal et Niger*.
48 *Ibid.* vol. III, pp. 1–2.
49 *Ibid.* p. 161.
50 *Ibid.* p. 163.
51 *Ibid.* p. 165.
52 *Ibid.* pp. 2–3.
53 *Ibid.* pp. 214–15.
54 Delafosse, *Maurice Delafosse*, ch. 7.
55 Marty's papers are not yet available, but I am grateful to the archivist of the Service historique de l'armée de terre in the chateau de Vincennes for allowing me to see a copy of Marty's official c.v..
56 For background to *dâhir*, see Ageron, *Politiques coloniales*, part II.
57 ANS 19 G 1, Gov.-Gen. AOF circular, 15 January 1913.
58 ANS 17 G 38, Gov.-Gen. AOF circular, April 1913.
59 ANS 19 G 1, Gov.-Gen. AOF circular, 1 August 1913.
60 O'Brien, *Saints and Politicians*, ch. 3, 'Chiefs, saints and bureaucrats', p. 90.
61 Arrêté, 1 September 1913, *JOAOF*, 1913, p. 894.
62 ANS 19 G 2, Gov.-Gen. AOF to Général Commt Supérieur, 23 March 1913; Médecin Principal, Garnier to Marty, 18 October 1913.
63 ANS J 85, Marty to Directeurs de l'Enseignement Musulman, Algérie et Tunisie, 2 September 1913.
64 ANS J 86, Marty, 'Rapport à M. le Gov.-Gen. sur les Ecoles coraniques du Sénégal', 20 November 1915.
65 See, for example, comments of Administrateur du Sine-Saloum to Marty, 21 June 1915, in ANS 13 G 67.
66 ANS 15 G 103, 'Rapport sur la politique musulmane suivie par le cercle de Djenné pendant l'année 1913'.
67 ANS J 94, 'La *Médersa* de Djenné', 16 June 1917.
68 Martin, *Muslim Brotherhoods*, pp. 141–5.
69 ANSOM AP 1402/20, Mouret, 'Rapport politique, 1ère trimestre', 1913.
70 ANS 9 G 30, Marty, 'Note à M. le Chef de Cabinet sur notre action politique dans les confins Maroco-Mauritaniens, 1913'.
71 ANS 9 G 30, Marty, 'Note à M. le Chef de Cabinet sur l'éventualité de la soumission d'El Hiba'.
72 Marty, *Les Mourides*, O'Brien, *Mourides*; *Saints and Politicians*; Coulon, *Le Marabout et le Prince*, are the best introduction to the subject.
73 Cited in Ba, *Ahmadou Bamba*, pp. 25–6.
74 F. Dumont, *La Pensée religieuse d'Amadou Bamba*, Dakar/Abidjan, 1975, is a comprehensive annotated collection of Bamba's religious poems.
75 ANSOM S et D IV/127, Leclerc to Directeur Affaires Politiques, 10 July 1895.
76 ANSOM S et D IV/127, Leclerc to Gov. S et D, 15 August 1895.
77 ANSOM S et D, Directeur Affaires Politiques to Gov. S et D 29 August 1895.
78 O'Brien, *Mourides*, p. 42; Ba, *Ahmadou Bamba*, pp. 81–7..
79 Ba, *Ahmadou Bamba*, p. 101.
80 Ba, *Ahmadou Bamba*, pp. 134–8; O'Brien, *Mourides*, pp. 44–5; Coulon, *Le Marabout et Le Prince*, pp. 76–7.
81 ANS 17 G 39, Ponty to Gov.-Gen. p. i, AOF, 12 January 1912 (emphasis added).

82 25,000 tonnes exported in 1885, 140,000 tonnes in 1900 and 508,000 tonnes in 1930. See Coulon, *Le Marabout et Le Prince*, p. 76.
83 Marty, *Les Mourides*, p. 28.
84 O'Brien, *Mourides*, p. 19.
85 Marty, *Les Mourides*, p. 19.
86 ANS 13 G 12 (17), Gov.-Gen. AOF to Lt.-Gov. Sénégal, 13 August 1912 (emphasis added).
87 See below, chapter 11.
88 ANS 13 G 12 (17), Gov.-Gen. AOF to Lt.-Gov. Sénégal, 8 November 1912.
89 The report was published unchanged as *Les Mourides d'Amadou Bamba*.
90 ANSOM S et D, Le Chatelier to Hardy(?)/Marty (?), 25 August 1913.
91 Marty, *Les Mourides*, pp. 9–10. Page references given in the following paragraphs refer to this volume.

7 The First World War

1 ANS 19 G 4, Clozel to Ponty, n.d.; Ponty to Clozel, 17 September 1914; Ponty circular, 20 September 1914.
2 ANSOM AP 907/3 *bis*, Min. Colonies to Gov.-Gen. Algérie, AOF, AEF.
3 ANS 7 G 69, Lt.-Gov. Guinée to *cercles*, 8 November 1914; SHAT AOF Niger 3/iii/d, Lt.-Gov. Niger to cercles, 10 November 1914, same to same, 18 November 1914.
4 ANS 5 G 62, Ponty to Admin. cercle Lagunes, 12 November 1914; Lt.-Gov. Côte d'Ivoire, to cercles, 16 December 1914.
5 See John Buchan, *Greenmantle*, London, 1916.
6 ANSOM AP 907/1, Gov.-Gen. AOF to Min. Colonies, 22 November 1914; ANSOM AP 1420/20, Lt.-Gov. Mauretanie to Gov.-Gen. AOF, 11 November 1914.
7 Cited in 'Les Musulmans français et la guerre', *RMM*, 1915, 17.
8 *Ibid*. p. 132.
9 *Ibid*. p. 107.
10 *Ibid*. p. 99.
11 ANS 19 G 1, Min. Colonies to Gov.-Gen. AOF, 21 December 1914.
12 ANS 19 G 4, Min. Colonies to Gov.-Gen. AOF, 21 October 1914.
13 ANS 19 G 9, Defrance (Plenipotentiary Minister in Alexandria) to Min. Affaires Etrangères, 23 July, 1915; Gov.-Gen. AOF to Min. Colonies, 14 October 1915; Min. Colonies to Gov.-Gen. AOF, 25 August 1915.
14 ANS 19 G 10, Min. Colonies to Gov.-Gen. p.i, AOF, 23 June 1916; Gov.-Gen. p.i. AOF circular, 28 June 1916.
15 See file in ANSOM AP 907 *bis* 5 for correspondence between Paris, Alexandria and Dakar in July 1916 and also IF Fonds Terrier 5917 for good collection of press cuttings relating to proclamation.
16 The Lieutenant-Governor of Niger said that el-Hajj Sliman was 'lukewarm' in his loyalty to France and therefore an unsuitable person to receive a copy of the proclamation. The interim Governor-General, on the other hand, thought that the proclamation would be a good influence. See ANS 19 G 10, Lt.-Gov. Niger to Gov.-Gen. p.i. AOF to Lt.-Gov. Niger, 14 September 1916.
17 Marty, *L'Islam en Guinée*, pp. 248–9.
18 Marty described Ahmed Baba as 'l'un des meilleurs artisans de notre occupation' in *Etudes sur l'islam et les tribus de Soudan*, vol. II, p. 12.
19 *Ibid*. p. 16.
20 Marty, *Etudes sur l'islam en Côte d'Ivoire*, p. 222. See also ANS 19 G 10, Min. Colonies to Gov.-Gen. AOF, 4 August 1916 and Gov.-Gen. AOF to Min. Colonies, 28 July 1916, for list of chosen leaders.
21 ANS 19 G 10, Min. Colonies to Gov.-Gen. AOF, 4 August 1916; same to same, 17 August 1916; Gov.-Gen. AOF to Min. Colonies, 18 August 1916. See also R. Bidwell, 'The

Bremard Mission in the Hijaz, 1916–17, A study in inter-allied cooperation' in Bidwell and Smith (eds.), *Arabian and Islamic Studies*, London, 1983.

22 ANS 19 G 10, Gov.-Gen. AOF to Lt.-Gov. Sénégal, 11 August 1916; same to same, 17 August 1916; Gov.-Gen. AOF to Min. Colonies, 18 August 1916.

23 ANS 19 G 10, Min. Colonies to Gov.-Gen. AOF, 19 August 1916; Lt.-Gov. Sénégal to Gov.-Gen. AOF, 17 August 1916; same to same, 18 August, 1916; Gov.-Gen. AOF to Min. Colonies, 28 August 1916; Min. Colonies to Gov.-Gen. AOF, 30 August 1916.

24 ANS 19 G 11, Lt.-Col. Bremond to Briand, 19 November 1916.

25 ANS 19 G 10, Min. Colonies to Gov.-Gen. AOF, 27 November 1916.

26 ANS 19 G 9, Min. Affaires Etrangères to Gov.-Gen. Algérie and Res.-Gen. Maroc, Tunisie, 3 April 1917. For Paris 'Levant lobby' see Andrew and Kanya Forstner, *France Overseas*.

27 See, for example, above pp. 31, 65 and ANSOM AP 907 *bis*/s, Min. Affaires Etrangères to Min. Colonies, describing France as 'la plus grande puissance musulmane arabe'.

28 IF Fonds Terrier 5917, Lyautey to Min. Affaires Etrangères, 16 June 1916 and see also in same file 'Note de M. Gaillard'.

29 Marty, *Les Mourides*, p. 43.

30 Details of the plans for the mosque and hospital are to be found in ANSOM AP 907 *bis*/5.

31 ANSOM AP 913/1, Gov.-Gen. AOF to Min. Colonies, 30 January 1916.

32 ANS 19 G 1, Arrêté, 28 April 1916.

33 ANS 7 G 69, Lt.-Gov. Guinée to Gov.-Gen. AOF, n.d.

34 ANS 13 G 17, Lt.-Gov. Sénégal to Gov.-Gen. AOF, 21 January 1915.

35 ANS 19 G 1, Gov.-Gen. AOF to Min. Colonies, 4 March 1915.

36 ANS 19 G 4, Min. Colonies to Gov.-Gen. AOF, 1 July 1916; Delafosse, 'Note pour M. l'Inspecteur des Douanes', 7 July 1916; same to same, 15 November 1917.

37 ANS 5 G 63, Joseph (Chef Bureau Politique) to Marty, 29 April 1916.

38 A good account of the internal politics of these years is to be found in Delafosse, *Maurice Delafosse*, pp. 264–341.

39 Marty, 'L'Islam et les tribus dans la colonie du Niger'.

40 Marty, 'Les Amulettes musulmanes au Sénégal', p. 319.

41 Marty, *Côte d'Ivoire*, p. 455.

42 Marty, *Trarzas*, p. 309.

43 Marty, *Soudan*, vol. II; *Soudan*, vol. IV, p. 210.

44 ANS 4 E 6 (NS), 'Le Groupement tidiani d'Al-Hadj Malick Sy', 1915, reprinted in Marty, *Mauretanie et Sénégal*.

45 Marty, *Mauretanie et Sénégal*, pp. 413–42. The quote is from p. 441.

46 ANS 19 G 4, Marty, 'Note pour M. le Chef du Cabinet', 11 May 1915.

47 ANS 13 G 26 (17) (NS), Marty, 'Note', 28 April 1919.

48 ANS M 241, Marty, 'L'Influence de l'islam dans le droit coutumier des peuples sénégalais', 1915.

49 Marty, *Soudan*, vol. IV, p. 1.

50 Marty, *Soudan*, vol. II, p. 221.

51 Marty, *Côte d'Ivoire*, p. 94.

52 IF Papiers Deharain 5629, 'Notes', July 1921.

53 Marty, *Mauretanie et Sénégal*, p. 467.

54 Marty, *Côte d'Ivoire*, p. 7.

55 See Marty's description of coastal Agni '... forts intelligents, mais paresseux au delà de tout ce qu'on peut imaginer, dans un pays prodigieusement riche elles n'ont qu'un besoin, l'alcool', *Côte d'Ivoire*, p. 1.

56 *Ibid.* p. 13.

57 ANS 5 G 62, Gov.-Gen. AOF to Admin. cercle Lagunes, 12 April 1914; Lt.-Gov. Côte d'Ivoire to cercles, 16 December 1914; Marty, *Côte d'Ivoire*, pp. 16–18.

58 Marty, *Dahomey*, p. 30.
59 Marty, *Mauretainie et Sénégal*, pp. 467–8.
60 Marty, *Côte d'Ivoire*, p. 273.
61 Marty, *Soudan*, vol. II, p. 293.
62 Marty, Trarzas, p. 289.
63 *Ibid.* p. 308.
64 Marty, *Soudan*, vol. III, p. 263.
65 *Ibid.* p. 148.
66 *Ibid.* pp. 150–1.
67 Marty, *Brackna*, pp. 121–2.
68 Marty, *Soudan*, vol. III, pp. 444–5.
69 *Ibid.* p. 270.
70 *Ibid.* pp. 253–4.
71 Marty, *Brackna*, p. 140.
72 ANS 13 G 67, Marty, 'De l'influence religieuse des Cheikhs Maures au Sénégal', n.d.
73 Marty, *Mauretanie et Sénégal*, p. 101 (Marty's emphasis).
74 *Ibid.* p. 400.
75 ANS 19 G 2, 'Politique et colonisation: l'influence musulman', *AOF-ECHO*, 24 October 1916.
76 ANS 13 G 67, Leroux to Gov.-Gen. AOF, 2 April 1917; Gov.-Gen. AOF to Lt.-Gov. Sénégal, July 1917.
77 Marty, *Côte d'Ivoire*, p. 400.
78 ANS 5 G 64, handwriten questionnaire, cercle of Odienné, n.d.

Part IV Introduction

1 On the war, see special edition of *JAH*, 'World War I and Africa', especially R. Rathbone's 'Introduction' and Andrew and Kanya Forstner, 'France, Africa and the First World War'; M. Michel, *L'Appel à l'Afrique: contributions et réactions à l'effort de guerre en A.O.F. (1914–1919)*, Paris, 1982. On hope and *mise en valeur*, see R. Giradet, *L'Idée coloniale en France*, Paris, 1971; C. R. Ageron, *France coloniale ou parti colonial*, Paris, 1978. The monthly magazine *Bulletin du Comité de l'Afrique Française* gives an excellent insight into the minds of the colonial enthusiasts during this period.
2 'L'Age de l'air en Afrique', *BCAF*, Oct.-Dec. 1922; *BCAF*, Oct. 1927.
3 See Andrew and Kanya Forstner, *France Overseas*, chs. 8, 9; Bertrand, *La Fin d'un monde*, Paris, 1973, pp. 131–78; C. S. Maier, *Recasting Bourgeois Europe*, Princeton, 1975, ch.4, 'The politics of reparation'; A. Toynbee, *Survey of International Events, 1920–23*, London, 1924.
4 A. Lebrun, 'La France coloniale devant le monde', BCAF, April, 1930, 159–62; see also M. Lakroum, *Le Travail inégal: paysans et salariés devant la crise des années trente*, Paris, 1983, pp. 23–7, on French suspicions of International Labour Office.
5 E. H. Carr, *The Bolshevik Revolution, 1917–23*, Harmondsworth, 1966, vol. III, pp. 253–71.
6 *BCAF* Sept.-Oct. 1920, p. 261.
7 *BCAF*, Jan. 1922, p. 43.
8 It tells the story of Kossi's passage through a violent life ending in a violent death as, escaping from a horde of cannibals, the hero jumps carelessly into the jaws of a hungry crocodile.
9 *BCAF*, June 1934, p. 353.
10 See above, p. 4. See also Asad (ed.), *Anthropology and the Colonial Encounter*, especially editor's 'Introduction' and Wendy James, 'The anthropologist as reluctant imperialists', pp. 41–70.
11 *BCAF*, June 1920.

12 On timing of French investment in Africa, see C. Coquery-Vidrovitch (ed.), 'L'Afrique et la crise de 1930 (1924–38)', *RFHOM*, LXIII (232–3), 1976.
13 The paradoxes of colonialism in the inter-war period are most eloquently and suggestively stated in J. Berque, *Le Maghrib entre deux guerres*, Paris, 1962 (Trans. *French North Africa*, London, 1967).

8 Post-war attitudes to Islam

1 ANSOM AP 1418, Min. Colonies to Gov-Gen. AOF, 15 October, 1919; Gov.-Gen. AOF to Min. Colonies, 21 October, 1919; Min. Colonies to Gov-Gen. AOF, 29 October 1919; Marty to Directeur de l'Afrique (rue Oudinot), 22 October 1919.
2 ANS 17 G (NS) 239 (180), Cheikh Ibra Fall to Gov-Gen. AOF, 21 October 1921. I am grateful to Jim Searing, Princeton, for showing me this reference.
3 ANSOM AP 170/3, M. Delafosse, 'De la participation des indigènes de l'AOF à l'administration locale', *Dépêche Coloniale*, 3,5,9,11,16 April 1918.
4 ANSOM AP 170/3, Gov.-Gen. AOF to Min. Colonies , 16 May 1918.
5 See Cohen, *Rulers of Empire*, ch. 6, 'Era of lost opportunities'.
6 Delafosse, 'Sur l'orientation nouvelle de la politique indigène', p. 146.
7 M. Michel, 'Un Programme réformiste en 1919: Delafosse et "la politique nouvelle" en AOF', *CEA*, 1975, 313–27.
8 H. Labouret, 'La Politique indigène en Afrique', *BCAF*, June 1930–April 1931; J. Brévié. *Circulaires sur la politique et l'administration indigènes en AOF*, Gorée, 1932. These are discussed in Auchnie, 'The *commandement indigène* in Senegal'.
9 Delafosse, 'L'Animisme nègre', pp. 143–60.
10 *Ibid.* pp. 139–41.
11 'Bien que professant pour l'islamisme un respect que mérite … cette religion, je ne puis concevoir qu'il réponde à l'idéal normal des sociétés noires, et je suis obligé à réfléchir aux difficultés qui pourraient résulter pour les puissances européenes de l'extension à l'ensemble de l'Afrique noire d'une religion qui, quoique dérivant des mêmes sources que la nôtre, en est trop éloignée historiquement pour ne pas être une rivale', Delafosse, 'L'Orientation nouvelle', p. 151.
12 The term *'naturisme'* appears to have been peculiar to Brévié. 'Naturalisme' was the term used by Durkheim to describe religions based on nature as opposed to 'animisme' which was based on spirits – although he admitted that in practice both types of religion existed side-by-side. See, *Les Formes élémentaires de la vie religieuse*, Paris, 1912, p. 68. Brévié intended 'naturisme' to be descriptive of a period in time in the development of society: 'Cette enfance des sociétés qui va de l'époque où l'homme vivait isolé dans la brousse à celle où se constituent les premiers groupements; famille patriarchale et matriarchale, clan, tribu etc. – ce que nous appelerons "naturisme".' Brévié, *L'Islamisme contre 'Naturisme'*, p. 6.
13 Delafosse preface to Brévié, *L'Islamisme contre 'Naturisme'*, p. ix.
14 Brévié, *L'Islamisme contre 'naturisme'*, pp. 38–9.
15 *Ibid.* p. 110.
16 *Ibid.* p. iii.
17 *Ibid.* pp. 125, 146.
18 *Ibid.* p. 181.
19 *Ibid.* p. 184.
20 *Ibid.* p. 293.
21 *Ibid.* p. 304.
22 *Ibid.* p. 307.
23 A nice example of this aspect of his character is his circular on the importance of the upkeep of libraries in each *cercle*: 'Il faut rappeler qu'il n y a pas désaccord entre l'action la plus

immédiate et la culture la plus en plus profondie, que c'est un devoir de développer en soi une rigueur intellectuelle', ANS 17 G 335 (NS), Gov.-Gen. AOF to colonies, 28 August 1931.
24 Durkheim also based his theories of religion on the work of British and American anthropologists in Australia and Polynesia.
25 See Vincent Monteil's ironic comments on the certainty of Giraule's explanation of the cosmology of the Dogon for an eloquent warning of the dangers of constructing too large a theory on the basis of insufficient evidence. *Islam noir*, p. 30.
26 Delafosse preface to Brévié, *L'Islamisme contre 'Naturisme'*, p. xi.
27 See Spiegler, 'Aspects of nationalist thought amongst French-speaking West Africans', ch. 6, especially pp. 144–52.
28 Delafosse, 'Les points sombres de l'horizon en Afrique occidentale', pp. 279–83.
29 *Ibid.* p. 278.
30 Ageron, *Politiques coloniales au Maghreb*, part II, ch. 2, 'La Politique berbère du Protectorat marocain de 1913 à 1934'.
31 This account is based on R. Cornevin, *La République populaire du Bénin*, Paris, 1981, pp. 273–410; Marty, *Dahomey*; D. Ross, 'Dahomey', in M. Crowder (ed.), *West African Resistance: The Military Response to Colonial Occupation*, London, 1971, pp. 144–69.
32 This paragraph is based on Marty, *Dahomey*, pp. 53–83.
33 ANS 8 G 51 (NS) 23, 'Note du Lt.-Gov. Dahomey', 17 January 1920.
34 Marty, *Dahomey*, p. 61.
35 Ballard, 'The Porto Novo incidents'.
36 ANS 8 G 51 (NS) 23, Doizy to Min. Colonies, 21 October 1919; Min. Colonies to Gov. Gen. AOF, 25 November 1919; 'Note du Lt-Gov. Dahomey', 17 January 1920.
37 Marty, *Dahomey*, p. 74.
38 ANS 8 G 51 (NS) 23, Marty to Lt.-Gov. Dahomey, 7 February 1921.
39 ANS 8 G 52 (NS) 23, Lt.-Gov. Dahomey to Gov.-Gen. AOF, 8 April 1922.
40 On Ligue des droits de l'homme and its activities in Dahomey where a branch was set up by the early Dahomean nationalist, Louis Hunkanrin, see Spiegler 'Aspects of nationalist thought', ch. 2 and Ballard, 'The Porto Novo incidents', pp. 64–8.
41 ANS 8 G 52 (NS) 23, Lt.-Gov. Dahomey to Gov-Gen. AOF, 19 February 1923; Gov.-Gen. AOF to Lt.-Gov. Dahomey, 23 February 1923; Gov.-Gen. AOF to Lt.-Gov. Dahomey, 26 February 1923.
42 ANS 8 G 52 (NS) 23, Min. Colonies to Gov.-Gen. AOF, 28 February 1923; Gov.-Gen. AOF to Lt.-Gov. Dahomey, 26 February 1923.
43 ANS 8 G 52 (NS) 23, M. l'Inspecteur des Affaires Administratives de cercles du Bas-Dahomey, 'Mémoire introductif d'enquête sur les incidents de Porto Novo en Février-Mars', 7 March 1923.
44 ANS 8 G 52 (NS) 23, Min. Colonies to Gov.-Gen. AOF , 7 March 1923. On Hunkanrin, see Spiegler, 'Aspects of nationalist thought', ch. 2.
45 ANS 19 G 22 (NS), Articles are filed in 'Extrait d'une note de renseignement du ministère du 23 Janvier 1923 sur la propagande bolchévique aux colonies'.
46 ANS 8 G 52 (NS) 23, Comité d'action franco–musulman d'Afrique du Nord to Carpot, 2 March 1923; *L'Humanité*, 9 March 1923.
47 ANS 8 G 52 (NS) 23, Lt.-Gov. Dahomey to Gov-Gen. AOF, 14 March 1923; same to same, 25 March 1923.
48 ANS 8 G 52 (NS) 23, Lt.-Gov. Dahomey to Gov-Gen. AOF, 11 April 1923; Gov.-Gen. AOF to Min. Colonies, 14 February 1923; Lt.-Gov. Dahomey to Gov-Gen. AOF, 21 April 1923; Gov.-Gen. AOF, to Lt.-Gov. Dahomey, 23 April 1923: same to same, 28 April 1923; Gov.-Gen. AOF to Min. Colonies, 27 May 1923; Gov-Gen. AOF to Lt.-Gov. Dahomey, 22 June 1923; arrêté, 23 July 1923, lifted the state of siege.
49 ANS 8 G 52 (NS) 23, Delafosse, 'Considérations sur les causes lointaines de certaines manifestations de mécontentement de la part des indigènes', *Dépêche Coloniale*, 16 April 1923.

50 ANS 8 G 52 (NS) 23, Lt.-Gov. AOF, to Lt.-Gov. Dahomey, 5 April 1923.
51 In ANS 5 G 5 (NS).
52 André, *L'Islam et les races*, vol. II, pp. 160–67.
53 ANS 19 NG 5 (NS), Capt. P. J. André, 'Rapport à M. le Gov.-Gen. de l'AOF ...', 5 January 1923.
54 'Arrêté instituant à la Direction des affaires politiques et administratives un service de renseignement et des affaires musulmanes', *JOAOF*, 15 March 1923, 241–2.
55 'Arrêté constituant les services du Gov.-Gen.', *JOAOF*, 1 July 1920, 391.
56 ANS 19 G 26 (NS), André, 'Rapport à M. le Gov.-Gen. ...', 26 March 1923.
57 ANS 19 G 23 (NS), André, 'Rapport à M. le Gov.-Gen. ...', 10 April 1923.
58 ANS 8 G 52 (NS) 23, Min. Colonies to Gov.-Gen. AOF, 28 February 1923.
59 ANS 19 G 23 (NS), André, 'Rapport à M. le Gov.-Gen. ...', 29 April 1923, 8 May 1923. See also A. Hughes and R. Morley 'The "Mallam Sa'id conspiracy" of 1923: British reactions to Mahdism in Northern Nigeria' (unpublished). I am very grateful to A. Hughes for showing me a copy of this article which demonstrates that the British to a very large extent shared French anxieties about possible Islamic rebellion at this time. H. R. Palmer, Resident of Bornu Province, sent reports as alarming as those written by André about the threat posed by *mahdi*sm. As in the earlier Satiru rebellion, the local Muslim establishment appear to have encouraged British suspicions in order to secure their help against the growing power of the new Muslim communities grouped around leaders such as Mallam Said who posed a direct challenge to the established order of the northern emirates.
60 ANS 19 G 23 (NS), André, 'Rapport à M. le Gov.-Gen. ... sur les musulmans à la colonie du Niger', 25 May 1923.
61 ANS 19 G 23 (NS), André, 'Rapport à M. le Gov.-Gen. ...', 16 June 1923.
62 ANS 19 G 23 (NS), Administrateur Martin to Lt.-Gov. Haute Volta, 21 July 1923.
63 ANS 19 G 23 (NS), Chatelain, Chargé du Service de Renseignement au Niger, 'Rapport à M. le Lt.-Gov. Niger', 22 August 1923. In fairness to André it should be said that Palmer at least was as worried about *mahdi*sm. See, Hughes and Morley, 'The "Mallam Sa'id conspiracy"'.
64 ANS 19 G 23 (NS), Chatelain, Chargé du service de renseignement au Niger, 'Rapport à M. le Lt.-Gov. Niger', 22 August 1923.
65 ANSOM AP 591/15, 'Rapport en fin de mission du Capt. P. J. André', 25 September 1923.
66 ANS 19 g 23 (NS), Gov.-Gen. AOF to Min. Colonies, 18 October, 1923.
67 ANS19 8 g 23 (NS), Min. Colonies to Gov.-Gen. AOF, 19 November 1923.
68 André, *L'Islam noir*, p. 58.
69 See Fisher, *Ahmadiyyah*.
70 The AOF administration was itself interested in Indian nationalism. See, ANSOM AP 518/19, Gov.-Gen., p. i, AOF to Min. Colonies, 10 August 1922, enclosing a copy of a Hindu newspaper which had been intercepted but which no one in Dakar was capable of translating. The Gov.-Gen. was worried by the fact that 'the name of the agitator Gandhi' appeared several times in the paper which suggested to him that it was 'an Indian nationalist pamphlet'. Min. Colonies replied (n.d.) that it was merely a commercial Sunday supplement of a local Indian paper and that its content was entirely apolitical.
71 Gen. P. J. André and Gen. J. Buhrer, *Ce que devient l'islam devant le monde moderne*, Paris, 1952.

9 The French stake in Islam

1 ANS 19 G 1 (NS) has details of all the various appointments. Martin's colleagues included Lt. Riehl, Capt. Rocaboy, Lt. Aune, Commts Borricand, Destaing and Michelangeli.
2 The correspondence is filed in ANS 19 G 26 (NS).
3 ANS 19 G 22 (NS), Gov.-Gen. AOF circular, 13 January 1925.
4 ANS 19 G 22 (NS), Gov.-Gen. AOF to Min. Colonies, Feb. 1925.

5 IF Terrier 5917, 'Rapport présenté par le Gen. Aubert au Comité consultatif de défense des colonies sur la propagande musulmane dans les troupes indigènes', Jan. 1923.

6 ANSOM AP 598/2, 'Rapport politique, Sénégal, 1926'.

7 In June 1926 the Conseil colonial debated the suggestion that Senegal should make this contribution but rejected it partly because it was felt that Senegalese individuals such as Ahmadu Bamba had already made substantial contributions to the fund. See ANS 4 E 17 (NS) 135, 'Procès verbal du séance du Conseil colonial', 12 June 1926. I owe this reference to Jim Searing (Princeton).

8 ANSOM AP 598/2, 'Rapport politique, Sénégal, 1926'.

9 *Ibid.*

10 See ANS 4 E 3 (NS) for these files.

11 ANSOM AP 598/3, 'Rapport politique, Sénégal, 1928'.

12 ANS 13 G 12 (NS) 17, Carde, 'Note pour M. le Gov.-Gen. p. i. AOF', 23 July 1929.

13 ANS 13 G 12 (NS) 17, 'Rapport sur l'incident de Diourbel: affaire Cheikh Anta M'Backé', 14 February 1930; see also ANSOM AP 598/3, 'Rapport politique, Sénégal, 1930'.

14 ANS 21 G 48 (NS) 17, 'Note au sujet de l'affaire Cheikh Anta', April 1933.

15 ANS 13 G 12 (NS) 17, 'Note', 28 July 1933.

16 Notably O'Brien, *Mourides*; Coulon, *Le Marabout et Le Prince*.

17 ANS 21 G 143 (NS) 108, 'Renseignements', 27 February 1939.

18 ANSOM AP 598/2, 'Rapport politique, Sénégal, 1926'.

19 The bank statements are filed in ANS 13 G 12 (NS).

20 ANS 13 G 12 (NS) 17, Spitz (Directeur du Cabinet du Gov.-Gen.) to Gov.-Gen. AOF, 24 July 1927; Brumauld to Tallerie, 25 July 1927.

21 ANS 4 E 3 (NS), Commt cercle Baol, 'Note', 20 January 1930.

22 IFAN Monteil I Lt. Nekkach, 'Le Mouridisme depuis 1912', St. Louis, 1952 (typescript).

23 ANS 13 G 19 (NS) 17, Lt.-Gov. p. i. Sénégal to Gov.-Gen. AOF, 20 July 1936.

24 See, for example, De Belvert, 'L'Exode d'une race'. De Belvert admitted that the rights of the Fulbe would have to be overlooked in the interests of following a 'realistic and unsentimental policy' in Senegal.

25 Chansard, 'Les Mourides du Sénégal'.

26 See above, p. 45.

27 See Brenner, *West African Sufi*, chs. 1–2, for a good summary of Tijani reaction to French conquest.

28 There are no satisfactory biographies of Seydou Nourou Tall. The following biographical details are taken from Kane and Cissoko, 'Une Grande Figure africaine'.

29 Marty, *Mauretanie et Sénégal*, p. 357.

30 ANS 19 G 43 (NS), 'L'Oeuvre de Seydou Nourou Tall en Afrique française' (typescript).

31 Cau, 'L'Islam au Sénégal'.

32 ANS 17 G 260 (NS) 108, 'Message radiodiffusé en AOF', 14 July 1939.

33 Traoré, 'Cheikh Hama houllah'; Brenner, *West African Sufi*, pp. 45–59. The following paragraph is based largely on these two sources, although Marty, *Soudan*, vol. IV, part III, 'Le Sahel de Nioro', also contains much valuable information.

34 Marty, *Soudan*, vol. IV, pp. 210–11.

35 Brenner, *West African Sufi*, pp. 47–50, contains the best summary of these versions.

36 Traoré, 'Cheikh Hama houllah' pp. 18–52.

37 Marty, *Soudan*, vol. IV, part III, p. 218.

38 *Ibid.* p. 220.

39 *Ibid.* p. 222.

40 Brenner stresses the importance of Malick Sy's death in *West African Sufi*, p. 54.

41 ANS 19 G 26 (NS), Lt.-Gov. Soudan to Gov.-Gen. AOF, 11 May 1925.

42 Cited in Traoré, 'Cheikh Hama houllah', p. 145.

43 Gillier, *La Pénétration française en Mauritanie*.

44 ANSOM AP 1415/4, Carde, 'Note au sujet de la politique suivie en Mauretanie', 20 September 1928.
45 ANSOM AP 1415/4, Gov.-Gen. AOF to Min. Colonies, 25 September 1928. The voluminous correspondence concerning Reine and Serre is in this file.
46 ANSOM AP 1054/1, 'Rapport de mission dans les territoires du sud de l'Algérie', 1928. The author had been sent on the mission by Carde to investigate Tijani links across the Sahara and concluded that 'Nothing which happens in southern Morocco should leave AOF indifferent'.
47 ANSOM AP 2258/3, Commt de cercle, Charbonnier, 'Compte rendu du cercle de Gorgol, Mauretanie', 5 September 1929.
48 Traoré, 'Cheikh Hama houllah', pp. 164–78.
49 ANSOM AP 2258/3, Gov.-Gen. AOF circular, 3 March 1930.
50 ANSOM AP 2258/3, Gov.-Gen. AOF to Min. Colonies, 31 August 1934 (emphasis added).
51 ANSOM AP 2258/3, Beyries, 'Note', 14 December 1934.
52 ANSOM AP 2258/3, Admin. de cercle d'Agneby to Lt.-Gov. Côte d'Ivoire, 11 March 1935; Gov.-Gen. AOF to Min. Colonies, 23 April 1935.
53 ANS O 82 (NS), Interprète Lt. Long, 'Rapport sur la diffusion en Adrar de la pratique dite "des deux rekâas" ', 1 September 1936.
54 ANSOM AP 2258/3, Gov.-Gen. AOF circular, 27 February 1937.
55 ANS 17 G 60 (NS), 17, Gov.-Gen. AOF circular, 6 August 1937.
56 Traoré, 'Cheikh Hama houllah', pp. 193–234.
57 ANS 19 G 7 (NS), Haut Commissaire de l'Afrique Française (Boisson) to Commt Supérieur des Troupes en AOF (Barrau), 17 February 1941; Barrau to Boisson, 8 March 1941. Montezer's pamphlet was called *L'Afrique et l'islam*, Dakar, 1939.
58 See Traoré, 'Cheikh Hama houllah', pp. 194–216, for details of Hamallah's imprisonment and death.
59 Brenner, *West African Sufi*.
60 D'Arbaumont, 'La Confrérie des Tidjania', p. 24 (emphasis added). Cf. Brenner's comment 'Hamallah was punished not for what he did but for what he failed to do', *West African Sufi*, p. 54.
61 For a discussion of the impact of colonialism on metropolitan politics, see R. Girardet, *L'Idée coloniale en France de 1871 à 1962*, Paris, 1972, chs. 7–9; C. Liduzu, *Aux Origines des tiers-mondismes: colonisés et anticolonialistes en France 1919–1939*, Paris, 1982.

10 The 'rediscovery' of Islam

1 'Arrêté fixant l'organisation de l'enseignement en AOF', 1 May 1923 in *Textes portant sur la réorganisation de l'enseignement en AOF*, Gorée, 1924.
2 ANS 0 82 (NS), 'Décision', 27 December 1930; see especially Article 2.
3 See above, pp. 63.
4 ANS 0 92 (NS), Gov.-Gen. AOF to Lt.-Gov. Soudan to Gov.-Gen. AOF, 6 October 1932; Arrêté, 12 September 1933; Bulletin d'inspection, 30 January 1934 – 2 February 1934.
5 ANS 0 92 (NS), 'Bulletin d'inspection; étude sur la *médersa* des fils des chefs et notables maures de Timbédra, 20 March 1934 – 12 January 1935'. The concern about food was entirely serious and probably justified. In 1939 five pupils were reported to have left the St Louis *médersa* because of the unusual food, see ANS 0 122 (NS), Gov. Mauretanie to Gov.-Gen. AOF, 8 March 1940.
6 ANS 0 92 (NS), Gov. Soudan to Gov.-Gen. AOF, 10 December 1935.
7 ANS 0 82 (NS), 'Décision', 13 January 1936.
8 J. Brévie, *Circulaires sur la politique et l'administration indigène en AOF*, Gorée, 1932.
9 For a discussion of these issues see Auchnie 'The *commandement indigéne* in Senegal.'
10 ANS 0 82 (NS), 'Décision', 13 January 1936.

11 ANS 0 82 (NS), Gov. Mauretanie to Gov.-Gen. AOF, 24 March 1936; Directeur des Affaires Politiques et Administratives, 'Note pour M. l'Inspecteur Général de l'Enseignement', 10 April 1936.

12 ANS 19 G 1 (NS), Gov.-Gen. AOF circular, 15 February 1937. *Tabaski* is the Wolof name for the Muslim feast, *al-Kabir*, celebrating the start of the new year.

13 ANS 19 G 1 (NS), Gov.-Sénégal to Gov.-Gen. AOF, 23 February 1937.

14 ANS 19 G 1 (NS), Imam, Grande Mosquée d'Abidjan to Gov.-Gen. AOF, 4 March 1937.

15 For full text of speech, see ANS 19 G 1 (NS).

16 ANSOM AP 598/4, 'Rapport politique, 1937'.

17 ANS 19 G 1 (NS), 'Président Fraternité Musulmane to Perrin, 26 February 1937. It is not clear from the sources why M. Perrin was chosen to receive this letter.

18 ANS 21 G 43 (NS) 108, *qadi*, Président Tribunal Musulman de St Louis to Gov.-Gen. AOF, 31 May 1937.

19 ANS 19 G 1 (NS), Abd el-Kader Diagne to Gov.-Gen. AOF, 19 January 1938; Gov. Sénégal to Gov.-Gen. AOF, 7 February 1938; Admin. p. i. Dakar to Gov.-Gen. AOF, 9 February 1938; Gov.-Gen. AOF; to Abd el-Kader Diagne, 21 February 1938.

20 ANS 19 G 1 (NS), Admin. p. i. Dakar to Gov.-Gen. AOF, 17 January 1940; 'Note', 21 January 1940. For 1944 celebrations see reports in same file.

21 ANS 19 G 6 (NS), Gov.-Gen. AOF to Min. Colonies 2 March 1937; 'Renseignements', 20 February 1938.

22 ANS 19 G 6 (NS), Gov.-Gen. AOF to Besson, 3 March 1938.

23 ANS 19 G 6 (NS), el-Hadj Ibrahim Niasse to Gov.-Gen. AOF, 27 March 1937; Directeur du Cabinet, 'Note', 2 March 1937; Inspector Travaux Publiques, 'Note', 3 May 1937; Gov.-Gen. AOF to Inspecteur Travaux Publiques, 12 May 1937; el-Hadj Oumar Kane to Gov.-Gen. AOF, 18 February 1938; Director des Affaires Politiques et Administratives, 'Note', 22 February 1938; Gov. Gen. AOF to el-Hadj Oumar Kane, 23 February 1938.

24 ANS 19 G 6 (NS), Habitants musulmans de l'avenue el-Hadj Malick Sy to Gov.,-Gen. AOF, 5 July 1938; Gov.-Gen. AOF to el-Hadj Omar Kane, 8 July 1938; Gov.-Gen. AOF to Admin. Dakar, 9 July 1938; Admin. Dakar to Gov.-Gen. AOF, 2 August 1938.

25 ANS 0 92 (NS), Gov.-Gen. AOF to Min. Colonies 13 June 1937.

26 ANS 0 92 (NS) 'Rapport à M. le Directeur des Affaires Politiques et Administratives', 10 August 1937.

27 ANS 0 92 (NS), Gov.-Gen. AOF to Min. Colonies, 28 August 1937.

28 See correspondence in ANS 19 G 6 (NS) concerning mosques in Medina (Dakar), Dagana and Guingiuneau (Sine-Saloum) for example of refusal of assistance beyond a token donation.

29 ANS 4 E 8 (NS), see 'Dossier Ibrahim Niasse' (1937) and 'Dossier; impression de voyage' for French records of Ibrahim Niasse's appreciation.

30 ANS 0 94 (NS), Ibrahim Niasse cited in Gov.-Gen. AOF circular, 24 May 1937.

31 See M. Lakroum, *Le Travail inégal: paysans et salariés sénégalais face à la crise des années trente*, Paris, 1982, for a full analysis of changing labour patterns.

32 See replies from Govs. to Gov.-Gen. Guinée, 21 September 1937; Côte d'ivoire, 21 July, 1937; Dahomey, 21 October, 1937; Mauretanie, 14 June 1937; Niger, 20 September 1937. It is interesting to note that in his reply to de Coppet, the Governor of the Ivory Coast wrote at length about the superiority of Islam over animism – an uncharacteristic attitude amongst administrations of this colony.

33 ANS 0 94 (NS), Lt.-Gov. Niger to Gov.-Gen. AOF, 20 September 1937.

34 ANS 0 94 (NS), Min. Colonies to Gov. Gen. AOF, 8 January 1937; Kleinschmidt, 'Les Ecoles coraniques dans les villages indigènes du Sénégal'; Bernadou, Inspecteur Adjoint de l'Enseignement, 'Note pour M. de Directeur des Affaires Politiques', 5 February 1937.

35 ANS 0 94 (NS), Gov.-Gen. AOF to Min. Colonies, 12 October 1937.

36 ANS 17 G 174 (NS), 28, 'Rapport annuel sur le fonctionnement du Service Central de Sûreté et de Renseignements Généraux', 1938. The statistics in this paragraph are taken from this source.
37 ANS 17 G 174 (NS) 28, 'Rapport annuel . . . renseignements généraux', 1937.

11 Epilogue 1940–1960

1 Hoisington Jr, 'The colonial factor'. Paper presented to the conference on 'The Second World War and Africa'. This paper gives a good summary of the attitudes of both the Free French and Vichy governments towards north-west Africa. M. Crowder, 'The 1939–45 War and West Africa' in J. F. A. Ajayi and M. Crowder (eds.), *History of West Africa*, 2nd edn, London, 1987, vol. II, is a good introduction to the subject.
2 R. Schacter Morgenthau, *Political Parties in French-speaking West Africa*, Oxford, 1964, 1970, remains the fullest account of political developments in post-war AOF. For more detailed local accounts, see Fugelstad, *Niger*, ch. 6; O'Brien, *Mourides* and *Saints and Politicians*; Coulon, *Le Marabout et le Prince*. For a general introduction, see M. Crowder and D. Cruise O'Brien, 'French West Africa, 1945–60' in J. F. A. Ajayi and M. Crowder (eds.), *History of West Africa*, 2nd edn, London, 1987, vol. II.
3 See, for example, ANSOM AP 2258/5, 'Note de M. le Gouverneur Beyries', 25 July 1948. It appears that the Minister of Colonies wholeheartedly approved of the grant; see in same file, Delavignette, 'Note pour le Ministre', 31 July 1948.
4 SHAT AOF Niger IX/1a, Lt. Frèrebeau, 'Etude succincte sur le hamalisme et son extension au Niger', April 1956.
5 See, for example, the three monographs produced between 1941 and 1947: D'Arbaumont, 'La Confrérie des Tidjania en Afrique française'; Lafeuille, 'Le Tidjanisme onze grains ou Hamallisme'; Rocaboy, 'Une Confrérie du Sahel soudanais'.
6 Triaud, 'Abd al-Rahman l'Africain (1908–1957)'. Paper presented to conference on 'Les Agents religieux'.
7 See, for example, Amselle, 'Le Wahabisme'. Paper presented to conference on 'Les Agents religieux'.
8 Kaba, *The Wahhabiya*, gives the fullest account of the origins of the Wahhabiyya in West Africa and of the operation of the 'Subbanu' movement.
9 Gov. Louveau, 'Rapport politique, 1946', quoted in Kaba, *The Wahhabiya*.
10 Amselle, 'Le Wahabisme', p. 4.
11 Kaba, *The Wahhabiya*, pp. 233–42.
12 However, it should be noted that many of the richer members were affiliated to the less radical Parti Soudanais du progrès (PSP). See Amselle, 'Le Wahabisme', pp. 7–8.
13 These events are described in Amselle, 'Le Wahabisme', pp. 8–9; Kaba, *The Wahhibiya*, pp. 202–18.
14 The following section is based on O'Brien, *Mourides*, ch. 12, 'The Brotherhood in Senegalese Politics' and Coulon, *Le Marabout et le Prince*, pp. 191–207.
15 ANSOM AP 2258/1, Cardaire, 'Note', 26 April 1956.

Bibliography

ARCHIVAL SOURCES

Archives nationales de la république du Sénégal (ANS), Building administratif, avenue Roume, Dakar

Archives du gouvernement général de l'AOF

Series D – Affaires militaires
 F – Affaires étrangères
 G – Politique et administration générale
  Subseries 2 G – Rapports périodiques
    5 G – Côte d'Ivoire
    7 G – Guinée
    8 G – Dahomey
    9 G – Mauretanie
    11 G – Niger
    13 G – Sénégal
    15 G – Soudan
    17 G – Affaires politiques
    19 G – Affaires musulmanes
Series J – Enseignement
 M – Justice
 O – Enseignement 1920–1940
Fonds de St Louis, Series E – Affaires politiques (Sénégal)

These are the archives of the federal government of AOF. Classification of documents has been in two series: the first containing all documents prior to 1920 has been indexed by J. Charpy (*Répertoire des archives* 7 vols., Rufisque, 1954–5) and has been micro-filmed. The second series of documents from 1920 to 1940 follows the same system of classification but the detailed list of contents can only be consulted in the library of the archives in Dakar. To date only the sub-series 2 G has been microfilmed. In the footnotes to this book the post-1920 classification codes have been identified with the letters NS.

Archives nationales, section Outre-Mer (ANSOM), Aix-en-Provence

Series: Affaires politiques (AP)
 Afrique
 AOF
 Sénégal et Dépendances
 Soudan
 Mauretanie
 Côte d'Ivoire
 Guinée

229

Bibliography

Archives privés
     5 PA – Camille Guy

Service historique de l'armée de terre (SHAT), chateau de Vincennes, Vincennes
Series 0 – 22 Mauretanie
        AOF – Niger
        AOF – Soudan

Institut de France (IF),
23 quai de Conti, Paris 75006
Fonds Terrier
Papiers d'Henri Deherain

Institut fondamental de l'Afrique noire (IFAN),
Université de Dakar
Fonds Vieillard (Fouta Djallon (F–D))
     Gaden
     Monteil

Institut catholique (IC),
21 rue d'Assas, Paris 75006
Dossier Levé

UNPUBLISHED MONOGRAPHS AND THESES

Amselle, J.-L. 'Le Wahabisme à Bamako (1945–1983).' Paper presented to conference on 'Les Agents religieux islamiques en Afrique tropicale', Maison de sciences de l'homme, Paris, 1983.
Anon, 'L'Oeuvre de Seydou Nourou Tall en Afrique française.' Typescript in Archives nationales, Senegal, n.d.
Arbaumont, Lt. de 'La Confrérie des Tidjania en Afrique française.' CHEAM, no. 1411, 1941.
Aubinière, Y. 'La Hierarchie sociale des Maures.' CHEAM, no. 1496, 1949.
Auchnie, A. 'The *commandement indigène* in Senegal, 1919–1947'. Ph.D. thesis, University of London, 1983.
Barrett, Lt. 'Les Peuls du Fouta Djallon.' CHEAM (R), no. 1412, 1948.
Cardaire, Capt. M. 'Contribution à l'étude de l'islam noire.' Mémorandum II du centre IFAN-Cameroun, 1949.
Cau, M. 'L'Islam au Sénégal.' CHEAM (R), no. 949, 1945.
Chansard, Capt. 'Les Mourides du Sénégal.' CHEAM (R), no. 1301, 1948.
Chapelle, Capt. 'L'Islam en A.O.F. et A.E.F.' CHEAM, no. 1335, 1948.
CHEAM 'Notes et études sur l'islam en Afrique noire.' Paris, 1962.
Delmond, M. P. 'Un Aspect de l'islam peuhl: Dori.' CHEAM (R), ńo. 1103, 1947.
Dubie, P. 'L'Organisation du commandement chez les maures du Trarza' CHEAM, no. 562, 1937.
Feral, G. 'Remarques sur l'islam en Guinée.' CHEAM (R), no. 1022, 1945.
Goerg, O. 'Echanges, réseaux, marchés. L'impact colonial en Guinée (mi XIXe – 1913).' Thèse dé z^e cycle, University of Paris VII, 1981.
Harding, L. 'Französische Religionspolitik in West Afrika "Soudan français" 1895–1920.' Inaugural Dissertation zur Erlangung des Grades einer Doktor der Philosophie der Freien Universität, Berlin, 1972.

Harrison, C. 'French attitudes and policies towards Islam in West Africa, 1900–1940.' Ph.D. thesis, University of London, 1985.

Hoisington, Jr., W.A. 'The colonial factor: France and North Africa during the Second World War.' Paper presented to conference on 'The Second World War and Africa'. SOAS, 1984.

Lafeuille, R. 'Le Tidjanisme onze grains ou Hamallisme.' *CHEAM*, no. 1189, 1947.

Mark, P.A. 'Economic and religious change among the Diola of Boulof (Casamance) 1896–1940: trade, cash-cropping and Islam in south western Senegal.' PhD thesis, University of Yale, 1976.

Martin, Lt.-Interprète H. G. 'L'Islam maure.' CHEAM, no. 163, 1937.

'Une Tribu marocaine en Mauritanie: les Oulad bou Sba'. CHEAM, no. 3108, 1937.

Michel, M. 'Le Concours de l'A.O.F. à la France pendant la première guerre mondiale.' Thèse de Doctorat, University of Paris, 1979.

Nekkach, Lt. L. 'Le Mouridisme depuis 1912.' Typescript, St Louis, 1952.

Rocaboy, Chef. de Bataillon 'Une Confrérie du Sahel soudanais: le hamallisme.' CHEAM (R), no. 958, 1947.

Sagna, S. 'Cherif Younousse Aidarara, 1832–1917.' Mémoire de maîtrise, University of Dakar, 1979–80.

Spiegler, J. S. 'Aspects of nationalist thought among French-speaking West Africans, 1921–1939.' D.Phil. thesis, University of Oxford, 1968.

Traoré, A. 'Contribution à l'étude de l'islam; le mouvement Tijanien de Cheikh Hama houllah.' Thèse de 3ᵉ cycle, University of Dakar, 1975 (now published).

Triaud, J.-L. 'Abd al-Rahman l'Africain (1908–1957), pionnier et précurseur du Wahhabisme au Mali.' Paper presented to conference on 'Les Agents religieux islamiques en Afrique tropicale', Maison de sciences de l'homme, Paris, 1983.

Voisin, Commt C. 'L'Islam maure' CHEAM (Questions Sahariennes), no. 1009, 1946.

PUBLISHED SOURCES

Books

Adeleye, R. A. *Power and Diplomacy in Northern Nigeria: 1804–1906*. London, 1971.

Ageron, C.-R. *Les Algériens musulmans et la France, 1871–1914*. 2 vols., Paris, 1968.

Ageron, C.-R. *Politiques coloniales au Maghreb*. Paris, 1972.

Andrew, C. and Kanya Forstner, A. F. *France Overseas: The Great War and the Climax of French Imperial Expansion*. London, 1981.

André, P. J. *L'Islam et les races*. 2 vols., Paris, 1922.

André, P. J. *L'Islam noir: contribution à l'étude des confréries religieuses islamiques en Afrique occidentale suivie d'une étude sur l'islam au Dahomey*. Paris, 1924.

Anon *Histoire militaire de l'A.O.F.*, Paris, 1931.

Arcin, A. *Histoire de la Guinée française*, Paris, 1911.

Arnaud, R. *Précis de politique musulmane* vol. I *Pays maures de la rive droite du Sénégal*. Algiers, 1906.

Asad, T. (ed.) *Anthropology and the Colonial Encounter*. London, 1973.

Audoin, J. and Daniel R. *L'Islam en Haute Volta à l'époque coloniale*. Paris and Abidjan, 1978.

Ba, O. *Ahmadou Bamba face aux autorités coloniales (1889–1927)*. Dakar, 1982.

Baier, S. *An Economic History of Central Niger*. Oxford, 1980.

Barot, Dr *Guide pratique de l'européen dans l'Afrique occidentale*. Paris, 1902.

Behrmann, L. C. *Muslim Brotherhoods and Politics in Senegal*. Cambridge, Massachusetts, 1970.

Bernard, P. *La Fin d'un monde, 1914–1929* (Nouvelle Histoire de la France contemporaine, vol. XII). Paris, 1975.

Bibliography

Bernus, E. *Touaregs nigeriens. Unité culturelle et diversité régionale d'un peuple pasteur.* Paris, 1981.

Binger, L.-G. *Esclavage, islamisme et christianisme.* Paris, 1891.

Binger, L.-G. *Le Péril de l'islam.* Paris, 1906

Bouchad, J. *L'Eglise en Afrique noire.* Paris, 1958.

Bouche, D. *L'Enseignement dans les territoires français de l'Afrique occidentale de 1817 à 1920. Mission civilisatrice ou formation d'une élite?* 2 vols., Paris, 1975.

Brenner, L. *West African Sufi: The Religious Heritage and Spiritual Search of Cerno Bokar Saalif Taal.* London, 1984.

Brévié J. *Islamisme contre "naturisme" au Soudan français: essai de psychologie politique coloniale.* Paris, 1923.

Buell, R. *The Native Problem in Africa.* 2 vols., New York, 1928.

Caillié, R. *Voyage à Tombouctou.* Paris, 1830, vol. I.

Carles, F. *La France et l'islam en Afrique occidentale.* Toulouse, 1915.

Chassey F. de *Mauritanie 1900–1975, de l'ordre colonial à l'ordre neo-colonial entre Maghreb et Afrique noire.* Paris, 1978.

Clarke, P. *West Africa and Islam.* London, 1982.

Clozel, F. and Villamur, R. (eds.) *Les Coutumes indigènes de la Côte d'Ivoire.* Paris, 1902.

Cohen, W. B. *Rulers of Empire: The French Colonial Service in Africa.* Stanford, 1971.

The French Encounter with Africans: White Response to Blacks 1830–1880. Bloomington, 1980.

Coulon, C. *Le Marabout et le Prince.* Paris, 1982.

Curtin, P. *The Image of Africa: British Ideas and Actions, 1780–1850.* London, 1964.

Delafosse, L. *Maurice Delafosse, le berrichon conquis par l'Afrique.* Paris, 1976.

Delafosse, M. *Haut-Sénégal et Niger.* 3 vols., Paris, 1912.

Depont, O. and Coppolani, X. *Les Confréries religieuses musulmanes.* Algiers, 1897.

Désiré-Vuillemin, G.-M. *Contribution à l'histoire de la Mauritanie, 1900–1934.* Dakar, 1962.

Diallo, T. *Les Institutions politiques du Fouta Dyallon au XIXeme siècle.* Dakar, 1972.

Djait, H. *L'Europe et l'islam.* Paris, 1978.

Dubief, H. *Le Déclin de la Troisième République (1929–1938)* (Nouvelle Histoire de la France contemporaine, vol. xiii). Paris, 1975.

Dubois, F. *Notre Beau Niger.* Paris, 1911.

Duveyrier, H. *Les Touareg du Nord.* Paris, 1884.

Evans-Pritchard, E. E. *The Sanusi of Cyrenaica.* Oxford, 1948.

Faidherbe, L. *Le Sénégal: la France dans l'Afrique occidentale.* Paris, 1889.

Fisher, H. J. *Ahmadiyya: A Study in Contemporary Islam on the West African Coast.* Oxford, 1963.

Forget, D. A. *L'Islam et le christianisme dans l'Afrique centrale.* Paris, 1900.

Froelich, J.-C. *Les Musulmans d'Afrique noire.* Paris, 1962.

Fugelstad, F. *A History of Niger, 1800–1960.* Cambridge, 1983.

Gillier, Commt *La Pénétration française en Mauritanie.* Paris, 1926.

Gouilly, A. *L'Islam, dans l'Afrique occidentale.* Paris, 1952.

Gouraud, Col. H. *La Pacification de la Mauritanie.* Paris, 1910.

Hardy, G. *Une Conquête morale. L'Enseignement en A.O.F.* Paris, 1917.

Hiskett, M. *Development of Islam in West Africa.* London, 1984.

Julien, C.-A. *Histoire de l'Algérie contemporaine, 1830–1871.* Paris, 1964.

Kaba, L. *The Wahhabiya. Islamic Reform and Politics in French West Africa.* Evanston, 1974.

Kanya Forstner, A. S. *The Conquest of the Western Sudan: A Study in French Military Imperialism.* Cambridge, 1969.

Klein, M. A. *Islam and Imperialism in Senegal: Sine-Saloum 1847–1914.* Edinburgh, 1968.

232

Le Chatelier, A. *L'Islam en Afrique occidentale*. Paris, 1899.
   Politique musulmane. Tours, 1907.
Lovejoy, P. E. *Transformations in Slavery: a History of Slavery in Africa*. Cambridge, 1983.
Lukes, S. *Emile Durkheim: His Life and Work*. Harmondsworth, 1973.
Machat, J. *Les Rivièrès du Sud et le Fouta Djallon: géographie physique et civilisations indigènes*. Paris, 1906.
Maran, R. *Bataouala*. Paris, 1921.
   Le Livre de la brousse. Paris, 1934.
Marks, S. *Reluctant Rebellion. The 1906–8 Disturbances in Natal*. Oxford, 1970.
Martin, B. G. *German–Persian Diplomatic Relations*. Gravenhage, 1959.
Martin, B. G. *Muslim Brotherhoods in Nineteenth-century Africa*. Cambridge, 1976.
Marty, P. *Les Mourides d'Amadou Bamba*. Paris, 1913.
   L'Islam en Mauretanie et au Sénégal. Paris, 1916.
   L'Emirat des Trarzas. Paris, 1918.
   Etudes sur l'islam, et les tribus du Soudan. 4 vols., Paris, 1920.
      vol. I   *Les Kounta de l'est – les Berabich – les Iguellad*
      vol. II *La Région de Tombouctou – Macina et dépendances*
      vol. III *Les Tribus maures du sahel et du Hodh*
      vol. IV *La Région de Kayes – le pays Bambara – le sahel de Nioro*
   L'Islam en Guinée. Fouta Diallon. Paris, 1921.
   L'Islam et les tribus maures. Les Braknas. Paris, 1921.
   Etudes sur l'islam en Côte d'Ivoire. Paris, 1922.
   Etudes sur l'islam au Dahomey. Paris, 1926.
Maze J. *La Collaboration scolaire des groupements coloniaux et des missions*. Algiers, 1933.
Monteil, C. *Les Khassonké. Monographie d'une peuplade du Soudan français*. Paris, 1915.
Monteil, V. *L'Islam noir*. 3rd edn, Paris, 1980.
Morgenthau, R. S. *Political Parties in French-speaking West Africa*. Oxford, 1964.
O'Brien, D. C. *The Mourides of Senegal*. Oxford, 1971.
   Saints and Politicians. Essays in the Organisation of a Senegalese Peasant Economy. Cambridge , 1975.
Prost, A. *Les Missions des Pères Blancs en Afrique occidentale avant 1939*. Paris and Ouagadougou, n.d.
Quellien, A. *La Politique musulmane dans l'Afrique occidentale française*. Paris, 1910.
Randau, R. *Un Corse d'Algérie chez les hommes bleus: Xavier Coppolani, le pacificateur*. Algiers, 1939.
Rebérioux, M. *La République radicale? 1898–1914* (Nouvelle Histoire de la France contemporaine, vol. 11). Paris, 1975.
Renault, F. *Lavigerie, l'esclavage africain et l'Europe*. 2 vols., Paris, 1971.
Richer, Dr A. *Les Oulliminden*. Paris, 1924.
Rinn, L. *Marabouts et Khouan: étude sur l'islam en Algérie*. Algiers, 1884.
Roberts, S. H. *The History of French Colonial Policy, 1870–1925*. 2 vols., London, 1963 (1st edn, 1929).
Robinson, D. *Chiefs and Clerics: Abdul Bokar Kan and the Futa Toro, 1853–1891*. Oxford, 1975.
   The Holy War of Umar Tal: The Western Sudan in the Mid-Nineteenth Century, Oxford, 1985.
Rodinson, M. *La Fascination de l'islam*. Paris, 1980.
Rouget, F. *La Guinée*. Corbeil, 1906.
Said, E. *Orientalism*. London, 1978.
Sanneh, L. O. *The Jakhanke: The History of an Islamic Clerical People of the Senegambia*. London, 1979.
Stewart, C. (with Stewart, E.K.) *Islam and the Social Order in Mauretania: A Case Study from the Nineteenth Century*. Oxford, 1973.
Tauxier, L. *Le Noir de la Guinée*. Paris, 1908.

Bibliography

Terasse, H. *Histoire du Maroc*. Casablanca, 1950.
Tomlinson, G. J. F. and Letham, G. J. *History of Islamic Political Propaganda in Nigeria*. London, 1927.
Trimingham, J. S. *Islam in West Africa*. Oxford, 1959.
A History of Islam in West Africa. Oxford, 1962.
Waardenburg, J.-J. *L'Islam dans le miroir de l'occident*. Paris and The Hague, 1963.
Weiskel, T. C. *French Colonial Rule and the Baule Peoples; Resistance and Collaboration*. Oxford, 1980.
Wesley Johnson, G. *The Emergence of Black Politics in Senegal*. Stanford, 1971.
Zeldin, T. *France 1848–1945*. 5 vols. (University paperback edition), Oxford, 1980.

Articles

Alexandre, P. 'A West African Islamic movement: Hammalism in French West Africa' in A. Mazrui and R. I. Rotberg (eds.), *Protest and Power in Black Africa*. New York, 1970, pp. 497–512.
Andrew, C. and Kanya Forstner, A. 'France, Africa and World War I.' *JAH*, xix (1), 1978, 11–23.
Anon 'La Confrérie musulmane de Sidi Mohammed ben Ali-es-Senoussi.' *Bulletin de la Société de Géographie et d'Archéologie de la Province d'Oran*, 1891, 319–31.
Arnaud, R. 'L'Islam et la politique musulmane française en Afrique occidentale'. *RCBCAF*, 1912, 3–20, 115–27, 142–54.
Asiwaju, A. I. 'Anti-French resistance movements in Ohori-Ije (Dahomey), 1895–1960.' *Journal of the Historical Society of Nigeria*, vii (2), 255–69.
Ballard, J. 'The Porto Novo incidents of 1923: politics in the colonial era.' *University of Ife Journal of African Studies*, ii (1), 1965, 52–74.
Barrows, L. C. 'The merchants and General Faidherbe: aspects of French expansion in Senegal in the 1850s.' *RFHOM*, lxi (223), 1974, 236–88.
'Faidherbe's Islamic policy in Senegal, 1845–65.' *French Colonial Studies*, 1977, 34–53.
Becker, C.-H. 'Ist der Islam eine Gefahr für unsere Kolonien?' *Kolonialen Rundschau*, 1909, 266–93.
Behrmann, L. C. 'French Muslim policy and Senegalese brotherhoods' in D. McCall and N. Bennett (eds.), *Aspects of West African Islam*. Boston 1971, pp. 185–208.
Belvert, J. de 'L'Exode d'une race.' *Outre-Mer*, 1937, 331–38.
Bouche, D. 'L'Ecole française et les musulmans au Sénégal de 1850 à 1920' *RFHOM*, lxi (223), 1974, 218–35.
Burrows, M. 'Les Origines de la Mission laïque' in A. Gourdon (ed.), 'Eléments pour une histoire de la Mission laïque française, 1902–1982.' *Dialogues* (Bulletin de l'enseignement des professeurs français à l'étranger), 1983, 35–7.
Chailley, Commt 'Xavier Coppolani.' *Cahiers Charles de Foucauld*, 1955, 84–114.
Clozel, F. 'Lettre de Korbous: politique musulmane au Soudan. Pacification du Sahara français.' *BCAF*, Feb.–March 1913, 60–2, 106–9, 150–2, 182–5.
Colombani, F. M. 'Le Guidimaka.' *BCEHSAOF*, 1931, 365–432.
Cooper, F. 'The problem of slavery in African studies.' *JAH*, xx (1), 1979, 103–25.
Cornevin, R. 'Alfa Yaya Diallo fut-il un héros national de Guinée ou l'innocente victime d'un règlement de compte entre gouverneurs?' *RFHOM*, lvii (208), 1970, 288–96.
Delafosse, M. 'Les Etats d'âme d'un colonial.' *BCAF*, 1909, 52–5, 102–5, 127–31, 162–5, 240–2, 288–9, 311–3, 338–9, 373–5, 414–6.
'L'Etat actuel de l'islam dans l'A.O.F.' *RMM*, xi (5), 1910, 32–54.
'Le Clergé musulman de l'Afrique occidentale.' *RMM*, xi (b), 1910, 177–206.
'Les Confréries musulmanes et le maraboutisme dans les pays du Sénégal et du Niger.' *RCBCAF* (4), 1911, 81–90.

234

'Sur l'orientation nouvelle de la politique indigène.' *RCBCAF*, 1921, 124–53.

'Les Points sombres de l'horizon en Afrique occidentale.' *BCAF*, June 1922, 271–84.

'L'Animisme nègre et sa résistance à l'islamisation en Afrique occidentale.' *RMM*, xlix, 1922, 121–63.

'L'Ahmadisme et son action en A.O.F.' *RCBCAF*, 1924, 32–36.

Désiré-Vuillemin, G.-M., 'Coppolani en Mauritanie.' *Revue d'Histoire des Colonies*, xlii (148–9), 1955, 291–342.

Doutté, E. 'Les Causes de la chute d'un sultan.' *RCBCAF*, 1909, 129–36, 163–8, 185–9, 220–5, 246–50, 262–7.

'L'Islam noir.' *La Revue Contemporaine*, May 1923, 188–95.

Dupuch, C. 'Essai sur l'emprise religieuse chez les Peulh du Fouta Djallon.' *Annuaire du Comité d'Etudes Historiques et Scientifiques de l'A.O.F.*, 1917, 210–309.

Harrison, C., Martin, M. and Ingawa, T. C. 'The establishment of colonial rule in West Africa, c. 1900–1914' in J. F. A. Ajayi and M. Crowder (eds.), *History of West Africa*. 2nd edn, London, 1987, vol. II.

Hughes, A. and Morley, R. 'The "Mallam Sa'id conspiracy" of 1923: British reactions to Mahdism in northern Nigeria.' (Unpublished.)

Ita, J. M. 'Frobenius in West African history.' *JAH*, xiii (4), 673–88.

Johnson, R. W. 'Educational progress and retrogression in Guinea (1900–1945)' in G. N. Brown and M. Hiskett (eds.), *Conflict and Harmony in Education in Tropical Africa*. London, 1975, pp. 212–28.

Jones, D. H. 'The Catholic mission and some aspects of assimilation in Senegal, 1817–1852.' *JAH*, xxi (4), 1980, 323–40.

Kane, O. and Cissoko, S. M. 'Il y a un an disparaissait une grande figure africaine, Thierno Seydou Nourou Tall.' *Afrique Histoire* (2), April–June 1981.

Klein, M. and Roberts, S. 'The Banamba slave exodus of 1905 and the decline of slavery in the western Sudan.' *JAH*, xxi (4), 1980, 375–94.

Labonne, R. 'L'Islam et les troupes noires.' *La Revue de Paris*, April 1923, 575–601.

Laforgue, P. 'Une Secte hérésiarque en Mauritanie: les Ghoudf.' *BCEHSAOF*, 1928, 654–665.

Laizé, Officier-Interprète 'L'Islam dans le Territoire Militaire du Niger.' *BCEHSAOF*, ii, 1919, 177–83.

Last, M. 'Reform movements in West Africa' in J.F.A. Ajayi and M. Crowder (eds.), *History of West Africa*, 2nd edn, London, 1987, vol. 2.

Le Chatelier, A. 'Le Panislamisme et le Progrès.' *RMM*, i (4), 1907, pp. 465–71.

'Politique musulmane.' *RMM*, xxi, 1910, (special issue).

'Introduction à "La Politique musulmane d'Hollande" par. M. Snouck Hurgronje.' *RMM*, xiv (6), 1911, 377–79.

'La Conquète du monde musulman.' *RMM*, xvi, 1911, 5–11.

'L'Assaut donné au monde musulman.' *RMM*, xix, 1912, 280–86.

'Nos Musulmans d'Afrique.' *La Grande Revue*, Nov. 1915, 1–7.

Ly-Tall, M. and Robinson, D. 'The Western Sudan and the coming of the French' in J.F.A. Ajayi and M. Crowder (eds.), *History of West Africa*. 2nd edn, London, 1987, Vol. II.

Malinowski, B. 'Practical anthropology.' *Africa* (2), 1929, 22–38.

'The rationalisation of anthropology and administration.' *Africa* (3), 1930, 405–29.

Mangeot, Col. P. and Marty, P. 'Les Touareg de la boucle du Niger.' *BCEHSAOF*, 1918, 87–136, 257–86, 432–75.

Marty, P. 'Les Amulettes musulmanes au Sénégal.' *RMM*, xxvii, 1914, 319–68.

'L'Islam et les tribus dans la colonie du Niger (ex-Zinder).' *Revue des Etudes Islamiques* (4), 1930, 333–429; (5) 1931, 139–237.

Mauss, M. 'L'Ethnographie en France et à l'étranger.' *La Revue de Paris* (19, 20) 1913, 537–60, 815–37.

Bibliography

Mitchell, P. 'The Anthropologist and the Practical Man: a reply and a question.' *Africa* (3), 1930, 217–33.

Monteil, V. 'Les Bureaux arabes au Maghreb (1833–1961).' *Esprit*, Nov. 1961, 575–606.

N'Diaye, M. 'Rapports entre Qâdirites et Tijânites au Fouta Toro aux xixeme et xxeme siècles à travers *Al-Haqq al-Mubîn* de Cheikh Moussa Kamara.' *Bulletin IFAN* (ser. B), 1979, 190–207.

Newbury, C. W. 'The formation of the Government-General of French West Africa.' *JAH*, I (1), 1960, 111–28.

O'Brien, D. 'Towards an "Islamic policy" in French West Africa, 1854–1914.' *JAH*, VII (2), 1967, 303–16.

Otton Loyewski, Lt. de 'Coppolani et la Mauritanie.' *Revue d'Histoire des Colonies*, 1938, 1–169.

Pasquier, R. 'L'influence de l'expérience algérienne sur la politique de la France au Sénégal (1842–1869)' in *Perspectives nouvelles sur le passé de l'Afrique noire: mélanges offerts à Hubert Deschamps*. Paris, 1974, pp. 263–84.

Sanneh, L. 'The origins of clericalism in West African Islam', *JAH*, XVII (1), 1976, 49–72.

'Tcherno Aliou, the wali of Goumba: Islam, colonialism and the rural factor in Futa Jallon, 1867–1912' in N. Levtzion and H. J. Fisher (eds.), *Rural and Urban Islam in West Africa*. Special issue of *Asian and African Studies*, 20 (1), 1986, 73–102.

Schnapper, B. 'Les Tribunaux musulmans et la politique coloniale au Sénégal (1830–1914).' *Revue Historique de Droit Français et Etranger*, (1), 1961, 90–128.

Stewart, C. C. 'Southern Saharan scholarship and the Bilad al-Sudan.' *JAH*, XVII (1), 1976, 73–93.

Suret-Canale, J. 'A propos du Ouali de Goumba.' *Recherches Africaines*, 1964, 160–64.

'Un Aspect de la politique coloniale française en Guinée. Le mythe du "complot féodal et islamique" de 1911.' *Bulletin de la Société d'Histoire Moderne*, 1970, 13–19.

'Touba in Guinea – Holy Place of Islam ' in C. Allen & R. W. Johnson (eds.), *African Perspectives*, Cambridge, 1970 pp. 53–82.

'The Fouta-Djallon chieftancy' in M. Crowder and O. Ikime (eds.) *West African Chiefs*, Ife, 1970, pp. 79–97.

Summers, A. and Johnson, R. W. 'World War I, conscription and social change in Guinea.' *JAH*, XIX (1), 1978, 25–38.

Thompson, F. M. L. 'Social control in Victorian Britain.' *Economic History Review* (2), 1981, 189–208.

Triaud, J.-L. 'La Question musulmane en Côte d'Ivoire (1893–1939).' *RFHOM*, LXI (225), 1974, 542–71.

Verdat, M. 'Le Ouali de Goumba.' *Etudes Guinéennes* (3), 1949, 3–83.

Webb, J. L. A. 'The trade in gum Arabic: prelude to French conquest in Senegal.' *JAH*, XXVI (2, 3), 1986, 149–68.

Wesley Johnson, G. 'William Ponty and Republican paternalism in French West Africa' in L. Gann and P. Duignan (eds.), *African Proconsuls*. New York, 1978, pp. 127–56.

Willis, M. R. 'The Torodbe clerisy: a social view.' *JAH*, XIX (2), 1978, 195–212.

Index

237

Index